Taking Morality Seriously

In *Taking Morality Seriously: A Defense of Robust Realism* David Enoch develops, argues for, and defends a strongly realist and objectivist view of ethics and normativity more broadly. This view—according to which there are perfectly objective, universal, moral, and other normative truths that are not in any way reducible to other, natural truths—is familiar, but this book is the first in-detail development of the positive motivations for the view into reasonably precise arguments. And when the book turns defensive—defending Robust Realism against traditional objections—it mobilizes the original positive arguments for the view to help fend off the objections.

The main underlying motivation for Robust Realism developed in the book is that no other metaethical view can vindicate our taking morality seriously. The positive arguments developed here—the argument from the deliberative indispensability of normative truths, and the argument from the moral implications of metaethical objectivity (or its absence)—are thus arguments for Robust Realism that are sensitive to the underlying, pre-theoretical motivations for the view.

David Enoch is Professor of Philosophy and Jacob I. Berman Professor of Law at the Hebrew University of Jerusalem.

Taking Morality Seriously

A Defense of Robust Realism

David Enoch

OXFORD
UNIVERSITY PRESS

OXFORD
UNIVERSITY PRESS

Great Clarendon Street, Oxford OX2 6DP,

United Kingdom

Oxford University Press is a department of the University of Oxford.
It furthers the University's objective of excellence in research, scholarship,
and education by publishing worldwide. Oxford is a registered trade mark of
Oxford University Pressin the UK and in certain other countries

First published in 2011
First published in paperback 2013

British Library Cataloguing in Publication Data
Data available

Library of Congress Cataloging in Publication Data
Data available

ISBN 978–0–19–957996–9 (Hbk)
ISBN 978–0–19–968317–8 (Pbk)

To Naomi, Rakefet, Ronnie, and Yonyon, and in memory of Reuven,

With love

Contents

Acknowledgments

I almost can't believe that there is finally a book. I don't know how many book-writers share this feeling, but to me the thought that there really is a book, *this* book, is quite amazing. So I am genuinely grateful to all who helped in getting here.

This project started as my dissertation project at NYU, where I started in 1998 and graduated in 2003. Getting my PhD at NYU was a terrific opportunity and experience for me, and so I want to start by thanking those who helped me get there – my teachers in Tel Aviv University, and especially those who were kind enough not just to teach me philosophy but also to write reference letters when I applied to PhD programs: Chaim Gans, Andrei Marmor, and Ruth Weintraub.

At NYU I had an ideal dissertation committee: Hartry Field, Tom Nagel, and Derek Parfit. I am sure their influence will be apparent in many places in this book, and I acknowledge with pleasure my gratitude to them. I also benefited tremendously from my other NYU teachers, and just as much from my fellow graduate students. When I think back of my NYU years, I miss the conversations and arguments with fellow graduate students most. I want to thank especially Josh Schechter. Josh and I hit it off philosophically from very early on, and conversations that started when we were first-year students eventually became two papers, and a major part of my dissertation. Our interaction is also present here, in Chapter 3. I am grateful for all his help.

My work environment at the Hebrew University in Jerusalem has been very supportive (much support came from the HU Faculty of Law, even though no one there is quite sure how work on metaethics is relevant to things that are more traditionally of interest to law schools; I am especially grateful for that attitude). I also had the privilege to spend six months at the Hebrew University Institute for Advanced Studies, coordinating a research group on metaethics. I gratefully acknowledge the support of the Institute, and the valuable intellectual interaction with (and feedback I received from) the other members of the group: Hagit Benbaji, David Heyd, Nadeem Hussain, Yair Levi, Mark Schroeder, Sigrún Svavarsdóttir, Mark van Roojen, Ralph Wedgwood, and Ruti Weintraub.

While at the HU, I also benefited from the support of two grants of the Israel Science Foundation (the more recent of which is grant 136/09), for which I am grateful.

The HU environment is supportive, as I just said, but also quite demanding and time-consuming. So I'm pretty sure that this book would not have been written if it weren't for a kind invitation I received some time ago – initiated by John Deigh, Larry Sager, and Mitch Berman – to spend a year as a Harrington Fellow at the University of Texas, Austin. Though work on this project started many years ago, as I already mentioned, the actual Taking-Morality-Seriously folder on my computer was launched at the beginning of my UT year, and by the time that year was over, the publisher already had the first version of my manuscript. I am grateful to UT and to the Harrington Fellows Program for all their help, and my UT colleagues for a lot of valuable feedback and for a great intellectual (and other) environment.

I acknowledge specific debts when they are relevant in the book. But let me mention here all of those who gave me comments, made suggestions, those with whom I've had conversations and the like – all of which, needless to say, improved this book tremendously: Erez Aloni, Dan Baras, Stephanie Beardsman, Hagit Benbaji, Hanina Ben-Menahem, Thérèse Björkholm, Paul Boghossian, Ray Buchanan, Terence Cuneo, Jonathan Dancy, Stephen Darwall, Stephen Davey, John Deigh, Josh DiPaolo, Jamie Dreier, Cian Dorr, Ronald Dworkin, Melis Erdur, Hartry Field, Stephen Finlay, Ernesto Garcia, Ruti Gavison, Pete Graham, Moshe Halbertal, Alon Harel, Ulrike Heuer, David Heyd, Nadeem Hussain, Jens Johansson, Peter Kung, Noa Leibowitz, Yair Levy, Ofra Magidor, Ofer Malcai, Andrei Marmor, Tristram McPherson, Tom Nagel, Jonas Olson, Derek Parfit, Joseph Raz, John Richardson, Josh Schechter, Mark Schroeder, Russ Shafer-Landau, Nishi Shah, Assaf Sharon, Yonatan Shemer, Brad Skow, Sharon Street, Bart Streumer, Sigrún Svavarsdóttir, Julie Tannenbaum, Sergio Tenenbaum, Kevin Toh, Teemu Toppinen, Mark van Roojen, Pekka Väyrynen, Peter Vranas, Ralph Wedgwood, Ruti Weintraub, Crispin Wright, Masahiro Yamada.

When previous versions of the book were ready, I was lucky enough to get some feedback on the manuscript as a whole from Stephen Finlay, Tristram McPherson, Jonas Olson, Russ Shafer-Landau, and Mark van Roojen. They were not just generous with their time but also extremely helpful with their comments, and I am grateful for that. I am especially grateful to Jonas Olson who organized a faculty workshop on the whole manuscript in Stockholm in April 2010, to Martin Turner who organized a reading group about the manuscript in Washington University in St. Louis in the spring of 2011, and to Russ Shafer-Landau who discussed the manuscript with his graduate students in his seminar in the spring of 2010. All of these resulted in greatly appreciated feedback.

Let me say a few more words about Russ. The influence of his work should be apparent on many, many pages of this book. But his influence goes much further than that of his work. As won't surprise anyone in metaethics today, Russ has been tremendously helpful, generous, kind, and encouraging throughout these years. Ever since we first met at the realism-support-club-table at a Madison Workshop lunch, he's been encouraging me to turn this project into a book; I suspect he threw in a good word with the OUP people; and he's been giving me advice and feedback on my work whenever I asked for it. His presence makes the field a better place.

Several of the chapters are based on previously published material. I have edited all this material to make it a more integral part of the book. Where I make substantive changes (this is pretty rare), I note it explicitly. The relevant published work is:

- Chapter 2 is based on (2010c) "How Objectivity Matters," *Oxford Studies in Metaethics*, vol. 5 (Oxford: Oxford University Press), 111–52.
- A part of Chapter 3 is based on (2007a) "An Outline of an Argument for Robust Metanormative Realism," *Oxford Studies in Metaethics* vol. 2, 21–50.
- Another part of Chapter 3 is based on Enoch, D. and Schechter, J. (2008) "How Are Basic Belief-Forming Methods Justified?" *Philosophy and Phenomenological Research* 76(3), 547–79.
- Chapter 6 is based on (2009a) "How Is Moral Disagreement a Problem for Realism?", *Journal of Ethics* 13(1), 15.
- Chapter 7 is based on (2010a) "The Epistemological Challenge to Metanormative Realism: How Best to Understand It, and How to Cope with It," *Philosophical Studies* 148(3), 413–38.

I thank the different publishers for permission to use this material, and the journals' anonymous referees for their input. In fact, let me take this opportunity to also thank some anonymous referees for *other* journals. Though the verdicts of these other referees have often been less flattering than those of the journals that eventually accepted the papers, their comments have sometimes been just as helpful.

When it came to the production stage, my experience with Peter Momtchiloff and his OUP staff has been so positive it almost made proofreading a pleasure. I don't have much experience with this kind of thing (okay, I don't have any experience), but I can't imagine a better publishing experience. And I am also grateful to Netanel Lipshitz for his excellent help with proofreading and with creating the index.

And then there are those who haven't helped much – certainly not directly – in the writing of this book, but whose presence in my life makes such projects worthwhile. I dedicate this book, with love, to Naomi and Rakefet (who haven't read this book, and probably won't), to Ronnie and Yonyon (who haven't read this book – though this did not stop Ronnie from insisting that her name *must* be mentioned in the book – and who perhaps one day may browse through it, just to make sure I haven't embarrassed them too much), and in memory of Reuven (who would have read this book, I'm pretty sure).

1

The View, the Motivation, the Book

I believe that there are irreducibly normative truths and facts, facts such that we should care about our future well-being, that we should not humiliate other people, that we should not reason and form beliefs in ways we know to be unreliable. These are, of course, just examples: even if I am wrong about them, I believe there must be *some* examples of this sort, examples of normative (and indeed moral) truths that are irreducibly normative, truths that are perfectly objective, universal, absolute. They are independent of us, our desires and our (or anyone else's) will. And our thinking and talking about them amounts not just to an expression of any practical attitudes, but to a representation of these normative truths and facts. These normative truths are truths that, when successful in our normative inquiries, we discover rather than create or construct. They are, in other words, just as respectable as empirical or mathematical truths (at least, that is, according to scientific and mathematical realists).

"Robust Realism" is my name for the view just sketched. And it is the business of this book to defend it.

1.1 The view

Robust Realism is primarily a view of, or about, normativity (it is also, though not primarily, about morality; I return to this shortly). Before proceeding to say something about Robust Realism, then, let me say a few words about the normativity I am a robust realist about.

Normative truths (or facts, propositions, properties, claims, sentences, and the like) are, at a first approximation, those that fall on the ought side of the is–ought distinction, the value side of the fact–value distinction, and the analogous side of analogous distinctions. These distinctions admit of vagueness and borderline cases, and they are not, of course, uncontroversial. But the controversies regarding them are mostly about how best to make theoretical sense of them, not about whether they have any content. Not much more than this first approximation will be given here – I do not think that more is needed at this stage, and if Robust Realism is true and my arguments for it sound, there is no reason to expect that much more is to be had. Paradigmatic examples may, however, help clarify the kind of things I refer to as normative. That we ought to give money to famine relief is a normative proposition (and, given that it's true, it's also a normative truth, and a normative fact); so are that I should go on a diet, that you have a reason to read Kant, that pursuing graduate studies in philosophy is the thing it makes most sense for her to do, that he is a good person, that pain is pro-tanto bad for the person whose pain it is, that you shouldn't form your beliefs on the basis of wishful thinking, that if he has inconsistent beliefs he's irrational, that it's unreasonable to expect everyone to convert to your religion, that we should all care more for our own children than for other people's children, that it's your duty to obey the laws of your country, that I have a moral right to free speech, and so on.

These examples should suffice, I think, to give an intuitive feel of the normative realm about which I'm a robust realist. In my mouth, then, the term "normative" is used rather liberally, encompassing also what some others prefer to characterize as *evaluative* rather than normative discourse. My reasons for this choice of words are two. First, by and large, the relation between the evaluative and the normative (more narrowly understood, perhaps as essentially tied to (normative) reasons) will not be my topic here. And second, it seems to me that the most interesting distinction – the one that better captures what may be thought of as a philosophical kind – is that between the normative (thus understood) and the non-normative, not that between the normative (more narrowly understood) and the evaluative.

Many of these intuitively normative claims, though, can be misunderstood in a relevantly important way. As Korsgaard (1996, 42) notes, different thinkers use different terms as their "normatively loaded words" – roughly, those for which it is analytically true that they carry normative force. Thus, a word that is understood as normatively loaded by one may be understood differently by another. Consider, for instance, the word "good" in "She is a good person". One may treat this claim as a normative one; but one may – treating "good" as normatively *un*loaded, and, say, "reason" as normatively loaded – treat this as a perfectly descriptive claim, one that leaves the relevant normative question – Do I have reason to be a good person, or to be (relevantly) like her? – entirely open. So in characterizing the normative I should say – somewhat vacuously, of course – that it is the discourse that comprises propositions (sentences, truths, facts) of the kind of the examples given above, when these are understood as normatively loaded.[1]

Ethical or moral facts (terms which in this book I use interchangeably) are a subset of normative facts. And it is an increasingly appreciated lesson of the recent decades' metaethical literature that many of the concerns and arguments traditionally thought to be about morality are really easily and naturally generalizable to metanormative concerns and arguments. This is true of most of this book as well. For the most part, it engages the more general metanormative issues, sometimes focusing on meta*ethics* just as an example. But seeing that Robust Realism is an existential rather than a

---

[1]   The point in the text here is closely related to Parfit's (2011, for instance vol. 2, section 88) insistence that the normativity he's interested in is normativity in the reason-implying, not the rule-implying sense.

universal thesis – it insists that *there are* irreducibly normative response-independent truths – Robust Meta*normative* Realism is consistent with a denial of Robust Meta*ethical* Realism: it cannot be ruled out without argument that though there are some such normative truths, none of them is recognizably moral. Nevertheless, I want to defend both the metanormative and the metaethical versions of Robust Realism. At times, then, my discussion of morality will have to be more systematic than merely the use of some examples. And one of my points here will be that Robust Metaethical Realism – though not entailed by Robust Metanormative Realism – still gains significant support from it.

So much, then – for now, at least – for what it is I am robust realist *about*. But what does a commitment to Robust Realism amount to?

The term "realism" is of course notoriously ambiguous. Without attempting anything like a comprehensive survey, then, let me start my characterization of Robust Realism with what Rosen (1994, 281) calls "minimal realism". Minimal realism about a discourse amounts to the following conjunction: Sentences in that discourse are truth-apt, and some of them are (non-trivially) true. It seems plausible to assume that – whatever exactly your favorite way of understanding "realism" is – it is a necessary condition to qualify as a realist to reject all versions of noncognitivism or expressivism about the relevant discourse (such as Ayer's about the moral and Gibbard's about the normative[2]), and it is another such necessary condition to reject an error-theory about it (such as Mackie's about the moral, the Churchlands' about the mental, and Field's about mathematical objects). Robust Realism is committed, then, to Rosen's minimal realism.

As Sayre-McCord notes (1988b, e.g. at 16), however, such minimal realism is compatible with a kind of relativism or subjectivism that Robust Realism is clearly meant to exclude. Let us add, then, that, in addition to satisfying the requirements of minimal realism, Robust Realism is an objectivist, response-independence view of normativity. Unfortunately, these characteristics are themselves hard to characterize. The intuitive idea – for which I will settle for now – seems to be the conjunction of observer-independence[3] and agent-independence: Whether or not a given normative statement applies (for instance) to a given action does not depend on what attitudes regarding it – cognitive or otherwise – are entertained by those judging that it is (or is not) or by anyone in their environment, nor does it depend on the attitudes, desires, and the like of the agent whose action it is or of anyone in *her* environment.

There is a complication here. The attitudes of those making the relevant judgments or of the relevant agents may be among the normatively relevant circumstances. For instance, when I pronounce the normative judgment "I am not irrational", its truth

---

[2] I know, I know: If something like Blackburn's (and now also Gibbard's) quasi-realist project is successful, then it is no longer as clear that realism is inconsistent with noncognitivism, or expressivism, or projectivism. I actually stand by the point in the text here, but my defense of it will have to await the next chapter.

[3] See Svavarsdóttir (2001, 162). See also Milo's (1995, 192) discussion of "stance-independence" as a necessary condition for realism.

may depend on my attitudes regarding it, for inconsistency in my beliefs – the one expressed by this very sentence included – may make this normative judgment false. But such judgment-dependence does not threaten the objectivity of the normative (in the intended sense of these words). Similarly, it may be wrong to spit in the direction of a person in some societies but not in others, simply because in the former, but not the latter, such an act would constitute a conventional expression of contempt and will thus cause humiliation, and it is (universally, objectively, response-independently) wrong to express contempt and cause humiliation. Such sensitivity to normatively relevant circumstances – circumstances which often include people's attitudes – again does not threaten objectivity or realism in the sense we are after. Let me say, then, that on Robust Realism normative truths do not *constitutively* depend on our responses or attitudes or desires. The extent to which they do depend on these things is the extent to which these things are normatively relevant – according, that is, to the more fundamental normative truths, themselves not response-dependent in any relevant way.[4]

Robust Realism is, then, an objectivist, non-error-theoretical, cognitivist, or factualist position, it states that some normative judgments are objectively[5] non-vacuously true. But Robust Realism goes further than that. It asserts that some normative truths are *irreducibly* normative. Again, it is not completely clear what a reduction is (I discuss this in more detail below, in Chapter 5). But for my purposes here the point is best put intuitively: Robust Realism rejects the naturalist claim that – in a sense yet to be precisified – normative facts are nothing over and above natural ones. Normative facts are just too different from natural[6] ones to be a subset thereof. The (somewhat) more precise details relevant here will have to await the discussion of reduction in Chapter 5.

Robust Realism is thus the thesis that there are objective irreducibly normative truths.

Notice further that Robust Realism as characterized above is prima facie neutral on the epistemology of the normative, and is thus compatible with even the most thoroughgoing epistemological skepticism about the normative. This, I think, is as it should be: at least since Descartes' realist skepticism about the external world and Berkeley's idealist (and, we would say, antirealist) reply to this skepticism, skeptical positions have been motivated by realist intuitions (and antirealist retorts have been motivated by anti-skeptical convictions). It would thus be a mistake to use the term "realism" so as to make realism incompatible with skepticism. Arguing for Robust Realism and defeating the normative skeptic – *this* normative skeptic, at least, the one claiming that no moral belief is justified, or amounts to knowledge – are thus two

---

[4] I take the point in the text to be a natural extension of Darwall's (1998, 65) distinction between the context of (the making of) the judgment and the context of the evaluated object. The reason Darwall's distinction cannot be enough here is that as stated it only seems to apply to observer- or speaker-dependence, not to agent-dependence.

[5] I do not pretend that I have here given an account of how objectivity is best understood. All I take myself to have done here is make it reasonably clear what it is that I have in mind when using this loaded word. I will have more to say on objectivity in the next chapter.

[6] It's not as if the natural–nonnatural distinction is very clear either. I have more to say about it – and consequently, about the nature of Robust Realism – in Chapter 5.

different, though related, tasks:[7] different, because Robust Realism is compatible with skepticism; related, because if the apparatus needed for a rejection of normative skepticism is unavailable to the robust realist, and if normative skepticism is highly implausible, this may count as a reason to reject Robust Realism after all. For now, then, let me note the compatibility of Robust Realism and skepticism, and postpone discussion of the epistemological problems to which Robust Realism may give rise to Chapter 7.

I've been characterizing Robust Realism in terms of propositions, properties, facts, truths, and the like. But these too are not beyond metaphysical controversy. Some people do not believe in facts, some do, but not in propositions, yet others don't believe in properties. At the end of the day, there may be interesting relations between a metanormative view and a view of, say, the metaphysics of properties. But I think it best not to build such relations into the very characterization of Robust Realism. I want to remain neutral, then, on such general metaphysical issues, at least at this starting point. Let me say, then, that according to Robust Realism, and *general doubts about properties aside*,[8] there are irreducibly normative properties; similarly, *general doubts about facts aside*, there are irreducibly normative facts; and so on. It seems to me I can afford this metaphysical nonchalance: for even a nominalist about, say, facts, must account for our everyday use of fact-talk; by doing that, she will have already accounted for our talk of *normative* facts – at least, that is, if Robust Realism is true. Similarly for other kinds of nominalists. And this nonchalance will allow me to speak rather loosely – sometimes about normative facts, sometimes about normative truths, and so on. The crucial point is that, in whatever sense there are physical facts, there are normative ones; in whatever sense there are truths in biology, there are in normative discourse; in whatever sense in which there are mathematical properties, there are normative ones. When, in following chapters, I talk about ontological commitment to facts and properties, this talk should be understood as subject to the metaphysical nonchalance explained here: if you'd rather avoid such entities, feel free to substitute "a commitment to a kind of truths" (or whatever) for "ontological commitment". And let me add that the metaphysical nonchalance endorsed here applies only to the most general metaphysical discussions of, for instance, the reality of properties, or truths, or facts. As I explain in Chapter 5, I am not at all metaphysically nonchalant about the normative and moral properties and facts themselves.

---

[7] The sentence in the text may seem false because of different understandings of the terms "normative skeptic" or "moral skeptic". Such terms are sometimes used to depict relativists, subjectivists, error theorists, amoralists, and perhaps others as well. I use it in the text in the more precise epistemological sense: A normative skeptic is someone who questions our entitlement to claim the status of knowledge or justification or warrant (or any other privileged epistemological status) for our normative beliefs. Brink (1989, 155) also notes that realism is compatible with skepticism (thus understood).

[8] I thank Cian Dorr for introducing me to such operators. Brink (1989, 16 n. 1) has a similar disclaimer about facts.

Much more can be said, of course, about the nature and details of Robust Realism. But it will prove useful to say more only when more is needed: the arguments for Robust Realism (in Chapters 2–5), and my replies to objections to Robust Realism (in subsequent chapters) will serve to motivate such further details. Thus, the precise view I want to defend is that view – whatever exactly its details – that satisfies the somewhat general characterization in this section, that answers to the concerns fleshed out in the positive arguments for the view, and that has the resources needed to deal with the objections to the view. The general argument of this book shows – if it works – that there is indeed such a view. And for now, the characterization above will do.

When I first offered a (very partial) defense of Robust Realism (in Enoch 2003a), I claimed the great philosophical advantage of being in the ridiculed minority, putting forward a view many don't think is even worth considering: it is a view that Gibbard (1990, 154), for instance, thought should be debunked rather than argued against, and that Miller (2003) didn't think merited discussion in a competent and widely used introduction to contemporary metaethics. But things seem to have changed, and views in the vicinity of Robust Realism are now making an impressive comeback.[9] I cannot here, of course, discuss in detail all closely related views. But it may be useful to indicate very briefly how my Robust Realism compares to some of them. The point of the following sentences, then, is not deeply philosophical, but rather heuristic: it is an attempt to help the reader locate my view in the current debate. Anyway, here it goes: unlike Cornell Realists (sometimes also called non-reductive moral naturalists) like Sturgeon (e.g. 1984), Boyd (1988), and Brink (1989) my Robust Realism is non-naturalist. My Robust Realism is much closer to that of Shafer-Landau (2003), though mine is more shamelessly non-naturalist: Shafer-Landau insists on a close metaphysical connection between the normative and the natural facts, closer than seems right to me.[10] But the nature of this connection – both according to Shafer-Landau and according to my Robust Realism – needs more discussion, and I therefore postpone it to Chapter 5. Bloomfield (2001) is also a naturalist-realist. We differ, then, regarding his naturalism, and also in that my Robust Realism is not Footean-Aristotelian in anything like the way Bloomfield's is.[11] Wedgwood (2007) is a non-naturalist realist about normativity,[12] but unlike him I want to have nothing at all to do with the idea

---

[9] Finlay (2010, 57 n. 1), for instance, classifies this as the now dominant view, also noting that its adherents still like to describe themselves as swimming against the current. And notice the change in tone regarding this kind of view from Gibbard (1990) to Gibbard (2003). Also see Stratton-Lake's "Introduction", in his 2002.

[10] For the suggestion that there may be less of a difference between Shafer-Landau and naturalists, see Cuneo (2007b, 871). Also, it seems that now Shafer-Landau is also committed to the causal efficacy of moral properties (see Shafer-Landau (2007)). If so, this is another difference between us, though this difference may come down not to a difference in the understanding of moral properties but rather to a difference in the understanding of what it takes to be causally efficacious.

[11] See here also Hursthouse (2004), and the references there to many of Philippa Foot's relevant texts.

[12] But see his discussion of the way in which he is nevertheless a naturalist (2007, 221), and his important (and for me, disappointing) disclaimers about some of the important metaphysical issues (2007, 135 n. 1). In conversation, though, Wedgwood assured me that on these matters too he and I are on the same page – the

that the intentional is normative, an idea which he takes to be "the key to metaethics" (2007, 2). Because of the centrality of this idea to his entire project, very little of the similarity between our views will be apparent in what follows. Indeed, when I do rely on him (in section 7.6 in Chapter 7), it will take an effort to see that the way in which I do this can be abstracted away from his relying on the normativity of the intentional. Unlike Oddie (2005), my Robust Realism is not committed to the causal efficacy of normative facts. This also means that I am not committed to Oddie's interesting (but ultimately, I would say, implausible) view of desires as perceptions of value.[13] In certain respects there are strong similarities between my Robust Realism and the views of Nagel (1986; 1997), Parfit (2011), Scanlon (1998, ch. 1; and more recently 2009), Dworkin (1996 and forthcoming), and Kramer (2009). But all of these writers – in different ways, and some more clearly than others – think that a fairly robust metaethical and indeed metanormative realism can nevertheless be metaphysically light, ontologically uncommitted, and so also (to an extent) immune to some of the traditional objections to such a view, objections that are (to an extent) based on a misunderstanding of this view. I have no such illusions. My Robust Realism wears its ontological commitment on its sleeve. I believe that if we are to take morality seriously, we must go for such an ontologically committed view, precisely as understood by some of the traditional objections to such a view. The thing for us realists to do, I believe, is not to disavow ontological commitment and pretend that this solves (or dissolves) problems for our realism. Rather, we must step up to the plate, and defend the rather heavy commitments of our realism. This, any way, will be what I attempt to do in this book. My view is closer to (the relevant parts of) those expressed by Tännsjö(2010), Fitzpatrick (2008), Cuneo (2007a), and Huemer (2006) – except that these writers, because their main order of business lies elsewhere (very roughly speaking: establishing that there is only one kind of obligation and reason, rejecting naturalist realism, establishing the analogy between epistemic and practical normativity, and refuting all alternatives to Robust Realism, respectively) do not develop their positive view in detail,[14] and so it is hard to determine to what extent precisely my view and theirs are alike.

I have just mentioned seventeen (!) philosophers whose views are at least somewhat close to my Robust Realism. The impatient reader may take this as evidence not for the livelihood of the debate but rather for the redundancy of yet another book on the topic. But this, I think (and hope), would be a mistake, for reasons I give toward the end of section 1.2 below.

---

disclaimer is there not because he doesn't believe these stronger claims, but merely because he doesn't argue for them in that book.

[13] My Robust Realism *is* committed, however, to the other four tenets of robust realism Oddie (2005, ch. 1) specifies, namely (in his terms) propositional content, presupposition fulfillment, mind-independence, and irreducibility.

[14] Though see Tännsjö 1990. And both Cuneo and Fitzpatrick have told me they are working on a more comprehensive development and defense of their views.

Finally, a point about terminology. Robust Realism and views in its vicinity go by many different names, names which I prefer not to use. "Platonism" as well as "Moorean Realism" suggest historical commitments which I would rather avoid (partly because I am not competent to evaluate them). "Rational Intuitionism" may also have such historical overtones. Furthermore, it uses an epistemological characterization of the view. I, on the other hand, characterized the view differently, leaving it to further discussion (here, in Chapter 7) to see what the epistemological commitments of the view are. "Non-naturalist realism" or simply "Non-naturalism" could do, I guess, though these terms suggest a negative characterization of the view, and I see no reason to opt for such a characterization. And while "Objectivism" is not completely misleading, it is also under-specific and highly ambiguous. This is why I think it is better to use a somewhat new[15] but also at least minimally informative term, "Robust Realism", and be reasonably clear and explicit about what it means (in this book, at least). But here as elsewhere, nothing hinges on the choice of terminology. If switching to a different terminology helps you as you go through this book, feel free to do so. I will not be offended if you call me a Platonist.[16]

1.2 The motivation

I suspect that as a psychological matter, I hold the metaethical and metanormative view I in fact hold not because of highly abstract arguments in the philosophy of language, say, or in the philosophy of action, or because of some general ontological commitments. My underlying motivations for holding the metaethical view I in fact hold are – to the extent that they are transparent to me – much less abstract, and perhaps even much less philosophical. Like many other realists (I suspect), I pre-theoretically feel that nothing short of a fairly strong metaethical realism will vindicate our taking morality seriously. Now, such inchoate pre-theoretical feelings are, I agree, philosophically suspicious. They certainly fall well short of an adequate argument for a philosophical view. But they are, I submit, good as starting points. The philosophical challenge then becomes either to vindicate them by presenting detailed views and arguments that answer to those initial concerns, or to explain them away.

My two main positive arguments for Robust Realism – the argument from the moral implications of metaethical objectivity (in Chapter 2) and the argument from deliberative indispensability (in Chapter 3) – constitute my attempt at facing up to this

---

[15] In my (2003a) I picked up this term from Boghossian (1989, 547), who uses it in the context of a discussion of meaning-skepticism to refer to a position about meaning analogous to mine about normativity. In the meanwhile, it has been used in the metanormative context by Oddie (2005), to depict a closely related (but, as stated above, not identical) view, and by Fitzpatrick (2008) to pick out a view that may very well be identical to mine. And I thank Sigrún Svavarsdóttir for the suggestion to use "Robust Realism" as a suitable name for my view.

[16] As I already said, I am not competent to evaluate the similarities between my view and Plato's. But at least one Plato scholar (Matt Evans) assures me that this term would not be totally out of place here.

philosophical challenge, by converting the general suspicion that without a fairly strong realism morality cannot be taken seriously into reasonably precise and clear arguments. They answer to different – though related – concerns, both members of the taking-morality-seriously family. The first is an interpersonal concern, and of the two it is the one most directly related to morality, and indeed – when push comes to shove – to politics. Here the thought is that had morality not been objective in a fairly strong sense (made clearer in Chapter 2), the moral constraints applying to the resolution of some conflicts would have been different than they actually are. In particular, under non-objectivist metaethical assumptions, conjoined with some fairly plausible moral premises, it would be morally impermissible to stand one's moral ground in any number of conflicts or disagreements where it does seem permissible (perhaps even required) to stand one's moral ground.

The second concern – that underlying the argument from deliberative indispensability in Chapter 3 – is more first-personal. The main thought there is that objective, irreducibly normative facts are indispensable (in a sense made there reasonably precise) for deliberation, and that this indispensability suffices to justify belief in their existence. This argument, then, is not primarily about ethics or morality at all: this is where my discussion is most clearly a metanormative rather than a metaethical discussion.

My positive arguments for Robust Realism aim not just at soundness but also at sincerity in the following sense. Often when reading philosophy one gets the feeling that the writer cares more deeply about his or her conclusion than about the argument, so that if the argument can be shown to fail, the philosopher whose argument it is will simply proceed to look for other arguments for the same conclusion rather than take back his or her commitment to the conclusion. And there need be nothing wrong with arguing in this way. The main thing that should interest us about philosophical arguments is how good they are, not what the motivations are of those putting them forward. And perhaps we have a general philosophical interest in philosophers doing the best they can to support their views – it is not impossible that philosophical progress is better served by such an adversarial practice. To risk what may be considered by some an admission of philosophical naivety on my part: this is how I think of the increasingly clever discussions of the Frege–Geach problem (and related problems) for expressivist theories.[17] Expressivists putting forward a suggested solution to the Frege–Geach problem will – if God whispers in their ears that their solution fails – proceed to look for another one, rather than convert to cognitivism (or some such). And the problem itself, while possibly a devastating objection to expressivism, is in a certain way a fluke – it does not, I think, answer to the deeper worries some of us have about expressivism. If God whispers in the ears of all cognitivists that the Frege–Geach problem can be very

---

[17] Very roughly: the problem of accounting for the content of normative judgments (such as "Lying is wrong") in non-assertoric contexts (such as "She thinks that lying is wrong", or "It is not the case that lying is wrong"), where they cannot plausibly be understood as expressing the relevant conative attitude (say, disapproving of lying). For a good introduction and survey, see Schroeder (2008b).

neatly solved, I do not foresee a trend of conversion to expressivism. And to repeat, there need be nothing wrong with proceeding in this way: there has recently been much progress, I think, on the Frege–Geach problem, perhaps more so than on the issues I take to be of deeper significance. But it nevertheless seems to me that there is something to be said for an argument in which the underlying concerns are put in clear view. And the arguments I develop in this book are, if I am successful, of this kind. The argument against expressivism in Chapter 2, for instance, is an attempt at fleshing out the deep worries we've always had about expressivism (and other non-robust-realist views). If my arguments in the next two chapters can be rejected – if, in other words, the denial of metaethical objectivity does not have any consequences that are objectionable on first-order moral grounds, and furthermore if normative truths robust-realistically understood are after all not indispensable for deliberation – then I no longer care whether Robust Realism is true, and am then happy to reject my argument's conclusion rather than look for other arguments that can better support it.

I can now address the question raised earlier: Why yet another book defending some rather strongly realist metaethical view? In reply I want quickly to mention three points.

First, I think that we realists have not – by and large – done a good enough job of addressing objections to our view, sometimes because we have failed to understand them in the most charitable way. This alone suffices to justify further discussion.

But much more pressing is the need for a positive argument for the view. As many critics are quick to note, much of the work by advocates of such strongly realist views consists either in criticizing alternative views or in responding to traditional objections to realism. There is very little by way of positive argument for Robust Realism (or related views) in the current literature.[18] The implicit – and sometimes explicit[19] – assumption of many realists seems to be that something like Robust Realism is the default view, that the burden of argument lies on the shoulders of those putting forward competing views. If so, rejecting alternative views and responding to objections may very well be all that robust realists need to worry about. I am not unsympathetic to this line of thought, but I am also painfully aware of its limitations: placing the burden of philosophical argument is often very hard, and rarely useful – we would like, after all, to have all arguments and evidence in front of us, and to make up our philosophical minds directly on the merits of the relevant case, not (merely) by using such philosophical analogues of rules from the law of evidence. And apparently, to

---

[18] Where there is more by way of characterization of the relevant kind of realism and positive arguments for realism, the results are rather idiosyncratic. The examples that come to mind here have already been mentioned: Wedgwood's relying centrally on the idea of the normativity of the intentional and Oddie's view of values as causally effective and of desires as perceptions of value make Wedgwood's and Oddie's arguments unusable to many card-carrying members of the rather-strongly-realists' club.

[19] See for instance, McGinn (1997, 8). And this seems to be the tone both in Parfit (2006, see for instance 330–2) and in Shafer-Landau (2003; see for instance 2–3). For a more explicit statement, see Shafer-Landau (2005, 264).

some Robust Realism is very far from being the default position. At any rate, it would be better – more dialectically effective, perhaps, and more intellectually satisfying even if not more dialectically effective – to have positive arguments for Robust Realism. This is the gap this books tries to fill. I hope you will agree it is a good enough reason to write a book.

Last, though it is hard to find positive arguments for Robust Realism, it is even harder to find arguments for the view that are sincere in the sense explained above – arguments that answer, that is, to the underlying concerns that make (some of) us hope and pre-theoretically believe that Robust Realism is true. If my attempt at abiding by this restriction throughout this book is successful, this too, I think, fills a gap in the now rather densely populated realism literature.

1.3 The book

The rest of this book is divided into two main parts. Chapters 2–5 consist of the positive argument for Robust Realism. Chapters 6–9 consist of replies to common objections to Robust Realism. And Chapter 10 concludes.

In Chapter 2 I argue that any non-objectivist metaethical theory will have – when conjoined with a plausible moral principle – implications that are unacceptable on first-order, moral grounds. In particular, I argue that a plausible principle governing the resolution of conflicts that are due to mere preferences (or other subjective attitudes of this kind) – the principle I call IMPARTIALITY – entails, under non-objectivist metaethical premises, objectionable moral conclusions. This suffices, I argue, to reject such non-objectivist metaethical theories. The argument in this chapter is – if successful – an argument for objectivity that is sensitive to why it is that objectivity matters, and because of this it also helps in understanding what the objectivity we are after comes to. Interestingly, the discussion in this chapter also helps to capture the sense in which expressivist theories are not objectivist – a suspicion many of us have had for a while, but one that it has proved remarkably hard to flesh out in any detail. In an appendix, I show how the discussion in this chapter can contribute to discussions of the normative neutrality of metaethics.

In Chapter 3 I put forward my argument from deliberative indispensability to Robust Metanormative Realism. The argument here is modeled after arguments from explanatory indispensability in the sciences or in the philosophy of mathematics. Such arguments are taken by most philosophers to justify ontological commitments (to, say, electrons, and – more controversially – numbers and sets). For the most part I take it as given that these philosophers are right (though I also say something about why I think that this is so). The crucial point to notice, I argue, is that such arguments from explanatory indispensability are really particular instances of a more general kind of argument, a kind of argument that has other, non-explanatory instances as well. Deliberative indispensability, I argue, is just as respectable as explanatory indispensability, and can equally ground ontological commitment. And indeed, I argue that thinking about deliberation naturally leads to the conclusion that irreducibly normative facts are indispensable for deliberation. This, I conclude, gives sufficient reason to believe that they exist.

As already noted, there is a discrepancy in the conclusions of Chapters 2 and 3: the former is metaethical, the latter metanormative; and the former establishes only some kind of objectivity, while the latter (if successful) goes all the way to Robust Realism. I want to concede even at this early stage that my positive arguments in Chapters 2 and 3 do not entail – even when combined – Robust Meta*ethical* Realism. Nevertheless, the combined force of these two arguments leaves any metaethical view other than Robust Realism utterly unmotivated. Or so, at least, I argue in Chapter 4.

Even if, at the end of Chapter 4, you are convinced that something in the vicinity of Robust Realism is probably true (or at least well-motivated), you may still think that we can have what is important in Robust Realism without the metaphysical extravagance of irreducibly normative, non-natural, normative truths. You may think, in other words, that even given the underlying concerns of Chapters 2–4, we may still be able to do with less, metaphysically speaking. In Chapter 5 I argue against three general strategies for doing with less: a naturalist reduction, several kinds of error theories and fictionalist views, and the currently fashionable attempts at a quietist, metaphysically nonchalant and uncommitted kind of realism. This chapter concludes, then, my positive case for Robust Realism. But it is also the first part of the metaphysical discussion that continues in Chapter 6, where I defend Robust Realism against the accusation of being committed to unacceptable metaphysics.

I do what I can to deal with objections to the arguments for Robust Realism in Chapters 2–5. But this leaves the task of dealing with objections to Robust Realism itself – objections, that is, attempting to show that Robust Realism itself is untenable, perhaps regardless of the considerations that can be mobilized in motivating it. The four chapters that follow deal with such objections, and the list is unlikely to surprise you, for the problems with Robust Realism and closely related views are ones we have been familiar with – in some form or other – for a while. Except for being yet further attempts – *my* attempts – at responding to these objections, these chapters are special in that the influence of the positive arguments of Chapters 2–5 is still present in them: the fact that I have available to me these positive arguments puts me in a better place (in certain crucial points in the dialectic) to respond to these objections.

Chapter 6 deals with the accusation that Robust Realism is committed to unacceptable – perhaps "queer" – metaphysics. My defense against the accusation of unacceptable metaphysics proceeds not by denying the commitment, but rather by denying the unacceptability. I argue that especially given the discussion in Chapter 3 sufficient reason has been given to include irreducibly normative facts in our ontology. In other words, I argue that Naturalism – understood as a metaphysical thesis – is false. In this chapter I also discuss the more focused objection to Robust Realism from the supervenience of the normative. I argue that the normative does supervene on the non-normative, that it is nevertheless not reducible to the non-normative, that this does indeed give rise to an explanatory challenge the robust realist must face, and that this challenge can by and large be coped with, given some other plausible assumptions.

In Chapter 7 I respond to the (or "the") epistemological objection to Robust Realism. As things turn out, it is entirely unclear what the challenge precisely comes to. Much of the work done in that chapter consists in presenting what I take to be the strongest version of the challenge, and distinguishing it from other, weaker versions. The stronger version is one that realists (of the fairly robust kind) have been remarkably good at ignoring. The real challenge, I argue, is that of explaining the correlation between our normative beliefs and the independent normative truths, a correlation in the absence of which we should adopt a skeptical position regarding normative judgments. I then suggest a way for Robust Realism to cope with this challenge: I argue that the correlation that needs to be explained is not as striking as it seems, and that whatever by way of correlation does need explaining can be explained consistently with Robust Realism, by a godless (and so speculatively evolutionary) pre-established harmony kind of explanation. In a final section I deal in a preliminary and unsatisfactory way with the claim that the robust realist lacks the resources to explain our ability to have semantic access to – say, to refer to – the normative facts and properties she is a robust realist about. Drawing on Ralph Wedgwood's work, I offer a sketch of a semantic account that is consistent with Robust Realism, and several arguments (partly utilizing the discussion of epistemic access in the earlier sections of this chapter) showing that there is reason to be cautiously optimistic about the prospects of Robust Realism dealing with this challenge in a satisfactory way.

Chapter 8 again consists in large part in clarifying an objection to Robust Realism, on the way to rejecting it. This time it is the objection from disagreement. I distinguish several different versions of "the" argument from disagreement appearing in the literature, arguing that some of the appeal of "the" argument comes from various shifts and equivocations between the different arguments. Once clearly distinguished, the different arguments can be critically assessed. The results of such an exercise, I argue, are mixed, but on the whole quite encouraging for Robust Realism: some versions of the argument can be shown to fail without remainder; others pose more serious challenges, but really challenges that have nothing essentially to do with disagreement, and that are (therefore) discussed in other chapters in this book; and yet others do leave the robust realist paying some price in plausibility points – but not a sufficiently high price for the realist to worry too much about it.

In Chapter 9 I engage the literature on the relation between morality, normative reasons, and motivation. I do this not in an attempt to uncover the complete and ultimate truth regarding these matters, but only with a much more focused aspiration, that of showing that Robust Realism can accommodate whatever in this area needs accommodating. This is of significance, because some think that it is here that Robust Realism's failure is most clearly present – it fails to account for the practicality of morality, or for the relation between morality and reasons, or perhaps between reasons and motivation, or between the making of a normative judgment and motivation, or something along these lines. In response, I argue that there is indeed a necessary connection between morality and normative reasons. I thus accept what is sometimes called Moral Rationalism. But, I argue, there is no (sufficiently strong, not normatively mediated) necessary connection between reasons and motivation. I thus reject most versions of what are sometimes called both judgment- and existence-internalist views. This leaves me with the task of explaining away the appeal of the kinds of internalism I reject. I argue that their appeal comes from the broadly Williamsian constraint that if an agent has a reason to act in a certain way, then it must be possible for the agent to act *for* that reason. I distinguish between this constraint and the stronger Williamsian constraint, namely, that if an agent has a reason to act in a certain way it must be possible for the agent to be motivated by that reason. The former – sound – constraint can be accommodated by the externalist robust realist who rejects the latter, I argue, once greater care is given to what it is to act for a reason.

1.4 How I do philosophy

It would be great if all non-robust-realist views of ethics and normativity could be decisively refuted (say, by showing they entail contradictions), or if Robust Realism could be decisively proved in some other way. I don't think anything like this is likely to happen any time soon – indeed, I think it is highly unlikely ever to happen, here as elsewhere with big philosophical debates. So we should settle for less.

It would be great if one view of ethics and normativity – greater still if it happened to be Robust Realism – had *everything* going for it, if, in other words, whenever you compared it to any alternative view in any respect, this view always seemed the more attractive one. But this too seems to me unlikely to be the case: after all, highly intelligent, good philosophers can be found on all sides of the metaethical and the metanormative debate, and had there been a view that scored higher than any alternative on *each and every* relevant issue, chances are the philosophical debate in this area would have been much less lively. So in trying to decide the metaethical and metanormative issues, we should settle for even less than an explanatory knockout.

What we should look for, I submit, is the philosophical theory that is best as a theory overall – and this is consistent, of course, with its losing some plausibility points on this or that issue, as long as it makes up for this loss with the plausibility points it honestly earns on other issues.[20]

So it is consistent with offering a defense of Robust Realism to admit that this view does lose plausibility points in dealing with some of the objections to the view. And this, anyway, seems to me the intellectually honest thing to do. It is in this spirit that I ask that you read the second part of the book (Chapters 6–9). Even when the polemical tone seems to indicate otherwise, the game being played is still that of

---

[20] This view of how we do – and also should do – philosophy is inspired by David and Stephanie Lewis (1983, 8–9).

overall plausibility points, where the robust realist is playing defense, attempting to reduce the loss in plausibility points due to the relevant objection. The point is not, for instance, that the robust realist has a better account of normative disagreement, better than that of any alternative metanormative theory. Quite possibly, some other meta-normative views score more plausibility points on this issue than Robust Realism. The point is, rather, that the loss for Robust Realism in plausibility points on this issue is – if there is one – not *that* significant, not significant enough to justify rejecting the view, given its other advantages, and given the other disadvantages (of which I say very little in this book) of alternative views. Of course, I do not in this book settle for only playing defense: I play offense in Chapters 2–5. But from then on, it's all about defense, minimizing the loss of plausibility points.

In Chapter 10 I try to keep score, briefly going through the advantages of Robust Realism for which I've argued in previous chapters, and the disadvantages I've conceded in them. It's not always easy to keep score in this way and tally the plausibility points – it would have been easier, say, to count *arguments*,[21] though given this book's division into chapters, this would have spelled doom for Robust Realism. So I do not expect unanimity or even significant convergence on this (or on anything else). But this too, I think, is just a part of how we do (and should do) philosophy: We should present all of the relevant arguments and considerations in plain view, and then just see which theory seems to make better sense (to us) overall. When the project is understood to be modest in this way, I think that Robust Realism emerges victorious.

---

[21] Here's the proof-that-*p* attributed to Katz (for instance, here: http://consc.net/misc/proofs.html): "I have seventeen arguments for the claim that *p*, and I know of only four for the claim that not-*p*. Therefore *p*."

2

The Argument from the Moral Implications of Objectivity (or Lack Thereof)

My first positive argument for a view in the vicinity of Robust Realism is the argument from the moral implications of objectivity, or indeed its absence. The intuitive idea underlying this argument is rather simple: Metaethical positions that are not objectivist in some important, intuitive sense have – in the context of interpersonal disagreement and conflict – implications that are objectionable on first-order, moral grounds, and should therefore be rejected. In this chapter, then, I do not look into the metaethical significance of moral disagreement directly (I do this, to an extent, in Chapter 8), but rather into the metaethical significance *of the moral significance* or implications of moral disagreement and conflict. And if I am right, focusing on the metaethical significance of the moral significance of disagreement and conflict can serve to vindicate the philosophical hunch – shared by many, I think – that there *must* be something objectionably non-objectivist about response-dependence and expressivist metaethical theories, that there *must* be some important way in which such views fail to take morality seriously, a suspicion that it has proved remarkably hard to precisify and establish.

Here is how my attempt at filling in the details of this intuitive thought will proceed. In section 2.1 I state, defend, and elaborate on the moral principle I will be using in my argument for objectivity, the principle I call IMPARTIALITY. In section 2.2 I show that a certain caricaturized metaethical position (Caricaturized Subjectivism) entails – when combined with the IMPARTIALITY principle from section 2.1 – highly implausible normative results. By the end of this section, then, Caricaturized Subjectivism – a paradigmatically metaethical theory – is shown to be false (because some of its normative implications are false). In the following sections I generalize the argument and inquire about the scope of its conclusion. In section 2.3 I argue that the argument from section 2.2 applies to many (non-caricaturized) response-dependence metaethical theories. In section 2.4 I generalize the argument even further, claiming that it applies to expressivist (and related) metaethical positions. In section 2.5 I discuss ways in which the argument can*not* be further generalized, and so I state the limited scope of its conclusion. Thus, Caricaturized Subjectivism is, of course, a caricature, and it is introduced here as a heuristic device, one that is intended to help in introducing the more interesting philosophical discussion – the one that does the real metaethical work – in sections 2.3 through 2.5. After the concluding section (2.6), I discuss – in an appendix – metaethics' purported neutrality on normative, moral, first-order questions. I put forward an interpretation of that thought, and claim that the argument in this chapter shows that – at least with neutrality thus understood – metaethics is not morally neutral.

First, though, two inevitable preliminaries, for it is not at all clear what objectivity is (in general, or even just in the metaethical context),[1] nor is it clear how to delineate the moral and the metaethical.[2] I have already had something to say on my understanding of objectivity in the previous chapter. Let me not say more now, for two reasons. First, what I do say in Chapter 1 (the relation to response-independence) is largely motivated by what will be my conclusions at the end of this chapter. So it would be awkward to try and say more at this point. And second, we do not need to say more at this point. Instead of doing that, I am deliberately going to avoid using the word "objectivity" for most of this chapter. Nothing at all in the first two sections – and at most very little in the following sections – will depend on how objectivity is understood. Though the term "objectivity" will not be doing any work in what follows, then, the conclusion supported by the argument developed here can, I think, rather naturally be described in terms of objectivity: I argue, that is, for the objectivity of morality, in at least *one* perfectly natural sense of this loaded word. And this, for present purposes, is quite enough. I briefly return to this issue in the concluding section of the chapter.

As for the moral, the metaethical, and the line between them: I suggest that we avoid this problem by focusing our attention on just paradigmatically moral and paradigmatically metaethical propositions. We can thus postpone for another occasion – to a large extent, at least – worries about more precise ways of delineating the moral and the metaethical (a topic I will briefly revisit in Chapter 4).

2.1 The normative premise: IMPARTIALITY

We're spending the afternoon together. I want to go catch a movie I've been looking forward to seeing. You'd rather play tennis. But both of us really want to spend the afternoon together. How should we proceed?

It seems clear that some loosely speaking egalitarian or impartial solution is called for. Perhaps we should flip a coin, thus giving equal chances to the movie and the tennis match. Or perhaps we should take turns – so that you get to choose what we do today, and I get to choose what we do next time we're spending an afternoon together. Or perhaps we should let some impartial spectator decide for us. But anyway, it would be wrong for me to stand my ground, and just insist that we go to the movie theater.

---

[1] For some discussion, see Rosen (1994) and Svavarsdóttir (2001).
[2] For some discussion in a relevant context, see Fantl (2006, 25).

Doing so – without some rather special further story, at least – would be wrong, unreasonable if anything is. Why is that so?

Here's one plausible explanation. You and I are, in a sense, equally morally important. In a situation of the kind described, and absent some distinguishing story, our preferences should count equally. After all, in the example of this friendly conflict of interests, it is just preferences that are involved. Now, each one of us should acknowledge that we are equally morally important, that our preferences should – other things being equal – count equally. Putting the point Nagelianly,[3] you should be willing to step back, and view the situation as just a situation of a conflict between two persons, one of whom happens to be you; you should be willing to abstract from your indexical knowledge here – that the preference for tennis is *your* preference – and treat your preference for playing tennis as just the preference of one among several, the one who happens also to be you. Similarly, of course, for my stepping back from my preferences. If I choose to stand my ground and just insist that we catch that movie (without offering some further justifying story), I refuse to step back in this way, and so I refuse to treat you and your preferences as equally important to mine.

The point is not, of course, that there is something morally wrong in just acting on my own preferences. If I am spending the afternoon by myself, there is no problem in my going to the movies simply because, well, I want to (or would enjoy doing so, or some such). The point is, rather, about a constraint on the appropriate way of settling some interpersonal conflicts. And what I've so far claimed is that in at least some cases of conflicts that are due to a mere preference, the right thing to do is to step back in this Nagelian sort of way, and endorse an impartial solution.[4] And the same principle holds, I now want to suggest, for conflicts that are due merely to other attitudes or feelings.

---

[3] This is a major theme in Nagel (1986; and for its applications to political philosophy, see his 1991). When Nagel talks in the political context about the impersonal point of view (which each person occupies alongside the personal point of view) he sometimes just means the point of view from which people's *interests* count equally, one without which "there would be no morality, only the clash, compromise, and occasional convergence of individual perspectives" (1991, 3–4). At other times, though, he seems to suggest that from the impersonal point of view we also step back from our *beliefs*, including our moral beliefs (1987; and to a lesser extent also 1991, ch. 14). I think Nagel is importantly right about the case of interests, and (at least partly) importantly wrong about beliefs, moral beliefs included (Nagel himself is painfully aware of the distinction between the two cases, and of the fact that it's much harder to justify the latter kind of impartiality (for instance, 1991, 158: "Impartiality among persons is one thing, but impartiality among conceptions of the good is quite another") but he nevertheless thinks this can be done). This point will be crucial in what is to come.

[4] Put in reason-talk, this may be either because in cases of interpersonal conflicts of this sort others' preferences too give you reasons (just like your own), or – perhaps somewhat more plausibly – because even though you have stronger first-order reasons to act on your own preference, still you have a second-order reason not to act on that balance of reasons. For my purposes in this chapter I do not have to decide between these two reason-talk explanations, because in both of them IMPARTIALITY – the moral principle I am about to get to in the text – does explanatory work. In the second, it is the source of the said second-order reason. And in the first, it is what explains why even though often others' preferences do not give you reasons (certainly not as strong as those given by your own preferences), in cases of interpersonal conflict they often do.

You may be worried that I'm underestimating the normative force of preferences, or feelings, or attitudes. In a somewhat different context, Simon Blackburn expresses a related worry:

Does the lover escape his passion by thinking "Oh, it's only my passion, forget it"? When the world affords occasion for grief, does it brighten when we realize that it is we who grieve? (1993, 176)

There's a sense in which Blackburn is clearly right: some feelings or attitudes can give me powerful reasons, reasons that are perfectly consistent with my realizing that they depend in some strong sense on these feelings or attitudes being very much mine. The answer to Blackburn's rhetorical question is very much as he expects it to be: the world does not brighten when we realize that it is we who grieve. But in our context, we need to think about another question,[5] we need to think of a case in which grief somehow gives rise to an interpersonal conflict. Usually, when someone is grieving we should go out of our way to accommodate them. So for instance, if you and I are the only physicians in town, and you are grieving, I should cover for you, work your shift, and so on. But now suppose that the world affords an equally serious occasion for grief for *both* of us. In this case, there *is* a sense in which I should step back, just like in the movie-or-tennis case. If I stand my ground, insisting that because I am grieving I should be accommodated, if I am unwilling to see the situation more impersonally, as one where two people (one of whom happens to be me) are equally entitled to accommodation – if, in other words, I am insisting that you cover my shift, then I am acting wrongly. In this sense, then, I *should* step back from my grieving, and it is important that I understand that it is just me who is grieving. The point is not that this fact brightens up the world, or makes the grief any less serious, or takes anything from its reason-giving force. The point is, rather, one about the significance of grief in certain interpersonal conflicts.

I suggest, then, the following approximation of a moral principle:

IMPARTIALITY: In an interpersonal conflict, we should step back from our mere preferences, or feelings, or attitudes, or some such, and to the extent the conflict is due to those, an impartial, egalitarian solution is called for. Furthermore, each party to the conflict should acknowledge as much: Standing one's ground is, in such cases, morally wrong.

Now, I am pretty sure that IMPARTIALITY does not hold in full generality. Perhaps, in other words, one of the ways in which it is permissible for us to be partial towards ourselves is to give extra weight, in some circumstances, to our own preferences

---

[5] Because I am suggesting a different question here, it is not immediately clear that what I am about to say amounts to a criticism of Blackburn. But I think it does: for in their context, Blackburn's rhetorical questions about love and grief are meant to answer a very general worry about his quasi-realism, and they cannot do that if I am right about the other question that follows in the text. I return to Blackburn's metaethics later in the text.

For a somewhat similar response to Blackburn's rhetorical questions, see Fantl (2006, 40).

compared to those of others, even in cases of conflict. Indeed, perhaps partiality should be seen as the rule, and IMPARTIALITY the exception that only applies in some special cases[6] (say, cases that involve a certain kind of interaction). But for now none of this matters. What does matter is that for a significant, roughly recognizable class of cases of interpersonal conflicts, IMPARTIALITY does seem to hold.

In circumstances in which IMPARTIALITY holds for preference-based conflicts, does something like it hold when a conflict is due to a perfectly factual disagreement about perfectly response-*in*dependent matters? I think it does not, but things are tricky here. Suppose that we've already agreed about going to the cinema, but we differ regarding the best way to get there. We agree that we should pick the quickest way, but we disagree about the facts: you think the quickest way would be to take a cab, while I think the quickest way would be to take the subway. How should we proceed? Well, it seems that truth – or sufficient reason to believe – makes a difference here, and so one perfectly sensible way of proceeding could be for me to try and convince you that taking the subway would be quicker, and for you to try and convince me that really, we should take a cab. But suppose that we still disagree, and that it seems like there is no point in continuing the discussion. A decision has to be made. What should we do? In this case, I think there is considerable pressure in the direction of an impartial solution of sorts. Perhaps, for instance, we should both agree to flip a coin, giving equal chance to our respective suggested solutions. So in this case, something like the analogue of IMPARTIALITY for factual beliefs seems to hold – we should both step back, view our beliefs as just the beliefs of someone who happens to be us, and so go for an impartial solution.

But I think the example is not clean enough as it stands, and that once we are more careful about some of the details, the analogue of IMPARTIALITY relevant here can be seen to fail. One complication is epistemological. For often when you find out that others who are (roughly) your epistemic peers disagree with you, this is some evidence that you are wrong. Epistemologists differ regarding the appropriate way of revising one's beliefs given peer disagreement, and I cannot discuss this controversy here.[7] But for our purposes here we need to abstract from the epistemic significance of the disagreement – it may be *epistemically* unreasonable for you to stand your epistemic ground and continue believing just as confidently as before that the quickest way to get to the movie theater is to take a cab, given that I differ. But it is not *epistemic* reasonableness we are interested in here. Rather, we are to assume that you remain epistemically justified in your belief (perhaps because you know that I am not as reliable as you are on the relevant matters, and so that we are not after all precisely each other's

[6] Sam Scheffler made this point to me in an especially powerful way.

[7] For my own view, and for references, see my "Not Just a Truthometer" (2011). Tristram McPherson noted that at least some theorists' views on peer disagreement may be thought of as incorporating an epistemological analogue of IMPARTIALITY. The point in the text is that in order to isolate the effect of IMPARTIALITY in the practical domain, we have to think of the significance of peer disagreement as already accounted for.

peers), and then proceed to ask how you are justified in proceeding *practically*, given our disagreement and (moderate) conflict.[8]

A second complication arises from the fact that in many real-life cases there are going to be other consequences, and perhaps also other normatively relevant factors, that will bear on how we are to proceed, factors that for our purposes we want to abstract from. For instance, standing my ground and insisting that we should take the subway (rather than take a cab) may harm our friendship in the future. Or your feelings may be hurt. Or some such. If such conditions hold, then they may give me excellent reasons not to act on what I take to be the truth of the matter (namely, that it's best if we take the subway).

But let's assume these complications away. Assume, then, that I am right – it would be quicker to take the subway. Assume further that I know as much, or at least that I justifiably believe as much, and that this justification survives the factoring-in of the peer disagreement (in other words, assume that even after reducing my confidence to the extent perhaps required given the peer disagreement involved, I am still epistemically justified in holding this belief). And assume further that I can act on my true judgment here without my doing so having any other bad consequences – perhaps I know that you are very forgetful about such things, or that you won't really mind. In such a case, it seems to me, it is no longer true that I should step back from my true belief, and support an "impartial" solution[9]. Truth *does* make a difference, it seems to me, but in the normal, messy cases the difference the truth makes may be overshadowed by other factors.

Another way of seeing that truth does matter here, and so that it's not the case that the analogue of IMPARTIALITY holds for factual beliefs, is to think about cases where the relevant truth is extremely important. In the quickest-way-to-the-movie-theater example, after all, the relevant truth didn't matter that much, and so other normatively relevant factors could outweigh it rather easily. But now suppose we're trying to neutralize a bomb: you think we should cut the red wire, and I think we should cut the blue one. And suppose that I am right, and that I am rational in believing as I do, even given the relevant peer disagreement. How should I proceed? Well, if much is at stake, it seems to me I should act on what I (rightly, and rationally) take to be the truth of the matter. Perhaps this will offend you, and if so, this counts against my proceeding in this way, and for my opting for an impartial procedure (like perhaps flipping a coin). But this reason is overwhelmingly outweighed by the reason I have to neutralize the bomb, that is, the reason I have to cut the blue wire (and not flip a coin about it). It seems to me, then, that the thing to do in this case is to act on the relevant truth, rather than on a solution that is neutral as between my true belief and your false one – and this, even if you're just as confident in your belief here as I am in mine. If so, this

---

[8] Kalderon (2005, ch. 1) consistently conflates the epistemic and the practical questions relevant to proceeding in cases of disagreement and conflict. This is one of the reasons why his conclusions regarding disagreement (moral and otherwise) are so different from mine.

[9] Even if there is something problematic in standing one's ground here, it is not because of a violation of IMPARTIALITY. Perhaps – a point I owe Dan Greco and Tristram McPherson – in some circumstances such behavior would be objectionably paternalistic or some such. But IMPARTIALITY still does not seem to apply.

strengthens the point from the previous paragraph – truth does matter here, even if it is not the only thing that matters. Sometimes other considerations are more important, and then it may look as if something like an analogue of IMPARTIALITY holds. But in fact it does not, for sometimes other considerations do not outweigh the significance of the relevant truth. In fact, in such cases it seems clear that IMPARTIALITY has no weight whatsoever. (And notice, of course, that in the mere-preference cases, IMPARTIALITY delivers intuitively plausible results even in cases where we neutralize other factors.)

Things would have been different if my reason for the relevant action – for instance, for cutting the blue wire – was *that I believe that cutting it will neutralize the bomb*. If this was my reason for action, then given that *you* believe that cutting the *red* wire will neutralize the bomb, there may be an IMPARTIALITY-style reason to go for a symmetrical solution. After all, if my reason for action is indexical in this way (that *I* believe . . .), then perhaps I should step back, and think of my beliefs as just the beliefs of someone who happens to be me, and so go for a solution that is impartial between your beliefs and mine. But my reason for cutting the blue wire is not the indexical *that I believe that cutting it will neutralize the bomb*; rather, my reason is *that cutting it will neutralize the bomb* (as I believe).[10] It is this feature of the situation that I take to be normatively significant.[11] If I imagine a case in which cutting the blue wire will neutralize the bomb but I don't (in that hypothetical situation) believe it will, I still (actually) think I should (in that hypothetical situation) cut the blue wire; if I imagine a case in which I (in that hypothetical situation) believe that cutting the blue wire will neutralize the bomb, but this belief is false, I no longer (actually) think that I should (in that hypothetical case) cut the blue wire. So while there may be a normative symmetry between the fact that I have a certain belief and the fact that you have a certain other belief, there is no normative symmetry between the true proposition (that cutting the blue wire will neutralize the bomb) and the false one (that cutting the red wire will do so).

Let me not pretend that things are either simple or uncontroversial here. Indeed, I think some political philosophers are profoundly mistaken about the significance of disagreement, partly because they fail to appreciate the point from the previous paragraph.[12] But I think enough has been said to show that – in at least a fairly recognizable class of interpersonal conflicts – there are important differences between the appropriate way of proceeding in cases where the conflict is primarily due to mere preferences (or

[10] Dancy (2000) emphasizes something like this insight, but proceeds to develop it in directions to which I do not want to commit myself. For this point in the political context, see Raz (1998, 27; 1990, 37). For a discussion of some of its broader epistemological significance, see Schroeder (2008a). And for its significance in the context of peer disagreement, see my "Not Just a Truthometer".

[11] So the sense of "reason" I am working with here is neither that of a normative reason nor that of a motivating reason (of which more in Chapter 9). Rather, it's *the agent's* reason, that is, the feature of the situation the agent takes (rightly or wrongly) to be normatively significant. For more details here, again see my "Not Just a Truthometer". For what seems to be the same notion of an agent's reason, see also Setiya (2007, 30).

[12] Here I side with Raz (1998; 1990) as against Rawls and, well, almost everyone else. See, for instance, Nagel (1987). It is not clear to me whether these claims are ones Nagel includes under the title "the epistemological argument", which he no longer thinks works (1991, 163 n. 49).

attitudes, or feelings), and cases in which the conflict is primarily due to disagreement about descriptive matters of fact.[13] This point may be dramatized using the device of a fair adjudicator.[14] Clearly, in the tennis-or-a-movie case, such an adjudicator would opt for an impartial solution (remember, we're assuming that there's no non-indexical information that can break the symmetry here, like for instance a difference in the intensity of the relevant preferences). In cases like the bomb case, and perhaps also the subway-or-cab one, such a fair adjudicator should have no problem relying on the relevant truth.

Now consider cases of *moral* disagreement. Suppose that I believe that there is nothing wrong in causing animals (say, dogs) serious pain. It's not that I hold the factually mistaken belief that dogs are automata that don't have minds and don't feel pain. I believe they do feel pain, but I also believe that morally their pain just doesn't count. You, on the other hand, believe that there *is* something morally wrong in subjecting dogs to serious pain. And suppose that we find ourselves in the kind of situation where IMPARTIALITY would have applied to a conflict based on mere preferences, and that we need to decide about a joint course of action, with one alternative involving causing serious pain to dogs, and the other involving no such thing (but which is, perhaps, a little more pricey in some way; and these are the only normatively relevant differences between the two cases, so that all other things are held equal). Suppose further that your relevant moral belief (dog-pain counts) is true, and that you are epistemically justified in holding it, even after taking into account the epistemic significance of this peer disagreement. Further assume that no seriously problematic consequences will follow if you stand your ground. With all these assumptions in place, then, should you stand your ground, as in the case of purely factual disagreement? Or should you opt for an impartial solution, say flipping a coin, or letting me decide this time and you decide next time? It seems intuitively clear that you are justified in standing your ground, making sure that we don't proceed in the way that will subject the dog to serious pain. Similarly, it seems (to me) intuitively clear that in some cases of inter-social or inter-cultural conflicts that are due to moral disagreement (say, about the status of women) we are required – at least if we are right about the substantive issues in dispute – to stand our moral ground.[15] Going for an impartial solution will be – unless

---

[13] Some conflicts may be due both to mere preferences and to other factors (like perhaps factual beliefs). In such cases, IMPARTIALITY entails that we should step back from the preferences, but not necessarily from the other factors.

[14] I thank Moshe Halbertal for suggesting this dramatization device. Notice that I do not think of this dramatization as *an argument* for the point in the text, but rather as an especially useful way of finding out what we intuitively think here. It is, in other words, a useful intuition pump.

[15] I have focused on cases where the disagreeing parties then have to perform a joint action. Some real-life cases that involve inter-social or inter-cultural conflicts involve not so much joint action, but rather a possible intervention of one party in the actions of the other. Now, when the disagreeing parties are cultures or societies or even states, I am no longer sure there is a normatively significant distinction between a joint action of two parties, and an intervention of one party in the actions of the other. But I am not sure about this, and anyway I don't have to decide this issue here: For if anything, cases of intervention are even clearer than cases of joint action in emphasizing the distinction I want between preference-based and moral disagreements and

it can be justified by other factors – morally wrong. And so it seems to me that (when other things are equal) the right way to proceed in cases of interpersonal conflicts due to moral disagreement is analogous to the right way to proceed in cases of interpersonal conflicts due to factual disagreement, and not to the right way to proceed in cases of interpersonal conflicts due to mere preferences (and the like).

Now, the truth in the vicinity of IMPARTIALITY is, as I have already indicated, messier than the discussion here seems to imply.[16] Perhaps – though I doubt it – there are cases in which something like IMPARTIALITY holds even in cases of factual or moral disagreement. And as already stated, some partiality may be morally permissible even in some mere-preference cases. But what will be needed for the argument below is just that the two "messes" do not overlap, so that there are many sets of circumstances in which IMPARTIALITY would hold for a mere-preference conflict, but no analogous principle would hold for one that is grounded in a factual or moral disagreement. And this much does seem rather safe. We can again resort to the fair-adjudicator dramatization: in the causing-pain-to-a-dog example, a fair adjudicator should have no problem relying on the prima facie wrongness of causing pain to a dog in adjudicating the case. The situation is similar to that of conflicts due to purely factual disagreements, not to that of conflicts due to mere preferences (and the like).

I would have loved to have much more to say on IMPARTIALITY: for one thing, an account is badly needed of when I am – and when I am not – required to step back and view my own preferences (and attitudes, feelings, etc.) as just someone's preferences, someone who happens to be me. I do not have such an account up my sleeve. But the general idea IMPARTIALITY is meant to capture is, I hope, at least reasonably clear. And for now, what has been said will have to suffice.

2.2 A normative argument against Caricaturized Subjectivism

In this section I describe a certain (caricaturized) metaethical view – the one I call Caricaturized Subjectivism – then proceeding to argue that this metaethical view – conjoined with IMPARTIALITY – entails false moral conclusions. If the details of this argument work, two interesting results follow. The first, of course, is that Caricaturized

---

conflicts: it seems even more clearly wrong to intervene in the actions of another based on mere preferences than it is to give one's own preferences extra weight when it comes to joint action. See also note 17, below.

[16] Here is another kind of mess I won't be discussing (I thank Julie Tannenbaum and Mark van Roojen for drawing my attention to this point). In the tennis-or-a-movie example, it seems that it is permissible – perhaps even virtuous – to let your friend have it their way. And in order to do that, you have to know which preference is yours and which is your friend's, so it can't be morally required that you step back and consider your (and your friend's) preference as just someone's preference. All of this seems right, but I think I can bypass this complication for my purposes. All I need from IMPARTIALITY is that it is not permissible for you to just stand your ground in such cases. For what follows, it is not necessary that letting the other party have it their way be impermissible.

Subjectivism is false. The second is that metaethics – or at least Caricaturized Subjectivism – is not morally neutral in one important sense of this problematic term. In other words, though I do not show that Caricaturized Subjectivism (or any other metaethical view) *all by itself* entails first-order, moral conclusions, I nevertheless argue that when conjoined with a true moral premise (namely, IMPARTIALITY) it does entail new, and highly non-trivial moral conclusions. This suffices, I think, for a violation of neutrality, but in order to establish this claim I have to present and defend an interpretation of the idea of neutrality. Because doing so would take me too far from the main line of argument in this chapter – and indeed this book – I do so in an appendix. Here, I settle for the first result: Refuting Caricaturized Subjectivism. In the sections that follow I generalize this result to other, less caricaturized, metaethical views.

Consider, then, the following metaethical view:

Caricaturized Subjectivism:

Moral judgments report simple preferences, ones that are exactly on a par with a preference for playing tennis or for catching a movie.

An example of a specific caricaturized subjectivist view would be the theory according to which an utterance of "Abortion is wrong" just means "I prefer that people not have abortions", with the "prefer" here understood as picking out a simple, non-special straightforward preference.

I don't know of any contemporary philosopher who accepts Caricaturized Subjectivism. But for now this doesn't matter. Caricaturized Subjectivism is, after all, explicitly introduced here as a caricature of a metaethical view rather than a serious metaethical contender. For now, it will be helpful to focus on this caricature. Less caricaturized metaethical views will be discussed in following sections.

Consider, then, the following *Reductio* Argument:

(1) Caricaturized Subjectivism. (For *Reductio*.)
(2) If Caricaturized Subjectivism is true, then interpersonal conflicts due to moral disagreements are really just interpersonal conflicts due to differences in mere preferences. (From the content of Caricaturized Subjectivism.)
(3) Therefore, interpersonal conflicts due to moral disagreements are just interpersonal conflicts due to differences in mere preferences. (From 1 and 2.)
(4) IMPARTIALITY, that is, roughly: when an interpersonal conflict (of the relevant kind) is a matter merely of preferences, then an impartial, egalitarian solution is called for, and it is wrong to just stand one's ground.[17]

[17] Similar arguments can be constructed with several more specific moral premises. Fantl (2006), for instance, repeatedly talks of violent intervention and it being justified in order to prevent some serious moral wrongs, but not because of reasons merely of moral disapproval. I think that IMPARTIALITY is the general principle underlying more specific examples, Fantl's included. Also, putting things in terms of IMPARTIALITY is more transparent, placing the underlying moral concern in full light. (For the most part Fantl does not attempt to argue for the specific moral judgment he's assuming. But see Fantl (2006, 39).)

(5)   Therefore, in cases of interpersonal conflict (of the relevant kind) due to moral disagreement, an impartial, egalitarian solution is called for, and it is wrong to just stand one's ground. (From 3 and 4.)

(6)   However, in cases of interpersonal conflict (of the relevant kind) due to moral disagreement often an impartial solution is *not* called for, and it is permissible, and even required, to stand one's ground. (From previous section.)

(7)   Therefore, Caricaturized Subjectivism is false. (From 1, 5, and 6, by *Reductio*.)[18]

I think that the *Reductio* Argument is sound. It shows that – given some plausible background moral assumption (IMPARTIALITY) – Caricaturized Subjectivism has unacceptable moral implications. We should thus reject Caricaturized Subjectivism on (partly) first-order, normative grounds.[19]

At this stage, three objections come to mind.

First, (6) may be rejected on normative grounds. Someone may argue, that is, that something like IMPARTIALITY does hold for conflicts grounded in moral disagreement, that it after all *is* morally wrong to stand one's moral ground in all these cases. I have done what I can to argue against this claim – at least in its general form – in the previous section (by taking pains to neutralize the influence of other, irrelevant factors, and inviting you to reflect on an example in which this claim is rather implausible). Furthermore, note that for the argument to go through, it is sufficient that there are *some* cases of conflicts due to moral disagreements in which standing one's ground is morally permissible, and in which IMPARTIALITY would have applied in mere-preference cases. It is not necessary that this hold of *all* such conflicts. And it is even harder to deny, I think, this existentially quantified reading of (6).

A second objection starts from the (true) observation that (6) itself is a moral statement. So, assuming (6) – *read in a way inconsistent with* Caricaturized Subjectivism – amounts to begging the question against the Caricaturized Subjectivist.

---

[18]   It is sometimes suggested – though more often in the classroom than in philosophical texts – that realist metaethical views will lead to intolerance, and that this gives reason to reject them. I believe this line of thought is confused in several ways (so there's good reason why it is not common in serious philosophical texts). But I also believe that there is something right about it, something captured by the argument in the text: on non-objectivist views of morality, it is harder to justify standing one's moral ground in the face of both disagreement and conflict. But, of course, I think of this as an *advantage* of objectivist views. For a somewhat similar point, see Sturgeon (1986b, 127).

[19]   There are well-known doubts about whether views like Caricaturized Subjectivism can even accommodate interpersonal moral disagreement in a plausible way. In the text I assume they can. If they cannot, they can be rejected for this very reason, of course. A related worry may arise, according to which – at least on caricaturist subjectivist grounds – metaethical claims enjoy some kind of metaphysical priority compared to first-order moral ones, and so it can never be justified to change one's mind about the former because of arguments with the latter as premises. But first, I don't see why we should accept this kind of priority, and second, if the subjectivist puts forward something like this line of thought, this renders him especially vulnerable to (a relative of) Cian Dorr's wishful-thinking problem for noncognitivism. For the problem, see Dorr (2002). For my suggestion of a response (one that does not vindicate the move just mentioned), see my "How Noncognitivists Can Avoid Wishful Thinking" (2003b).

This is true enough, of course, but the *Reductio* Argument only assumes (6) as a premise, it does not assume any specific metaethical understanding of (6). This point can be conveniently put dialectically: The Caricaturized Subjectivist is free to understand (6) in accordance with his Subjectivism. He either accepts or denies (6), thus understood. If he accepts it, he has yet to find a way of dealing with the *Reductio* Argument. If he does not, this second objection collapses into the previous one. Either way, there is no good independent objection here to the argument against Caricaturized Subjectivism.

A third objection is more serious. For the argument assumes that all preferences (and the like) are on a par when it comes to IMPARTIALITY. In particular, it assumes that the Caricaturized Subjectivist cannot claim that the preferences to which he reduces morality are special in certain ways, special in ways that make a difference to the appropriate way of proceeding in cases of interpersonal conflict. Why can't the Caricaturized Subjectivist argue that there is no generally appropriate way of proceeding in cases of interpersonal conflict grounded in preferences? What the appropriate way of proceeding is will depend, he can argue, on the nature of the relevant preferences. Some preferences are such that we are required to step back from them (in the appropriate circumstances), and others aren't; and the ones to which morality is reducible are of the latter kind.

As an objection to the *Reductio* Argument, this objection fails, because Caricaturized Subjectivism was stipulatively defined so as to rule out such a response (because it reduces morality to preferences *that are on a par* with the preferences relevant to the movie-or-tennis case). This objection will not, then, save Caricaturized Subjectivism. But it is still extremely important. For it may be taken to show just how caricaturized Caricaturized Subjectivism really is. This objection, in other words, is best seen not as an objection to the *Reductio* Argument above, but rather as an objection to any attempt at generalizing the argument to less caricaturized, still non-objectivist metaethical positions. Such attempts will be our topic in the rest of this chapter, where I will revisit this objection.

2.3 Generalizing: response-dependence

No one writing in metaethics today, as far as I know, is a Caricaturized Subjectivist. The discussion of Caricaturized Subjectivism is not, then, of much interest in itself. It *is* interesting, I hope, for two other reasons. First, it illustrates how a metaethical position can fail to be morally neutral. Second, the argument against Caricaturized Subjectivism can serve as a productive start, a step in the right direction for constructing similar arguments against other, not at all caricaturized, metaethical positions.

Some ways in which the argument can be generalized are quite straightforward. For instance, if you want a theory that is in certain respects much like Caricaturized Subjectivism, but you hope to avoid the rather obvious counterfactual counter-examples (had I preferred seasickness, seasickness would have been of value) using the rigidifying trick[20] – by introducing an actuality operator that ties the truth of moral judgments even in other possible worlds to the relevant preferences in the actual world – the argument against Caricaturized Subjectivism applies pretty much as it stands.[21] Because I was careful to avoid any counterfactuals in stating the argument and the IMPARTIALITY premise it rests on, rigidifying is just beside the point.[22]

But I want much, much more. I want to argue that the argument against Caricaturized Subjectivism can be generalized to apply to (almost) all response-dependence metaethical views. And to show this, more work needs to be done.

The first thing to note here is that though in the previous section when differentiating the case of disagreement in beliefs from the case of disagreement that is due to preferences I spoke in terms of truth mattering, really it's not *truth* per se that matters. To see what it is that does matter here, think again about IMPARTIALITY, and what seems to have motivated it. So long as it's all about people – their attitudes, preferences, desires, feelings, interests, and even their beliefs[23] – then the IMPARTIALITY intuition kicks in, because, well, there's an important sense in which people should count equally. The role the truth of certain factual beliefs played was simply that of *some* standard that is independent of the responses of people, responses which arguably should count equally. But once this is noticed, it becomes clear that truth need not be the only thing that can play this role, and also that not any old truth can play this role.

Start with the latter point. Even Caricaturized Subjectivism, after all, allows for rather straightforward moral truth. According to Caricaturized Subjectivism, the judgment "Abortion is wrong", coming from my mouth, is true if and only if I prefer that people not perform abortions. And so, since there is no problem with truths about which preferences I have, Caricaturized Subjectivism unproblematically allows for moral truth. But this moral truth won't do as a standard neutralizing the IMPARTIALITY intuition, because this truth depends[24] on responses to which the IMPARTIALITY intuition applies, and therefore so does the relevant disagreement or conflict. Another way of making the same point is by returning to the stepping-back metaphor: I suggested that the sometimes-required stepping back involves an abstraction from indexical knowledge, knowledge of who (among those in conflict) is me, or of which

---

[20] The seasickness example comes from Lewis, as does the characterization of the rigidifying trick as a trick (1989, 88).

[21] For an explicit discussion of rigidification as a way of avoiding neutrality-failure (though not, of course, with the precise understanding of neutrality I defend in the Appendix), see Dreier (2002).

[22] If the rigidifying trick is indeed a trick, then that it is beside the point is precisely as it should be. See here also Copp (2006, 13).

[23] Here, again, it is important to note the difference between the relevant reason for action being the fact that one believes (and then the underlying IMPARTIALITY intuition holds) and the content of the belief (and then it does not).

[24] It is not completely clear or uncontroversial how to understand this dependence. In the context of an argument against response-dependence, though, I think I can safely avoid this issue – I am happy to work with whatever understanding of dependence those I argue against work with. In the context of a discussion of expressivism, though, such nonchalance may no longer be affordable. So I return to this point in the next section.

responses (among those of the people engaged in the conflict) are mine, and so on. If so, it is not just action on the personal preferences that is ruled out when we are required to step back, but also action on the belief that *my* preference is so-and-so (rather than the belief that *someone's* preference is so-and-so). So really, the argument from IMPARTIALITY (or the generalization of the argument against Caricaturized Subjectivism) is best seen not as an argument for moral truth, but rather as an argument against response-dependence theories of moral truth.

But we have to be careful here, as not all versions of response-dependence theories are even prima facie vulnerable to this argument. Think, for instance, about a social relativist position of sorts, according to which moral judgments are reducible to judgments about social approval of some kind.[25] According to such a metaethical view conjoined with IMPARTIALITY, what is the appropriate way of proceeding in a situation of a conflict (of the relevant kind) that is due to a moral disagreement? In particular, is an impartial solution called for, or is it morally permissible for the disputing parties (or for some of them) to stand their moral ground? The answer, it seems to me, is "it depends". If the disputing parties are members of the same society, then according to this relativist theory the same moral standards apply to both, and so the disagreement between them is presumably an instance of purely descriptive, factual disagreement. If, however, the disagreement and conflict are *inter*-social, then it seems to me IMPARTIALITY applies. And so, if we think (as I think we should) that sometimes it is morally permissible to stand one's (or one society's) ground in the face of such inter-social disagreement and not go for an impartial solution, then a version of the argument against Caricaturized Subjectivism works against this relativism as well. But – returning now to the discussion of response-dependence theories which are not vulnerable to my argument – if there are some responses that are necessarily shared by *all*, then a response-dependence view of morality that only referred to those necessarily-shared responses would treat all moral disagreements in the same way the sketched relativist position treats *intra*-social disagreements and conflicts. So my argument does not apply to constitutivist theories, response-dependence theories that only refer to responses that are necessarily shared by all agents (although, of course, such theories may be subject to other criticisms[26]).

This, then, is one kind of a response-dependence view to which my argument does not apply. There may be others. Some response-dependence theorists, for instance, include a *normative* element in their analysans, reducing, say, moral judgments not to people's actual responses (of a relevant kind), but to people's *rational* responses. What implications, if any, do such views have with regard to the practical significance of

---

[25] For my purposes here it does not matter whether the relevant social approval is determined by the social context of the agent or of the speaker (or in some other way). In the text that follows I focus on agent-relativism.

[26] For my own criticism of constitutivist views, see "Agency, Shmagency" (2006). For constitutivist responses, see Velleman (2009, 135–46) and Ferrero (2009). I reply in "Shmagency Revisited" (2010b).

moral disagreement in a case of conflict? The answer depends, I think, on whether –
according to the relevant theory – rational responses may differ. If the answer is yes,
then in cases of a conflict due to rational-responses differing, the IMPARTIALITY intuition
seems to apply (why, in other words, should *my* ideal advisor have privileged normative
status over *yours?*). Such normative response-dependence theories are thus not off the
hook. But if rational responses cannot (on the relevant theory) differ, then when it
comes to the moral significance of moral disagreement this picture is not different from
that of the response-*in*dependence, objectivist, Platonist.[27] Such objectivist response-
dependence theories are not vulnerable to the generalized version of the argument
against Caricaturized Subjectivism.[28]

Another version of a response-dependence view that may – I am genuinely not sure
about this – be immune to my argument is a no-priority view. On such views, though
there is a sense in which the relevant moral truth depends on the relevant responses, the
dependence is not asymmetrical in any interesting way. Depending on how such
interdependence is supposed to work, perhaps it can rule out the IMPARTIALITY intuitions that feed the argument against Caricaturized Subjectivism and its generalization.[29]

Where does the discussion leave us at this stage, then? What directly mattered for the
underlying IMPARTIALITY intuitions, I've argued, was not truth (or the absence thereof)
but response-dependence. And so the argument against Caricaturized Subjectivism
rather straightforwardly generalizes to many other response-dependence theories,
though not to all of them (constitutivist response-dependence theories, some normative
ones, and perhaps some no-priority ones are off the hook). But the implications of the
point about truth (or its absence) not being what the underlying IMPARTIALITY intuitions
are directly motivated by are not restricted to just this generalization. The generalization
relied on truth not being sufficient to defeat the IMPARTIALITY intuition (if the relevant
truth is response-dependent). But we should still address the possibility that truth is not
necessary for defeating IMPARTIALITY and its underlying intuitions. This thought – that
perhaps response-independent truth is not necessary for defeating IMPARTIALITY – brings
us back to the objection that concluded the previous section – namely, the claim that the
subjectivist need not, and should not, treat all preferences alike.

Here is one way of making this point. The feature of Caricaturized Subjectivism that
made it especially susceptible to the *Reductio* Argument was not the reduction of
morality to preferences, but rather the decision to treat the preferences to which

---

[27] I take it Michael Smith's version of a dispositional theory is one that aspires to this status – for it clearly
incorporates a normative condition in the dispositional analysis, and Smith at least conjectures that the
relevant rational responses (the desires of ideally rational advisors) will converge. For references, and for a
criticism of this point (and others from Smith), see my (2007b). For Smith's response, see Smith (2007).

[28] Certainly, response-dependence theories that include a "whatever-it-takes" clause (see, for instance,
Johnston (1989, 145)) are not vulnerable to my argument. But they have their own problems.

[29] See, for instance, Wiggins (1987) and McDowell (1985) (I'm not sure I understand these texts, so let me
qualify things here – at least they *can* rather naturally be read as putting forward no-priority views). For a
general – and compelling, I think – critique of no-priority views, see Sosa (2001).

morality is reducible as exactly on a par with a preference for playing tennis or for catching a movie. But why accept this further condition? Furthermore, how is this "on a par" to be understood? I used it as a part of my characterization of a metaethical view (Caricaturized Subjectivism), but isn't this cheating? Isn't this "on a par" a paradigmatically first-order, normative judgment, something to the effect that some preferences are not *more important* than others? If so, what prevents the (non-caricaturized) subjectivist from rejecting the on-a-par clause on first-order, normative grounds? The subjectivist, after all, is not an eliminativist – she is perfectly happy to enter first-order normative discussion, it's just that she has a subjectivist view of what it is that is going on in such a discussion. So in saddling my subjectivist with this problematic normative commitment haven't I just set her up for the *Reductio* Argument? There is nothing surprising or informative, of course, about a metaethical theory entailing problematic normative conclusions, if the metaethical theory is first itself saddled with some objectionable normative baggage.

The point can also be put thus. For it seems that the subjectivist can rely on *normative* propositions to do the job the objectivist wants response-independence truth to do. What the subjectivist needs in order to escape the *Reductio* Argument is a way of distinguishing in a normatively relevant way between the preferences involved in the tennis-or-movie case (where IMPARTIALITY applies) and those to which morality is supposedly reduced (IMPARTIALITY does not apply), and then, in the moral case, between the (preference-reducible) moral views of two disagreeing parties. Perhaps she cannot do so by relying on a response-independent truth. But she can certainly say that some preferences are more important than others, or that some moral views (or, for that matter, some preferences) are *better* than others, thereby (purportedly) reporting yet more preferences, and rejecting the supposed parity between the preferences to which morality is reducible and preferences for playing tennis or for catching a movie (where presumably she does not think that some preferences are better than others). And if some preferences are better than others, then why be impartial among them?

Once we leave Caricaturized Subjectivism behind, then, a line of reply opens up for the response-dependence theorist. She can treat the responses to which she reduces morality as – normatively, though perhaps not metaphysically – special, not on a par with (some) other more mundane responses.[30] And she can then distinguish between the (morally relevant) responses of disagreeing parties not by tying them to some response-independent truth, but rather by insisting that some of these responses are normatively better than others. And this allows her, the objection concludes, to escape

---

[30] Similarly, the response-dependence theorist may insist that some preferences are simply bad and some good, and that for this reason there is no symmetry between them. But if this goodness or badness of preferences is itself understood in response-dependence terms, then my main argument seems to apply at that step: for why should the goodness or badness of preferences – itself subjectively understood – escape the force of IMPARTIALITY?

the generalization of the *Reductio* Argument unharmed: true, in the movie-or-tennis example, IMPARTIALITY holds, and it's wrong to stand one's ground. But in the moral case, it is sometimes permissible to stand one's ground, and so the analogue of IMPARTIALITY fails. But this doesn't show that morality is not reducible to responses. It just shows that the responses to which morality is reducible are normatively special (compared to those relevant to the tennis-or-a-movie case).

I want to emphasize that there is nothing mistaken about this line of thought. Indeed, I think that this is precisely what the response-dependence theorist who feels the force of IMPARTIALITY, but who nevertheless wants to avoid moral spinelessness, should say. But I now want to show that relying on this line of thought is not without cost.

The realist, or objectivist, or anyway response-independence theorist, also – like the non-caricaturized subjectivist – wants to distinguish normatively between, say, the movie-or-tennis case (we should step back, standing one's ground is unreasonable) and the causing-pain-to-a-dog example (we should not step too far back, standing one's ground is morally permissible, and even required). Suppose we ask this theorist why it is that the analogue of IMPARTIALITY doesn't hold for the latter, or why it is that she distinguishes between these cases. She has a rather obvious answer – the causing-pain-to-a-dog example is, on her theory, more like that of the purely factual disagreement, where truth matters. IMPARTIALITY rests on normative intuitions about the equal moral significance of people and so of their responses. But the symmetry-breaker relevant in the causing-pain-to-a-dog example is a standard that is completely independent of persons and their responses. So the underlying motivations for IMPARTIALITY simply don't apply.

Getting back to the response-dependence theorist: he too, we now say, will want to distinguish normatively between the movie-or-tennis case and the causing-pain-to-a-dog case. So far, so good. But when we ask him what his rationale for this distinction is, what can he say? Clearly, he cannot give anything like the reply available to the objectivist. It seems like the best he can do is insist on the normative intuitions themselves, or on some intra-normative support for them: we do, after all, think it's morally wrong for one to stand one's ground in the movie-or-tennis case. And we do, after all, think it is not morally wrong for one to stand one's ground in the causing-pain-to-a-dog case. What further motivation can one ask for distinguishing between the responses relevant in both cases?

But at least in our context, such a move would be objectionably ad hoc. Remember the dialectical situation: we are asking for an explanation of a normative difference (between movie-or-tennis preferences and the responses morality is arguably reducible to). The realist (or objectivist, or Platonist, or whatever) seems to have something to say. The response-dependence theorist, however, simply has no further explanation. In order to avoid normatively problematic consequences, he explicitly introduces the normative input needed to get the right normative output. But he has nothing to give by way of rationale for this normative input. We knew all along, after all, that *there was* this normative difference. The question was *why* it is that there is such a difference. And here the response-dependence theorist just has no answer.

Perhaps an example will help to make this point more clearly. Suppose, then, that two theorists want to defend the distinction between eating shrimp (morally permissible) and eating beef (morally wrong). Now suppose that one of them does so by directly relying on intuitions with regard to which animals count, or the interests of which animals count, or some such. The other theorist, though, tells another kind of story, about the nature of the relevant creatures and the differences between them. Perhaps, for instance, she says that cows have a central nervous system, and so are rather clearly capable of feeling pain, whereas shrimp do not have a central nervous system, and so are highly unlikely to be able to feel pain. This theorist then proceeds to put forward a general moral principle, according to which it is morally wrong to kill and eat creatures that can feel pain. She offers the conjunction of her biological claims (about central nervous systems), her folk philosophy of mind (about the relation between having a central nervous system and feeling pain), and her cited moral principle (about it being wrong to kill and eat pain-feeling creatures) as an explanation of the moral distinction between eating shrimp and eating beef. In this example, both theorists agree on the moral distinction between eating shrimp and eating beef. And it's not as if the first theorist has nothing to say in defense of this distinction. But it can hardly be denied that the second theorist has *much more* to say. She offers an explanatory layer the first theorist does not offer, and so her theory is (other things being equal) better. Analogously, then: the response-dependence theorist can happily participate in the normative discussion, defending (to an extent) the moral distinction between mere-preference disagreements and conflicts (IMPARTIALITY applies) and conflicts based on moral disagreements (IMPARTIALITY does not apply). But she can offer very little by way of rationale for this distinction, and anyway much less than can be offered by the response-independence theorist, who can cite the metaphysical difference between the two as further explanation. And just as the more general commitment of the second vegetarian theorist renders the biological and philosophy-of-mind facts morally relevant to her explanation, so too the general moral commitments of the objectivist I am imagining (possibly shared by the response-dependence theorist) make the metaethical facts morally relevant to her explanation. And so, compared to the story offered by the response-dependence theorist, the objectivist has – just like the second vegetarian theorist from this little example – more to offer by way of an explanation of the moral distinction between different kinds of disagreement and conflict. And this difference in explanatory power counts in favor of the objectivist.

Of course, here as anywhere else when an explanatory advantage is claimed by one party to a philosophical debate, the other party may also want to argue that there is really nothing in the vicinity that calls for explanation. This too, then, is an option (of sorts) for the response-dependence theorist. But it is not, I think, an attractive one. It is, after all, also an option for the first vegetarian theorist from the example in the previous paragraph – he can insist that there are these intuitive judgments about the difference in normative status between shrimp and cows, and that that's the end of the matter. But, though moral arguments too come to an end somewhere, in the face of the second theorist's explanation, such insistence sounds highly implausible (and also quite possibly insincere). At the very least, if the first vegetarian theorist is committed to such insistence, his theory thereby loses plausibility points compared to that of the second vegetarian theorist. Similarly for our response-dependence theorist: he too can insist that there are these intuitive judgments about the difference in normative status between conflicts due to the preferences in the tennis-or-a-movie case and those due to moral disagreement, and that that's the end of the matter. But here too such insistence seems highly implausible. At the very least, if this is the best the response-dependence theorist can say, his theory thereby loses plausibility points compared to response-independence theories.

Perhaps this is too quick, though, because I haven't shown that the response-dependence theorist has no further explanatory story to tell. I've only shown that he can't help himself to the kind of story the response-*in*dependence theorist can help herself to. Can the response-dependence theorist come up with some other explanation of this normative difference? I cannot rule out this possibility. But nor can I think of a plausible explanation of this kind (in a footnote I quickly discuss two suggestions[31]). And let me remind you that the mere strength of the relevant preferences or other responses will clearly not do as a way of distinguishing between the responses to which IMPARTIALITY applies and those to which it does not: this much we've already seen from the example of the two grieving physicians who are the only two physicians

---

[31] First suggestion: perhaps morality is reduced to attitudes (or some such) that are in a sense closer to our identity. The distinction between tennis-or-movie cases and moral disagreement cases then becomes that between attitudes that are closer to and those that are further from our very identity. And this distinction, the subjectivist can argue, is far from being ad hoc, even on subjectivist grounds. (I thank Ronald Dworkin for this suggestion.) But this suggestion can be understood in two different ways. The relevant identity may be the kind of identity that is necessary for – indeed, constitutive of – agency. If so, the sketched view is a constitutivist one, to which the argument in this chapter does not apply (as I note earlier in the text). Or it may be understood as one's contingent identity. In such a case, though, it seems to me that IMPARTIALITY and its underlying intuitions straightforwardly apply: in a case of conflict due to some tension between what is a part of my (perfectly contingent) identity and yours, why should mine take precedence?

Second suggestion: perhaps the subjectivist can claim that IMPARTIALITY is only supposed to apply *within* morality, not, as it were, *about* morality. So suggesting that the subjectivist is required to apply IMPARTIALITY to moral disagreements – including, for instance, to disagreements about IMPARTIALITY itself – constitutes a misunderstanding of IMPARTIALITY. The force of IMPARTIALITY is exhausted, it may be thought, within morality. The suggestion that IMPARTIALITY also implies that in certain cases we should be impartial between IMPARTIALITY and its denial is not one the subjectivist can be saddled with. (I thank Tom Nagel, Ronald Dworkin, and Moshe Halbertal for this suggestion.) I agree, of course, that we should not be impartial between moral truths and moral falsehoods. My point is simply that the subjectivist (of the kind I'm imagining) has no non-ad-hoc way of supporting such a claim. If morality comes down to preferences, attitudes, and the like, then IMPARTIALITY does seem to apply to morality (and to itself). But this conclusion is false. And therefore so is subjectivism. An attempt by the subjectivist to restrict the scope of IMPARTIALITY so as not to apply to itself is – without some further story – as objectionably ad hoc as, say, an attempt by someone who puts forward the theory "All generalizations are false" to escape contradiction by shifting to the theory "All generalizations *except this one* are false".

in town (in section 2.2), where the relevant responses can be presumed to be maximally strong, but still IMPARTIALITY applies.[32]

So my argument from the normative significance of moral disagreement does not amount to a knock-down argument against response-dependence theories (honestly, though – did you expect one?). But it is not without force. For it highlights an explanatory challenge response-dependence theorists face if they are to escape it. And if they cannot cope with it successfully – if, in other words, they cannot come up with a rationale for treating differently conflicts that are due to moral disagreements and those that are due merely to preferences – then at the very least they are at an explanatory disadvantage compared to response-independence theorists. Response-dependence theories, then, are not *refuted* by my argument. But they do lose plausibility points.[33]

2.4 Generalizing even further: expressivism

If expressivist theories are response-dependence theories, then they are already covered by the discussion of the previous section. However, contemporary expressivists (most clearly, perhaps, Simon Blackburn, whom I'll use as my main interlocutor in this section) like to deny that their view is a response-dependence view in any interesting sense of this theoretical term. So we need to dedicate a separate section to expressivism.

If Blackburn's quasi-realism is right, then he can – on expressivist, or Humean projectivist grounds – give the realist all she could reasonably want, including things like moral beliefs, moral truths, and indeed *objective* moral truths. So it seems like the argument in this chapter just doesn't threaten quasi-realist expressivism: either it can be shown – independently of the argument in this chapter – that quasi-realism cannot after all deliver the promised goods, or it cannot so be shown; if this can be shown, then presumably quasi-realism is refuted independently of the argument in this chapter. If this cannot be shown, then presumably Blackburn can reject the analogue of IMPARTIALITY for moral beliefs, and can justify (in the relevant circumstances) standing

---

[32] In correspondence, Steve Finlay insisted that everything can after all be done here in terms of strength of preferences. On his suggestion, IMPARTIALITY itself gains its significance from the preferences that back it up (say, preferences for the good will of others, and for others believing that we are good-willed). And what explains the difference between the movie-or-tennis example and the causing-pain-to-a-dog example is just that our preferences for IMPARTIALITY are stronger than the preferences relevant for the movie-or-tennis, but weaker than those relevant for the causing-pain-to-a-dog case. But this won't do, for a number of reasons, the clearest of which being that on this suggestion, there is even in the causing-pain-to-a-dog case a reason (perhaps even a moral reason) to go for an impartial solution, except it is outweighed by other reasons. As I have argued, though, IMPARTIALITY simply does not apply in the causing-pain-to-a-dog case at all, so there is not even an outweighed reason to go for an impartial solution.

[33] This explanatory advantage of response-independence is somewhat reduced by the already-mentioned messiness of the truth in the vicinity of IMPARTIALITY. Because of this messiness, the response-independence theorist also cannot claim that her explanation of the relevant normative distinction is completely clean. But still she has an explanatory advantage over the response-dependence theorist.

one's moral ground, in a way exactly similar to that of the Platonist. Either way, then, the argument in this paper does not make a serious dialectical difference.

But this, I now want to argue, is too quick. I do not want to quarrel with Blackburn about his success in delivering such things as moral belief and moral truth (I suspect he does not succeed in doing so, but I am willing to assume for the sake of argument that he does). I am even willing to grant that there is *a* sense of objectivity in which he succeeds in giving a quasi-realist understanding of objectivity. Granting all that, I want to now argue that expressivism – quasi-realist or otherwise – is still vulnerable to the argument from IMPARTIALITY.

The crucial point to notice is that the expressivist – even at the end of a hypothetical perfectly successful carrying-out of the quasi-realist project – still has to believe that morality somehow depends on us, that the ultimate explanation of why it is that certain moral claims are true has something to do with us and our feelings and attitudes. One way of insisting on this point is by insisting that expressivists are committed to problematic counterfactuals like, "Had I approved of bullfighting, bullfighting would have been morally permissible", or the more general and abstract, "Had our relevant conative attitudes been different, different moral claims would have been true". But it is important in our context to see that we do not even need to enter the wars over the readings of such counterfactuals.[34] The important thing is that – if the expressivist is going to have a distinctive metaethical position at all – she must continue to affirm the metaphysical story of projection, or some such analogous story, even while also engaging in first-order discourse with the realist. After all, Blackburn cannot let his quasi-realist project be *too* successful, for if it is – if there really is *nothing* the realist wants to say that the quasi-realist cannot say – then rather than arguing against realism Blackburn will have argued against the distinction between realism and antirealism (of this kind).[35] But Blackburn repeatedly emphasizes[36] that his quasi-realism is *based on* his antirealism. So we have to see what difference remains, according to Blackburn, between the realist and his quasi-realist. Here is Blackburn:

> But sure we do have a serviceable way of describing the [realist–antirealist] debate, at least as far as it concerns evaluation and morals. It is about explanation. The projectivist holds that our nature as moralists is well explained by regarding us as reacting to a reality which contains nothing in the way of values, duties, rights, and so forth; a realist thinks it is well explained only by seeing us as able to perceive, cognize, intuit, an independent moral reality. He holds that the moral features

---

[34] For Blackburn's view, see, for instance, Blackburn (1988, 173). For criticism, see Cassam (1986) and Rasmussen (1985).

[35] For an especially clear presentation of this worry, see Rosen (1998, e.g. at 395). Johnston (1989, 141) seems to express a similar suspicion when he characterizes those who hold a view of colors analogous to Blackburn's metaethical Quasi-Realism as "delayed-reaction colour realists".

[36] As when he characterizes his view as "expressivism with quasi-realist trimmings" (1999, 213). Nevertheless, at times he is not as clear about this, apparently willing to accept realism as commonly characterized – see Blackburn (1991b, 42).

of things are the parents of our sentiments, whereas the Humean holds that they are their children. (1981, 164–5; see also 185–6)[37]

So the difference seems to come to a difference in explanatory priority.[38] One may, of course, question whether the explanatory claim Blackburn saddles the realist with is really essential to realism.[39] But let me grant Blackburn for the sake of argument this characterization of what is at issue.

Arguably, this explanatory priority of our normative emotions and reactions over the normative truths or facts – a priority the quasi-realist has to insist on if she is to have an independent metaethical position at all – suffices to show that Blackburn's quasi-realism is committed to a contingency (of moral truths) of the kind Blackburn is eager to avoid.[40] But again, I don't even need *this* much. For my purposes, it is sufficient that this priority suffices for IMPARTIALITY to have its force. If what explains certain moral truths is something about my emotions or reactions, and if my emotions are prima facie just as important as those of others, then it *must* be wrong to just stand one's ground in cases of conflict (of the relevant kind) due to moral disagreement. To use Blackburn's metaphor: if the moral features of things are our sentiments' children, then it is very hard to justify – in certain cases of conflict, cases where IMPARTIALITY would have applied to mere-preference conflicts – giving priority to the children of my sentiments over the children of yours.

Perhaps, though, I am making too much of a few sentences from Blackburn where he is not at his quasi-realist best.[41] Perhaps, in other words, though Blackburn *does* seem to say that the moral features of things are explained by our sentiments, this is not something he *should* say. Rather, he should insist – consistently with the most general expressivist strategy – on not saying anything about what (except for other moral claims) explains the moral truths or properties themselves (he does not, after all, have a truth-conditional theory). Even so, though, the expressivist will not be off the hook. For at the very least the expressivist should insist that at the most fundamental explanatory level, all there is in the vicinity of morality is people and their responses, that there is nothing more (at that fundamental explanatory level). But this much seems enough, it seems to me, in order to trigger the normative motivations underlying IMPARTIALITY.[42]

---

[37] For more recent statements of this kind, see Blackburn (1995, 84): "It is true that in some sense there is only we, the subjects, and our attitudes"; and Blackburn (1998, 310): "Remember that for quasi-realism, an ethic is the propositional reflection of the dispositions and attitudes, policies and stances, of people."

[38] See also Blackburn (1999, 216). For a similar point made by Gibbard, in the context of replying to the worry that his view is a mere terminological variant of some cognitivist view, see Gibbard (1992, 971).

[39] Rosen (1998, 396) does, and to an extent so will I (in Chapter 3).

[40] For related points, see McDowell (1985, 124 n. 4) and Sturgeon (1992, 114 n. 2).

[41] I've heard suggestions of this kind (separately) from Michael Ridge and Nadeem Hussain. And I think (but I am not sure) I heard Blackburn himself concede as much in discussion.

[42] I am using Blackburn as my paradigmatic expressivist, and I am putting things in terms of responses. But I could have just as easily used Gibbard (2003), and put things in terms of plans. For an argument against Gibbard that is in some respects similar to the one in the text, see Fitzpatrick (2010, 19–24).

Indeed, Blackburn seems to agree that on his theory there is a sense in which moral truths and facts are really just a matter of our passions, that it is really *we* whose feelings explain morality. Blackburn denies not these claims, but rather their normative significance. To quote again from the telling paragraph already quoted in section 2.1:

Does the lover escape his passion by thinking "Oh, it's only my passion, forget it"? When the world affords occasion for grief, does it brighten when we realize that it is we who grieve? (1993, 176)

Blackburn seems here to concede that there is a sense in which morality is just a matter of our passions (though he would deny the belittling of these passions presumably pragmatically implicated by this "just"), and to argue (by rhetorical questions, presumably coding a *reductio* argument) that morality is none the worse for that. But as already noted, though Blackburn is right to insist that there are some normative consequences that are *not* implied by the characterization of the love as just my passion and the grief mine, he is wrong in suggesting that there are no normative implications that *are* sensitive to these characterizations. The implications associated with IMPARTIALITY clearly are.

Of course, the main line of reply that was available to the response-dependence theorist is also available to the expressivist – the latter can insist, just like the former, that some of our responses (or passions, or attitudes, or feelings, or whatever) are unique, and that it is *those* that are (to use Blackburn's metaphor) the parents of the moral features of things. And the expressivist can further insist that the classification of responses as special (or as non-special) is itself a normative matter, about which her expressivism implies nothing one way or another, so that she can join this part of the normative discussion with the rest of us.[43] And here too this would show that my argument does not amount to a refutation of expressivism. But here too expressivism will be losing plausibility points, as it cannot explain this distinction among our relevant responses, and so stands at an explanatory disadvantage compared to more objectivist views.[44]

2.5 Generalizing further still?

The argument that started as an argument against Caricaturized Subjectivism can be generalized so as to apply to many response-dependence theories and expressivist theories as well (or so, at least, I've argued in the last two sections). True, some of them may have a possible reply available to them, but that reply too is not without cost. How much further – if at all – can it be generalized?

---

[43] I take it this is what Blackburn says in related contexts (1993, 156; 1998, 306). See also Horgan and Timmons (2006, 95–6).

[44] For a family of recent attempts at another way of showing that expressivism is not an objectivist position, see Suikkanen (2009), and the references there. I am not optimistic about the prospects for success of these attempts.

The argument in this chapter – even if entirely successful – cannot alone support Robust Realism. In section 2.3 I have already mentioned several response-dependence views to which the argument does not apply – constitutivist ones, some normative ones, and perhaps also some no-priority ones. And if such response-dependence theories have expressivist analogues, then perhaps those too are immune to my argument here.

Another family of metaethical theories that aren't robustly realist but to which the argument doesn't apply are objectivist naturalist reductions. If moral truths or facts just are natural facts that do not depend in any constitutive way on people's responses, then moral disagreements are not significantly and relevantly different from disagreements about matters of natural fact, and we've already seen that nothing like IMPARTIALITY applies to those.

A more interesting question is whether anything like the argument developed in this chapter has any weight at all against error theories. I think the answer may depend on the details of the relevant error theory. Eliminativist (or abolitionist) error theorists – those who argue not just that our moral discourse is systematically mistaken, but also that it should be discarded – are entitled, it seems, to object to my argument for objectivity because it employs a moral premise (IMPARTIALITY) which they believe is just as problematic as all other parts of moral discourse. Using a moral premise in an argument against this kind of metaethical error theory would be a case of begging the question, tantamount to using a premise committed to the existence of witches in an argument against an error theory about witch-discourse. But in fact I think that things are complicated here, and that at the end of the epistemological day such an argument does not objectionably beg any question, not even against the eliminativist. I do what I can to support this assertion in Chapter 5 (section 5.2.2). How about non-eliminativist error theories, error theories that in some sense allow (and perhaps even recommend) that we continue to engage in the systematically erroneous moral discourse? Does the argument from IMPARTIALITY apply to them as well? Again, I think, the answer may differ according to the details of the relevant view. A fictionalist view (of the error-theoretic kind), for instance, with severe restrictions on admissible fictions, may be immune to my argument. If, for instance, you believe that moral discourse is systematically erroneous, but that we can talk about what is and what is not true in the objective-value story, and furthermore if you think there is some objective sense in which it is *this* story (rather than others) that we must be telling, then you may not be vulnerable to the argument from IMPARTIALITY: after all, according to such a view moral questions have objectively correct (if not true) answers. But if your fictionalism allows for a plurality of fictions that are, in some sense, on a par, then it is hard to see how your view can avoid the argument from the normative implications of objectivity. I discuss fictionalism and error theory in more detail in Chapter 5.

The argument from IMPARTIALITY to objectivity, then, cannot support Robust Realism. As has been seen, quite a few other metaethical views are not vulnerable to it. But the argument does strongly count against a rather wide range of theories. And the theories that are not vulnerable all merit being called objectivist, I believe, in at least one sense of this term. To this I now turn.

2.6 Objectivity again

As already mentioned, the term "objectivity" is notoriously ambiguous, even when considered just in the metaethical context. And because of this, I chose to conduct my discussion largely without using this term. But I want to suggest, in conclusion, that the concern expressed by IMPARTIALITY manages to capture at least one good understanding of this problematic concept.

Think again about the (rough) division of metaethical views into those that are and those that are not prima facie vulnerable to my argument. Roughly: many response-dependence theories, relativist theories, expressivist theories, and at least some error theories on one side; Robust Realism, objectivist naturalist realism, and constitutivism on the other side. This division nicely fits, I take it, our pre-theoretic distinction between objectivist and non-objectivist metaethical theories (to the extent that we have pre-theoretic beliefs about such things). Indeed, it is an advantage of the understanding of objectivity that seems to underlie my argument that it gives a rather clear sense in which expressivist theories are not objectivist: a suspicion many of us have had for a while, but one it has proved very hard to support.[45]

Furthermore, objectivity does seem closely related to the availability of standards of correctness that can settle (in some sense) disputes, standards of correctness that do not depend on the relevant persons and their responses. And my argument for objectivity makes use of precisely this feature of certain conflicts and disagreements. It thus seems reasonable to conclude that what I have in effect been arguing for is the objectivity of morality, in at least one legitimate sense of this term.

---

[45] Russ Shafer-Landau (2003, 30–3) claims that noncognitivists are closet relativists. I think that his arguments for this claim do not, at the end of the day, withstand criticism as stated. But I think the intuition underlying them is exactly right: it is that noncognitivist views are not objectivist in something like the sense suggested in the text.

Paul Bloomfield (2003) expresses what seem to be similar thoughts. But unlike Shafer-Landau, he cannot plausibly be read as putting forward an underdeveloped version of the argument in this chapter, because he is explicitly committed to the normative neutrality of metaethics (see his (2009)).

For a noncognitivist defense against accusations such as Shafer-Landau's and Bloomfield's, see Horgan and Timmons (2006) and the references there. Horgan and Timmons understand the issue as one about truth or correctness. But if I am right, the real problem is a first-order, moral one, starting with IMPARTIALITY. There is no reply in Horgan and Timmons's paper to this kind of worry.

For Gibbard's list of things that could be meant by objectivity, and for his attempt at supplying them on expressivist grounds, see Gibbard (1990, 155). Of the three issues he mentions, the third one (authority) is closest to the kind of objectivity I think my argument captures. His attempt to accommodate such objectivity is in terms of conversational demands and higher-order norms, an attempt that – if the argument in section 2.4 works – cannot succeed.

For Blackburn's similar attempts, see his (1998, 307–8).

Now, objectivity is sometimes understood as a metaphysical issue, perhaps one about the existence of objects. At other times, it is understood as primarily an epistemological issue, or as an issue involving both metaphysical and epistemological concerns.[46] And there may be yet other ways of understanding objectivity. But it seems to me that the best way of proceeding in discussing objectivity is to start with a clear understanding of why it is that objectivity matters, of why it is an interesting question to ask about morality whether it is objective, and about a metaethical theory whether it is objectivist. And objectivity is important, I want to suggest, precisely because of its moral significance in cases of interpersonal conflict. So while the discussion above was a discussion of how it is that objectivity (or anyway one thing worth the name) matters, it can contribute in the suggested way to a better understanding of what objectivity is.

2.7 Appendix: neutrality

The suggestion that metaethical theories can be rejected on normative grounds naturally raises worries about the supposed moral neutrality of metaethics. But I don't think that there is in the (limited) literature on metaethical neutrality a good enough understanding of this idea.[47] In this appendix I try to develop an account of neutrality, one that – as I proceed to show – is very relevant to the argument in the main text in this chapter. It will not be a part of what I argue for, however, that this is the only possible or productive understanding of neutrality. Indeed, it is limited in ways that I mention below. But still, it nicely captures at least one central family of ideas often associated with talk of metaethical neutrality. And thinking about neutrality in those terms is, I believe, productive, in ways that tie this appendix with the main argument of this chapter, and indeed, of the book as a whole.

What does it mean for metaethics to be – or to fail to be – morally neutral? Indeed, what does it mean for one discourse, D_1, to be neutral with regard to another, D_2?

One thing that would rather clearly seem to constitute a failure of neutrality is if some D_1-propositions entailed, all by themselves, some D_2-propositions. If a valid argument can be constructed with only D_1-premises and a D_2-conclusion, then it seems that D_1 is not neutral with regard to D_2.[48] And so, if there are valid arguments with purely metaethical premises and a first-order moral conclusion, then metaethics, it seems, is not morally neutral.

Before proceeding to show that the criterion for neutrality seemingly implied by such observations is far too weak – even if there are no such implication relations, still

---

[46] This is probably the right characterization of Wright's (1992) tests for objectivity (sometimes put as tests for realism).

[47] Throughout this appendix, I refer to the recent literature that I found addressing this issue. But this issue was more vividly discussed in the 1950s and 1960s. For references, see Sumner (1967, 106 nn. 1 and 5).

[48] There may be complications here, but not, I think, ones we need to worry about in our context. See Dreier's (2002, 247) distinction between commitment and implication. Fantl (2006, 28) also nicely bypasses these complications in our context.

metaethics may very well fail to be morally neutral – I want to note that this criterion is also too strong. D_1 may be neutral with regard to D_2 in an important sense even if there *are* valid arguments from only D_1-premises to a D_2-conclusion.

To see this, think about an error theory about mathematical objects, of the kind defended by Hartry Field (1980). Is it neutral with regard to number theory? If we employ the criterion suggested above, the answer is clearly "no". For it follows from the error theory itself that there are no prime numbers between 13 and 16, or indeed between 10 and 20 (because, well, there are no numbers), and these are number-theoretic propositions if anything is. But, I now want to argue, it would be far too quick to conclude that the philosophy-of-mathematics error theory is not in an important sense neutral with regard to basic number theory. Field's error theory still seems number-theoretically neutral in something like the following intuitive sense: practicing mathematicians needn't worry about it. While the error theory may have first-order implications, it does not have *discriminating* first-order implications; it cannot, for instance, settle any number-theoretic disputes.[49] Indeed, this is *why* practicing mathematicians need not worry about it, even if it shows that many of their beliefs are false: if a mathematician wonders whether, say, there is a largest prime, or if two mathematicians differ on this question, then despite the fact that Field's error theory entails that there is no largest prime, still it is not relevant to the mathematicians' concerns, and it would be an obvious *faux pas* for a practicing mathematician to rely on Field's error theory (instead of the number-theoretic proof) in defending her claim that there is no largest prime. We can conveniently put the point in fictionalist terms: if Field's error theory is right, then what practicing mathematicians are interested in is the number-theoretic fiction (which they may think of as non-fictional). And while the relevant error theory does say *that* the number-story is a fiction, it has no implications *within* that fiction. And so those studying what's true *in* that fiction need not worry about Field's error theory. In this sense, then, Field's error theory is (or at least, for anything thus far said may very well be) number-theoretically neutral, even though it entails number-theoretic propositions (and sometimes rather surprising ones). It is, in a perfectly understandable, though not perfectly precise, sense not something the practicing mathematician needs to worry about.[50]

The same may be true of some metaethical positions, like some versions of metaethical error theory. Noticing this can help solve a puzzle in reading Mackie

---

[49] This non-discrimination does not mean that the error theory assigns the same truth-value to all first-order propositions. It cannot consistently do that, of course.

[50] Not all error theories share this feature. All those engaged in first-order witch-discourse *should* be worried about the possible truth of a second-order error theory about witch-discourse. This is so, presumably, because our now commonsensical error theory about witch-discourse is *eliminativist*; we think that people should just stop engaging in witch-discourse. But Field's error theory about mathematical objects is not eliminativist in this way. And it seems clear that neither is Mackie's error theory about morality, to which I turn in the text. This suggests the following plausible generalization: While eliminativist error theories are not completely neutral with regard to the discourse they are about (even though they are still non-discriminatory), non-eliminativist error theories may very well be.

(1977).[51] Mackie is commonly taken to have argued for a metaethical error theory (at least about objective values). But he also claimed first-order neutrality for his "second-order skepticism", claiming that first- and second-order claims are "not merely distinct but completely independent" (1977, 16). Given the obvious implication relations between his error theory and numerous first-order claims (it's not the case that love is of value; it's not the case that murder is wrong, etc.), how could Mackie seriously claim neutrality for his metaethical theory? A plausible answer is suggested, I think, by the previous paragraphs: perhaps Mackie thought that his metaethical error theory is not something people thinking about first-order morality should worry about, because – though it has first-order implications – it does not have discriminating implications, in the sense outlined above.

So $D_1 \rightarrow D_2$ implication relations do not suffice for neutrality-failure. Perhaps more importantly, nor are such implication relations necessary for neutrality-failure. To see this, think again about the metaethical case. Now suppose that there are no valid arguments with only metaethical premises and a moral conclusion, but that there are valid arguments with one metaethical premise and one factual, descriptive (neither moral nor metaethical) auxiliary premise, and a moral conclusion. And suppose, crucially, that the auxiliary factual premise is true (or at least very plausible), and that it does not entail the moral conclusion all by itself. In such a case, the metaethical premise clearly makes a moral difference – with it, the moral conclusion follows, and without it, it doesn't. In a clear sense, then, in such a case there is a failure of metaethical neutrality, even though there are no valid arguments from purely meta-ethical premises to a normative conclusion. More generally and abstractly: D_1 can fail to be neutral with regard to D_2 even in the absence of $D_1 \rightarrow D_2$ implication relations, if there are $(D_1 \& D_3) \rightarrow D_2$[52] implication relations, where the relevant D_1-premises are not redundant.

But there's more. Suppose there is a valid argument with one metaethical premise and one first-order, *moral* auxiliary premise, and a moral conclusion, and assume that the moral conclusion would not have followed from the moral premise alone. In such a case, though a moral premise is needed for the moral conclusion to follow, still the metaethical premise makes a moral difference:[53] for the moral conclusion would not have followed without it. Here too, then, there is a failure of metaethical neutrality. More generally: D_1 can fail to be neutral with regard to D_2 even in the absence of $D_1 \rightarrow D_2$ implication relations, and even in the absence of $(D_1 \& D_3) \rightarrow D_2$ implication relations, if there are valid $(D_1 \& D_2) \rightarrow D_2$ implication relations where the D_1-premise is non-redundant, in the way just sketched.

---

[51] A disclaimer: I do not do history, recent history included. I do not want to commit myself, then, to the claim that what I am about to say is a good interpretation of Mackie. Perhaps it is – I do not know. But my reason for making the point I am about to make in the text is not that it's a good piece of Mackie-interpretation, but that it is (I think) of independent interest.

[52] Throughout I assume that $D_1 \neq D_2 \neq D_3$.

[53] For a similar observation, see Smith (2006, 440, 443).

These considerations suggest, I now want to argue, that a productive way of thinking about neutrality will be in terms of one discourse being (or failing to be) a *conservative extension* of another. In the proof-theoretic terms in which the idea of a conservative extension is usually discussed: a theory T_1 conservatively extends a theory T_2 if and only if all the theorems of T_2 are also theorems in the extended theory (T_2 & T_1), and all of the theorems of (T_2 & T_1) that are stated purely in T_2-terms are also theorems of T_2. Intuitively, while a conservative extension allows to prove more theorems in the extended language, it does not allow to prove more theorems *in the original, non-extended language*. An example may make this clearer: arguably, mathematics conservatively extends physics.[54] What this means is that there are no *purely physical* results that are provable in the combined language of mathematics and physics that are not already provable in the language of physics alone. If mathematics conservatively extends physics, then while mathematics may make a huge difference to our way of doing physics (perhaps, for instance, some mathematics facilitates much easier or shorter proofs), still there is a clear sense in which mathematics doesn't matter to physics: any purely physical result that is provable given the extension (that is, including mathematics) is already provable in the non-extended language of physics. In principle, then, mathematics doesn't teach us any new things about physics.[55]

The idea of a conservative extension gives us a way of thinking about neutrality in general, and metaethical neutrality in particular. Perhaps the proof-theoretic talk is not very helpful when it comes to the moral significance of metaethics, but the underlying idea is easily generalizable. For we can replace talk of proofs with talk of good arguments, referring to whatever standards of good arguments are appropriate in the context. We then get that D_1 conservatively extends D_2 if and only if any D_2-proposition that is supported by a good argument in D_2 is also supported (to the same degree) by a good argument in the extended (D_2 & D_1), and any purely D_2-proposition that is supported by a good argument in the extended (D_2 & D_1) is already supported (to the same degree) by a good argument in the original D_2, so that the support it gets in the extended language does not add anything to the support it already has in the non-extended language.[56] Put more intuitively, focusing on the second conjunct, and now applying it to the case that is of interest to us here: metaethics conservatively extends ethics only if there are no moral propositions that can only be supported (to a certain degree) by a good argument with at least one metaethical premise, only if the degree of support any moral proposition gets in the extended

---

[54] Field (1980, ch. 1).

[55] Needless to say, I do not want to commit myself one way or another on the question whether mathematics conservatively extends physics. Even if mathematics extends physics non-conservatively, still the example is helpful in getting my point across.

[56] If a purely D_2-proposition p is supported to degree d in the extended (D_2 & D_1), and if there is also a purely D_2-argument supporting p to degree d, this does not suffice for the extension to be conservative, because it's possible that the two arguments *together* support p to a degree greater than d. In such a case, the extension still makes a difference to the warranted credence in the purely D_2-proposition p. The wording in the text is supposed to rule out this possibility.

THE ARGUMENT FROM OBJECTIVITY'S IMPLICATIONS   45

language of ethics and metaethics together is identical to that it gets in the language of normative ethics alone. And the discussion above suggests that if metaethics does *not* conservatively extend ethics, and furthermore if the way in which metaethics non-conservatively extends ethics is discriminating (so that it's not a case where the implications are ones ethicists need not worry about), then in an important sense metaethics is not morally neutral.

Notice that it falls out of what has been said that for metaethics to fail to be morally neutral, metaethical premises must play the relevant role in *good* arguments, that is, arguments the moral premises of which are true, or at the very least plausible. Consider the following argument, which I'll call Simon Says:

(1)   If Simon's philosophical views are right, then you ought to always do as Simon says.
(2)   Simon's philosophical views are right.
(3)   Therefore, you ought to always do as Simon says.

Here, premise (1) is a paradigmatic moral premise (in the sense in which "moral" is the opposite of "non-moral", not of "immoral"). Premise (2) is a paradigmatic metaethical premise, at least given a suitable specification of Simon's philosophical views, which include his metaethical views. The conclusion follows from (1) and (2), but we may safely assume that it doesn't follow from (1) alone, or indeed from any argument that does not have something like (2) as a premise. But if merely stating the Simon Says argument is enough to show that metaethics is not morally neutral, then the discussion over neutrality has been trivialized, and furthermore then no discourse is neutral with regard to any other one (just replace "Simon's philosophical views" with "Simon's macroeconomic views", or "Simon's views regarding the existence and nature of God", or whatever).[57] What has to be shown, then, in order to show that metaethics extends ethics non-conservatively is that there is a *good* argument from a metaethical premise – perhaps conjoined with other *true, or at least plausible* moral premises – to a moral conclusion that wouldn't be supportable without the metaethical premise. A cooked-up moral premise (like (1) in Simon Says) is just not good enough for that. And this is in line, of course, with other contexts in which the idea of a conservative extension is productive: when asking whether mathematics conservatively extends physics we do not, I take it, wonder whether any cooked-up proposition that could be classified as a part of physics can render a mathematical premise physics-relevant in a way that violates conservativeness. Rather, we ask whether there is any *true* physics-proposition that does so, or perhaps whether there is any physics-proposition that is in the game for

---

[57] Here's Dreier (2002, 247) making a similar point: "We were hoping for a sense of carrying moral commitment in which metaethical theories do and Newtonian mechanics does not carry any."

Fantl (2006) notices that on his understanding of neutrality, no discourse is neutral with regard to any other. He takes this not as a reason to understand neutrality differently, but rather as a reason to think that neutrality is only interesting when the relevant further premise is plausible or true.

being true – one that seems plausible to us, and about whose truth-value we are not confident, or something like that – that can do so.

Indeed, this understanding of neutrality suggests that we should restrict the relevant arguments not to just those with true (or at least plausible) *moral* premises, but also to just those with true (or at least plausible) *metaethical* premises. But I suggest that at this stage we do not go this way, because I am here ultimately interested in using first-order moral insights in order to help us decide between competing metaethical views. So I suggest that at this point we suspend – for the sake of argument – metaethical judgment, and just proceed to see whether any metaethical theory – true or false – can be shown to have moral implications, in the sense that *if* the metaethical theory is true, it extends first-order ethics in a non-conservative way.

This, then, is how I suggest that we understand the question of metaethical neutrality:[58] the question is whether there are good, discriminating arguments with a moral conclusion, and at least one indispensable metaethical premise, that is, whether there are any moral propositions such that the degree of support they enjoy given the partly metaethical argument is greater than the degree of support they get from purely first-order arguments.[59]

This way of understanding the question of metaethical neutrality has several notable advantages. First, it is reasonably precise. Second, as has been argued above, it nicely answers to the intuition regarding whether or not metaethics makes a moral difference. Third, it is itself to a large extent neutral as between different ways of delineating the moral and the metaethical. Indeed, it can be easily generalized so as to apply to any two discourses, and seems to me like a promising initial way of thinking about neutrality elsewhere as well: Does religion conservatively extend political philosophy? Does the philosophy of mathematics conservatively extend mathematics? Does the philosophy of science conservatively extend science? Does philosophy conservatively extend, well, everything else? Does normative discourse conservatively extend non-normative discourse?

Notice also that this way of understanding the issue – and this is its fourth advantage – includes other ways as particular instances. After all, perhaps some metaethical theories do imply (in a discriminating way), all by themselves, moral conclusions. Analytic Utilitarianism is an example that comes to mind, though I have doubts about its playing

---

[58] I am going to have to make one last revision below. And let me again stress that I am not invested in the claim that this is the *only* way in which neutrality can or should be understood. I am insisting only on this being *one* interesting, theoretically productive way of understanding it.

[59] This way of understanding the neutrality issue draws on Sturgeon's (1986b, 125) suggestion that realists and noncognitivists have to differ ethically when they both accept "any ethical principle whose application *depends* on whether there is moral truth or moral knowledge". Sturgeon then proceeds to mention some ethical principles of this kind, without much argument. I do not find his examples compelling, and I think his discussion is imprecise at points. Nevertheless, I am indebted to his discussion. Indeed, my argument in this chapter can be seen as an attempt carefully to fill in the details in the intuition that Sturgeon got right.

For Sturgeon's focus on good – but not necessarily deductively valid – arguments here (on which I also draw), see Sturgeon (1986b, 135).

this role.[60] If so, metaethics is – or at least *these* metaethical theories are – certainly not morally neutral. But in these cases it is also true, of course, that metaethics doesn't conservatively extend ethics.

A final advantage I want to mention of this way of understanding the neutrality issue is that if metaethics turns out not to be neutral in this way – if metaethics extends ethics non-conservatively – then this conclusion will constitute a sane middle-ground between neutralists and quietists.[61] Quietists (as I understand this term in this context) argue, roughly, that there just is no metaethical discourse that is at all distinct from good old first-order moral discourse. I will discuss quietism in some detail in Chapter 5 (section 5.3). Let me just note that quietists often spend significant effort in establishing implication relations between supposedly metaethical propositions and paradigmatical-ly moral ones, and then take themselves to have shown that metaethics *just is* ethics.[62] This move cannot, I think, be defended. And the idea of a (non-)conservative extension nicely shows why: if, say, mathematics non-conservatively extends physics, then mathematics is not completely physically neutral, but on the other hand this clearly does not count in favor of a reduction of mathematics to physics.

Before proceeding to show how the discussion of IMPARTIALITY nicely exemplifies a violation of neutrality thus understood, let me quickly address a worry about my suggested understanding of the neutrality debate.[63] For it may be thought that there is after all a sense in which this understanding of neutrality makes the issue trivial: after all, in the sense in which I understand neutrality, *purely factual* discourse ends up not being morally neutral, for surely facts make a moral difference, and some specific moral judgments can only be supported (to the degree that they can be supported) given some factual premises. Indeed, pretty much anything can be morally relevant, and so pretty much nothing is morally neutral in the sense of neutrality suggested above. And my discussion can be criticized for its attempt to borrow an understanding of neutrality from other discourses precisely because pretty much anything can be morally relevant, but it's not the case that pretty much anything can be mathematically or proof-theoretically relevant.

I agree that pretty much anything can be morally relevant: consider "Jamie promised to φ if *p*." For just about any *p*, if Jamie promised to do something if *p*, then *p* becomes

---

[60] Analytic Utilitarianism certainly does have moral implications, but I would be reluctant to classify it as a metaethical position. It has a metaethical element, of course – analytic naturalism. This element is paradig-matically metaethical. But this element alone does not, it seems to me, have moral implications. Be that as it may, I do not need to decide this issue here.

[61] See Gewirth (1960, 188) for a related point. I think that Gewirth's rejection of metaethical neutrality is motivated – much like mine – by thoughts about what it would take to take morality seriously (see, for instance, 204), but the details of his discussion are very different from mine.

[62] This is perhaps clearest in Dworkin (1996). In conversation, Dworkin agreed that this kind of argumen-tative move is unsound. He insisted that he was not guilty of it, though, as he relied on some supposedly metaethical propositions entailing *all by themselves* some paradigmatically substantive, moral judgments. I discuss this further in Chapter 5.

[63] For pressing me on this point, I thank Melis Erdur and Jamie Dreier.

morally relevant.[64] But this is not the kind of relevance that is needed for neutrality, for this kind of relevance is too contingent (on the content of Jamie's contingent promises). The intuitive idea in dispute between those taking metaethics to be morally neutral and those denying this neutrality is about some *internal* connections, as it were, between metaethics and morality, or some non-contingent, at least morally necessary connections of this sort. In *this* way, of course, it is not the case that pretty much anything is morally relevant. This qualification does not take away anything, I think, from the advantages I detailed above of my understanding of the neutrality issue.

With neutrality thus understood, then, is metaethics morally neutral? The discussion in the main parts of this chapter shows that it is not. To see this, return to the *Reductio* Argument, but focus now on just its first five stages, which constitute what I will call the Simple Argument:

(1)   Caricaturized Subjectivism.
(2)   If Caricaturized Subjectivism is true, then interpersonal conflicts due to moral disagreements are really just interpersonal conflicts due to differences in mere preferences. (From the content of Caricaturized Subjectivism.)
(3)   Therefore, interpersonal conflicts due to moral disagreements are just interpersonal conflicts due to differences in mere preferences. (From 1 and 2.)
(4)   IMPARTIALITY, that is, roughly: when an interpersonal conflict (of the relevant kind) is a matter merely of preferences, then an impartial, egalitarian solution is called for, and it is wrong to just stand one's ground.
(5)   Therefore, in cases of interpersonal conflict due to moral disagreement (of the relevant kind), an impartial, egalitarian solution is called for, and it is wrong to just stand one's ground. (From 3 and 4.)

This Simple Argument has a first-order, moral (that is, not non-moral) conclusion. Of its two interesting premises, one (1) is metaethical, and the other (4) a true, or at least plausible, first-order, moral premise. And it is clear that in this argument, the metaethical premise is indispensable. So if no purely normative argument – argument without any metaethical premises – can support (5) (to the same degree) it is supported (also) given the Simple Argument, Caricaturized Subjectivism non-conservatively extends first-order morality. And I think it is plausible that no purely normative argument can do that, for the following reasons. First, remember that what would be needed are normative arguments that support (5) *to the same degree*, so that the availability of the Simple Argument in no way increases the plausibility of (5). So long as the Simple Argument makes a difference with regard to (5)'s plausibility, Caricaturized Subjectivism still makes a moral difference. And even if you can think of some purely normative argument that supports (5), it is hard to believe it would render the Simple Argument entirely irrelevant. Second, let me remind you that with regard to purely factual beliefs,

---

[64]   I thank Jamie Dreier for a version of this example.

we've seen that (5)'s analogue fails. So in order to argue for (5) in the moral case, it seems that a metaethical disanalogy between moral and non-moral, factual disagreement has to be relied on. Third, and relatedly, on more realist views, (5) is deeply mysterious. If moral judgments are representations of Plato's Forms, say, then why on earth think that there's even a prima facie symmetry between accurate and inaccurate representations thereof? But if on such a metaethical view (5) is that surprising, then it seems highly unlikely that a convincing argument for (5) can be constructed that does not include something like a denial of such a metaethical view as a premise.[65] For these reasons, then, I believe that we can safely conclude that Caricaturized Subjectivism extends morality non-conservatively.

Note also that (5) is a highly interesting moral conclusion, one that may very well be in dispute among people only interested in normative ethics. So it cannot be said that the normative implications of Caricaturized Subjectivism are ones that those engaging in normative ethics need not worry about. And so – given the discussion earlier in this appendix – Caricaturized Subjectivism is not morally neutral.

In sections 2.3 and 2.4 above I generalized the *Reductio* Argument (of which the Simple Argument is a part) to many other metaethical views. If the argumentation works, we can apply it here to conclude that not just Caricaturized Subjectivism but in fact many other metaethical theories are not morally neutral.[66] And this suffices, I believe, to render the following conclusion not too premature: in at least one important sense of "neutrality", metaethics is not morally neutral.

Recall the brief discussion above of the sense in which Field's error theory about numbers can be number-theoretically neutral. As I put it there: while Field's theory clearly implies that number theory is fictional, it arguably has no implications *within* the fiction. The nice thing about the argument from IMPARTIALITY is that if it works it shows that morality is in this regard unlike mathematics. For while there presumably are no mathematical theorems that render Field's error theory relevant within the mathematical story (or fiction) itself, there *is* a moral "theorem" that could – within certain restrictions – render certain metaethical views morally relevant. IMPARTIALITY thus renders (some) metaethical theories morally relevant, in a way that has no plausible analogue (as far as I know) in the mathematical case.

---

[65] You may recall that when presenting the *Reductio* Argument I argued on first-order, normative grounds directly that (5) is false. If so, and assuming the consistency of first-order morality, it follows that there cannot be a good moral argument for (5). But I do not want to deny the dialectical awkwardness of relying on the denial of (5) in arguing that the Simple Argument shows that Caricaturized Subjectivism extends morality non-conservatively.

[66] Kramer (2009, 4–5) rightly emphasizes that from the ethical neutrality of *some* metaethical view the neutrality of *all* simply does not follow.

3

The Argument from the Deliberative Indispensability of Irreducibly Normative Truths

The argument of the previous chapter was a (partly) moral argument for metaethical objectivity. I now turn to an argument that attempts to do more in some respects, less in others. It attempts to do more, because it attempts to support Robust Realism, and not just some possibly weaker kind of objectivity. It attempts to do less, because the Robust Realism it supports (if successful) is about normative truths in general, and so it is consistent with the denial of Robust Realism (or even objectivism) about morality. In this chapter I focus on this other argument. I discuss the relation between the two arguments – and what happens, if I'm right, when we combine them – in Chapter 4.

My argument in this chapter is modeled after arguments from explanatory indispensability common in the philosophy of science and the philosophy of mathematics. I argue that irreducibly normative truths, though not explanatorily indispensable, are nevertheless deliberatively indispensable – they are, in other words, indispensable for the project of deliberating and deciding what to do – and that this kind of indispensability is just as respectable as the more familiar explanatory kind. Deliberative indispensability, I argue, justifies belief in normative facts, just like the explanatory indispensability of theoretical entities like electrons justifies belief in electrons.

My discussion starts with an antirealist challenge – the one I call Harman's Challenge – that claims that moral truths or facts are explanatorily redundant, and that we therefore have no reason to believe they exist. Having presented the challenge (in section 3.1), I proceed to reject the explanatory requirement on which it is based. I then show – in section 3.2 – how doing so is compatible with a rather strict requirement of ontological parsimony. In section 3.3 I argue that indispensability – the kind of indispensability that purportedly justifies ontological commitment – need not be explanatory, and that deliberative indispensability may be just as respectable as explanatory indispensability. In section 3.4 I leave metaethics and metanormativity behind, and proceed to do some epistemology – this is where I do what I can to justify the move from indispensability to belief. I explain, in other words, why we should take the indispensability of something (explanatory or otherwise) as reason to believe that it exists. In section 3.5 I say more about what indispensability is, dividing the discussion into an account of what I call instrumental and intrinsic indispensability. In the following two sections – 3.6 and 3.7 – I characterize the phenomenology of deliberation, arguing that it satisfies the desiderata needed for my argument for Robust Realism to go through. In section 3.8 I hint at why it is unlikely that any other metanormative view can supply all that is needed for deliberation, thus further supporting the indispensability premise of my argument. I state the conclusion that I take this chapter to establish in section 3.9.

3.1 Harman's Challenge

Seeing a vapor trail in a cloud chamber, a physicist thinks to herself: "There goes a proton". That she makes the observation that she does is at least some evidence for there having been a proton in the cloud chamber, Harman argues plausibly, because the best explanation of her observation involves the fact that there really was a proton in the cloud chamber at the relevant time. If the physicist's observation is best explained by an alternative explanation, one that does not involve the proton in an appropriate way, her observation gives no reason to believe that there was a proton in the cloud chamber.

Seeing a few children set a cat on fire you think to yourself "That's wrong". How is the fact that you immediately make this judgment best explained? Harman argues that it is best explained by psychological, sociological, historical, cultural, and other such facts about you. Whether or not what the children are doing really *is* wrong is not at all relevant, Harman says, for the best explanation of your immediate moral judgment. Seeing that the relevant observation or judgment is best explained without assuming the existence of the relevant purported (irreducibly) moral fact, Harman concludes, we have no reason to believe there are such (irreducibly) moral facts. Realism refuted.[1]

The general thought seems clear enough: moral facts do not play an appropriate explanatory role (the No Explanatory Role Thesis), and, given that playing such a role is necessary for justified belief in the existence of a kind of fact (the Explanatory Requirement), we are not justified in believing in moral facts. But despite the simplicity of the thought this argument attempts to capture, much work needs to be done if we are to have here a reasonably precise argument against Robust Metanormative Realism. Which possible explananda, for instance, count in shouldering the burden of the Explanatory Requirement? Only observations, as Harman himself seems to suggest? Why this restriction? Maybe explaining non-observational beliefs, or desires, or actions, or non-action sociological events, or more purely causal events suffices for satisfying the Explanatory Requirement or the intuitive condition it is meant to capture?[2] Do *moral* facts count as respectable explananda, such that if moral

---

[1] For his original statement of the problem, see Harman (1977, ch. 1). Harman does not claim originality for the general problem his text tries to capture.

[2] For discussion of these issues, see Sturgeon (1984, 54–5), Lycan (1986, 89), Railton (1986a, 192), Brink (1989, 186–9), Sayre-McCord (1992), Wright (1992, 197–8), Shafer-Landau (2003, 102–3).

facts are required in order to explain other moral facts, moral realism is vindicated? This seems like cheating, but can moral facts be declared less than respectable explananda without begging the question against the realist?[3] What assumptions about the individuation of kinds of fact is it reasonable to read into the Explanatory Requirement? What kind of explanatory role must be played by a kind of fact in order to satisfy the Explanatory Requirement? And if the argument is generalized from the metaethical to the metanormative,[4] doesn't it flirt with self-defeat, given that the Explanatory Requirement itself is normative through and through?[5] These are some of the questions in need of answers if Harman's Challenge is to become a complete threat to Robust Realism.[6]

As I am not here specifically interested in Harman's Challenge but am rather using it as a way of introducing my argument for Robust Realism, for my purposes no such detailed discussion is needed. For regardless of the details, an intuitive challenge remains: we have, it seems, good reason to believe in electrons, and perhaps also in numbers, because they play an appropriate role in the best explanation of a respectable explanandum. Can belief in normative facts – or, say, in values – be justified in a similar way? If not, what reason *do* we have for believing in them? Shouldn't we avoid multiplying kinds of entities, facts, and truths without sufficient reason?

Broadly speaking, two realist response-strategies suggest themselves.[7] The realist can, first, reject the No Explanatory Role Thesis, and argue – usually, by citing examples – that normative facts indeed do play an appropriate role in the best explanation of a respectable explanandum. Or, second, the realist can reject the Explanatory Requirement, arguing that we have reason to believe in normative truths even though (or even if) they do not play such an explanatory role.

The former strategy has been far more common in the literature.[8] Though one can find in the literature some hints and brief comments suggesting the second strategy,[9] it

---

[3] For some discussion, see Nagel (1986, 146), Brink (1989, 182–3), and Shafer-Landau (2003, 104).

[4] A generalization along these lines has been suggested by Sayre-McCord (1988a, 278; 1992, 70 n. 21). It is also clear that normativity – and not just morality – is at stake in Nagel's (1986, ch. 8) and Dworkin's (1996) relevant discussions.

[5] For similar points, see Quinn (1986, 539), Simon (1990, 113 (n. 27)), Putnam (1995, 71), McGinn (1997, 13–14), and Shafer-Landau (2003, 113).

[6] This is not necessarily a criticism of Harman. First, it's not clear he is interested in the metanormative generalization of his argument. And second, perhaps even without answering some of the questions in the text, Harman's Challenge poses a serious threat to some other kind of realism, like the Cornell Realist's. Indeed, much of the discussion of Harman's Challenge in the literature is by such naturalist realists as Sturgeon and Brink.

[7] Zimmerman (1984, 81–2) and Leiter (2001a, 88) draw a similar distinction between two strategies of coping with Harman's Challenge, as does (perhaps more implicitly) Shafer-Landau (2007).

[8] And an extensive literature it is. For some of it, see: Audi (1997, ch. 5); Blackburn (1991a; 1991b); Brink (1989, 182–97); Copp (1990); Harman (1977; 1984; 1986a; 1998); Harman and Thomson (1996, chs. 6, 9, 10); Leiter (2001a); Lycan (1986); McDowell (1985, 117–20); Moore (1992); Quinn (1986); Railton (1998); Sayre-McCord (1988a; 1992); Shafer-Landau (2003, 98–115); Sturgeon (1984; 1986a; 1991; 1992; 1998); Wiggins (1990); Wright (1992, ch. 5); Yasenchuk (1994); Zimmerman (1984).

[9] Remarks that are somewhat suggestive of the second strategy, either in rejecting the Explanatory Requirement, or in interpreting it liberally enough, can be found in Lycan (1986, 89); Wiggins (1990,

has not, to the best of my knowledge, been pursued systematically. In a moment I will proceed to pursue the second strategy and so I can afford to remain largely neutral regarding the prospects of the first strategy, about which I am rather pessimistic. Very briefly, then, and without pretending that the following comment is a serious argument: my pessimism regarding the first strategy of vindicating Robust Realism comes not only from the implausibility, as it seems to me, of the claim that normative facts play an appropriate role in the best explanation of relevantly respectable explananda, but also from two further points. First, I suspect that even if normative facts do play such a role, the first strategy for coping with Harman's Challenge could at most vindicate a naturalist kind of realism, not the Robust Realism I am out to defend (this, of course, is not a reason to think the first strategy must fail, only that it can't get me all that I want). And second, and more importantly, it seems to me that even if normative facts do not play such an explanatory role, still this doesn't compromise their respectability in any way. If this is so, a serious attempt at the second strategy is certainly called for.

Let me put the first strategy to one side, then, and focus on the second.

3.2 Parsimony

A worry immediately threatens: what underlies the Explanatory Requirement is, after all, a highly plausible methodological principle of parsimony: Kinds of entities should not be unnecessarily multiplied, redundancy should be avoided.[10] And, it seems, without such a principle it is exceedingly hard – perhaps even impossible – to justify many of our negative existential beliefs. Taking this methodological principle as given, then, how can the Explanatory Requirement be consistently rejected? Assuming that (irreducibly) normative facts play no appropriate explanatory role, are they not redundant, and then isn't belief in them unwarranted?

In order to allay this worry, it is necessary to distinguish two different requirements of parsimony. First, there is the most general requirement not to multiply ontological commitments without sufficient reason. This requirement places a prima facie burden

---

85); McDowell (1985, 118–19); Nagel (1986, 144–5); Dworkin (1996, 119–22); Platts (1980, 79); Korsgaard (1996, 96); and Shafer-Landau (2003, 114–15). A clearer statement of the second strategy and an initial attempt at pursuing it can be found in Simon (1990, 105–6) and Sayre-McCord (1988a, 278–80). An emphasis on the point of view of the deliberating agent – central to my employment of the second strategy of coping with Harman's Challenge – can be found in Regan (2003) and Rosati (2003). At times, Regan's claims are very close to my own, except he thinks such line of thought only defends realism "for practical purposes" (2003, 656). I am not sure I understand this phrase, and to the extent that I do, I want more. And for an emphasis on the practical, deliberative relevance of the realist truth of normative judgments, see Fitzpatrick (2005, 685–6).

[10] Let me remind you of a point made in Chapter 1: if for some reason you find talk of normative *truths* rather than facts, or normative *properties* rather than objects much less threatening, feel free to paraphrase accordingly. Nothing much will then be changed. Notice, for instance, that the appeal of the parsimony requirement survives such a paraphrase.

of argument on the party arguing for a belief in the existence of entities or facts of a certain disputed kind. Call this *the Minimal Parsimony Requirement*.

Often, though, more is packed into the methodological principle of parsimony than the Minimal Parsimony Requirement. It is often assumed that the only way of satisfying the Minimal Parsimony Requirement is by showing that the relevant kind of fact is *explanatorily* useful.[11] With this assumption, the Minimal Parsimony Requirement becomes the Explanatory Requirement.

I want, then, to reject the Explanatory Requirement while adhering to the Minimal Parsimony Requirement. And, as is by now clear, the way to do this is to reject the assumption that the Minimal Parsimony Requirement can only be satisfied by explanatorily indispensable facts, truths, properties, and entities.[12] In other words, I suggest we restrict, in accordance with the Minimal Parsimony Requirement, our ontological commitment to just those things that are indispensable. But I suggest that we consider other – non-explanatory – kinds of indispensability as satisfying this requirement. So the line I'm about to take does not have the unacceptable counterintuitive result of admitting objectionable – and completely, not just explanatorily, redundant – things into our ontology.

3.3 Indispensability – explanatory and otherwise

Why should we believe in, say, electrons? One common – and plausible – answer runs like this: There are many inferences to the best explanation the conclusion of which entails the existence of electrons: our best scientific theories quantify over electrons; we ought to believe that these theories are at least approximately true (they are, after all, our *best* theories, our best explanations of numerous phenomena; and they are also – now in non-comparative terms – fairly good), and so we ought to believe that electrons exist. If electrons play an appropriate role in the best (and good enough) explanation of respectable explananda – and it seems they do – we're justified in believing that electrons exist. Of course, Inference to the Best Explanation (IBE, for short) is not

---

[11] In a somewhat different context (that of characterizing the realist–antirealist debate, not that of deciding it), Wright (1993, 73) notices this often-made assumption (explicitly referring to Harman), and expresses his doubts about it.

[12] Slors (1998, 243) makes a similar point about the mental, when he writes: "But why shouldn't mental regularities have some other function than a causal-explanatory one? It might just be possible that the mental justifies its place in our ontology by other means than its causal efficacy." And here is Grice (1975, 31): "My taste is for keeping open house for all sorts and conditions of entities, just so long as when they come in they help with the house-work. Provided that I can see them at work, and provided that they are not detected in illicit logical behaviour . . . I do not find them queer or mysterious at all. To fangle a new ontological Marxism, *they work therefore they exist*, even though only some, perhaps those who come on the recommendation of some form of transcendental argument, may qualify for the specially favoured status of *entia realissima*. To exclude honest working entities seems to me like metaphysical snobbery, a reluctance to be seen in the company of any but the best objects." Honest working entities are, of course, those that satisfy the Minimal Parsimony Requirement. And I would add only that explanatory work is not the only kind of work around the house that needs doing.

uncontroversial. For now, though, let us assume that IBE suffices to justify ontological commitment. (I will reopen this issue, to an extent, in the next section.)

As I understand inferences to the best explanation, they are really particular instances of indispensability arguments.[13] Electrons are indispensable for our best explanations; so, by IBE, electrons exist. And it is important to note here, that instances of IBE are arguments from *explanatory* indispensability. Electrons are indispensable for our explanatory project, and for this reason we are justified in believing they exist.

As has already been argued, the availability of the second strategy of coping with Harman's Challenge depends on there being other, non-explanatory, kinds of indispensability that suffice to justify ontological commitment. Later on I will suggest one such other kind, deliberative indispensability. For the moment, though, I want to make the following preliminary point: given some other purportedly respectable kind of indispensability, the proponent of the Explanatory Requirement (who is also a proponent of IBE) must find a non-arbitrary way of distinguishing between explanatory and that other kind of indispensability. She must show, in other words, why it is that explanatory indispensability ought to be taken seriously, but other kinds of indispensability ought not to be so taken; she must present a reason for taking explanatory indispensability to justify ontological commitment that does not generalize to other kinds of indispensability.[14] Now, my way of justifying the move from indispensability to belief – described in the next section – will not be of that sort. It will apply to explanatory indispensability just in case it applies to other, non-explanatory, kinds of indispensability, and in particular to deliberative indispensability. This does not show, of course, that *no* rationale can be given for restricting respectable status to explanatory indispensability alone. So think of my point here as a challenge: can you think of any reason for grounding ontological commitment in explanatory indispensability that is not really more general, a reason for grounding ontological commitment in indispensabilities of other kinds as well?[15]

---

[13] This relation between IBE and indispensability arguments has been noticed by Field (1989, 14) and Colyvan (2001, 7–8, esp. n. 17). Interestingly, Harman (1977, 10) mentions indispensability arguments for mathematical realism as support for his *dis*analogy between mathematical and ethical facts. If I am right in what follows, these arguments in fact supply the material for an important analogy between the two.

[14] Thus, I think Simon (1990, 105–6) accurately characterizes the dialectical situation when she writes: "What one would like from the anti-realist is an argument for using explanatory necessity as a criterion of reality which is more compelling than the absence of a better one. On the other hand, what one would like from the realist is, if not an alternative criterion, at least some indication of how one is to go about evaluating claims concerning the reality of different purported existents." My argument can be seen as an attempt to give Simon what she wants from the realist.

Later on, Simon writes (1990, 108): "And, one might ask, is not the necessity of saving morality as compelling as explanatory necessity? Perhaps it is a necessity which itself warrants multiplying entities." It is not entirely clear to me what Simon has in mind, but she may very well be anticipating here an argument similar to my argument from deliberative indispensability.

[15] You may think that the obvious difference is that explanatory indispensability is *epistemic*, or perhaps *paradigmatically* epistemic, or perhaps *truth-related*, in a way that deliberative indispensability – being entirely pragmatic – is not. I thank Mark van Roojen, Tristram McPherson, and Jonas Olson for related objections. The answer that emerges from the next section is that, first, at the most basic level, the epistemic status of IBE

If there is no reason for taking explanatory indispensability seriously that is not a reason for taking some other kinds of indispensability seriously, then the move from the Minimal Parsimony Requirement to the Explanatory Requirement is arbitrary and so unjustified.[16] If any other kind of indispensability can be defended, then the second strategy for coping with Harman's Challenge becomes promising: all that is then left to do is to show that (irreducibly) normative truths are indispensable in this other, non-explanatory, way.

3.4 The move from indispensability to (justified) belief

In the next few sections I am going to say much more on what indispensability comes to, and on the deliberative indispensability of normative truths. But there is a very general and natural worry about my argumentative strategy, one that can be appreciated before more details are introduced, and that it will prove useful to discuss already at this stage: why think that indispensability – explanatory or deliberative – is any guide at all to ontology, or to truth? "Even if everything you are about to say about indispensability and deliberation is true", my interlocutor can say, "all you will have shown is that, in some sense, we *need* normative truths. But how is this any reason at all to believe that there are such things? Perhaps you will establish that it would be nice if there were normative truths, or that we deeply want them to exist. But concluding from this to the *belief* in normative truths is a clear instance of wishful thinking."[17]

The first thing to note in reply to this objection is that it applies just as forcefully to arguments from explanatory indispensability: "Even granting you the explanatory indispensability of numbers, or electrons, or whatever", someone may argue, "all you've shown is that, in some sense, we *need* there to be electrons and numbers if we are going to make sense of the world. But how is this any reason at all to believe that there are such things? Perhaps you've established that it would be nice if there were electrons, or that we deeply want them to exist (because we want the world to make sense to us). But concluding from this to the *belief* in electrons is a clear instance of wishful thinking." Of course, had we had independent reason to believe that the

---

too depends on some pragmatic stuff; and second, in the case of deliberation too what we end up with – based on the pragmatic stuff – is a perfectly kosher epistemic status. Here too, then, at the end of the day (that is, at the end of the epistemological story of section 3.4) there is no disanalogy between arguments from explanatory and deliberative indispensability.

[16] I suspect this is what McGinn has in mind when he accuses Harman's Explanatory Requirement of being arbitrary and dogmatically empiricist (1997, 13; see also at 17, 36). For a similar point, see Putnam (1995, 70).

[17] Here is a similar accusation from Korsgaard (1996, 33): "Having discovered that he needs an unconditional answer, the realist straightaway concludes that he has found one." (Korsgaard doesn't, of course, address my argument; this sentence is taken from her criticism of realists (primarily Nagel) whose views and arguments are distinct from mine, but are nevertheless closely related to them.) Zimmerman (1984, 95) makes a similar point in criticizing Platts. And Russ Shafer-Landau (2003, 29 n. 11) makes a similar point against Wiggins's different but related critique of (what he calls) noncognitivism.

universe was such as to make sense to us, that it was at least by and large intelligible, that it was explanation-friendly, this problem would go away. Similarly, if we had independent reason to believe that the universe was deliberation-friendly, the analogous worry about my own argument would go away. But it does not seem like we have – or indeed can have – independent reason to believe such things. And so the worry stands.

Now, justifications come to an end somewhere. And perhaps this is where: we usually take that something is theoretically useful to be reason to believe it, and perhaps we should rest content with that as a fairly basic epistemic procedure, as one place where epistemic justification comes to an end.[18] And in a sense, I think this *is* where epistemic justification comes to an end. But as always, the justifications-come-to-an-end-somewhere reply is not very satisfying. More needs to be said here.

Before I proceed to say more, though, let me warn you: things are going to get pretty epistemological now. The rest of this section, that is, engages with fairly basic issues in general epistemology, and I won't return to metaethics or anything clearly resembling it until section 3.5. If, then, you do not have a taste for the most general epistemological discussions, and if, furthermore, you are at this point happy to concede the point from the previous paragraph – namely, that indispensability of the explanatory kind, and of relevantly similar kinds, can justify belief and ontological commitment – feel free to go directly to section 3.5.

3.4.1 Where epistemic justification comes to an end[19]

When I wonder what time it is, usually I turn to my watch. If my watch says it's 2:24 I update my time-belief accordingly, coming to believe that it's 2:24. Deferring to the watch, in other words, is my method for forming beliefs about the time of day. If a watch-skeptic comes along and requires some epistemic justification for this method of mine, I am not without words: I might be able to explain to her the watch's mechanism and why it is that it is very likely, once set to the right time, to keep at least reasonably accurate time thereafter; I can just note that my watch has never failed me before and that I have no reason to believe it will start now; and so on. If the watch-skeptic then asks about the belief-forming methods I'm using in giving this reply – the deductive or inductive rules of inference, for instance, or relying on my memory – and why it is that I am epistemically justified in employing them, I may again have something to say. But sooner or later (most often, it seems, embarrassingly sooner) justifications come to an end. Some belief-forming methods are just basic for me, they are fundamental in how

---

[18] David Lewis, for instance, is not terribly worried. In introducing his argument for modal realism – a rather surprising ontological thesis, initially no less surprising than Robust Metanormative Realism, I would hope – he says: "I begin the first chapter by reviewing the many ways in which systematic philosophy goes more easily if we may presuppose modal realism in our analyses. I take this to be a good reason to think that modal realism is true, just as the utility of set theory in mathematics is a good reason to believe that there are sets" (1986, vii).

[19] The rest of this section (up to section 3.5) draws rather heavily on Enoch (2003a) and on Enoch and Schechter (2008).

I think: I don't employ them because I employ other methods, but rather I employ other methods because they are licensed by these basic ones.

For inferential belief-forming methods, relying on the rule known as *modus ponens* (From p and *if p then q* infer q) seems like a plausible candidate for a belief-forming method that is basic for most of us. For non-inferential belief-forming methods, plausible candidates for basicness are relying on perception and on memory. These and other basic belief-forming methods are where epistemic justification comes to an end, and if the most radical kind of skepticism is to be avoided, noticing this fact should not compromise our warrant in using them. If we are ever justified in any of our beliefs, then, there must be basic belief-forming methods we are epistemically justified in employing even though we do not – and perhaps cannot – possess an epistemic justification for so employing them. (One way of making this point is to think of these basic methods as *default-reasonable*, methods that are, roughly, reasonable in the absence of a case either for or against them.[20])

If total *inductive* skepticism is to be avoided, there had better be some rules of *ampliative* inference we are justified in using. And, given the desperate prospects of grounding such rules in purportedly more basic rules of deductive inference, it seems clear that there is going to be some rule of ampliative inference that is going to be *basic* for us. Arguably, IBE is just such a rule. We infer to the best explanation, not because doing so is licensed by some other, more basic, belief-forming method, but rather basically. Indeed, other rules of inductive inference – such as some version of Enumerative Induction – can plausibly be seen as based on, derived from, some version of IBE.[21]

If this is so, then IBE is one place where epistemic justification comes to an end. And this would mean, it seems, that there is something wrong about asking for further justification for employing IBE. The question "Why are you epistemically justified in employing IBE?" is then – like "Why are you epistemically justified in using *modus ponens* or relying on perception?" – one I cannot give a non-trivial answer to without taking back my commitment to classifying them as basic belief-forming methods. Something, it seems, is wrong with the question, or at least with understanding it literally.[22]

If IBE is a basic belief-forming method for me, and if furthermore it is one I am *justified* in employing as basic, then it is not required, for me to be justified in employing it, that I antecedently form a justified belief regarding the explanatorily-friendliness (or, in Lipton's (1991) helpful terms, the *loveliness*) of the universe.[23] And this is undoubtedly a piece of good news, for it is hard to see how we could arrive

---

[20] For some discussion of default-reasonableness, see Field (2000).

[21] For such claims, see, for instance, Harman (1965), and Lycan (1985).

[22] Lycan (1985), to whose discussion I'm very much indebted in this context, therefore suggests reading the question differently, as a request (somewhat roughly) for a *pragmatic* justification of employing IBE. But Lycan (2002) also illegitimately belittles the challenge – more on this below.

[23] A worry remains, one that is perhaps best put in terms of the doubtful *reliability* of IBE, or the doubtful connection between epistemic justification (if IBE is indeed justified) and truth. I address this worry below.

at a justified belief in the world's loveliness without being antecedently justified in employing some method of ampliative inference.[24] (This is, of course, an analogue of the observation that underlies Hume's critique of induction.[25]) Indeed, if I can justifiably employ IBE without being antecedently justified in believing that the world is lovely, perhaps – depending on what we end up saying about rule-circular arguments[26] – I can then come to have a justified belief that the universe is lovely by employing IBE.[27]

3.4.2 The need for a vindication

But that IBE is one of the places where epistemic justification comes to an end does not mean that nothing else – not even nothing else that is of epistemic significance and interest – can be said here. And indeed, more *needs* to be said. For among the many different possible belief-forming methods (even possibly basic ones) that could be employed some, such as *modus ponens*, IBE, and relying on perception, we are presumably justified in employing. Others, such as Affirming the Consequent, Counter-Induction, and Inference to the Worst Explanation we would presumably not be justified in employing.[28] It is highly implausible that the only thing distinguishing justified from unjustified basic belief-forming methods is their justificatory status. It seems much more plausible that there is some other, deeper, difference *in virtue of which* some basic methods are, and some are not, justified.[29] And ideally, we would want this distinction to be principled, one that we would be reasonably happy to consider the ultimate justification-relevant distinction. What is needed, then, is a principled way of drawing the distinction between belief-forming methods we are justified in employing as basic, and those we are not justified in so employing. If you like to think of some methods as default-reasonable, what is needed is a principled way of distinguishing between methods that are, and those that are not, default reasonable.[30] Perhaps such a distinction cannot after all be found. Perhaps we will have to settle for a "brute-list"

---

[24] Unless, that is, we are willing to follow Leibniz and argue that God, in His perfection, has created the world which is simplest in hypotheses (1686, section 6). I assume we are not. An analogous line may be taken by some idealists or Kantians, who may argue that it is guaranteed a priori that the world is lovely because we confer loveliness on it. (For an example of a contemporary view of this sort, see Kitcher, 1989, 494–500). Whatever the merits of such a line, clearly it will not do for the purpose of arguing – partly by analogy – for Robust Realism.

[25] Fumerton (1992) explicitly notices this similarity.

[26] See Enoch and Schechter (2008, 576) and the references there.

[27] Here's a sketch of such an instance of IBE: We've been using – when doing science, and also in our everyday commonsensical reasoning – IBE; and we've been tremendously successful in our endeavors; but, if the world is not lovely, this success of ours would be utterly mysterious. So, *by IBE*, the world is lovely.

[28] Affirming the Consequent is the rule of inference that licenses the inference from q and *if p then q*, to p. Counter-Induction is the rule of inference that licenses the inference to the denial of any claim (some reasonable version of) Enumerative Induction licenses, given the same initial beliefs. Inference to the Worst Explanation licenses inferences to the worst explanation of some initially believed propositions.

[29] Boghossian (2000, 239) and Peacocke (2004) make similar points.

[30] Boghossian (2000, 239) makes this point as an objection to the idea of default-reasonableness, because he sees no way in which the proponents of default-reasonableness can cope with this challenge.

view of justified basic belief-forming methods. But I see no reason for giving up so soon. And if a brute-list view can be avoided, if a principled way of drawing the relevant distinction can be found, then equipped with it we can turn back to arguments from deliberative indispensability and see whether relying on them as basic satisfies the criteria for justification of basic belief-forming methods.

If such a unified account of justified basic belief-forming methods can be found, and if, furthermore, it presents belief-forming methods we're justified in employing as basic in a positive light, such that we're happy to treat the account as zeroing in on the ultimately justificatorily-relevant features of a belief-forming method, I will say that the account is a *vindication* of our basic belief-forming methods.[31] It will not be, of course, an epistemic justification of the employment of these methods – nothing will be *that*, for they are methods we employ as basic. Epistemic justifications really do come to an end somewhere, and basic belief-forming methods are where they come to an end. But that doesn't mean there's no legitimate concern to be addressed about them. The concern is that of vindicating them, by drawing a principled distinction between them and methods we are not justified in employing as basic, a distinction that presents them in a positive light.

Extensional adequacy is going to be one adequacy constraint on such a purported vindication: if relying on perception and memory, or using *modus ponens*, are not vindicated by a suggested account, or if relying on clairvoyance or Affirming the Consequent are, this would count strongly against the suggested account. So we're looking for a non-ad-hoc, not merely list-like, vindication of basic belief-forming methods that is at least reasonably extensionally adequate.

3.4.3 A (somewhat) pragmatic account of vindication

What's common to all the examples of basic belief-forming methods, I want to argue next, is that their possible success is our only (relevant) hope of successfully engaging in some extremely important project. Think again of IBE. Now, the explanatory project is one of tremendous importance for us. We are explaining, understanding creatures, creatures that try to make sense of themselves and the world around them. Perhaps the explanatory project is even a project we *cannot* disengage from (so long as we are physically able to think). But even if we *can*, it seems we *should* not so disengage. In an important sense, the explanatory project is non-optional for us, it is one we are rationally required to engage in. Now, at least given our constitution, it seems our only hope of ever succeeding in making the world intelligible is if (some version of) IBE is at least reasonably reliable. So, even independently of an antecedently justified belief in the reliability of IBE, we are pragmatically justified in employing it. This is so simply because if not even IBE works, all is lost. This, then, is the idea: given a project which is non-optional in the relevant sense, and given a belief-forming method that

---

[31] I borrow the term from Feigl (1952) who coins it in a very similar context. Nevertheless, there are some important differences between his use of the term and mine, differences I cannot discuss here.

we, given our constitution, have to employ if we are to have any chance of successfully engaging in that non-optional project, we are prima facie epistemically justified in employing it as basic.

Notice that the suggested account, although it doesn't epistemically justify the use of our basic belief-forming methods, nevertheless does justify them *pragmatically*. And, given the rational weight of pragmatic justification (and given the non-optionality of the relevant project), this line of thought also justifies the rational force of our basic belief-forming methods. So the suggested account amounts to a vindication in the above given sense: it draws a principled distinction between methods that we are and those that we are not justified in employing as basic in a way that presents the former in a rationally positive light.

Note also that this (initial) account of the justification of basic belief-forming methods is an account of a *sufficient* condition for epistemic justification. All the underlying intuition directly supports is the claim that if a basic belief-forming method is one we cannot avoid using if we are successfully to engage in some non-optional project, then it is justified. I suspect that the pragmatic account of vindication yields also a necessary condition for the justification of basic belief-forming methods. But, seeing that the underlying intuition as stated does not (directly) support the necessity requirement, and that the sufficiency is all that is needed for my indispensability argument for Robust Realism, I will not pursue this point further here.

To see better what the said non-optionality of projects consists in, notice that usually, facing a valuable project and a method without the success of which the project is bound to fail, there is more than one possibly justified way of proceeding. The ultimately justified way of proceeding here may depend on the likelihood of the relevant method actually succeeding and on the value of the project (and on other factors as well). If, for instance, the only method that could possibly lead to your successfully engaging in the relevant project is itself highly unlikely to succeed, and if the project is not of that much value anyway, it seems the rational thing to do is to discard the project. If, on the other hand, the method is at least somewhat likely to succeed, the project of sufficient value, and engaging with it not too costly, then the rational thing to do is to employ the method (and hope for the best).

What does *not* depend on these factors, though, seems to be this: given such a project and such a method, you are pragmatically justified in *either* employing the method, *or* discarding the project. Now, the pragmatic account invokes the non-optionality of the relevant project in order to block the second disjunct, thus leaving only the first: if discarding the project is not a rationally acceptable option, then employing the relevant method is the only rationally open option.[32]

---

[32] Here is an argument with a similar structure, attributed to Hobbes by Darwall (1992, 162): "As *agents*, unavoidably viewing the world *sub specie* the end of self-preservation, our conclusions regarding how our lives are 'best preserved,' give rise to dictates, to 'ought to do's. Of course, could we give up this end, the most

Notice that the kind of non-optionality directly relevant here is *normative*. The point is that the project is one we have strong reason not to disengage from, perhaps one that we rationally ought not to disengage from. In previous work (2003a), I thought that non-normative essential non-optionality could also do the trick: that, in other words, if we just *cannot* disengage a project, that suffices to render methods that are needed for success in it to be justifiably employed as basic. But I no longer believe this, or at least I do not believe that such non-normative non-optionality can all alone do the work here. If such essential, non-normative non-optionality can have the implications suggested by this account of the justification of basic belief-forming methods, this has to be because of some general principle of rationality according to which we are justified in pursuing projects we cannot disengage from. Here as everywhere else, normative input is needed if normative output is to be secured.[33]

When I speak of a method being the only one that has any chance of making one's relevant non-optional endeavor successful, what exactly does this "the only one that has any chance" come to? The intuitive idea can be understood as involving two requirements. First, employing the relevant method, it must be possible successfully to engage in the relevant project. Second, it must be impossible successfully to engage with it otherwise.[34] If a method satisfies these two requirements – and, it seems, only if it satisfies them – then employing it gives a chance, and the only chance, of succeeding. And the kind of modality involved here is the kind associated with natural-language "I-can" locutions, and can be called *pragmatically relevant* possibility,[35] so that for a belief-forming method to be such that without it all is lost, there must be a sufficiently

---

we could conclude would be that we ought either to do what is necessary for self-preservation or renounce it as end, but the latter, Hobbes believes, is not an option that is open to us."

[33] The sketchy argument in the text explaining why non-normative non-optionality will not do echoes my criticism of constitutivism (in my "Agency, Shmagency" (2006), and "Shmagency Revisited" (2010b)), which – I now think – applies (with some modifications) to the use to which I tried to put non-normative non-optionality in my (2003a).

This means that my indispensability argument for Robust Realism will rely on a normative premise (that the deliberative project is rationally non-optional). But isn't it problematic – question-begging, perhaps – to use a normative premise in an argument for Robust Metanormative Realism? Against most alternative views, the answer is "no", for the premise is the normative proposition itself, not a robust realist understanding of it. But against error theorists there may be some question-begging involved, but not of an objectionable kind, as I argue in Chapter 5.

[34] This needs to be qualified so as to take into account the following possibility: assume two distinct methods M_1 and M_2 that would each allow successful engagement with the relevant project. Now suppose that if M_2 is successful, M_1 is likewise guaranteed to be successful (but not the other way around). Then, though it is not impossible successfully to engage with the relevant project without employing M_1 (one can employ M_2, which may also succeed), one is still pragmatically justified in employing M_1, for it is at least guaranteed to work *if anything does*. Strictly speaking, then, what is needed is not the impossibility of success without employing the relevant method, but the impossibility of success *if that method fails*. (This point mirrors Reichenbach's arguments, which were designed to show, not that Enumerative Induction is the only predictive method that might succeed, but rather that it succeeds if any method does. See his 1938.) For my purposes here I think I can safely ignore this complication, and so in what follows I do.

[35] For some alternative ways of understanding the relevant modality, and for reasons not to endorse them here, see Enoch and Schechter (2008, section 4.4 (p. 561 and on)).

close metaphysically possible world in which one successfully engages in the relevant project employing the method; and there must be no sufficiently close metaphysically possible world in which one successfully engages in the project without employing the method. The qualification to *sufficiently close* possible worlds is needed both for extensional adequacy and in order to maintain the initial intuitive appeal of the suggested account. Consider the case of IBE and the explanatory project. It seems fairly clear that there are some – very far, perhaps – possible worlds in which very different belief-forming methods render our explanatory endeavor successful. Perhaps, for instance, some version of mystical contemplation can – on a sufficiently far possible world – make everything intelligible for us in a flash. But we want IBE to be a method we are justified in employing as basic. So if the pragmatic account is to be extensionally adequate, a qualification to sufficiently close possible worlds is in order. Furthermore, the very distant possibility of success without employing the relevant method doesn't seem to undermine the otherwise-all-is-lost intuition. And if, even employing the method, the possibility of success is extremely distant, this does seem to undermine some of the force of the intuition that pragmatically justifies us in employing the relevant method. After all, it's not as if this distant possibility captures another way in which I can successfully engage in the explanatory project. So the qualification to pragmatically relevant – or sufficiently close – possible worlds is needed also in order to preserve the pragmatic account's intuitive appeal. Of course, this way of putting things relies on the obviously metaphorical apparatus of a closeness-metric between worlds. And there is no denying that this apparatus gives rise to some indeterminacy. But the sufficiently-close qualifier is meant to capture an intuitive idea: in the context of a pragmatic justification, we are only interested in those metaphysically possible worlds that are not so far as to be rendered pragmatically irrelevant. So, for instance, it seems plausible in this context to consider only those possible worlds in which our constitution is held more or less fixed: other worlds are, perhaps, possible, but they do not seem to be relevant for pragmatic considerations. Furthermore, the closeness-metric is highly context-sensitive: for me, a world that is very much like ours except that a different sperm cell "won the contest" and so not I but a genetic brother of mine was born, may be *further* from the actual world than a world in which I exist, but that is otherwise very different from the actual world.[36] Nevertheless, the idea of a sufficiently close possible world is, though vague and highly context-dependent, not without content. And it will do, I think, for my purposes here.[37]

Here, then, is the more precise formulation of the pragmatic criterion for belief-forming methods we are justified in employing as basic: *A thinker T is prima facie epistemically justified in employing a belief-forming method M as basic if there is for T a rationally*

---

[36] I owe this example to Tom Nagel. In the text I assume (as many today do) that (genetic) origin is essential. I have my doubts about this doctrine, but will not pursue them here.

[37] If you dislike the closeness metaphor, feel free to return to just talk of pragmatically relevant possibilities, or to just using I-can locutions.

non-optional project P such that it is (pragmatically-relevantly) possible for T to succeed in engaging in P using M, and it is (pragmatically-relevantly) impossible for T to succeed in engaging in P without using M.

We are reasoning creatures, and the reasoning project, it seems safe to assume, is not a rationally optional one (perhaps because it is also one we cannot disengage from). Furthermore, it seems that, if we cannot even use *modus ponens* (or some other deductive rule close enough to it), this project of ours is doomed from the start to systematic failure. There is no sufficiently close possible world in which we successfully engage in the reasoning project but do not use *modus ponens*. On the other hand, using *modus ponens* it does seem possible to reason at least somewhat successfully. So according to the suggested account, we are justified in using *modus ponens* as a basic rule of inference. Affirming the Consequent, on the other hand, is not needed for successful engagement with the reasoning project. Nor is it necessary, it seems to me, for successful engagement with any other non-optional project. So the pragmatic account does not yield an unwanted result that justifies employing Affirming the Consequent as a basic rule of inference. (If the pragmatic account supplies also a necessary, and not just sufficient, condition for the justification of basic belief-forming methods, then we can conclude that using Affirming the Consequent as basic is unjustified.)

The project of trying to find out what is going on in the world outside our minds also seems rationally non-optional. If we rely on perception, there is at least some chance we can succeed in this project. If we don't – or if even perception fails across the board – then in terms of this project, all is lost. So according to the suggested account we are justified in employing as basic the method of relying on perception.

I will not discuss any further examples. More can and should be said here, of course.[38] But for my purposes here what has been said seems sufficient to give a feel for how the account would apply to natural candidates for belief-forming methods we are justified in employing as basic.

3.4.4 A remaining worry about truth and reliability

A worry remains. For whatever exactly epistemic justification comes to, surely it has to be at least closely related to truth and reliability. And now it may seem as if I've saved the status of the relevant basic belief-forming methods as epistemically justified only at the price of severing the necessary tie between epistemic justification and truth. "You may use words as you wish", someone may argue, "and so you can present the pragmatic account as a stipulated definition for a technical term 'epistemic justification'. But don't pretend this is the justification we have been concerned about all

---

[38] Particularly important here is the suspicion that this pragmatic account is vulnerable to the difficulty that devastated Reichenbach's pragmatic justification of induction, namely, that it lacks the resources to distinguish between infinitely many different possible deductive and inductive rules of inference and focus just on the (intuitively) right ones. Schechter and I do what we can to address this worry (and several others as well) in "How Are Basic Belief-Forming Methods Justified?" (2008).

along. For a method can satisfy the conditions of the pragmatic account without being at all reliable, without being at all likely to yield true beliefs. Perhaps you've shown that there is *some* sense in which we are rationally justified in relying on the methods that satisfy your account. But this is not a sense that entitles us to the *belief* that their conclusions are *true*."

There are here, really, two distinct objections. The first can be dealt with fairly quickly. It argues that all I've shown, at most, is that we are *pragmatically* justified in employing the methods vindicated by the pragmatic account, but that I haven't shown that we are *epistemically* justified in so doing. But this is not how the pragmatic account is to be understood. True, I have emphasized the pragmatic value of employing a method when doing so is your only chance of avoiding failure. But this story was not meant as an (epistemic) *justification* of the relevant belief-forming methods, but rather as a *vindication* of them, as showing that they are belief-forming methods that do not need further epistemic justification in order to be justified.

The second, related, objection is more troubling. This is an objection to the pragmatic account as a purported vindication, and it proceeds by drawing attention to an important feature of epistemic justification that seems inconsistent with the pragmatic way of drawing the distinction between belief-forming methods we are and those we are not justified in employing as basic. This is the relation – whatever exactly its details – between epistemic justification and truth.

True, on the pragmatic account the relation between epistemic justification and truth is not as straightforward as may be thought. Nevertheless, the pragmatic account is consistent with the thought that, at least in reasonably fortunate circumstances, epistemic justification and truth are reliably correlated. (And we wouldn't want a stronger relation anyway: think, for instance, of your Brain-in-a-Vat counterpart, whose beliefs are presumably justified if yours are,[39] but are nevertheless radically unreliable.[40]) There are two important points to make here.

First, it does not seem mysterious that there is, in general, some correlation between the deliverances of the methods we employ as basic and the truths. Given the pragmatic value of having reasonably reliable beliefs, we would expect – on evolutionary grounds – the creatures around us to have belief-forming methods that are at least reasonably reliable. This is so simply because the creatures whose basic belief-forming methods were radically unreliable are probably no longer with us. And the same applies, it seems, to us as well. We have this (speculative) evolutionary reason

---

[39] This is not obviously so. For some discussion, see Enoch and Schechter (2008, 567 and on).

[40] In her world, at least. Depending on how you individuate belief-forming mechanisms and on your understanding of reliability, and assuming that the methods you and your BIV-counterpart use are at least reasonably reliable in the actual world, you may want to say that your BIV-counterpart is using reliable mechanisms alright, but she's radically unlucky in using them (hers are, as it were, exactly the rare circumstances in which these reliable mechanisms fail). I find it more natural to say that her methods are unreliable, and her misfortune consists in this being so through no (epistemic) fault of hers. But I cannot seriously discuss these matters here.

to believe that our basic belief-forming methods are at least reasonably reliable.[41] Otherwise, we wouldn't have been doing as well as we do.[42]

Second, given the previous point, the only remaining mystery can be topic-specific, and so topic-specific solutions to it should be entirely acceptable. However reliable our (basic) belief-forming methods in general, then, we can still ask questions about specific topics, or specific belief-forming methods (even ones we employ as basic).[43] If, with regard to a specific belief-forming method vindicated by the pragmatic account, the correlation with truth cannot be explained, this fact may very well defeat the default-reasonableness of employing that method as basic (remember that the pragmatic account is only an account of *prima facie* justification). And if the correlation between the deliverances of another vindicated method and truth *can* be explained, that method is off the hook. So if I can offer an explanation of such a correlation in the case of normativity – if, in other words, I can explain how it is that there is likely to be at least some correlation between our normative beliefs that are justified, at least partly, by an argument from deliberative indispensability and the normative truths – then the current challenge has been successfully coped with. And what this means is that there is no *further* challenge here, over and above the most general epistemological challenge to Robust Realism, at least once appropriately understood. Because I address this challenge at length in Chapter 7, I do not have to say more here.

This has been a long section. And I cannot say I am confident in all of its epistemological details. Let me end this section, then, by reminding you of the general dialectical point, which stands regardless of the details of this section: if you accept arguments from explanatory indispensability – inferences to the best explanation, that is – but you want to reject arguments from some other kind of indispensability (like deliberative indispensability), you have to present and defend a

---

[41] An evolutionary story such as the one in the text does not support a claim about the *optimality* of our belief-forming methods, but that is perfectly all right, as we don't have any reason to think they *are* optimal. As Lycan (1985, 158) puts it: "All's for *nearly* the best, in this next best of all possible worlds."

[42] Notice that although relying on (speculations based on) empirical science, I am not here making my argument – a vindication of, among other things, the very method of empirical science – objectionably circular. For remember the dialectical position: I have already argued for the pragmatic account of the vindication of basic belief-forming methods. I am here facing an objection to that account, a claim that it cannot accommodate something that needs accommodating, namely, the relation between epistemic justification and truth. If I can show – now already assuming the account – that the relevant data can be accommodated from within the pragmatic account, the objection is rendered powerless. Had I relied on the evolutionary speculations here as positive support for the pragmatic account, circularity would have ensued. Using it as I do only as a reply to an objection that is, as it were, further down the road from the positive argumentation supporting the pragmatic account, no circularity threatens.

[43] This is the sense I can make of the question – with regard to IBE – what reason we have to believe that we inhabit the loveliest (that is, most explanation-friendly) of all possible worlds (see Lipton (1991, ch. 4)). Lycan (2002) is right that we do not need an answer to this question in order to be prima facie justified in inferring to the best explanation – for IBE is presumably a method we are epistemically justified in employing as basic, one place where epistemic justification comes to an end. But Lycan is wrong to think that no challenge remains. For if we have no reason to believe that we inhabit at least a reasonably lovely world – if, in other words, we have no explanation of the (assumed) reliability of IBE – this fact would defeat our prima facie justification for employing IBE.

principled way of drawing the distinction between types of indispensability that can ground ontological commitments, and those that do not. The account suggested in this section applies – as I am about to argue – to deliberative indispensability just as it does to explanatory indispensability. But even if it is wrong, still showing that this is so does not amount to a defense of the claim that explanatory indispensability does – and other kinds of indispensability do not – justify ontological commitment. And this dialectical point will suffice for most of what follows (unless, that is, you reject all IBEs too).

But in order to see whether the suggested account can vindicate arguments from deliberative indispensability, more needs to be said about indispensability and about deliberation.

3.5 Indispensability: some details

As has been noted in the philosophy-of-mathematics literature,[44] where discussions of indispensability are typically located, indispensability is always indispensability *for* or *to* a certain purpose or project. Quantifying over numbers and sets is arguably indispensable *for* doing physics. Quantifying over (possibly other) abstracta is arguably indispensable *for* doing metalogic.[45] And of course, one thing may be indispensable for one purpose or project but not for another.

Once this is noticed, it becomes clear that in order fully to understand what (the relevant kind of) indispensability comes to, two distinct questions must be answered. First, it must be determined what it takes, given a purpose or a project, for something to be indispensable for it. As I will put things, the first thing that is needed is an account of *instrumental indispensability*. Second, it must be determined which purposes or projects are such that indispensability for them suffices to ground ontological commitment. That is, an account of what I will call *intrinsic indispensability* is likewise needed. And the details of both of these accounts should be filled in with the previous section in mind. The question this section is meant to answer, then, is: How is indispensability (both intrinsic and instrumental) to be understood if indispensability arguments can be belief-forming methods we are justified in employing as basic?

3.5.1 Instrumental indispensability

Given a purpose (such as explaining) or a project (such as the scientific project), what does it take for something to be indispensable for it, in the sense relevant for ontological commitment?

Of course, being helpful is not enough. If, for instance, mathematical objects are only used in scientific theories as a means of simplifying inferences which could be drawn without numbers as well, then, it seems, mathematical objects are not indispensable for the scientific project in the relevant sense. What is needed here is

---

[44] See, e.g., Field (1989, 14), Colyvan (2001, 6).
[45] See Field (1991, 1).

something like Field's (1989, 59) distinction between being useful in, e.g., facilitating inferences on the one hand, and, on the other hand, being useful in being theoretically indispensable.[46] However exactly the latter is to be understood, it seems intuitively clear that the former cannot justify ontological commitment, even assuming that the relevant project is intrinsically indispensable; it is perfectly compatible, for instance, with a fictionalist attitude towards mathematics and a nominalism about abstract objects. Mere usefulness does not suffice for instrumental indispensability.

Nor does what I will call (merely) *enabling* indispensability. Presumably, we cannot successfully engage in the scientific project without sufficient sleep. But sleep is not indispensable to the scientific project in the sense that suffices for the justification of ontological commitment. Of course, if we cannot successfully engage in the scientific project without sufficient sleep, then that we have in fact so engaged in the scientific project is evidence that we did get sufficient sleep. But our engaging in the scientific project – though evidence for sufficient sleep – does not *commit* us to any claims about us having had sufficient sleep. The account of instrumental indispensability I am after should have this result. So enabling indispensability is not what I am after.

An initially attractive recourse is to restrict instrumental indispensability – indispensability for a *theory*, for now – to just those things that are ineliminable from the theory. However, as Colyvan (2001, 76–7) argues, this too will not do, for the following two related reasons. First, it is not entirely clear what ineliminability is. Surely, just noting that once the disputed entities are eliminated the theory that is left is different from the one we started with is not sufficient for ineliminability, for this requirement is satisfied by all entities a theory invokes, talks of, or quantifies over. Second, it may very well be the case that once we relax our criteria for the individuation of theories to cope with the previous problem, no entity is strictly ineliminable for any theory, because the theory can be reformulated and reaxiomatized such that any given entity is eliminated.[47] Ineliminability as a criterion for instrumental indispensability thus also fails.

I want to follow Colyvan in offering the following criterion for instrumental indispensability. If a scientific theory T_1 quantifies over, say, electrons, and T_2 is the theory we get after eliminating all references to electrons from T_1, *and if T_2 is all-things-considered at least as attractive as T_1* (or is, at least, sufficiently attractive), then it seems clear that electrons are not instrumentally indispensable for our scientific project.[48]

---

[46] Brink (1989, 192) makes a similar distinction in the metaethical context between pragmatic and in-principle indispensability. For reasons that should be clear given the discussion of the previous section, I think Brink's terms are potentially misleading.

[47] Colyvan (2001, 77).

[48] This is a reformulation of Colyvan's (2001, 77) criterion. The term "instrumental indispensability", as well as the (explicit) distinction between instrumental and intrinsic indispensability are mine. Field nowhere puts an explicit definition or characterization of what it takes for an entity to be indispensable to a theory, but at times he says things that suggest that he too acknowledges something like Colyvan's condition. Colyvan (2001, 76 n. 16), for instance, quotes the following sentence from Field (1980, 8): "we can give *attractive* reformulations of [the theories of modern physics] in which mathematical entities play no role" (Colyvan's emphasis). In the metaethical context, Wiggins (1990, 84) hints at such a condition.

The relevant criteria of attractiveness are, of course, explanatory. An entity is explanatorily indispensable just in case it cannot be eliminated from our explanations without
loss of explanatory attractiveness. Colyvan's condition is intuitively appealing, and may
be considered simply a result of the policy of inferring only to the *best* explanation.

For my purposes, though, Colyvan's condition is not good enough as it stands, for
I am interested in more than just *explanatory* indispensability, and in more than just
indispensability *to a theory*. Luckily, though, Colyvan's condition – and its appeal –
generalize nicely. Something is instrumentally indispensable for a project, I suggest, just
in case it cannot be eliminated without undermining (or at least sufficiently diminishing) whatever reason we had to engage in that project in the first place; without, in
other words, thereby defeating whatever reason we had to find that project attractive.
The intuition underlying this criterion for instrumental indispensability is simple: The
project itself is (intrinsically) indispensable for a reason, and if the only way to engage in
it in a way that doesn't defeat that reason involves a commitment to an entity (or a fact,
or a belief, or whatever), then the respectability of the project confers respectability on
that commitment. Colyvan's condition is a particular instance of this condition, with
the relevant project being the scientific one, and the relevant criteria of attractiveness
being explanatory.

On this account, then, what is in the first instance indispensable to the scientific –
and more generally explanatory – project is not electrons and numbers but rather
whatever it is that our best explanations quantify over. The commitment to electrons
and numbers is both derivative (from the more general belief together with the specific
scientific findings and theories) and tentative (for better explanations may be found in
the future). We would lose whatever reason we had to engage in the explanatory
project, not if we ceased to believe in electrons, but rather if we ceased to believe that
whatever it is our best explanations quantify over is likely to exist. Indirectly, what is
indispensable for the explanatory project is (roughly speaking) the implicit belief in the
loveliness of the universe – the belief, that is, in the legitimacy of instances of reasoning
that follow IBE.

3.5.2 Intrinsic indispensability

So much, then, for instrumental indispensability. But that something is (instrumentally)
indispensable for a project cannot justifiably ground ontological commitment without
some restriction on the set of acceptable projects. Believing in evil spirits, for instance,
may be indispensable for the project of sorcery, but this is no reason to believe in evil
spirits (if anything, it is a reason not to engage in sorcery). And belief in God may be
indispensable for the project of achieving eternal bliss, but this does not give reason to
believe in God – unless, that is, the project of achieving eternal bliss is of the kind that
can justify ontological commitment; unless, in other words – in the terms I am
introducing here – it is an intrinsically indispensable project.

It has been noted in the philosophy-of-mathematics literature that some restriction
on the set of admissible purposes is needed. Nevertheless, to the best of my knowledge

no criterion for intrinsic indispensability has been suggested. Colyvan (2001, 7), for instance, asks the right question, but fails to answer it:

Which purposes *are* the right sort for cogent [indispensability] arguments?
I know of no easy answer to this question.

Nor does he suggest an answer to this question that is not easy. Now, in discussions of the Quine–Putnam indispensability argument for Platonism regarding mathematical objects, neglecting to offer a criterion for intrinsic indispensability is not a serious dialectical flaw: as is often noted,[49] the argument is put forward by the mathematical Platonist in an attempt to convince scientific realists. And with these as the major interlocutors, both parties to the debate are happy to assume that, whatever the criterion for intrinsic indispensability, at least the scientific project satisfies it, at least the scientific project is respectable enough to justify ontological commitment. The parties are typically so comfortable with such an assumption that it remains implicit.[50]

In our context, though, more needs to be done. I agree that the explanatory project is intrinsically indispensable. But I am not willing to grant that it is the *only* intrinsically indispensable project. And in order to establish the claim that our deliberative project is also intrinsically indispensable, it is necessary to answer the question Colyvan leaves unanswered. Which projects, then, are intrinsically indispensable, that is, are such that instrumental indispensability to them can ground ontological commitment?

It is here that the discussion from the previous section enters again. Some projects, I argued there, are rationally non-optional, they are such that disengaging from them is not a rationally acceptable option. This is, then, my suggestion for a criterion of intrinsic indispensability: a project is intrinsically indispensable if (and only if, quite plausibly; but my argument doesn't rely on the following condition being also necessary) it is rationally non-optional in the relevant sense. Instances of IBE are justified, then, because they are arguments from indispensability to the explanatory project, which is rationally non-optional.

3.6 Deliberation and intrinsic indispensability

But if that is right, it seems clear that our deliberative project is likewise intrinsically indispensable. For deliberation too seems a rationally non-optional project for us. Perhaps this is so partly because we are *essentially* deliberative creatures. Perhaps, in other words, we *cannot* avoid asking ourselves what to do, what to believe, how to reason, what to care about. We can, of course, stop deliberating about one thing or another, and it's not as if all of us have to be practical philosophers (well, if you're reading this book, you probably are, but you know what I mean). It's opting out of the

---

[49] See Colyvan (2001, e.g. 25).
[50] Colyvan (2001, 7) is a welcome exception, in that he explicitly notes this assumption.

deliberative project as a whole that may not be an option for us. But even if it is an option for us, it does not seem to be a *rational* option for us.

If I am right, then, about what makes projects intrinsically indispensable, the deliberative project is one such project. But I acknowledge that I've said very little on what rational non-optionality comes to,[51] and without saying more here there is something frustrating about the argument. Let me emphasize, then, that even if I am wrong, if you want to exclude deliberative indispensability as not-quite-as-respectable as explanatory indispensability, you face the challenge of distinguishing between the two. What reason is there, then, to take the explanatory project seriously that is not equally a reason to take the deliberative project seriously? I cannot think of one. And so I tentatively conclude that the deliberative project is intrinsically indispensable if the explanatory one is, that the explanatory project is in no relevant way privileged compared to the deliberative one.[52] And if so, there is an instability in a view that takes the former but not the latter as a respectable ground for ontological commitment. Though this is not enough to get me all the way to my argument for Robust Realism, it causes enough pressure to make the discussion of the rest of the argument, I believe, of value.

The deliberative project is, then, intrinsically indispensable (or at least – it is intrinsically indispensable if the explanatory one is). If it is instrumentally indispensable for the deliberative project that *p*, we are justified in believing that *p*. At least, we are every bit as justified in so believing as we are in believing the conclusions of inferences to the best explanation (from warranted premises). If, then, it can be established that irreducibly normative truths are deliberatively indispensable, we are every bit as justified in believing in them as we are in believing in the explanation-friendliness of the universe, and, derivatively, in electrons.

3.7 Deliberation and the instrumental indispensability of normative truths

What we need next, then, for the indispensability argument for Robust Realism is an account of deliberation that satisfies two desiderata. First, deliberation (as characterized and understood here) must be plausibly considered a rationally non-optional project. And second, irreducibly normative truths must be indispensable for deliberation. Unfortunately, though, these desiderata seem to pull in opposite directions. The thicker one's account of deliberation – the more one is willing to build into it as necessary conditions – the more plausible it is that irreducibly normative truths are

---

[51] Let's be honest: it's not that I've said so little because "saying more would take me too far astray", or any such thing. I just don't know what more to say.

[52] Indeed, there may even be some reason to think that the deliberative project is privileged compared to the explanatory one, because when explaining we *evaluate* competing explanations. See Sayre-McCord (1988a, 277–81) and Wiggins (1990, 66 n. 5).

indispensable for deliberation, but the less plausible it is that opting out of the (thickly understood) deliberative project is not a rationally acceptable option; the thinner one's understanding of deliberation, the more plausible it is that deliberation is rationally non-optional, but the less plausible it is that deliberation requires irreducibly normative truths. The challenge is to steer a middle course. In this section, then, I try to develop an account of deliberation that is sufficiently thick to require irreducibly normative truths without losing the plausibility of the claim (defended in the previous section) that deliberation is rationally non-optional.

Law school turned out not to be all you thought it would be, and you no longer find the prospects of a career in law as exciting as you once did. For some reason you don't seem to be able to shake off that old romantic dream of studying philosophy. It seems now is the time to make a decision. And so, alone, or in the company of some others you find helpful in such circumstances, you deliberate. You try to decide whether to join a law firm, apply to graduate school in philosophy, or perhaps do neither.

The decision is of some consequence, and so you resolve to put some thought into it. You ask yourself such questions as: Will I be happy practicing law? Will I be happier doing philosophy? What are my chances of becoming a good lawyer? A good philosopher? How much money does a reasonably successful lawyer make, and how much less does a reasonably successful philosopher make? Am I, so to speak, more of a philosopher or more of a lawyer? As a lawyer, will I be able to make a significant political difference? How important is the political difference I can reasonably expect to make? How important is it to try and make *any* political difference? Should I give any weight to my father's expectations, and to the disappointment he will feel if I fail to become a lawyer? How strongly do I really want to do philosophy? And so on. Even with answers to most – even all – of these questions, there remains the ultimate question. "All things considered", you ask yourself, "what makes best sense for me to do? When all is said and done, what should I do? What *shall* I do?"

When engaging in this deliberation, when asking yourself these questions, you assume, so it seems to me, that they have answers. These answers may be very vague, allow for some indeterminacy, and so on. But at the very least you assume that some possible answers to these questions are better than others. You try to find out what the (better) answers to these questions are, and how they interact so as to answer the arch-question, the one about what it makes most sense for you to do. You are not trying to create these answers. Of course, in an obvious sense what you will end up doing is up to you (or so, at least, both you and I are supposing here). And in another, less obvious sense, perhaps the answer to some of these questions is also up to you. Perhaps, for instance, how happy practicing law will make you is at least partly up to you. But, when trying to make up your mind, it doesn't feel like just trying to make an arbitrary choice. This is just not what it is like to deliberate. Rather, it feels like trying to make the *right* choice. It feels like trying to find the best solution, or at least a good solution, or at the very least one of the better solutions, to a problem you're presented with. What you're trying to do, it seems to me, is to make the decision it makes most sense for you to make. Making the decision is up to you. But which decision is the one it makes most sense for you to make is not. This is something you are trying to discover, not create.[53] Or so, at the very least, it feels like when deliberating.

Deliberation, then, is the process of trying to make the decision it makes most sense for one to make.[54] And, as the discussion above suggests, it has a distinctive phenomenological feel.

Thus, deliberation should be distinguished from the making of an arbitrary choice. You're in the supermarket, intending to get a cereal. You may have good reasons to pick Mini-Wheats rather than Raisin Bran (you just don't like Raisin Bran that much), perhaps even one brand over another (the Kellogg's one is usually fresher). But you have no reason, it seems, to pick one package of Kellogg's Mini-Wheats over another, and you know you don't. Of course, you have reason to pick one rather than none at all. But you've already decided you'll pick one rather than none at all. All that remains to be done now is just to pick a specific package arbitrarily. It should be uncontroversial that sometimes we just pick.[55] And it is one lesson of the unfortunate fate of Buridan's ass that picking arbitrarily may often be the rational thing to do.[56] But it is clear, I think, that the phenomenology of arbitrary picking is very different from that of deliberation, of trying to make the right decision.

It is worth noting how *similar* the phenomenology of deliberation is to that of trying to find an answer to a straightforwardly factual question: when trying to answer a straightforwardly factual question (like what the difference is between the average income of a lawyer and of a philosopher) you try to get things right, to come up with the answer that is – independently of your settling on it – the right one. When deliberating, you also try to get things right, to decide as – independently of how you end up deciding – it makes most sense for you to decide.

In the supermarket, you have no (normative) reason to pick one package of Mini-Wheats rather than another. With the only relevant decision to be made being which one to pick, there is no one option it makes most sense for you to pursue. More than

---

[53] "In deliberation we are trying to arrive at conclusions that are correct in virtue of something independent of our arriving at them" (Nagel, 1986, 149). For a similar point, though restricted to the case of making a moral choice, see Dancy (1986, 172).

[54] Notice that deliberation is not merely the process of trying to find out what the decision that it makes most sense for one to make is. Rather, deliberation consists in trying to find out what the decision is that it makes most sense for one to make, and then (trying to) make it. It is this latter part that gives deliberation its first-personal nature. (We can, after all, rather easily try to find out what the decision is that it makes most sense for someone else to make, but we cannot try to make it.)

[55] For a discussion of such cases – and for references to some who question that what I say in the text should be uncontroversial – see Ullmann-Margalit and Morgenbesser (1977), from which the example is taken (though somewhat modified). Ullmann-Margalit and Morgenbesser also introduce some helpful terminology: they suggest a distinction between choosing (for reasons) and picking (arbitrarily, in the kind of case described in the text), with "selecting" being the generic term. For similar distinctions see Darwall (1983, 69), Kolnai (1962, 213), and Railton (1997, 64 n. 12).

[56] The interesting questions regarding Buridan's ass are, I think, not *whether* we can just pick (we obviously can), and not *whether* cases of just picking can be beneficial (they obviously can), but rather *how* it is that, rational creatures that we are, we can just pick, and *how* it is that just picking can be the rational thing to do.

that, it isn't even the case that one option is at all better than any other. And you know all this. Now, as mentioned before, this doesn't preclude your just picking a package of cereal. Although if you come to reflect on your situation you may feel some discomfort, we are not typically – certainly not always – paralyzed in such situations. We can just pick in the face of a known (or believed) absence of reasons. But we cannot, it seems, *deliberate* in the face of a believed absence of reasons. Knowing that there is no decision such that it makes most sense for us to make it, we cannot – not consistently, anyway, in a perfectly commonsensical sense of "consistently" – try to make the decision it makes most sense for us to make. Deliberation – unlike mere picking – is an attempt to eliminate arbitrariness by discovering (normative) reasons, and it is impossible in a believed absence of such reasons to be discovered.

Thus, in deliberating, you *commit* yourself to there being (normative) reasons relevant to your deliberation.[57] Now, this sense of commitment need not entail an explicit belief that there are such reasons, and it certainly doesn't preclude an explicit belief in their non-existence (this is psychologically possible because people are often inconsistent). Nevertheless, in a perfectly good sense of "commitment", by deliberating you've already committed yourself to the existence of reasons. To see what I mean by commitment here,[58] think of a reasoner who routinely infers to the best explanation. Now, she may not be a very reflective reasoner, and so she may not have any beliefs *about* which inductive inference rules are valid and why. Or perhaps she's been convinced by some of the literature criticizing IBE, and she now explicitly believes that IBE is not a good rule of inference. Nevertheless, by routinely inferring to the best explanation, she commits herself to IBE being in some important way a good (reliable, perhaps, or justification-conferring, or knowledge-transmitting) rule of inference. If she believes that IBE is not a good inference-rule, she is being inconsistent (though perhaps in a somewhat generalized sense of this term) – unless, that is, she has some story available to her explaining how her use of IBE is compatible with her explicit rejection of it (perhaps, for instance, by showing that IBE is, though generally fallacious, actually harmless in a privileged class of cases, and by restricting her own use of IBE to such cases). Similarly, I want to argue, by deliberating you commit yourself to there being relevant reasons; if you also believe there aren't any, you are being inconsistent in exactly the same sense, and just as irrational, too.[59]

Notice that no such commitment is involved in cases of mere picking. Neither by picking one package of Mini-Wheats from all the others nor by going through some mental process beforehand, do you commit yourself to there being any reason that makes your package more worth picking than the others (you may commit yourself to there being reason to pick some package rather than none at all, but this is a different

---

[57] Actually, what immediately follows is the commitment to the possibility that there are reasons. I get back to this shortly.

[58] I thank Stephanie Beardsman and Derek Parfit for pressing me on this issue.

[59] For more on implicit beliefs and commitments, see section 9.1.2, in Chapter 9.

matter). It is, then, a result of the nature of deliberation – an attempt to eliminate the arbitrariness so typical in cases of mere picking – that by deliberating, by asking yourself which choice it would make most sense for you to make, you are committing yourself to there being reasons relevant to your choice. Suppose a friend of yours seems to undergo a process of deliberation, but then – when asked, perhaps – says that it really doesn't matter one way or another, that there is absolutely nothing to be said for or against any of the relevant alternatives, that there are no considerations counting in favor of any of his possible decisions. You would treat him either as having changed his mind ("Oh, he thought, until just a moment ago, that there was a point to his deliberation, but now he understands that this is not so"), or as being inconsistent. You would treat him as you would someone who professes to reject IBE and nevertheless infers to the best explanation – he has either changed his mind about IBE ("Oh, he thought, until just a moment ago, that we should not infer to the best explanation, but now he sees that he was wrong about that"), or he is being inconsistent. What explains this attitude of yours, I think, is precisely that both *are* being inconsistent. And this is also why, upon coming to believe that there are no relevant reasons, deliberation stops (though a decision may remain to be made).

Now, that something is a (normative) reason for you to join a law firm, a consideration that counts in favor of so doing, is a paradigmatically normative claim, as is that pursuing graduate studies in philosophy is the thing that makes most sense for you to do. So, by deliberating, you commit yourself to there being relevant reasons, and so to there being relevant normative truths (you do not, of course, commit yourself to the reasons *being* the normative truths). Normative truths are thus indispensable for deliberation.[60]

But I hear objections.

Don't we sometimes deliberate when we know that the weight of reasons is balanced, so that no option is the best? Yes, but by doing so we betray our lack of confidence in this normative judgment, and our suspicion that there may be reasons we've overlooked, or ones to which we haven't assigned the right weight.

Well, aren't our desires enough for deliberation? Why do we need normative truths to settle deliberation, when we are moved by desires? Because when you allow yourself to settle a deliberation by reference to a desire, you commit yourself to the judgment that your desire made the relevant action the one it makes most sense to perform. This may be either because, say, there is a general reason to satisfy your desires, or because you take

---

[60] "The ordinary process of deliberation, aimed at finding out what I should do, assumes the existence of an answer to this question" (Nagel, 1986, 149). For similar points, see Bond (1983, 60), Darwall (1983, 224) (though Darwall doesn't make this point regarding the deliberation of agents in general, but rather only regarding his "ISIS", an internally self-identified subject), Kolnai (1962) (though Kolnai, being a skeptic of sorts regarding normative truths, draws skeptical conclusions about deliberation as well), and Pettit and Smith (1998, e.g. 97) (who argue that deliberation is a kind of conversation one has with oneself, and that adopting this kind of conversational stance – to oneself as well as to others – involves assumptions, one of which is rather close to the one in the text).

having a reason to simply consist in having the relevant desire. But on either of these options, and even with desires at hand, you still commit yourself to a normative truth. Had we been here in the explanatory business – trying to explain action, or perhaps even deliberation, from a third-person point of view – perhaps desires would have been enough[61] (though I doubt it). But the whole point of the argument of this chapter is the focus on the first-person, deliberative perspective.[62] And from this perspective, desires are not often relevant,[63] and whether they are or are not, the normative commitment is – though perhaps implicit – inescapable.[64]

This idea is very Kantian, of course. Interestingly, the idea may not be limited to Kant's practical philosophy. In the *Prolegomena*, when addressing the (unstated) question of why we need the noumena in his metaphysical picture given that we know nothing about them, Kant says: "The world of sense contains merely appearances, which are not things in themselves; but the understanding must assume these latter ones, viz., noumena, because it knows the objects of experience to be *mere* appearances" (section 59, my italics). At the risk of taking things out of context, I would suggest the following analogy: we need normative truths even if, viewed from a third-person perspective, our desires suffice in order to cause our actions and then explain them, because, when deliberating, we know our desires are *merely* our desires.

Anyway, we don't necessarily explicitly invoke normative truths when deliberating. True, but that doesn't mean we don't commit ourselves to normative truths when deliberating.

---

[61] If desires themselves require a normative belief of sorts, if we can only desire things, as it is sometimes said, under the guise of the good, then the role of desires in deliberation and action would serve to strengthen the argument of this chapter rather than weaken it. But I shall resist the temptation to reply to the objection in this way. Though some desires may very well be responses to reasons, and some desires may very well be caused by normative beliefs, I find the claim that *all* desires necessarily involve normative reasons or judgments highly implausible. I would certainly not want my argument to hinge on this implausible claim.

[62] This is entirely in line with the analogy I rely on between explanatory and deliberative indispensability. In an explanatory indispensability argument, we are not in the business of explaining (say) *the scientist's engagement in the explanatory project*; rather, we're in the business of finding out what is indispensable *for her explanation itself*. Similarly, in a deliberative indispensability argument, we are not in the business of explaining *the agent's engagement in the deliberative project*; rather, we're in the business of finding out what is indispensable *for her deliberation itself*.

[63] A point accepted also by many who put forward a desire-based theory of normative reasons. See, for instance, Pettit and Smith (1990) and Schroeder (2007).

[64] Nagel (1997), to whose discussion I am indebted here, emphasizes similar points: "And I would contend that either the question whether one should have a certain desire or the question whether, given that one has that desire, one should act on it, is always open to rational consideration" (102–3); "Once I see myself as the subject of certain desires, as well as the occupant of an objective situation, I still have to decide what to do, and that will include deciding what justificatory weight to give to those desires" (109); "It is only when, instead of being pushed along by impressions, memories, impulses, desires, or whatever, one stops to ask 'What should I do?' or 'What should I believe?' that reasoning becomes possible – and, having become possible, becomes necessary. Having stopped the direct operation of impulse by interposing the possibility of decision, one can get one's beliefs and actions into motion again only by thinking about what, in light of the circumstances, one should do" (109); "It is not enough to find some higher order desires that one happens to have, to settle the matter: Such desires would have to be placed among the background conditions of decision along with everything else. Rather, even in the case of a purely self-interested choice, one is seeking the right answer" (110). And see also Bond (1983, e.g. at 54, 60) ("If valuing is really nothing but wanting, then deliberative rationality is a delusion" (54)).

The reasoner who routinely infers to the best explanation need not have explicit beliefs about IBE being a good rule of inference. But she is nevertheless committed to this claim.

Well, can't we deliberate even believing there are no normative truths, just like you can try to defeat a security system in order to test whether (as one believes) it is undefeatable?[65] Perhaps we can, but, first, this way of deliberating seems in an important sense parasitic on the more common one, where one believes that one is at least somewhat likely to succeed. So it's not clear that this line of thought can be applied to deliberation as a whole (rather than to some particular tokens of deliberation). And second, even if such deliberation is possible, it is clearly less attractive than the fuller deliberative projects, where one tries to find answers one believes are there to be found. And on the account of instrumental indispensability presented above, this suffices to establish the instrumental indispensability of the belief in normative truths.

So perhaps in order to deliberate you have to believe that there may be *normative truths to be found. This is still no reason to believe that* there are *such truths.*[66] Some delicate modal questions are relevant here. If, for instance, the modality invoked in the objection is something like the possibility of everyday, practical, "can-do" locutions, then at least given the robust modal status of normative truths (if they exist), the (practical) possibility of discovering them may entail their actuality. But even putting this point to one side, still the answer to the previous objection holds: for the retreat to the possibility (rather than actuality) of the existence of normative truths takes something, it seems, from the strength of the reason to engage in the deliberative project. And note, of course, that the line of thought expressed in the objection – whatever its ultimate strength – cannot serve to distinguish between the case of normative truths and the case of whatever is necessary for the explanatory project. If possibility suffices for the former, the mere possibility that the universe may be explanation-friendly should suffice for the latter.

But shouldn't we distinguish between trying to make up our mind, and trying to make the decision it makes most sense to make? The two are clearly distinct, as is evidenced by mere-picking cases. Perhaps normative truths are indispensable for trying to make the decision it makes most sense to make, but this is not a rationally non-optional project. Trying to make up our mind is plausibly considered rationally non-optional, but normative truths are not indispensable to it. So your argument can only seem plausible if we're equivocating on "deliberation" as between these two activities. (This objection, you may recall, is an instance of the tension with which I started this section – the two desiderata for an account of deliberation in the context of my indispensability argument pulling in opposite directions.) I certainly don't intend any such equivocation. This objection is right to highlight the distinction between the two different activities. And it is also right to insist that normative truths are often not indispensable for making up our mind. Where it goes wrong, I think, is in saying that

---

[65]   Harman (1986b, 370).
[66]   I thank Pete Graham and Josh Schechter for pressing me on this point.

deliberation more thickly understood – as phenomenologically characterized above, as an attempt to make the decision it makes most sense to make – is rationally optional. Think of creatures whose only decisions (or "decisions") amount to mere pickings. Such creatures would not be recognizably human, and we would not be inclined to classify them as agents (perhaps this is the right way to think of some animals). And what they are lacking – deliberation, thickly understood – seems rationally non-optional for us. Turning Gibbard's (2003, ix–x) main thesis on its head,[67] we can put the point by insisting that (as the phenomenology of deliberation indicates) thinking what to do comes down – often, and for creatures like us – to thinking what I ought to do. And this thinking too is rationally non-optional for us.

Wait – what exactly is indispensable here? You talk as if it's the normative truths themselves, but all you've shown – at most – is that belief *in them is indispensable. And it's hard to see how this helps in establishing the ontological conclusion you are after.* And it may be thought that this also marks an important disanalogy with the case of inferences to the best explanation, where arguably it is *electrons*, not *belief* in electrons, that are explanatorily indispensable.[68] But this disanalogy, I now want to suggest, is misleading. What is directly indispensable in the explanatory case too is the belief in electrons, or perhaps more generally the belief in the explanatory-friendliness of the universe. True, the explanation itself only speaks of electrons (and the like), not (except in unusual cases) of beliefs about electrons, and for this reason what is needed for the explanation to succeed is for there to be electrons. But this is true of deliberation as well. The content invoked in deliberation is in terms of the relevant normative truths, not (except in unusual cases) in terms of beliefs about them. And for this reason what is needed for the deliberation to succeed is for there to be normative truths. But in both cases, the indispensability of the relevant objective things (electrons, or normative truths) follows the indispensability of the belief in those things for the relevant projects. If I am right, this is how indispensability arguments *in general* work: it's the belief (or quantification, or some such) that is directly indispensable for the relevant project. But notice that the attitude that is indispensable is genuine *belief*, not some less-truth-directed surrogate for belief.[69] And you cannot *believe* that there are electrons, or normative truths, without believing *that there are electrons, or normative truths.*[70] Which is it, then, that is indispensable – normative truths or belief in them? Both, of course. The former are indispensable because the latter is.

---

[67] Gibbard (2003, 10) anticipates the possibility of so doing.

[68] I thank Russ Shafer-Landau and Mark van Roojen who were especially clear about the need to address this worry.

[69] I discuss *acceptance* in discussing fictionalism, in Chapter 5, section 5.2.1.

[70] Usually, one comes to a justified belief regarding *p* by thinking about *p*, not about the belief that *p*. If I am right, though, indispensability arguments work in the other directions. In such arguments, the conclusion that one is justified in believing *p* is epistemically prior to the conclusion *p*. I understand that this result may surprise you. But it is supported, I believe, by the general epistemological story in section 3.4.

Well then, what if deliberation is simply illusory? Perhaps what is needed in order to explain deliberation is not normative truths, but rather a good error theory.[71] The first thing to note in reply here is that I do not argue that normative truths are needed for the *explanation* of deliberation.[72] I want to remain neutral on this and all other explanatory questions (at this stage, at least). Normative truths are needed, so I've argued, not necessarily for the person observing the phenomenon of deliberation ("from outside", as it were), but for the deliberating agent herself. It is still possible, of course, that deliberation is illusory, that it essentially relies on a false belief in normative truths. But first, we would need a very strong argument to believe that, perhaps as strong as the argument we would need in order to believe that the universe is not even reasonably explanation-friendly (*Can* there even be such an argument?). And as I argue in the second part of this book, the arguments meant to show that there are no irreducibly normative truths show no such thing. Now, it's true that in some cases we are happy to continue in an as-if, or make-believe kind of way – perhaps our talk of the sun shining and setting is of this kind, and a color-skeptic can without problem (or inconsistency) follow our instruction to get us the red cup off the shelf. But in those cases, there has to be a story explaining why it is still a good idea to continue in this as-if kind of way. And in the case of the normative, such a further story would have to include a metanormative theory that is an alternative to Robust Realism. If no such alternatives succeed, then, we cannot continue deliberating without any problem or inconsistency even rejecting Robust Realism, in the way that the color-skeptic can still get the red cup. But this, of course, is a very big "If". I do what I can to support it in the next section.

3.8 (Further) supporting the indispensability premise: eliminating alternatives

One more step is necessary for the indispensability argument for Robust Realism. Alternative metanormative views must be rejected, and in particular, it must be shown that no alternative metanormative theory can deliver the goods that are deliberatively indispensable. For if a non-robust-realist view of normativity and normative discourse can supply all that is needed for sincere deliberation, irreducibly normative truths are after all not deliberatively indispensable. Think again of indispensability arguments

---

[71] My indispensability argument for Robust Realism may be thought of as a kind of a transcendental argument. And this objection – and the previous one – are close in spirit to Stroud's (1968) famous objection to transcendental arguments – namely, that at most they show that *belief* in the disputed claim is necessary, not that its truth is.

[72] My emphasis on deliberation is in some respects very close to some of the things Gibbard says in *Thinking How to Live* (2003), but our conclusions are very different. The point in the text explains, I think, why: one of Gibbard's major lines of argument against the realist is, I think, that expressivism can explain all that needs to be explained about deliberation ("we don't *need* queer properties to explain reasoning what to do"; 2003, 7). Even if this is so, though, my argument stands, for the reason given in the text: I do not claim that Robust Realism is what is needed in order to (third-personally) explain deliberation, but rather in order to (first-personally) engage in deliberation.

in the philosophy of mathematics: If a non-Platonist view of mathematical discourse and entities can supply all that is needed for scientific explanations (and is
adequate otherwise), numbers (Platonistically understood) are after all not explanatorily indispensable and the indispensability argument (as an argument for Platonism) fails.

In the context of my argument for Robust Realism, rejecting alternative metanormative views is thus not a luxury: it is not merely a further dialectical step, enhancing
the plausibility of one view by reducing that of others. Nor is it an instance of the
(purported) flaw that is typical of the writing of many realists – that of writing mostly
negatively, rejecting other views while having very little by way of positive argument
in support of their realism.[73] Rather, rejecting alternative views is part of the positive
argument – the argument from deliberative indispensability – for Robust Realism.

So what is needed here is nothing less than a survey of the metanormative field, and
arguments showing of each less-than-robust-realist view of normativity that it does not
suffice for deliberation (either directly, or indirectly, in that it fails in some other way,
and so on the whole cannot accommodate deliberation). And this would be quite a big
project – too big to fully engage in here. In the rest of this section, then, let me first hint
at reasons why I suspect that some major alternative views cannot accommodate what
is indispensable for deliberation, and second, do some geography – showing where else
in this book I say things that support the indispensability premise by rejecting alternative views.

Because only normative truths can answer the normative questions I ask myself in
deliberation, nothing less than a normative truth suffices for deliberation. And because
the kind of normative facts that are indispensable for deliberation are just so different
from naturalist, not-obviously-normative facts and truths, the chances of a naturalist
reduction seem rather grim. For similar reasons, the chances of a Neo-Aristotelian
metaethical or metanormative view that blurs the normative–natural distinction (perhaps utilizing, as Bloomfield (2001) does, an analogy with such concepts as *healthy*) do
not seem promising. The gap between the normative and the natural, considered from
the point of view of a deliberating agent, seems unbridgeable.

An honest noncognitivist or expressivist – even a quasi-realist – will have to agree
that there is *a* sense in which all normativity is grounded in the attitudes she just
happens to find herself with.[74] Such views, then, cannot eliminate the constitutive
role in shaping normativity of these normatively arbitrary attitudes. And while the

---

[73] See Korsgaard (1996, 31) (referring to Clarke and Price). And Russ Shafer-Landau too (2005, 264)
characterizes his defense of moral realism in his (2003) as essentially an argument from elimination.

[74] His many protests notwithstanding, this is true even of Blackburn. See his (1981, 164–5) parent
metaphor, and see also the discussion of this metaphor and related passages from Blackburn in Chapter
2 above. See also Gibbard's (2003, e.g. 82) characterization of expressivism in terms of such explanatory
priority. To repeat a point emphasized in Chapter 2 – I am not among those impressed by the ability of the
expressivist to accommodate everything the realist wants to say. If he is to have a distinct position, the
expressivist must concede *a* sense in which normativity is response-dependent (even if there are other senses
in which he can argue it is not). And denying response-dependence in *this* sense is one of the things the realist
wants to say.

unending ingenuity of expressivists can make this problem less obvious, it cannot, it seems to me, make it go away. Furthermore, even if somehow expressivist views can find a way of accommodating the full scope of deliberation, still the indispensability argument for Robust Realism stands. Remember, on the account of instrumental indispensability I endorsed (following Colyvan), for something to be instrumentally indispensable for a project it is not necessary that it cannot be eliminated from that project. Rather, it is sufficient that it cannot be eliminated without defeating whatever reason we had to find that project attractive in the first place. And the deliberative project loses much of its initial appeal, it seems to me, once normativity is viewed as dependent on our attitudes. (In this respect, *cognitivist* subjectivist theories, of course, do no better.)

Error theorists, as is widely noted, at least acknowledge the full strength of the commitment of normative discourse. In this respect, then, they are the robust realist's kindred spirits.[75] But it is important to note that the argument from deliberative indispensability is most directly an argument against global, metanormative error theory (just like the indispensability argument in the philosophy of mathematics is most directly an argument against straightforward error theory, and only indirectly against other ontologically thin views of number-discourse). More *local* error theories may very well still be in play – in particular, an error theory about morality need not be committed to an error theory about normativity in general, and even if my indispensability argument works I haven't shown that *moral* truths are indispensable for deliberation (and in fact I think they aren't). So such more local error theories deserve another discussion (in Chapter 4). But if the indispensability argument for Robust Realism establishes anything at all, it establishes the falsehood of the most general metanormative error theory.

But all of this, of course, is terribly sketchy. These sketches are not contentless, and I hope that they succeed in at least giving a feel of why it is that I am rather confident no non-robust-realist view can accommodate deliberation. But I do not want to pretend here that the views just mentioned have just been refuted, and I certainly don't want to pretend they are the only ones in logical space. So more work needs to be done. Let me finish this section, then, with indications of where this further job is done – some of it elsewhere in this book, some in other texts of mine.

I take the argument in this chapter to be effective against global metanormative error theory. In order to discuss a more local, metaethical, error theory, I need to discuss the relations between the moral and the normative, and indeed between the argument of this chapter and the argument of the previous one. I do this in Chapter 4. I also discuss fictionalism – in some versions, an instance of an error-theoretical view – in Chapter 5.

Obviously, there is more to be said about the just-too-different intuition underlying my rejection of a naturalist reduction of the normative. Though I am afraid I have less

---

[75] It is often instructive, I think, in trying to understand a philosopher's views and underlying motivations, to think about what her *second*-best view (of the relevant issue) would be. Mine would be, I think, an error theory.

to say here than I would want to, I say whatever more I can say in Chapter 5. In that chapter I also reject some other attempts at settling for less, metaphysically speaking, compared to Robust Realism. These include – except for a naturalist reduction and a global error theory – also non-error-theoretic fictionalism, and a kind of metaphysically laid-back quietist realism.

I discussed expressivism in more detail in the previous chapter. But note that there the discussion was just about morality, not about normativity in general. The rejection of expressivism as a metanormative theory, then, is constituted mostly by the discussion in Chapter 2 conjoined with that in Chapter 4 – the one that discusses the interaction between the argument from the implications of objectivity to metaethical objectivity and the argument from deliberative indispensability to Robust Realism.

Some response-dependence theorists think that they can get us pretty much all the objectivity worth having utilizing some idealization mechanism: they think, that is, that normativity (or perhaps morality) is reducible not to actual responses but rather to ones that are idealized in some way (perhaps the responses we would have if we were fully informed, or possessed full imaginative acquaintance, or deliberated rationally, or had undergone cognitive psychotherapy, or some such). And they also think that the distance between our actual and hypothetical responses leaves room for everything by way of deliberation that can be desired.[76] But as I argue at length elsewhere,[77] such idealization is always suspicious, and it is hard to see how it can be philosophically motivated – except, that is, as an ad hoc attempt at saving a response-dependence theory from obvious counterexamples.

Some (perhaps Kantian) response-dependence theorists think they can get all that is worth getting here by focusing on just the responses (or motives, or desires, or attitudes, or some such) that are constitutive of agency. And in the previous chapter I conceded that my argument from the moral implications of objectivity does not rule out such theories. As I argue elsewhere,[78] however, what does rule them out as the ultimate metanormative story is that even if there are some responses that are constitutive of agency, this in no way secures for them a privileged normative status.

Some people seem to believe that there is room somewhere in logical space for a constructivist view that avoids all of the problems above, perhaps by finding cracks in between the classification into all these different isms. But as I argue elsewhere,[79] there does not seem to be such room in logical space: no view can be both interestingly constructivist (that is, constructivist in a way that is not merely a particular instance of

---

[76] For instance, Williams's "Internal and External Rasons" (1981).

[77] In my "Why Idealize?" (2005). For a response, see Sobel (2009). For my response to Sobel, see my "Idealization Still Not Off the Hook" (manuscript).

[78] In my "Agency, Shmagency" (2006). For responses, see Velleman (2009, 135–46) and Ferrero (2009). For my reply, see "Shmagency Revisited" (2010b).

[79] In my "Can There Be a Global, Interesting, Coherent Constructivism about Practical Reason?" (2009b).

some other ism, of the kind already discussed), global (that is, applying to all normative reasons), and coherent.

There is, I understand, something frustrating about this section. Rather than fully defend the indispensability premise my indispensability argument relies on, I hint at why I think it is probably true, and refer to other places (in this book and elsewhere) where it is further defended, one alternative view at a time. And things get even worse, for I haven't given reason to believe that the alternative views mentioned above exhaust all possibilities here, nor do I think that such an argument can be given. If there are other alternative views, then, and if my indispensability argument is going to be complete, they too are going to have to be discussed and rejected piecemeal as failing to account for what is needed for deliberation. So the argument in this chapter is not completely independent of the argumentative moves elsewhere in this book, in other works of mine, and indeed in other works by others (some of which presumably yet to be written). But this, I think, is not unique to my indispensability argument – in the philosophy of mathematics as well, I guess, a full development of an indispensability argument would have to rule out fictionalist, metaphorical, and other understandings of the quantification over abstract objects that is involved in natural science. And in the metanormative context as well as the philosophy-of-mathematics one, even before this project is pursued to its completion, at the very least a challenge to alternative views has been presented: given the role of mathematical statements in the natural sciences, how can we reject mathematical Platonism? And given the role of irreducibly normative truths in our deliberation, how can we reject Robust Realism? Noting that no conclusive reasons have been given to believe that this question cannot be successfully answered falls well short of answering it.

3.9 Conclusion

We can now present my indispensability argument for Robust Realism in a more schematic form.[80] Here is, then, the Indispensability Argument:

(1) If something is instrumentally indispensable to an intrinsically indispensable project, then we are (epistemically) justified (for that very reason) in believing that that thing exists.

(2) The deliberative project is intrinsically indispensable.

(3) Irreducibly normative truths are instrumentally indispensable to the deliberative project.

(4) Therefore, we are epistemically justified in believing that there are irreducibly normative truths.

[80] I am grateful to Russ Shafer-Landau both for patiently reminding me how helpful it would be to do so, and for suggestions about how to do it best here.

I've supported premise (1) in the general epistemological discussion in section 3.4 (and to an extent, in the preceding sections as well). And by reflecting on the nature of deliberation I did what I could (in section 3.6) to support premise (2). As a fallback position here I suggested that deliberation is as respectable as explanation, and that arguments from deliberative indispensability are prima facie as respectable as the more common arguments from explanatory indispensability – this is why insisting on an ontological parsimony requirement does not entail the Explanatory Requirement underlying Harman's Challenge – so that even if you are not willing to accept the generalization in (1), so long as you accept instances of IBE you should accept (the fallback version of) my argument for Robust Realism. In section 3.7 I suggested an account of instrumental indispensability that – together with a phenomenological characterization of deliberation – supports premise (3). But the full support of premise (3) includes also the rejection of alternative views – a task I cannot complete here (though I do engage some of it elsewhere in this book, perhaps mostly in Chapter 5).

If all this works, the conclusion (4) follows, and we have strong (if defeasible) reason to believe that Robust Realism is true.

4

And Now, Robust Metaethical Realism

In Chapter 2 I presented an argument for metaethical objectivity. The argument, you may recall, was distinctly meta*ethical*, it had something to say distinctly about (and also within) morality. But, as you may also recall, the argument did not go all the way to *Robust* Metaethical Realism, because the objectivity it established was consistent with several other, non-robust-realist views of morality (like, for instance, certain constitutivist views, and objectivist naturalist reductions).

In Chapter 3 I presented an argument for Robust Metanormative Realism. The argument, you may recall, was generally metanormative, and had nothing to say specifically about morality – what was deliberatively indispensable, I argued there, was normative truths, not necessarily moral ones. On the up-side, though – and with only one caveat – that argument in Chapter 3 was supposed to lead all the way to Robust Realism, though Robust Metanormative, not Robust Metaethical Realism. (I return to the caveat below.)

Is there, then, a way of combining the force of the arguments of the two previous chapters, to reach a stronger conclusion than merely the conjunction of their respective conclusions? In this chapter, I argue that the answer is (pretty much) "yes", and indeed that together the arguments of the previous chapters can be seen to support Robust Metaethical Realism.

In order to do that, I have to say something about the relation between moral and normative truths. I do this in section 4.1. In section 4.2 I argue that the motivations underlying less than robustly realist views about morality do not in general survive the endorsement of Robust Metanormative Realism. A complication remains, though, for at least one such motivation (or family of motivations) arguably do survive – those having to do with the relation between morality and categorical reasons. But in section 4.3 I argue that this motivation does not survive the endorsement (following Chapter 2) of metaethical objectivity. In section 4.4 I return to the caveat mentioned two paragraphs ago – namely, that the indispensability argument for Robust Realism itself depended on the rejection of other views elsewhere in this book (and elsewhere), showing that this does not significantly damage my overall argument. I then conclude – in section 4.5 – that though the conjunction of metaethical objectivity (and my argument for it) and Robust Metanormative Realism (and my argument for it) does not *entail* Robust Metaethical Realism, still it makes it *very* hard to see what philosophical considerations could possibly motivate any alternative view.

4.1 Morality and normativity

Recall how liberal I am in using the term "normative": as explained in Chapter 1, I include what some others call the evaluative as a part of the normative. In this sense of "normative", then, it is pretty uncontroversial that moral truths are normative truths. By this I do not mean to say that their content is *exhausted* by the normative part of their content – perhaps, for instance, some moral concepts include both descriptive or empirical and normative components (thick concepts are the obvious thing that comes to mind here). Nor do I mean to beg any questions regarding moral rationalism, the claim (perhaps roughly), that as a matter of necessity morality gives reasons for actions, or that it is always at least prima facie irrational to behave immorally – I briefly address these issues in section 4.3 below. My point here is much less interesting: if we are roughly to divide all truths into normative (in this loose sense) and non-normative ones, clearly the moral ones are going to be there with the former.

With this point in mind, then, asking about the relations between the moral and the normative becomes the question of how to delineate the moral within the normative. What *more*, in other words, does it take for a normative truth (or falsehood) to qualify as moral? Morality is a particular instance of normativity, and so we are now in effect asking about its distinctive characteristics, the ones that serve to distinguish between the moral and the rest of the normative.

I do not have a view on these special characteristics of the moral. In fact, I think that for most purposes this is not a line worth worrying about. The distinction within the normative between the moral and the non-moral seems to me to be shallow compared to the distinction between the normative and the non-normative – both philosophically, as I am about to argue, and practically. (Once you know you have a reason to φ and what this reason is, does it really matter for your deliberation whether it qualifies as a *moral* reason?) What *would* make such a distinction interesting – in my context, at least – is if the arguments either for or against Robust Realism were sensitive to it. If this is not the case, then the distinction between the normative and the moral is not one that makes a relevant difference (in our context, that is). Well then, do any of the relevant arguments – for Robust Realism or views in its vicinity (as discussed in the previous chapters) or against it (as will be discussed in the next ones) – turn on the question whether the target truths are moral or (non-moral but still) normative?

I think – but I am not entirely sure – that the argument from the moral implications of objectivity (in Chapter 2) can be applied to other, non-moral normative claims as well, though possibly not to all. What would have to hold for this to be so is that there are some cases of conflicts due to non-moral but normative disagreement, where still nothing like IMPARTIALITY holds: where, in other words, it is morally permissible to stand one's ground, and the parties are not required to look for a more egalitarian or impartial way out. In Chapter 2 I restricted myself to conflicts due to paradigmatically moral disagreements, like for instance whether that an action will cause unnecessary pain to a dog counts morally. But think about other normative, but presumably not moral, cases. For instance, suppose you're a two-boxer and I a one-boxer when it comes to Newcomb's Problem.[1] Suppose further, in order to neutralize the factors neutralized in Chapter 2, that two-boxing is the uniquely rational policy in such cases, and that you know as much (even after factoring in to the extent needed the epistemic effect of peer disagreement here). Further suppose that we need to decide on a joint action here, and which decision we make will depend on how we go on Newcomb's Problem. Does something like IMPARTIALITY apply? Or does truth matter, so that you are entitled to rely on what you know is the truth here (at least when all other things are equal)? Or suppose that you and I differ in how we think of excitement – in general, or just in the practically relevant context. You think that the fact that performing a certain action will be exciting is a reason to do it, whereas I think that excitement is normatively inert – being exciting in this way is just neither here nor there. And suppose that you are right, and that you know as much. Further suppose that we need to decide on a joint action, and which decision we make will depend on whether we take excitement here to be a reason for action. Does something like IMPARTIALITY apply here? Or does truth matter, so that you are entitled to rely on excitement being a reason for action here (at least when all other things are equal)?

In both these cases, I am inclined to say that nothing like IMPARTIALITY applies, and if you agree, then we have what we need to apply the argument of Chapter 2 to such non-moral-but-still-normative cases. But I do not want to rely on this suggested judgment for the two cases sketched in the previous paragraph, for the following two reasons. First, I am *much* less confident about them than I am about the moral cases from Chapter 2. And indeed, when I try to strengthen these examples in order to get cases in which I am more confident, I find myself inadvertently returning to the moral or to things too close to it for comfort (for instance, imagining a disagreement not on whether excitement is a reason for action, but on whether pleasure and pain are). This alone indicates that morality – though perhaps not unique within the normative – is still somewhat special in ways relevant for the argument of Chapter 2. And second, though I find the examples above at least somewhat (if not fully) convincing, I can think of other cases of conflicts due to a normative disagreement where things are not (even) as clear, and so in order to responsibly rely on the examples above I would have to contrast them with others, and present an account of the distinction between the parts of the normative where an analogue of IMPARTIALITY applies and those where no such analogue applies. And I wouldn't know how to do that.

Fortunately, though, I do not need to attempt such a generalization of the argument of Chapter 2. Robust Realism, you may recall, is an existential, not a universal thesis.

---

[1] For one presentation, see Weirich (2008, section 2.1).

I do not believe – and certainly do not intend to argue – that *all* claims that are normative in the loose sense in which I am using this term are objective in the sense of Chapter 2. And as for the normative truths presumably vindicated by the indispensability argument in Chapter 3, they *must* be objective in the sense of Chapter 2, because they are to be understood robust-realistically, and this entails their objectivity.

More interesting for my purposes here, though, is the question whether the indispensability argument in Chapter 3 is sensitive to the moral–normative distinction, and in particular, whether the argument, assuming that it works, can be applied directly to some moral truths, thus supporting also Robust Metaethical Realism. And here it seems to me that the answer is "no", however exactly you want to delineate the moral within the normative. It just does not seem that moral truths are indispensable for deliberation. Consider, for instance, the example of a fairly serious deliberation I used in Chapter 3, that of trying to decide – after graduating from law school – whether to join a law firm or pursue graduate studies in philosophy. Here it seems very clear that I can conclude my deliberation with a normative truth that need not be moral, in (pretty much) whatever way exactly you choose to delineate the moral. Also, in noting that our deliberation need not invoke normative truths explicitly, I insisted that nevertheless, when we let ourselves conclude a deliberation relying on some consideration, we thereby commit ourselves (in a sense made suitably precise in Chapter 3) to that consideration counting in favor of the relevant action, or being a reason for it. But – and this is the point I want to stress now – there is nothing at all to suggest that in any such cases we also commit ourselves to the further claim that the relevant consideration counts *morally* for the relevant action. The point is not, of course, that we cannot conclude deliberation with a moral truth. The point, rather, is that we *needn't*, so that no analogous metaethical indispensability argument can be constructed. Deliberation, then, is insensitive to the distinction between the moral and the rest of the normative, regardless of how precisely this distinction is to be understood. And given that the indispensability argument supports an existential thesis, if it cannot distinguish between the moral and the non-moral normative, it cannot support any distinctly metaethical claim.

My indispensability argument for Robust Realism, then, is not sensitive to the precise way of delineating the moral and the normative. My other positive argument – the argument from the moral implications of objectivity – does seem to presuppose that there is a fairly recognizable set of paradigmatically moral judgments within the normative, though this set may be very vague, and the implications of the distinction between members and non-members of that set are not completely clear. How about the arguments *against* Robust Realism, though?

4.2 If you're already a Robust Meta*normative* Realist, why not also go for Robust Meta*ethical* Realism?

To see whether traditional objections to Robust Metaethical Realism are easily generalizable to the metanormative, we have to carefully go through these objections – one by one – and see whether they apply just as forcefully to Robust Metanormative Realism, or whether there is anything about them that is distinctly metaethical. But I will not do this now – there will be enough by way of discussion of these objections and their details in the chapters to come. What I want to do now, rather, is to very quickly go through the main suspicions that make many despair on Robust Metaethical Realism, and then show that these suspicions rather straightforwardly apply to the normative more generally. The rather quick discussion that follows, then, is to be understood as partly relying on a promissory note to be made good on in the next chapters – I hereby officially promise that nothing in the detailed discussion of the objections to Robust Realism in the next chapters will rely on anything that is particular to the moral (as opposed to the normative more generally). If so, this further supports the suggestion – partly already supported by the discussion in the previous section – that there is no distinction between the moral and the non-moral (within the normative) that is of much interest in our argumentative context. However, the discussion here will leave one main way in which you may think morality is relevantly special. This will be the topic of section 4.3.

Why *are* people so suspicious of morality, robust-realistically understood? Sometimes the worries are metaphysical – moral properties, or truths, or facts, or values, or duties, or some such are said to be metaphysically queer, not to find a comfortable place in a naturalistic worldview, and so on. The merits of such worries are a matter for Chapter 6, but my point here is much more limited: if you think that things like the purported fact that we ought not to humiliate others is metaphysically queer, you should be equally metaphysically suspicious of things like the purported fact that two-boxing is the uniquely rational policy in Newcomb's Problem. If you find it hard to metaphysically stomach things like the value of humanity (or the negative value of pain), you shouldn't (prima facie, at least) find the value of excitement more appetizing. If the scientific worldview can't find room for the wrongness of murder, it is hard to see how it can find room for the irrationality and (sometimes) irresponsibility involved in wishful thinking. The metaphysical worries about morality seem to just be instances of metaphysical worries about normativity more generally.

More or less relatedly, some suspicions about morality (robust-realistically understood) are epistemological in nature. If there are truths of the kind that the Platonist (say) envisages, how is it, it is sometimes asked, that we can have epistemic access to them? And if we can't, should we conclude that on this view none of our moral beliefs are justified? And isn't this a *reductio* of this kind of Platonism? Again, a discussion of the merits of this and related objections will be postponed, this time until Chapter 7. But for now the crucial thing to see is that the epistemological challenge – whatever exactly its details – seems to apply just as forcefully to other, non-moral normative truths and facts. So here too, the objection to Robust Metaethical Realism is just a particular instance of an objection to a similar view about the normative as a whole.

Similar points apply, it seems to me, to worries about the relation between normative reasons and motivation (discussed in Chapter 9). They also apply – though perhaps not quite as forcefully – to worries about disagreement as reason to be suspicious of moral truths robust-realistically understood (such worries are discussed in Chapter 8). Normative judgments in general seem to be often controversial, and the controversies over them seem to have many of the characteristics of moral disagreement that arguments from disagreements attempt to capitalize on – for instance, they seem to survive agreement on all non-normative facts, and seem to last even among otherwise seemingly reasonable people (think about Newcomb's Problem again). So if you're worried about disagreement, it seems you should be worried about normative dis-agreement as much as you're worried about moral disagreement. Or perhaps not quite *as* much – for it is not entirely implausible that some problems of disagreement are not as severe in the more general normative case as in the moral one. It is, after all, rather hard (if not impossible) to find people believing that we should often use wishful thinking, or form intransitive preferences, or be indifferent about our pain on future Tuesdays. (On the other hand, it is not all that easy to find many who believe that the unnecessary pain of innocent children counts in favor of a course of action either.) So I do not want to say that in the case of the objection from disagreement the metaethical worry is *just* a particular instance of a metanormative one – perhaps it's a particular instance that is somewhat stronger than others of its kind. But it is a particular instance of a more general metanormative worry all the same.

By and large, then, the common objections to Robust Realism are objections to Robust Metanormative Realism, and the objections to Robust Metaethical Realism are particular instances of the more general ones (and let me again stress that this statement partly depends on the details of these objections, to be presented and discussed in Chapters 6–9). But I now want to make a stronger point – I want to argue that once this fact is noticed, and assuming that we already have sufficient reason to accept Robust Meta*normative* Realism, these objections lose their force against Robust Meta*ethical* Realism as well.

This point may seem to follow rather immediately from the following observation: Once we've accepted Robust Metanormative Realism (perhaps on the strength of the indispensability argument in Chapter 3), we already know that the objections to it must fail.[2] And so all particular instances of them must also fail. So any objection to Robust Metaethical Realism that is also an objection to Robust Metanormative Realism fails. So the objections above fail. So given Robust Metanormative Realism, there is no reason to deny Robust Metaethical Realism.[3]

---

[2] Appearances to the contrary notwithstanding, this is *not* an instance of the dogmatism paradox. For crucially, I am here assuming that the belief in Robust Metanormative Realism remains *justified* even after considering the objections to it, and this is precisely the feature lacked by instances of that paradox – noticing this fact is arguably the first step towards solving it (see Sorensen (1988)). If we continue to be justified in believing Robust Realism in the face of these objections, then it unparadoxically follows that these objections fail.

[3] I am assuming here that there are no *other*, strong reasons – reasons not mentioned in the text – to reject Robust Metaethical Realism. This assumption may well be false. I partly address this worry in section 4.3, and I then revisit it in section 4.5.

But this line of thought would be too quick. That going on yet another vacation will cost money is an objection to going on vacation; this objection is a particular instance of an objection to many things we justifiably do all the time; but noticing this fact does not take away any of the force of the initial objection to going on yet another vacation. Perhaps somewhat similarly, though now on the theoretical rather than practical side: that a theory introduces a new kind of entity into our ontology is arguably an objection to it, a reason to prefer some other theory over it (if the two theories are equally good in all other respects); this objection is a particular instance of a very general objection, one that applies (at least prima facie) to many theories we do in fact justifiably accept; but noticing this fact does not take away any of the force of the initial objection – it's not as if once we've added some new kind of entity into our ontology all ontological hell breaks loose, and no parsimony requirement is any longer in force. What these examples show is that some considerations are such that even when we violate them or act against them, they still apply by requiring that we not violate them too much, or more than we have to (because of other important considerations). Can it be argued that this is also true of the objections to Robust Metaethical Realism? Perhaps, for instance, it can be argued that the fact that we're allowing these normative entities into our ontology (on the wings of the indispensability argument) is bad enough, but that it in no way justifies paying an even heftier ontological price by populating our ontology even further with moral entities.

For some considerations the price analogy holds. For others, though, it does not. Suppose I put forward an argument to the conclusion that a priori knowledge is impossible. You then present – by way of counterexample – mathematical knowledge. Suppose that I acknowledge this as a genuine counterexample, and proceed to take back my commitment to the impossibility of a priori moral knowledge. Suppose then I wonder about the possibility of modal knowledge. At this point, the price analogy no longer works – it does not make sense, at this stage, for me to insist that at least *this* a priori knowledge is to be denied, that it's bad enough that I had to concede the possibility of mathematical knowledge, but this is no reason to concede even further the possibility of modal knowledge as well. The appropriate response in the face of the mathematical-knowledge example is, it seems safe to assume, to abandon the general objection to a priori knowledge altogether – unless, that is, you have some reason to think of the mathematical case as a really special case, so that its vindication cannot project to other areas of purported a priori knowledge.

So the question we need to ask next is whether the objections to Robust Metanormative Realism are more like the price case or more like the a-priori-knowledge case. And the point I want to make now – I am sure this will come as a great surprise – is that they're much more like the latter than the former. In fact, one of them *just is* the latter, for the epistemological challenge to Robust Realism can be seen, I think, as a particular instance of a similar problem for (perhaps substantive) a priori knowledge more generally (I support this claim, and argue that this is still consistent with the metaethical and the metanormative case being special in relevant respects, in Chapter 7). If Robust

Metanormative Realism is true, and furthermore if this conclusion is consistent with the possibility of normative knowledge (this is a major "if", and nothing here is trivial; again see the discussion in Chapter 7), then this must be because the epistemological challenge can somehow be coped with. If you like thinking in terms of access, this must be because there is some way to secure epistemic access to the normative truths in Plato's heaven (so to speak). But of course, if you're already willing to accept this much, then it doesn't seem like there's any reason for you not to accept that there is a way of securing epistemic access also to the moral truths in the moral part of (the normative part of) Plato's heaven. Similar points apply, it seems to me, to the worries about semantic access, disagreement, and motivational force. In none of these does the price analogy hold.

It may be thought, though, that the metaphysical objection is different in this regard, and indeed an example rather similar to it served as an example of the price model. If we have sufficient reason to commit ontologically to the existence of some (not-necessarily moral) normative truths, the thought seems to go, so be it. But we should still be as parsimonious as we can (as parsimonious, that is, as the indispensability argument allows us), and so we should not commit also to the existence of specifically moral truths. It is, I think, in general true that the parsimony requirement functions according to the price model from a few paragraphs back. But it's important to note that the parsimony requirement functions at the level not of specific entities, but rather at the level of *kinds* of entities. If we already have sufficient reason to believe in electrons, then that a theory quantifies over electrons is no reason to reject it, or to prefer another theory that doesn't. And it just doesn't matter if the former theory quantifies over *more* electrons than the latter. The point is not a formalistic one about the wording of "the" parsimony requirement – there is no canonical text capturing it, and if there were, it would not go without argument that it merits our allegiance. The point, rather, is about the plausible idea the parsimony requirement is supposed to capture. And if you agree with me that once committed to the existence of electrons, it no longer counts against a theory that it is committed to the existence of more electrons compared to some alternative theory, then you agree that any plausible parsimony requirement works at the level of kinds of entities.[4]

Now, it seems to me that moral properties and facts are of the same kind – in the sense of "kind" relevant to the parsimony requirement – as normative properties and facts more generally. Partly because of how little the distinction between the moral and the (non-moral) normative matters philosophically, the case at hand seems to me to be analogous to the just-more-electrons case above. Or consider another analogy: suppose that under the pressure of the indispensability argument for mathematical Platonism you accept the existence of some abstract mathematical objects, like, say, sets. If you then also consider quantifying over, say, numbers (that are not, let's suppose, reducible to sets), should you think of this as *further* ontological price? Or should you think of

---

[4]   See Baker's (2004, section 2) distinction between quantitative and qualitative ontological simplicity, and the references there.

numbers as here more of the same, and the price of accepting them into your ontology as essentially a price you already paid by accepting sets into your ontology? Numbers are not sets, but still, I hope you share my feeling that numbers and sets are of a kind in the sense relevant to the parsimony requirement. And this is what I want to say about moral and (non-moral) normative facts and properties. They are not identical, but they are of a kind in the sense relevant to any plausible parsimony requirement. And so the metaphysical objection to Robust Metaethical Realism also comes down to merely a particular instance of Robust Metanormative Realism, and once we already (presumably) have sufficient reason to accept the latter, there is no good metaphysical motivation for denying the former.

4.3   Categorical reasons

But you may think that my discussion of the objections to Robust Metaethical Realism has left out the most obvious and important reason why morality is especially suspicious – why, as we may put it, there is *much* more reason to be suspicious about moral reasons than about normative reasons in general.[5] What's distinctive of moral reasons – if there are any, that is – is that they are *categorical*.[6] If there is a moral reason not to humiliate people (say), then this reason applies to each of us *whatever* our contingent motivations. It's not hypothetical, stating something like that we have reason not to humiliate people if we go for that kind of relationship, or if we want to keep them on our good side. Nor is it merely categorical in the more superficial sense that Foot (1972) famously recognized, the sense in which etiquette too is categorical, namely, that it's no defense against an accusation of a violation of etiquette that one doesn't really care about etiquette (as it is a defense against an accusation of irrationality in failing to pursue a means to note that one doesn't want to achieve the end). Moral reasons, if there are any, are categorical in the stronger sense of actually applying to you – calling upon you for an action – regardless of your contingent motivations and related states. And, it may now be argued, this is precisely what makes them so suspicious, and furthermore so *especially* suspicious compared to other reasons.[7] For though we can understand the relations between hypothetical reasons and motivation, it's very hard to understand the relation between categorical reasons and motivation. And though (perhaps) the relation to motivations you already have helps in finding room for your hypothetical reasons within the scientific worldview, no such room is available for categorical reasons. So even if we should be realists about normativity, this still falls well short of showing that we should be realists about

---

[5] So in this section I switch to reason-talk. But everything I say here using reason-talk can, I think, be put in other terms too, if you prefer them.

[6] Joyce's (2001) error theory about morality is motivated by the claims that categorical reasons are necessary for morality, and that there are no such reasons.

[7] This is clearly and explicitly the motivation for Olson's error theory about morality (though not about normativity in general). See Olson (2010).

morality. And so arguably a non-robust-realist view of morality is not only consistent with Robust Metanormative Realism and my argument for it, but it also retains its underlying philosophical motivation.

Now, pretty much everything here is controversial. Some will doubt that moral reasons *are* as a matter of necessity categorical in this sense, that, in other words, it's a part of the job description of moral reasons that they are categorical, so that no reason can qualify as moral without being categorical. I will not doubt this, though, for reasons that I am about to make clear later in this section. Others may wonder whether the categorical–hypothetical and the moral–non-moral distinctions (with regard to reasons) may not cut across each other. Even if *some* moral reasons are categorical, is it clear that *all* are? And even more plausibly, aren't there some reasons that we would be *very* reluctant to call moral, but that seem quite categorical (like the reason we have to be instrumentally rational, if we have such a reason;[8] or the reason we have not to have intransitive preferences)? And if this is so, then we still haven't found a neat way of delineating the moral within the normative (though presumably someone may advance an antirealist position about all categorical reasons, whether they are moral or not). Furthermore, it's not completely clear how the categorical nature of moral reasons interacts with the objections to Robust Realism mentioned above. If non-categorical reasons are sufficiently intimately related to motivations the agent already has, then perhaps this helps with the objections above – presumably, the objection from motivation disappears, the one from metaphysics becomes much more manage-able, and as a result accommodating epistemic access also seems more manageable. As for disagreement, perhaps it can be argued that there just isn't that much of it when it comes to non-categorical reasons. But the very first stage here – securing a close enough connection between non-categorical reasons and motivations the agent al-ready has – is neither unproblematic nor uncontroversial.[9] And if, perhaps in order to solve some of these problems, your favorite view ties the (hypothetical) reasons we have not to what we (roughly speaking) want but rather to what we would want under some idealized conditions, then it is again not clear that your view secures the necessary relation to (actual) motivation.[10] Once we are more realistic about the relation between hypothetical reasons and motivation, then, it becomes far less clear that categorical reasons are *especially* problematic among all reasons in ways the traditional objections mentioned above render relevant.

Let me not press this point further, though. I am willing to assume, for the sake of argument, that categorical reasons – and so, with perhaps some rough edges, moral reasons – *are* more problematic compared to non-categorical reasons, and so that even if you are already a committed metanormative realist there may still be a respectable

---

[8] There's a huge debate I am trying to bypass here. For some of it, see Schroeder (2007, ch. 3), Raz (2005, and the following symposium), Kolodny (2005), Broome (2007).

[9] See, for instance, Hampton (1998, 165–6).

[10] For some related points, and for references, see my "Why Idealize?" (2005, 768 n. 21).

philosophical motivation for you to stop short of metaethical realism. The point I want to emphasize next is that even if this is so, still we have the resources to reject such a position, using now the force of the argument of Chapter 2.

Assuming that the argument of Chapter 2 works, we already have sufficient reason to be objectivists (though not, let me remind you, robust realists) about morality. And so we should reject response-dependent theories of morality.[11] And any attempt to ground morality (or some such) in hypothetical reasons is bound to be response-dependent (for your hypothetical reasons depend on the motivations you already have).[12] Or think about it this way: if all the reasons you have are hypothetical reasons, then all conflicts due to a normative disagreement are of the kind to which IMPARTIALITY (or something like it) applies. But we've seen examples of such conflicts (namely, those that are due to a moral disagreement) to which nothing like IMPARTIALITY applies. So some reasons are categorical.[13]

Now, after the discussion in the previous section, the relation between morality and categorical reasons was the only remaining reason to be especially suspicious of moral truths (assuming we are no longer suspicious of normative ones more generally). But the argument of Chapter 2, I've just argued, gives us sufficient reason to believe in categorical reasons, indeed moral ones. Granted, that argument does not support directly *Robust* Metaethical Realism. But if you're already a robust metanormative realist, and furthermore you are already an objectivist, believing in objective moral truths that are intimately connected to categorical reasons, then it does become very hard to see why you would not go for a Robust Metaethical Realism as well. At this point in the discussion, any alternative view, it seems, would be under-motivated, and perhaps also objectionably disjunctive. To see this, let me sketch two such possible views.

---

[11] I qualify this in Chapter 2, but the qualifications there are not ones that cause problems for the argument here.

[12] Even if morality cannot be grounded in (or in some other way very closely related to) hypothetical reasons, it still doesn't follow that it has to be grounded in (or in some other way very closely related to) categorical reasons. It may just not be very closely related to reasons at all. This, presumably, is a natural way of reading Foot (1972). But I proceed to reject this way out of the little argument in the text later on, when I argue that morality has at least pretty good normative credentials.

[13] Mark Schroeder's "Hypotheticalism" (2007) is, so he says, capable of accommodating genuinely agent-neutral, and so moral, reasons, while at the same time grounding all reasons in desires. (Whether or not they are categorical depends on terminology, of course. If a reason's being hypothetical amounts just to it being grounded in a desire, and if being categorical is not being hypothetical, then these reasons are not categorical. But if all it takes for a reason to be categorical is for it to apply to an agent whatever she wants, then Schroeder's agent-neutral reasons would be categorical.) Two points are relevant here. First, I don't believe that this part of Schroeder's project succeeds; see my "On Mark Schroeder's Hypotheticalism" (forthcoming). I just note here the relevance of his project, if it does succeed. And second, if Schroeder does succeed in giving us (pretty much) categorical reasons on Humean grounds, then this is not in conflict with the more important point in the text, namely, that nothing like IMPARTIALITY applies in the moral case. I would still need to reject Schroeder's naturalist reduction of the normative in order to fully defend Robust Realism, but the problem would not arise in the context of this paragraph in the text.

Convinced by the arguments of the previous two chapters, a thinker may go for a robustly realist view of normativity in general, but an objectivist-which-is-not-robustly-realist view of morality. For instance, one could opt for an objectivist naturalist reduction of morality. Such a reduction is consistent, you may recall, with the argument from the moral implications of objectivity. But now consider what such a view would have to look like. Such a view incorporates an unattractive discontinuity between moral and other reasons. Indeed, because it accepts irreducibly normative truths, but on the other hand reduces moral truths to naturalistically specifiable ones (say, reducing the right to what maximizes overall happiness), it severs any necessary ties between moral and normative truths. In other words, on such a view whether you have a reason to do as morality requires that you do becomes a contingent question. Moral rationalism, on such a view, is false. To some this will be reason enough to reject such a view, but I know, of course, that to others it won't, and relying here on the plausibility of moral rationalism may be dangerously close to begging the question against some metaethical alternatives to Robust Realism. Let me not do that, then. The point I want to emphasize now, rather, does not *assume* moral rationalism, but rather *establishes* some (fairly weak) version thereof (utilizing the force of the arguments in the previous chapters). And here's how: if moral rationalism is false, then morality can be seen, for present purposes, as precisely analogous to etiquette, in that reasons must be given in support of its claims, claims which sometimes, but not always, generate *real* reasons. But then, following the discussion in Chapter 2, we can imagine a conflict that is due to a tension between two different systems of (something like) etiquette, E_1 and E_2. When the adherents of E_1 call an action rude, they are truly saying that it is $rude_1$ (that is, rude-according-to-the-rules-of-E_1), and when the adherents of E_2 say that that very same action is not rude, they are truly saying that it is not $rude_2$.[14] Now suppose a joint decision must be made with regard to that action. Clearly, just insisting that it is $rude_1$, and so it shouldn't be performed – or indeed that it's not $rude_2$, and so there is no objection to performing it – will not do. Noting how this action is classified by one etiquette system or another alone will not suffice to break the kind of symmetry Chapter 2 is concerned with. Rather, an argument should be put forward supporting the conclusion that it is E_1 that we should follow, or that it is E_2 to which we owe our allegiance, or some such. What is needed, in other words, is a normative distinction between E_1 and E_2, a reason to follow one or the other. Getting back to morality: if moral truth is to be able to serve its role in undermining the application of something like IMPARTIALITY to conflicts arising from moral disagreement, then moral truths must be normatively privileged, they must be essentially tied to normative truths.

---

[14] I do not want to enter the debate over Cornell Realism and the moral twin earth problem. This is why in the text here I resort to stipulation: I stipulate (unobjectionably, I think) that "rude" in the mouths of the E_1-followers refers to the property of being $rude_1$, and in the mouths of the E_2-followers refers to the property of being $rude_2$.

Now, it's not clear how exactly moral rationalism is to be understood, and so whether I've just argued for moral rationalism. What I think the previous paragraph establishes is that morality must have pretty good normative credentials, it must not be entirely contingent that we have reasons to do what morality requires that we do. I do not claim that morality must itself be the source of these reasons (in whatever precise sense we want to give this metaphor), or that the moral reasons themselves must be real reasons.[15] And perhaps the relation I argue for between morality and normativity is one that is consistent with *some* special cases where one has no reason to do as morality requires that one do. It is certainly consistent with the possibility of other considerations sometime overriding morality's normative force. So I certainly haven't argued for some of the stronger ways of understanding moral rationalism. But the term doesn't matter. What does matter is that morality has pretty good normative credentials, that it isn't entirely contingent that we have reasons to do what morality requires that we do.

Notice that I do not take back here my acknowledging that the argument of Chapter 2 *on its own* is consistent with an objectivist naturalist reduction. My point now is, rather, that if you go for an objectivist reduction of morality, you had better go for a similar reduction of normativity in general, because for moral truth to have the significance it (according to the argument of Chapter 2) has it must be very closely tied to reasons and normativity. But this means that if, under the force of the indispensability argument in Chapter 3, you do *not* go for such an objectivist naturalist reduction of normativity in general, you shouldn't go for such a reduction of morality either. What defeats this view of morality is thus not the force of Chapter 2, but rather the *combined* force of Chapters 2 and 3.

Combining Robust Metanormative Realism with an objectivist, naturalist reduction of morality does not look very promising, then. How about a more radical disjunction, according to which non-moral normativity is understood along the lines of a subjectivist reduction, but the right theory of categorical normative statements – including only, or mostly, moral ones – is an error theory?[16] As noted in Chapter 2, whether the argument of Chapter 2 has force against a metaethical error theory depends on some intricate dialectical issues (like which cases of question-begging are objectionable). But the argument of Chapter 3 does have force – or so I've argued – against any reduction, subjectivist or otherwise. And if you already accept into your ontology these supposedly queer normative truths, and if you already need an epistemological and semantic story for them – again, when they are understood as I understand them in Chapter 3, not when they are understood as subjectively reducible, or some such – then what argument can you offer for a metaethical error theory? Error theory, after all, is rarely if ever the default position about an entrenched discourse, it is not a theory that is

---

[15] For Shafer-Landau's related distinction between intrinsic and extrinsic moral rationalism, see Shafer-Landau (2003, 204).

[16] Joyce (2001) is clearly an error theorist about morality, and not about rationality, but I am not completely sure whether the description in the text applies completely accurately to his view about reasons.

immediately plausible, to the point of being endorsable without some rather strong positive argument for it. Again, what counts against a metaethical error theory here is, then, not the force of Chapter 2 alone, but only the combined strength of Chapters 2 and 3. Making essentially the same point, now in the other direction: the only kind of hypothetical reasons that can plausibly (that is, in a philosophically motivated kind of way) be accounted for by someone rejecting categorical reasons are just not enough for what is indispensable for deliberation.

4.4 In the other direction: if, for instance, you already reject metaethical expressivism, why not also reject metanormative expressivism?

Before concluding this chapter, I want to discuss another aspect of the interrelations between the arguments of the previous two. So far the discussion in this chapter took the conclusions of the previous two chapters as given, attempting to show what follows from their conjunction. But – especially given the incompleteness of the argument in Chapter 3 regarding rejecting alternative metanormative views – we can also wonder whether the results in Chapter 2 can help in completing the argument of Chapter 3. In particular, can the rejection of (most) response-dependence views and expressivist views of morality (in Chapter 2) be utilized to bolster the case for the deliberative indispensability of irreducibly normative truths?

   Once again, there is no quick entailment to this effect: that expressivism, say, is not acceptable as an account of moral discourse and practice does not entail that it is not acceptable as an account of some other parts of normative discourse and practice. But if we know that morality is indeed a particular instance of normativity more generally, then the failure of expressivism as a metaethical theory *does* entail its failure as a metanormative account with global scope. And this in turn means that any attempt at an expressivist account of (some parts of) normative discourse and practice is going to end up being disjunctive, offering one kind of account of morality, quite another of normativity more generally and its other instances. And it is the upshot of the discussion in the previous sections in this chapter that such a disjunctive account is going to be hard to motivate. Furthermore, any such disjunctive account is going to be especially unwelcome to expressivists, who typically *emphasize* the relations between the moral and the normative – think, in this context, of Gibbard's (1990) attempt to reduce talk of moral wrongness to talk of when certain responses would be rational, or of the general expressivist hostility towards naturalistic reductions. So expressivists, it seems, have especially powerful reasons not to go for a disjunctive account of the kind sketched. And if such disjunctive accounts are unlikely to be attractive – in general, or given some expressivist motivations – then that expressivism fails when it comes to morality should at the very least make us more suspicious of its chances of succeeding as an account of other, fairly basic parts of normativity. (This, of course, is consistent with the possibility that expressivism is the right theory of some other fairly local normative discourses, like perhaps that of the beautiful, or the disgusting, or the cool.) And the same holds, it seems to me, when it comes to cognitivist response-dependence theories as well.

Thus, it seems to me that the metanormative analogues of the metaethical views rejected in Chapter 2 do suffer a blow – they at the very least lose plausibility points – as a result of that metaethical discussion. And this strengthens their elimination as viable metanormative theories for Chapter 3 as well. In other words, this further strengthens the indispensability premise of the indispensability argument there developed.

4.5 Robust Metaethical Realism: going all the way

If the arguments of the two previous chapters work, then, we should accept not just metaethical objectivity (Chapter 2) and Robust Metanormative Realism (Chapter 3). We should also accept Robust Metaethical Realism. This is so, not because the former two theses entail the third (they don't). Rather, it's because none of the motivations for endorsing an alternative to this third thesis survives the acceptance of the former two. Or so, at least, I've argued in this chapter.

I want to be careful not to overstate my case here. For it's possible that there is some other consideration – one I haven't even mentioned in this chapter – that can serve to motivate a less than robustly realistic metaethics, even after we are already committed both to metaethical objectivity and to Metanormative Robust Realism. I cannot rule out this possibility. I can just mention the motivations I can think of (and can find in the literature), and conjecture that no such further consideration can be found. But my argument here is open-ended in this way, and so my conclusion can perhaps better be thought of as a challenge: if you cannot find a flaw with the arguments of the two previous chapters, but want to resist the further conclusion of Robust Metaethical Realism, you had better be able to come up with a rationale for the surprising combination of views you find yourself with.

5

Doing with Less

In this chapter I examine three attempts to satisfy metaphysically for much less than Robust Realism – a naturalist reduction (with "reduction" sufficiently loosely understood, as explained below), a host of error-theoretic and fictionalist views, and a recently popular kind of quietism that is very much like Robust Realism in some respects but also insists on its being metaphysically "light". This chapter should be seen, then, as a part of the positive case for Robust Realism, though it is the more negative part of the positive part of this book. This chapter helps to support the indispensability premise in the indispensability argument of Chapter 3, by showing some of the problems with views that may render irreducibly normative facts after all dispensable. But this chapter also serves as a natural introduction to the next one. In the next chapter, I discuss metaphysical objections to Robust Realism. And the metaphysical discussion starts in this chapter. In this chapter, in other words, I argue that what may seem like the metaphysically extravagant commitments of Robust Realism are not easily dispensed with. And in the next chapter I argue that the metaphysical extravagance is not that objectionable after all.

5.1 Naturalism, after all

I have been emphasizing – mostly, but not only, in Chapter 3 – how different the normative (and so also the moral) truths are from the natural, non-normative ones. Normative facts and properties, as I have been saying, are just too different from natural ones to be a subset of them. But it may be thought that I have been making uncalled-for metaphysical noise. Perhaps the convincing claim is not that normative *facts* or *properties* are too different from natural ones, but rather that normative *thoughts* or *concepts* are. This diagnosis may be strengthened by noting the kind of indispensability I've argued is relevant here. After all, I did not argue (and do not believe) that normative facts are *causally* indispensable. I've argued that they are *deliberatively* indispensable. But such indispensability – unlike causal ones – operates at the level of thoughts, and so that of concepts, not that of facts and properties. Can I get all that I want, then, by rejecting a *conceptual* naturalist reduction, and yet accepting a naturalist reduction (or some such) at the more metaphysical level?[1] Perhaps – under the pressure of the argument of Chapter

[1] Insisting on this distinction may also be attractive on historical grounds. For arguably, Moore's infamous Open Question Argument fails miserably when understood as trying to make the metaphysical point,

2 – subjectivist reductions are no longer an option to be considered now. But why aren't objectivist naturalist reductions still very much on the table? Unlike my Robust Realism, they would not lose plausibility points on account of having a non-naturalist metaphysics. Unless they can be shown to have some rather significant shortcomings compared to Robust Realism, then, aren't they to be preferred?

Now, as already hinted, it's not clear what the precise naturalist claim would be.[2] Suggestions in this area include things like the following: normative facts just are (*identical with*) natural facts; normative facts are *reducible to* natural ones; normative facts are *metaphysically grounded in* natural ones; normative facts are *constituted by* natural facts. And further distinctions may be relevant here. For instance, we may want to distinguish – even if we've settled on an identity claim – between type–type and token–token identity. Furthermore, it's not as if the terms just used (in any of these suggestions) are philosophically transparent. It is, after all, not at all clear, and far less is it uncontroversial, how reduction is best understood, or how grounding is to be distinguished from constitution, or – perhaps most clearly – how the natural is to be understood and delineated. So there are many, many suggestions that a fuller philosophical treatment would have to distinguish and evaluate piecemeal. Without pretending to cover everything in the neighborhood that needs covering, then, let me make a fairly concrete suggestion about how to capture the naturalist thought, and then argue against it. I have to concede, though, that nothing here will qualify as a conclusive argument, much less will it qualify as a conclusive argument against *all* possible roughly-speaking-naturalist positions here.

I am going to make use of the *nothing-over-and-above* relation.[3] I take the more philosophically-sounding relations of identity, reduction, constitution, and grounding to be attempts at precisifying this more intuitive relation (in different ways, in different contexts). And I take the issue between metaethical naturalists and non-naturalists to be conveniently put in terms of the more intuitive notion. Naturalists affirm, and non-naturalists deny, that normative facts are nothing over and above natural ones. And the

because, as we've known for a while now (but Moore may have failed to realize) the denial of the identity of concepts does not entail the denial of the identity of the corresponding properties. On the other hand, as is often noted, there does seem to be something true and important in the vicinity of the Open Question Argument. Perhaps what (if anything) can be salvaged from Moore's Open Question Argument, then, can only work at the level of concepts.

[2] As Åsa Wikforss insisted in conversation, some would treat accepting the (perhaps strong) supervenience of the normative on the natural as sufficient for qualifying as a naturalist. I do not think this is a helpful way of characterizing naturalism in our context. But let me note here that if this is how you think of naturalism, you should think of me as a naturalist. I discuss supervenience in the next chapter.

[3] Oddie (2005, ch. 6) also does. Some complain about this relation: "what does 'nothing over and above' mean? This slippery phrase has had a lot of employment in philosophy, but what it means is never explained by its employers" (van Inwagen (1994, 210)). But this complaint is made in the context of discussions where proponents of some kind of supervenience relation proceed to avoid (so they argue) ontological problems by claiming that supervening properties – while not identical to the subvening ones – are still nothing over and above them. (For discussion, see McLaughlin and Bennett (2005, section 3.4).) In that context, employing the nothing-over-and-above relation does look like cheating. I, on the other hand, am going to *reject* a nothing-over-and-above claim, thus *accepting* ontological implications, all the time while also accepting a supervenience thesis. I don't think, then, that my use of this relation is as suspicious as many others'.

reason I will not have to worry about the precisification suitable for our context is that I want to deny the nothing-over-and-above claim, *however* precisified.[4]

Thus, I take it to be a starting point for the debate over the relation between statues and "their" lumps of clay that there is *a* sense in which the statue is nothing over and above the lump of clay. But then further claims are made – perhaps, for instance, about the persistence conditions of both, or about some of their modal features – to push us in the direction of a constitution rather than an identity claim (because the former relation is consistent and the latter is not with different persistence conditions for the two relata). Perhaps somewhat similarly, it seems to me clear that chair-facts are nothing over and above the rather complex facts that include something about chairs' physical structure, their function, and so on. But – depending on your favorite way of using the term "reduction" – you may want to resist the claim that chairs are reducible to these other things if, for instance, you think that chair-generalizations are explanatorily useful in ways that the purported reduction base misses. Or you may think that mental facts are nothing over and above physical ones, but refuse to put the point in terms of an identity statement because you think that the physical facts are metaphysically more basic than the mental ones,[5] and that identity precludes such basicness-asymmetries.[6]

When I speak of irreducibly normative (and moral) facts, I use the term "reduction" and its relatives somewhat loosely, to pick out the nothing-over-and-above relation. According to Robust Realism, then, there are moral and other normative facts that are not merely natural ones; according to Robust Realism it is just false to say of (all) the normative facts that they are nothing over and above natural ones. The relation between the normative facts and the natural ones is not like that between statues and "their" lumps of clay, or between chair-facts and facts about their structure and function,[7] or between mental facts and physical facts (according to the monist).

But there is need for even more clarification, for it's not as if we have a character-ization of the natural we're all happy with.[8] The temptation, of course, is to ask whether

---

[4] Because I am about to accept a supervenience thesis (in Chapter 6), you may be worried that this suffices for some kind of ontological dependence. But you shouldn't be. For a quick overview of the differences between supervenience and ontological dependence, see McLaughlin and Bennett (2005, section 3.5). For the claim that supervenience does not suffice for the nothing-over-and-above relation in our context, see Majors (2005, throughout).

[5] Fine (2001) characterizes reduction as the conjunction of an identity and a basicness claim of this kind.

[6] The different metaphysical relations mentioned in the text differ interestingly with regard to symmetry. Identity is a symmetrical relation. Reduction, constitution, and grounding are arguably asymmetrical. The nothing-over-and-above relation is more permissive than those, and so is unsurprisingly non-symmetrical: it does not require symmetry, but nor does it preclude it (notice, for instance, that it is reflexive – for any x, x is nothing over and above x). Notice, interestingly, that all these relations are arguably transitive.

[7] Shafer-Landau (2003, 64) compares moral properties (on his kind of realism) to geological ones. I take it, though, that geological properties are nothing over and above the physical and chemical ones. This is where Shafer-Landau's realism is not sufficiently robust for me.

[8] I am not willing to assume that the natural and the physical are one and the same. Whether there's more to the natural than the physical is something our understanding of the natural should remain neutral on. And this makes most of Wedgwood's (2007) discussion of reduction irrelevant for my purposes – for he rejects the reducibility of the normative and the intentional (which he thinks are interdependent) to the physical.

the normative is reducible to the non-normative. But this temptation should be resisted, because reductionists argue – certainly, they *may* argue – that the normative is nothing over and above the thing to which they reduce (loosely speaking) the normative, and so they (may) argue that that thing *is* normative. Characterizing it as non-normative would not be a good way of asking the question about the feasibility of reduction – rather, it would be a way of making sure that the question cannot be fairly asked.[9] Another temptation is to put things linguistically, so that the question becomes whether normative facts can be captured in non-normative *terms*. But this temptation too should be resisted: for one thing, it would hold what seems to be a metaphysical question hostage to the contingencies of our natural language (and indeed, the answer may depend on *which* natural language is being referred to).[10] Also, this way of putting things makes the question we were hoping to ask (about normative properties and facts) too close to the question we were hoping to avoid (about normative concepts and thoughts).

I suggest, then, that we understand talk of the natural here in the following somewhat vague (and rather standard[11]) way. Facts and properties are natural if and only if they are of the kind the usual sciences invoke. This characterization inherits its vagueness mostly from the vagueness of the classification of facts and properties into kinds being assumed here, and to an extent also from the reference to the "usual sciences".[12] So I do not want to pretend that this characterization is precise or otherwise entirely unproblematic. Still, it is not contentless. And I do not know of a better characterization of the natural in our context.[13] For now, then, I think that this characterization should suffice.

[9] A point emphasized by Schroeder (2005, 9).

[10] Boyd's (1988) cardinality argument against the hope of a reduction (more narrowly understood than in the text) is an especially nice way of exploiting the point in the text.

[11] For a quick survey of the Moorean origins of this way of understanding the natural, and for other references, see Sturgeon (2007, 64).

[12] One legitimate worry is that this way of putting things renders what we thought of as a metaphysical distinction an epistemological one – so that natural facts and properties are characterized by the method of gaining knowledge about them (namely, the scientific method) (see here Shafer-Landau 2003, 58–61). The reference to *kinds* of facts and properties is supposed to partly allay this worry: presumably, facts can be of the same kind of facts that are scientifically known even if they themselves aren't scientifically known.

[13] Copp's (2003) characterization is entirely epistemic here. But this is inadequate as we are after a metaphysical one. (I also think that even as an epistemic one Copp's suggestion fails, but the details need not concern us here.) Ridge (2007) characterizes the natural – in the context of precisifying a supervenience claim – in terms of either the non-normative, or the descriptive. Given the problems with the first disjunct (at least in our context, if not in Ridge's), it is the second that does most of the work, and it is not, I think, significantly different from the characterization of the natural in the text. Cuneo (2007b) suggests a characterization in terms of *stances* – where naturalists give priority to "external accommodation" (reconciling our metaethics with science and the scientific world view) and non-naturalists to "internal accommodation" (reconciling our metaethics with moral practice and its phenomenology, etc.). As a sociological observation, I am sure Cuneo is on to something. As a characterization of naturalism, though, I cannot agree: The issue is metaphysical, not stance-related. And *my* stance is that of attempting an honest evaluation of all the relevant evidence, giving priority to neither internal nor external accommodation.

With these clarifications in mind, then, we can return to our main question: are normative facts (objects, properties) nothing over and above facts of the kind the usual sciences deal with? Indeed, how would we even argue for an answer – be it positive or negative – to the question thus understood?

One thing that can be done is to engage in piecemeal evaluation of specific reductive proposals or the arguments for them. If such a proposal comes up that nicely deals with all of the local objections, this will pull strongly in the direction of acknowledging the success of the reductionist project. If, on the other hand, the reductive suggestions of which we are aware are all found problematic, and if the arguments for them are found problematic,[14] this strengthens the suspicion that no naturalistic reduction is possible (though perhaps not by much, given that *any* metaethical view is subject to objections; as you may recall, it's all about overall plausibility points). This is especially so, if the difficulties faced by the reductive suggestions we know of are of a somewhat systematic nature. And I think they are: for any such reduction (loosely understood) would have to be either a priori, or a posteriori. If it is a priori, then it works at the level of concepts after all, and I take it we already have sufficient reason to be highly suspicious of views that are naturalist at that level, simply because (as emphasized at the beginning of this section) normative thoughts and truths are so different from natural ones.[15] And if it is a posteriori (roughly, along Cornell Realist lines[16]), then it is up against a host of familiar difficulties trying to accommodate genuine moral disagreement in some extreme cases where such disagreement seems nevertheless possible. Such difficulties have been emphasized at least since Hare (1952), and have fairly recently been given their definitive shape by Horgan and Timmons in their series of papers (e.g. 1992) dealing with Moral Twin Earth.[17] I don't have much to add about these thought experiments over what is already there in the literature, and so I will not discuss them in detail here. But let me make the following point (following the sincerity policy announced in Chapter 1): the problem here for a posteriori naturalist reductions is not a technical fluke of sorts. It is a precisification of the central worry that many of us have had about

[14] It is in this spirit, I think, that Parfit (2011, for instance vol. 2, 338) offers his criticism of naturalist arguments that work by analogy with reductionist strategies in the natural sciences.

[15] Michael Smith's (1994; and elsewhere) dispositional view is probably the best-known and best-developed attempt at (what is arguably) an a priori naturalist reduction. But his theory fails, I think, and for reasons that are closely related to the point made in the text. For my arguments to this effect, see my (2007b). For the ambiguity about Smith's naturalism, see there (106 n. 22). For Smith's reply, see Smith (2007).

[16] Cornell Realists like to deny that theirs is a reductionist view. Let me remind you, though, the loose sense of "reduction" with which I am working here, the one characterized by the nothing-over-and-above relation. I take it that Cornell Realists believe that normative (and so moral) facts are nothing over and above the natural ones – the relation between normative and natural facts according to such a view are roughly analogous to that holding between chair-facts and the physical and functional facts to which they are (loosely speaking) reducible. So their view qualifies as a reductionist one in my sense here.

[17] These worries may just be the implications of the fact that we do not, in the case of evaluative or normative terms, have the referential intentions of the kind we do have with natural-kind terms. For a development of this line of objection to a posteriori naturalism, see Gampel (1996).

naturalist reductions, namely, that they lose the normativity of normative and indeed moral facts – the very feature they were supposed to capture. This, after all, is precisely *why* such reductions seem to fail the moral-twin-earth thought experiment: The earthlings and twin-earthlings seem to genuinely disagree (rather than talk past each other) and use the target word ("wrong", for instance, or "good") in the same way, because the normative force of the target word is held constant on earth and twin-earth. The naturalist reduction fails because it loses precisely this crucial feature. Or so the thought goes.

But none of this is conclusive. Perhaps a posteriori naturalists can somehow deal with such worries. Or perhaps there are better a priori reductions that we just haven't thought of yet.[18] Is there anything that can be said here, anything more general, and that does not constitute merely insisting on the just-too-different intuition emphasized already in Chapter 3? Any *positive* argument that can be offered, supporting the irreducibility claim?

I do not have such an argument up my sleeve. Indeed, there is some reason to think that we find ourselves here in a dialectical predicament where no such argument is possible.[19]

To make this point, I am going to use Mark Schroeder's (2005) recent attempt at making sense of what is at stake in the debate over reduction. Schroeder starts with the plausible thought that attempts to naturalistically reduce[20] God-facts are non-starters, and are right off the bat much less plausible than attempts to naturalistically reduce normative facts (and this even if the latter too end up being irreducible). The rest of Schroeder's discussion is diagnostic in nature, attempting to explain why it is that God-facts are so clearly irreducible. The (plausible) diagnosis he comes up with is that a naturalist reduction of God-facts and theological discourse will either prevent us from saying some of the things we pre-theoretically take to be true (like, for instance, that God, if he exists, created the universe), or else will commit us to offering revisionary accounts of increasingly larger parts of our conceptual make-up (by offering, for instance, a weird, non-standard understanding of "create" and "universe") – in Schroeder's terms, we would have to "propagate implications". Because none of these options seems attractive, neither does a naturalist reduction of theological discourse.

---

[18] Kit Fine (2002) offers a related argument against naturalism, which also divides – in order to conquer – the opposition roughly along the lines of a priori and a posteriori naturalism; as against the latter, his argument comes down to the claim that no such naturalism can simultaneously accommodate the possibility of moral disagreement and (roughly) the apriority of moral knowledge. Though I accept the apriority premise, I find it hard to believe that anyone not already confident in the falsity of a naturalist reduction will be as accommodating.

[19] Parfit's "Triviality Objection" (2011, vol. 2, section 95) may be thought of as an argument of this kind. But for reasons that I can't get into here, I don't think it is a convincing argument (unless, that is, this objection at the end of the day comes down to yet another way of pressing the just-too-different intuition).

[20] Schroeder (2005, 12) too is clear about speaking of reduction in a fairly loose, relaxed sense, though it's not precisely mine that he has in mind, I think. The difference, though, to the extent that there is one, is not one that makes a difference for the limited use to which I put Schroeder's discussion in the text.

Armed with this diagnosis, we can now ask whether similar difficulties face attempts at a naturalist reduction of normative discourse. Schroeder suggests that the answer is "no". The reason is that there is an important distinction between theological and normative discourse that is relevant here. Many of the things we pre-theoretically want to say about God, Schroeder argues plausibly enough, are put in non-theological terms (like certain claims about the origin of the universe). This is why offering even a remotely plausible naturalist reduction of theological discourse would commit us to propagating implications. But normative discourse is different, argues Schroeder, in that most of the central commitments of normative discourse are "primarily set out at least in part in terms of other normative notions" (2005, 7). And this means that no implications will have to be propagated by the metanormative reductionist – none, that is, outside normative discourse itself. As for the implications propagated within normative discourse – these will presumably be plausibly dealt with by the reductionist account itself. Now, as Schroeder well knows, this is not a positive argument for a naturalist reduction – on his view, our reasons for going reductionist are going to be the theoretical payoffs of such a reduction, and the virtues of the *particular* reductionist position those of us who are reduction-aficionados are going to end up going for.[21] But the disanalogy between theological and normative discourse is supposed to disarm one line of worry about a naturalist reduction of the normative: for such reduction is not subject to the main reasons we have for rejecting a naturalist reduction in places where it is clearly implausible (as in the example of theological discourse). At the very least, then, we should be more open-minded about the prospects of a naturalist reduction of the normative, assessing particular reductionist suggestions on their particular merits.[22] So argues Schroeder.

I want to highlight two problems with Schroeder's reasoning here. The first is that the list of things we pre-theoretically want to say may itself include a denial of a naturalist reduction.[23] Indeed, the just-too-different point is precisely an attempt to capture such a pre-theoretical desideratum.[24] I don't know whether we want to say of this commitment that it too is "set out at least in part in terms of other normative notions", but we do not need to decide this issue here. For either way, so long as you're on board with the just-too-different intuition, you're already committed to a reduction either having strongly counterintuitive consequences or requiring propagating implications (by offering, for instance, a non-standard understanding of "too-different"). Of course, you may not already be on board with regard to the

---

[21] Schroeder's own reductionist account is developed in detail in his *Slaves of the Passions* (2007).

[22] Schroeder (several times throughout his article) is even willing to concede that there are modest inductive grounds to be suspicious of reductionist accounts. But they are not, he argues (and I agree), conclusive.

[23] It's not clear whether Schroeder's list is supposed to include only the things we want to say regarding the target for reduction but can't say about the reducing, or also things we do *not* want to say about the target for reduction but can't plausibly avoid saying about the reducing. If the latter, the point in the text becomes stronger still – for we really don't want (pre-theoretically) to say of the normative that it's natural.

[24] I'm not sure, but this may be a variant of what Schroeder (2005, 8) calls "Nagel's Worry".

just-too-different point. I take it most reductionists aren't. And so we find ourselves here at a dialectical impasse: either one accepts the just-too-different thought (at least as a defeasible starting point), or one doesn't. If one does, then one should reject the disanalogy Schroeder is after between theological and normative discourse, and with it any reason to believe that the normative is more readily amenable to naturalist reduction than the theological. And if one does not accept even initially the just-too-different thought, then one should stick to the disanalogy. Either way, then, no dialectical progress has been made.

For the second problem with Schroeder's reasoning, notice its peculiarity. For in effect, Schroeder enlists what may be called the (putative) autonomy of the normative – the fact, somewhat roughly, that there are no implications to or from normative discourse to non-normative discourse – as an (indirect) consideration *for* the reducibility of the normative. But I would have thought that the autonomy of the normative is, if anything, some reason to suspect that it can*not* be reduced, that it is, as it were, *sui generis*. And this peculiar feature of Schroeder's line of thought should make us suspicious that there's some cheating going on, that at most what Schroeder manages to show is not that the normative is more likely to be naturalistically reducible than the theological, but rather that it's going to be harder *to come up with an argument* against a naturalist reduction of the normative. This is an interesting dialectical result, and it may have some methodological implications (of which more shortly). But it certainly does not show anything about the plausibility of such reduction. If you're not yet convinced of this point, note that Schroeder's line can be used with regard to any discourse or domain of (putative) facts that are autonomous in this sense, *regardless of what the world is like*. So Schroeder's argument, if sound, gives us (indirect) reason to go for a naturalist reduction of *any* such discourse and domain, on any possible world. But surely the argument can't do this much. So as an indirect argument for the reducibility of the normative (by eliminating one kind of objection to naturalist reduction), the argument does not succeed.

Notice that the arguments in the last two paragraphs are by no means arguments for the irreducibility of the normative. They are at most[25] arguments against one (Schroeder's) argument against one line of thought that may be thought to support irreducibility. So where in the debate over the reducibility of the normative are we left?

Where we started, I'm afraid – with the just-too-different intuition. Normative facts sure seem different from natural ones, different enough to justify an initial suspicion regarding reductionist attempts. This is especially clear when considered – as it should be – from the point of view of the deliberating agent. When I ask myself what I should do, it seems that just answering "Oh, pressing the blue button will maximize happiness" is a complete non-starter, it completely fails to address the question. Of course, given some background commitments it can be a better answer. If, for instance, I am

---

[25] In fact, and despite the points just made, there may not be a deep disagreement between Schroeder's conclusion and mine, as I proceed to note below.

already a convinced utilitarian, willing to commit myself to something like "It always makes sense to perform the action that maximizes happiness", then "pressing the blue button will maximize happiness" seems like a reasonable answer to the question what should I do. But such background commitments are themselves paradigmatically normative, and themselves just too different from naturalist facts and beliefs. Absent such background commitments, "pressing the blue button will maximize happiness" seems just irrelevant to the question I ask myself, as does – in just the same way – any other purely naturalist answer. Rather than answering my question, such an answer simply changes the subject. It takes a normative commitment to render a naturalist answer to a normative question relevant. No natural fact by itself can have normative force.[26] Or so, at least, it seems to me.[27]

This is not satisfying – I would have preferred to have a more robust argument against reduction (it would have been especially nice to have just one crisp argument that refutes, at one blow, *all* reductionist attempts). But my discussion of Schroeder's contribution here gives reason to suspect that no such argument is possible. As made clear in the second critical point I made above, Schroeder's discussion, with its emphasis on the autonomy of the normative, rather than (indirectly) supporting reduction, in fact helps to show the constraints on our dialectical abilities here. And as the first critical point above shows, any argumentative move here will likely start either with accepting or with rejecting the just-too-different intuition, thus in a way begging the question against the other party to the reducibility debate. We may not be able to do here much more than just stare at the just-too-different intuition and try to see how plausible it seems to us, at least as a starting point. And to me, it seems very plausible indeed.

But that it's a plausible starting point does not mean it's the final word on the matter. And as I conceded earlier on, if a reductionist proposal comes along that scores sufficiently well on the list of theoretical virtues, this may in itself be a good enough reason to take back our commitment to the just-too-different thought. In a way, then, everything depends on the details and resulting attractiveness of specific reductionist proposals.[28]

In terms of plausibility points, then, I concede that naturalist reductions of the normative have some advantage over Robust Realism given their more parsimonious

---

[26] The intuition that no answer in terms of a naturalistic reduction succeeds in addressing the questions we ask ourselves in deliberation may be the intuition underlying Moore's Open Question Argument, only highlighted from the perspective of the deliberating agent. For an attempt to save what can be saved from the Open Question Argument by highlighting it from the perspective of deliberating agents, see Rosati (1995).

[27] For expressions of similar intuitions, see Donagan (1981), Johnston (1989, 157), Dancy (1996a, 180–2; and 2005, 132, 141), McGinn (1997, e.g. 11 and 25), Scanlon (1998, 57–8), Fitzpatrick (2008; 2010), Heathwood (2009, 89) and Parfit (2011, vol. 2, section 91). And perhaps Darwall, Gibbard, and Railton have a similar intuition in mind when they say (1992, 30): "... despite their protestation, they [such reductive naturalists] might turn out to be error theorists after all". For a similar intuition in another context (that of the normativity of meaning and suggested dispositional reductions) see Boghossian (1989, 532).

[28] It is here that my conclusion and Schroeder's converge. And here see also Gibbard (2003, 35).

ontology. But they lose plausibility points because they have to reject the just-too-different intuition. And the ones I am familiar with are also problematic on other grounds. So I am not optimistic about naturalist reductions of the normative. But I remain officially open-minded about the possibility of a reductionist position whose theoretical value will be worth its cost.[29]

5.2 Fictionalism and error theory

If I am right, then, a naturalist reduction will not allow the realist sensitive to the considerations I've been emphasizing to do with less by way of metaphysics. But this may give rise to two related (but distinct) responses. One would be an attempt to divorce the apparent commitments of normative discourse from any metaphysically heavy implications, by endorsing a hermeneutic,[30] non-error-theoretic fictionalism about it. The other would be another metaphysical insistence on the unacceptability of Robust Realism, in the form of an error theory. I discuss these in turn.

5.2.1 (Non-error-theoretic) fictionalism

A conversation among Sherlock Holmes enthusiasts may be very lively, and it may look (and perhaps also be) very serious. They may, of course, say things like, "In the Holmes fiction, Holmes smokes a pipe." But typically – in some contexts, at least – they are much more likely to say things like, "Holmes smokes a pipe." If someone says that Holmes smokes cigars, many will correct him (perhaps by saying things like "That's false!"), and if then someone else says that actually, Holmes smokes a pipe, many will respond approvingly (perhaps by saying "True!"). Inferences may be employed: for instance, someone may offer an inference to the best explanation supporting her conclusion that Moriarty was in fact smarter than Holmes (even though nothing explicit in Conan Doyle's text strictly implies this conclusion); and another may offer: "If Moriarty is smarter than Holmes, and Holmes is smarter than Watson, then Moriarty is smarter than Watson." And so on.

Even though Holmes does not exist, it would be silly, I take it, to insist that the discussion just sketched is systematically erroneous. A much more natural conclusion would be that the participants implicitly precede each statement they make with

---

[29] I don't know of anyone developing in detail a token–token naturalist reduction (loosely speaking) in the metanormative case, perhaps analogous to anomalous monism or other token–identity theories in the philosophy of mind (for some suggestions in this direction, see Scott (1980, 266), Jackson and Pettit (1995), Wedgwood (2007, 221), and see also related comments by Shafer-Landau (2003, 70, 76 n. 9)). This, to me, is a surprising fact, given the abundance of isms in current metaethics. It seems like an option worth pursuing – roughly, one according to which particular normative facts are nothing over and above particular natural facts, but there are no useful general laws regarding such reduction, and in particular no reductions of normative generalizations. Of course, in order to evaluate such a position we would need to see its details. And it would have to be shown how this view avoids difficulties analogous to those confronted by analogous views in the philosophy of mind. But to repeat, this seems to me like a direction initially worth pursuing.

[30] See, for instance, Eklund (2007, section 2.2) and the references there.

an in-the-fiction operator. This understanding renders much of what they say true (in the fiction, after all, Holmes does smoke a pipe rather than cigars), many of their controversies intelligible (for it is, I take it, an interesting question whether in the fiction Moriarty is smarter than Holmes), many of their inferences valid (for in the fiction too *modus ponens* necessarily preserves truth, and also, it necessarily preserves – really, not just in the fiction – truth-in-the-fiction).

And so we have a general, if modest, lesson here: a serious, disciplined, regimented, truth-evaluable discourse can be seemingly committed to unacceptable ontological claims (the existence of Sherlock Holmes, for instance), but avoid wide-ranging error by not being *really* committed to it. If we can understand the relevant discourse along fictionalist lines – analogously to the natural understanding of the Sherlock Holmes conversation, with wide use of an implicit in-the-fiction operator – all may still be well.

The suggestion now to be discussed, then, is that normative discourse be understood along similar fictionalist lines.[31] There are no irreducibly normative facts and properties, to which this discourse is seemingly committed. But normative discourse is still error-free, because normative statements are to be understood as preceded by an implicit in-the-fiction operator. Of course, such a fictionalism will allow us to get all we want for a metaphysical bargain – thus understood, normative discourse is not more committed to the denial of metaphysical naturalism than Holmes-enthusiasts are to the existence of Sherlock Holmes. And if you think that this understanding will prevent us from taking normative (and so moral) discourse seriously, I suggest that you pay more attention the next time Holmes-enthusiasts discuss a Holmes-related controversy.

Many details need to be filled in if we are going to have a complete view here.[32] For instance, when is it plausible to attribute the use of an implicit in-the-fiction operator to a speaker? When she does not believe the statement without that operator? When she disbelieves it? When upon reflection, or when challenged, she would disavow it? When by and large, her community will? We need an answer to this question, and it's not clear that an answer would be friendly to the suggestion of metanormative fictionalism. (For instance, would those engaging in moral discourse disavow their unqualified moral commitment when challenged, saying something like, "Oh, sure, I was just talking about what's true in the morality fiction"? In the Sherlock Holmes case, after all, this is the kind of response we would expect.[33]) Another issue fictionalists will have to discuss is how to draw the distinction between

---

[31] I think that everything I am about to say about this kind of fictionalism (sometimes (e.g. Eklund 2007) called content-fictionalism) can also be applied (with minimal changes) to a fictionalist view that employs not the apparatus of an in-the-fiction operator but that of pretense-assertion instead, that is, to force-fictionalism (as in Joyce 2001). And although in the text I keep helping myself to the in-the-fiction operator, and consequently the fictionalism I discuss may be an instance of what Yablo (2001) calls meta-fictionalism, I think everything I say can be rather straightforwardly applied to a metaethical instance of what he calls object-fictionalism (and also his reflexive fictionalism) as well.

[32] For many more details, see Eklund (2007) and the references there.

[33] Cuneo and Christy (2010) emphasize this apparent disanalogy. See also their discussion of Kalderon's attempt at a response to this worry – Cuneo and Christy (2010, 90–1), and the references there.

an apparent controversy amounting to a disagreement about the goings-on within a given fiction, and an apparent controversy amounting to the telling of two different (though perhaps closely related) fictions. Perhaps this is just an especially important particular instance of the general challenge facing fictionalists – to come up with a plausible account of what it is to be telling a fictional story in a way that may be relevant to cases like that of normative discourse, cases where there's no obvious author, or canonical text.[34]

I will not, then, discuss fictionalism in full detail. But enough has already been said to see that fictionalism poses an initial challenge to Robust Realism and my arguments for it. For what, we can ask, is lost if we shift from Robust Realism to a fictionalist view of this kind? We know what is gained – namely, more modest, naturalist metaphysics.[35] And we also know that it's not as if what is lost is the possibility to (in some sense) seriously engage in normative and moral discourse. What *is* lost, then? In what ways is a fictionalist view inadequate, or at least less adequate than Robust Realism, so that robust realists can claim to earn – in comparison to fictionalism – more plausibility points than they lose by their purportedly extravagant ontological commitments?

This, I take it, is a perfectly legitimate challenge even without the full details of the relevant fictionalist view in front of us. But of course, some ways of coping with it may depend on those further details. If, for instance, fictionalists have no way of filling in the details in a plausible way, this will be sufficient to justify rejecting fictionalism. But I want to grant fictionalists for the sake of argument most of the details here, and highlight an aspect of fictionalism that justifies rejecting it (pretty much) however the details are filled in. In a nutshell – fictionalism cannot accommodate the kind of objectivity argued for in Chapter 2, and (partly for this reason) normative claims that are only true in the relevant fiction do not suffice for deliberation. In these ways, then, fictionalism does not allow us to take morality sufficiently seriously.[36]

Start with objectivity. There is *a* sense of objectivity, of course, that is consistent with fictionalism. I take it that if someone in the Holmes-fans conversation says that Holmes lived on Oxford St, she is quite objectively wrong (in a way someone saying that Holmes lived on Baker St isn't). This holds for the kind of objectivity discussed in Chapter 2 as well: if two people disagree about the street where Holmes lived, their disagreement is perfectly factual (even if the facts are somewhat complicated, having to do with the telling of fictions), and should it somehow be relevant to a joint action the two need to perform, I take it nothing analogous to IMPARTIALITY will apply. And so it

[34] Which is not to suggest that there are no clear examples of fictions with these characteristics.
[35] Whether fictionalism does better than Robust Realism vis-à-vis other challenges – like the epistemological one, for instance – will depend on the details of the relevant fictionalist view.
[36] In other ways, it may – let me remind you the seriousness with which the Holmes-enthusiasts may treat their Holmes-controversies. But there may also be other ways – not the ones to be discussed in the text – in which it is hard to see how fictionalism can accommodate the seriousness with which morality is usually taken. As Stephen Finlay reminded me, it is much harder to find people willing to kill each other over (what they acknowledge) are matters of fiction than it is to find people willing to kill each other over (what they take to be) moral matters.

is possible to go fictionalist about morality[37] while retaining at least some objectivity. It may be, after all, that some things just are objectively true (or false) in the morality-fiction, just as in the Holmes-fiction.[38]

But this is not enough.[39] For there are infinitely many different fictions that can be told, and fictionalism lacks the resources to privilege one (or some) of them. Perhaps, in other words, in the morality-fiction cruelty is wrong, and this is quite objectively so. But there is some other fiction, call it the morality*-fiction, according to which cruelty is actually the single all-encompassing virtue (similarly, there is a Holmes*-fiction, where Holmes lives on Oxford St). Now, should a disagreement arise between a follower of morality and a follower of morality*, the fictionalist has no way of privileging morality over morality*, no way of rendering it objectively correct to follow morality rather than morality*, and so no way of rendering cruelty objectively wrong.[40] Now, perhaps there just aren't that many morality*-followers around. If so, and assuming for now *very* fictionalism-friendly assumptions about the individuation of fictions,[41] then this will not be a practical, political problem. But it will remain a theoretical one – for surely, we think that morality *is* privileged compared to morality*, and in a normatively relevant way.[42]

Now, it's not as if anything goes when it comes to fictions. Some fictions, for instance, are just better in some respects than others. And perhaps we can even say that some fictions are better – *sans phrase*, as it were – than others. Or perhaps in some other ways we have (in a certain context) reason to tell one story rather than another. So the fictionalist too can say that, say, we have reason to tell the morality-fiction rather than the morality*-one (this reason may or may not be related to the fact that it is the morality-fiction we *have* been telling).[43] But then, of course, this fictionalist has to give an account of this very normative statement (namely, that we have reason to tell this

[37] For the next few paragraphs, I am going to talk of morality rather than normativity, mostly because the argument of Chapter 2 was confined (pretty much; see the discussion in Chapter 4) to morality.

[38] Reynolds (2009, 327–8), for instance, makes a heroic effort to show some further constraints on what fictions can be told or on what can be told within a fiction (he uses here the apparatus of make-believe, rightly insisting that even with make-believe, there are admissible and inadmissible ways of going forward). But as he admits, and as I am about to emphasize in the text, still significant degrees of freedom remain.

[39] In the only place in their article in which they discuss objectivity, Nolan, Restall, and West (2005, 321) seem to say, if I understand them correctly, that the kind of fictionalist objectivity mentioned in the previous paragraph *is* quite enough. For the reason that follows in the text, I think they are wrong.

[40] The claim in the text should be qualified so as to make room for a fictionalist version of the reply on behalf of response-dependence theories I discussed in Chapter 2, section 2.3 (I thank Stephen Finlay for making me see this). The fictionalist may try to privilege the morality- over the morality*-fiction because it is better *in the morality-fiction*. Though this is a possible move, it is not a very promising one, I think, for the reasons discussed in section 2.3.

[41] Recall that one of the details we need from our fictionalist is a distinction between a disagreement within a fiction and the telling of an alternative fiction. The point in the text may depend on the plausibility of the way in which the fictionalist fills in the details here.

[42] For a somewhat similar point – though in the context of a discussion of a revisionary version of error theory, not fictionalism – see Lillehammer (2004, 108).

[43] See here Yablo's (2005) discussion of different possible developments of mathematical theories, with one alternative being more apt as a metaphor than the other.

story rather than that), and so she needs *this* to be objectively true, and so she needs to privilege the reasons-story over, say, the counter-reasons one,[44] and so on. You just can't accommodate objectivity while remaining a metanormative fictionalist all the way down.[45]

A similar point can be shown to undermine the possibility of normative judgments fictionalistically understood accommodating deliberation. For if there is no rational, normatively relevant way in which, for instance, reasons are preferred to counter-reasons, then all the deliberating agent is left with is the possibility of merely picking acting-on-reasons rather than on counter-reasons. Or perhaps the agent should simply think to herself something like, "Well, around here we follow the morality-fiction rather than the morality★-one." But then this fact will itself remain normatively arbitrary, and so unable to settle deliberation. Thus, someone who is a fictionalist all the way down cannot accommodate deliberation.

Can the fictionalist avoid both her problem with objectivity in the interpersonal case and her problem with deliberation in the intrapersonal case by relying on a fiction that is, as it were, *necessary* for us to tell? What, in other words, if we all necessarily find ourselves already telling the morality-fiction rather than the morality★-one? Does this help?[46] I don't see how it would. This is so not just because the idea of a necessary fiction seems to stretch the analogy with Holmes-like fictions too far,[47] but also because the nature of this necessity has to be either normative, or non-normative. If it is normative, it can solve the problems, but only at the price of generating the regress mentioned above. And if it is not normative, it doesn't generate the regress, but nor does it solve the objectivity and arbitrariness problems.

Here is another way of making my main point against fictionalism.[48] The fictionalist – or at least one kind of fictionalist[49] – challenges the robust realist to show what would be lost (for instance, in terms of taking morality seriously) if our

---

[44] Of which more in the next section.

[45] How about views that are fictionalist only some of the way down? They are rejected in Chapter 4 as under-motivated.

[46] The idea of a necessary fiction in this sense – where the in-the-fiction operator cannot be meaningfully cancelled – is closely related to Yablo's (1998) meaning-fictionalism and to Woodbridge's (2005) intrinsic pretense.

I am *really* not sure about this, but at times it seems that Scanlon's anti-metaphysical sort-of-realist view (which I discuss in the next section) should be understood as a terminological variance of *this* kind of fictionalism.

[47] Another thing we are entitled to get from our fictionalist is an account of how the implicit in-the-fiction operator works. It is perhaps plausible to say that almost always when we talk of Sherlock Holmes an in-the-fiction operator is included. But we know that it is cancelable, as in "Oh, he actually believes that Sherlock Holmes really exists, not merely in the fiction!" Indeed, there are also *implicit* ways of canceling the implicit in-the-fiction operator, as when we say "Sherlock Holmes is a fictional character." (This statement is true, I take it, but it is most certainly not true in the fiction – in the Holmes-fiction, Holmes is a flesh-and-blood person, not a fictional character at all.) It seems that such cancelability is a fairly central feature of in-the-fiction talk. The suggestion of a necessary or unavoidable fiction is barely intelligible.

[48] I thank Mark van Roojen for several challenges that helped me see it may be helpful to put things in the way that follows (as well as for the suggestion to compare fictionalism here with constructive empiricism).

[49] Namely, the fictionalist who emphasizes pretense rather than in-the-fiction operators.

engagement with normative truths is understood along some as-if lines. Perhaps, for instance, an analogy may be drawn with Bas van Fraassen's (1980) constructive empiricism about the empirical sciences. Perhaps, that is, deliberation no more requires belief in normative truths than doing science requires belief in theoretical entities. Perhaps in both cases *acceptance* is sufficient, where acceptance is understood as an attitude that is consistent with the absence of belief, indeed, even with a belief in the negation of the proposition accepted. Of course, if *acceptance* of normative beliefs suffices for deliberation, then the indispensability argument of Chapter 3 fails. Now, I will not here argue against constructive empiricism.[50] Rather, the points I've been making above against fictionalism should be seen as highlighting what is plausibly considered a disanalogy with the constructive-empiricism case, so that even if something like constructive empiricism can be made to work, still fictionalism about the normative cannot succeed. The crucial difference is that nothing *in* science is, as far as I know, sensitive to such views *about* science. This is why no problematic scientific statement follows from constructive empiricism. In the terms of the appendix to Chapter 2, constructive empiricism arguably conservatively extends science.[51] But the above thoughts about the morality- and morality*-fictions – together with the argument from IMPARTIALITY in Chapter 2 – show that this is precisely what is *not* going on in the case of the normative. Normative discourse – and more particularly moral discourse – most certainly *is* sensitive to such as-if thoughts *about* it, and in a way that makes the relevant kind of fictionalism highly implausible.[52] Hence the disanalogy.

Now, as you may have noticed – perhaps more clearly with regard to the application of the argument of Chapter 2 than to that of Chapter 3 – the arguments against fictionalism have normative premises. In Chapter 2, after all, I emphasized that the argument was one from the normative implications of objectivity (or lack thereof). So you may think that this causes a problem for the argument as an attempt to refute metanormative fictionalism. But this is not so. Recall that the fictionalism discussed in this subsection is not error-theoretic. Our fictionalist is happy to use an

---

[50] Full disclosure, though: I am not convinced. Surprised?

[51] Let me again emphasize how little I know about constructive empiricism, and so how qualified I want to be here. Perhaps what I say in the text is false, and if so, constructive empiricism rather clearly fails. My point here is that if it succeeds, there is an important disanalogy here between the scientific and the normative cases.

[52] How about indispensability, though? In Chapter 3 I developed (following Colyvan) an account of instrumental indispensability according to which something is instrumentally indispensable for a project just in case it cannot be eliminated without undermining (or at least sufficiently diminishing) whatever reason we had to engage in that project in the first place. One of the problems with endorsing some as-if relation to normative truths is that this would at the very least make deliberation much less attractive than it would otherwise have been, so that normative truths are instrumentally indispensable to deliberation, given this understanding of instrumental indispensability. Is there, then, here too a disanalogy with the case of constructive empiricism? The answer depends on whether constructive empiricism undermines – or at least sufficiently diminishes – whatever reason we had to engage in the scientific project in the first place. I would answer "yes", and reject constructive empiricism for this very reason. But I don't want to pretend that anything here is obvious.

implicit in-the-fiction operator and engage normative discourse with the rest of us. The crucial point is that if my arguments work, there is something special about the morality "fiction" compared to the more traditionally fictional Holmes-fiction. The content of the Holmes-fiction is in an intuitive sense independent of it *being* a fiction. Not so with the content of the morality "fiction". For its content is partly sensitive to the classification of certain claims as fictional. In the morality-fiction, in other words, true statements have one status (nothing like IMPARTIALITY applies), and statements that are only true-in-an-unprivileged-fiction have a different status (something like IMPARTIALITY sometimes applies). Furthermore, in the morality-"fiction" moral statements have the status that only true statements (and not merely true-in-a-fiction statements) have. And this means that we cannot coherently treat morality as a fiction. Fictionalism – *global* fictionalism, at least, of the kind that applies to all normative discourse – is false.[53]

This is a limited result. It does not entail Robust Realism, or anything like it. But it refutes non-error-theoretic fictionalism as an attempt to give the robust realist all she wants for a better ontological price. Of course, you may treat the unavailability of a satisfying metanormative fictionalism not as a reason to accept Robust Realism, but rather as further evidence that nothing can save morality and perhaps normativity from systematic error. Perhaps, in other words, error theory is the way to go.

5.2.2 Error theory

As you may have noticed, I have the philosophical temperament of an extremist. Compromise philosophical positions often seem to me like a philosophically under-motivated attempt to please everyone where a more clear-cut choice is called for. So it should not surprise you to find out that of all the non-robust-realist metaethical and metanormative options, it is a global metanormative error theory that, in a way, I find most respectable. Such error-theorists do not kid themselves about the commitments of normative discourse, and they proceed to boldly follow the argument from these commitments and the belief that they are unsatisfied to its natural, if extreme, conclusion.

The typical argument for an error theory thus proceeds by noticing a commitment of the target discourse (say, a commitment to the existence of an omnipotent, omni-benevolent being, or to Platonic mathematical objects, or to the convergence of the desires of all rational creatures, or to objective values), and then presenting an argument to the conclusion that this commitment is not satisfied (because of the problem of evil, or because there would be no way of explaining the reliability of our beliefs about

---

[53] Put in the terminology more commonly used in the context of fictionalism about mathematical objects, the argument in the text here amounts to the claims, first, that nothing like the premise of the "Oracle Argument" (according to which we would proceed as before if an oracle informed us that there were no abstract objects; see Burgess and Rosen (1997, 3); Eklund (2007, section 3.2 and the references there)) applies to the moral case, and second, that a part of the reason for this is itself moral.

Platonic mathematical objects,[54] or because it would be a miracle if the desires of all rational creatures converged,[55] or because objective values would be too queer[56]). Now, I am not here going to discuss the different arguments for a metaethical or a metanormative error theory – often, these are just versions of objections to Robust Realism and close views, and as such they are discussed elsewhere in this book. But the motivation for an error theory that is relevant here is clear enough: my interlocutor may think of the arguments of previous chapters as an elaborate argument establishing some of the commitments of moral and normative discourse; she may then treat the discussion in this chapter as showing that such commitments cannot be satisfied in a metaphysically naturalistic world; she can then plug in metaphysical naturalism as a premise (perhaps taken as basic, perhaps supported by some other arguments); and she may then conclude that the commitments of normative discourse are unsatisfiable,[57] and so that it is systematically erroneous. Is there anything I can say in reply to this way of treating my arguments?[58]

Well, the positive arguments for Robust Realism were *not*, after all, intended merely as attempts at fleshing out the commitments of moral and normative discourse. They were meant as attempts to *establish* Robust Realism. When someone puts forward an inference to the best explanation attempting to establish the existence of some theoretical entity, we do not treat her as merely fleshing out the commitments of a relevant scientific discourse. Rather, we take her to be presenting an at-least-initially powerful argument for the existence of the relevant theoretical entity. Similarly, my argument from deliberative indispensability (in Chapter 3) – if successful – positively supports Robust Realism, and not a weaker thesis (say, a tentative one about merely the commitments embedded in normative discourse). Similarly, the argument for objectivity in Chapter 2 assumed the *truth* of some version of IMPARTIALITY and some other normative judgments. I did not there settle for assuming the sort-of-sociological thesis

---

[54]   Field (1980).

[55]   Smith (1994, 164–77) believes that moral discourse is committed to such convergence, but he is optimistic about this commitment being satisfied. For my reasons for thinking that such a convergence would be miraculous – and so, for the suggestion that what more plausibly follows from Smith's analysis is an error theory – see my (2007b).

[56]   Mackie (1977, 38).

[57]   Depending on the modal nature of her commitment to metaphysical naturalism, she may conclude that these commitments *cannot* be satisfied (if naturalism is understood as a necessary truth), or merely that they *are* not satisfied (but may be satisfied in some other possible worlds, where naturalism is false).

[58]   There is a debate going on in this vicinity that I am going to ignore (except for this footnote). Error-theorists differ about how to proceed with regard to moral discourse – whether we should just do without it, or use it knowing full-well that it's systematically erroneous, or that we should from now on use the same words in some other way than the (erroneous) one we've been using them, though still somehow related to their traditional use (perhaps along fictionalist lines, thereby giving us revolutionary fictionalism), or some such. For representatives of this debate see Nolan, Restall, and West (2005, 310 and on), Garner (2007), Cuneo and Christy (2010, section 4), and Olson (forthcoming). I have two reasons to ignore this debate. First, it is to a large extent an internal debate among those already convinced of error theory, and so is of little interest in the context of this book. Second, to the extent that I understand this debate, pretty much all of it consists in empirical speculations about which consequences will follow if we speak in this or that way. I find it hard to get philosophically excited about such speculations.

that these were things we were committed to, or the somewhat more respectable-sounding conceptual thesis that these were things moral discourse was committed to. This argument too, then – again, if it works – establishes the objectivity of morality, not something weaker than this. The first line of response to the error-theoretic challenge in the previous paragraph, then, is simply to refer back to the positive arguments for Robust Realism from previous chapters.

I suspect, though, that you are not entirely happy with this way of responding to the error-theoretic challenge. The problem, you may think, is that the arguments of both Chapter 2 and 3 (and so also that of Chapter 4, which is parasitic on the preceding two) crucially depend on *normative* premises. This is clearest in the case of the argument from objectivity's first-order moral implications (in Chapter 2). As emphasized there, both the principle of IMPARTIALITY, and the intuitive judgments about where it plausibly does and where it plausibly does not apply, are straightforwardly moral judgments. And this, you may think, amounts to blatantly begging the question against the error-theorist. Using a moral premise in an argument that is supposed to refute a metaethical error theory is tantamount to using "But the bible says there's a God" as a premise in an argument for theism, or perhaps to using "But clearly, *she* is a witch" as a premise in an argument against a meta-witch error theory. Similarly, though perhaps not as clearly, for the indispensability argument in Chapter 3. For recall that a crucial part in that argument was played by the premise that the deliberative project is rationally non-optional for us, a paradigmatic normative judgment. Doesn't this argument too, then, beg the question, if not against all of its targets, at least against the metanormative error-theorist?

As if this is not bad enough, it may be thought that an even worse result follows. For either it is legitimate to use normative and moral premises in an argument against an error theory or it isn't. If it isn't, then my arguments all fail miserably (again, at least against the error-theorist). And if it *is* somehow legitimate to use (say) moral premises in an argument against a metaethical error theory, then my arguments, far worse than failing miserably, are just utterly uninteresting: after all, if we're entitled to use moral premises in such arguments, why not go for the following much more straightforward argument, with the *much, much* more plausible premise:

> The infliction of horrible pain on random victims is morally wrong; therefore, it's true that the infliction of horrible pain on random victims is morally wrong; therefore, some simple moral judgments are true; therefore, a metaethical error theory is false.

There is, of course, something suspicious about this argument (more on this shortly), which I'll call the Simple Moorean Argument,[59] but in what way is it *worse* than my arguments, which also rely on moral (or normative) premises?

---

[59] Olson (2010) calls a similar argument "The Moorean Argument". For a general discussion of Moorean arguments – in metaethics and elsewhere – see McPherson (2009), and the references there.

To see the advantage of my arguments over the Simple Moorean Argument, consider its mathematical analogue. Suppose, then, that attempting to refute an error theory about mathematical objects, someone argues as follows:

3+5=8; therefore, it's true that 3+5=8; therefore, some simple mathematical statements are true; therefore, an error theory about numbers is false.

Regardless of the suspicion about begging the question (to which I return shortly), it is hard to get excited about this argument. This is so, I think, because any remotely plausible error theory would have to explain why it is OK to continue doing mathematics (and accepting the premise of this little argument) even though there are no mathematical objects. Perhaps – again, following Field (1980) – it would point to the advantages of doing science with numbers (say, because this, compared to doing science without numbers, greatly simplifies inferences), and to the dangerlessness of so doing (perhaps because mathematics conservatively extends physics). And with this in mind, the mathematical analogue of the Simple Moorean Argument loses much of its force (though not all of it, a point to which I return). The error-theorist, in other words, allows us to say things very close to the premise of that argument, and indeed explains the intuitive appeal of that premise. And so the argument loses much of its force. What would be more exciting, of course, is if it could be shown, for instance, that something in the way we do (or should do) mathematics is sensitive to our endorsing a meta-mathematics error theory. I don't know if this can be done in the mathematical case. But this is precisely what the arguments of Chapters 2–4 attempt to do in the metanormative case. And so, if they succeed, they *are* after all more exciting than the Simple Moorean Argument.

Exciting or not, though, the worry about question-begging remains. What can be said in defense of the legitimacy of using moral premises in an argument against moral error theory?

Here is a related question. We all know that one person's *modus ponens* is another's *modus tollens*. Given a valid argument of this sort, then, when should you take it as a *modus ponens* (and proceed to accept its initially implausible conclusion), and when should you take it as a modus tollens (and proceed to reject at least one of its initially plausible premises)? I would have loved to have more to say in reply to this question, but all I have is as follows: If you are (justifiably) more confident, prior to thinking about the relevant argument, in the conjunction of the premises than you are in the negation of the conclusion, treat the argument as an instance of *modus ponens*. If you are (justifiably) more confident, prior to thinking about the argument, in the denial of its conclusion than in the conjunction of its premises, treat it as a modus tollens. This is just a long way of saying that given a set of propositions you believe, and a proof of their inconsistency, the one to be tossed aside is the one in which you are (justifiably) least confident. This does not seem like profound advice, but it seems sound nonetheless.[60]

---

[60] I am ignoring here possible complications regarding the scope of the relevant epistemic operator (is it that you should [if q is the one you're least confident in, discard q], or is it that if q is the one you're least

Return to my arguments for Robust Realism understood now as arguments specifically against error theory. Or indeed, consider the Simple Moorean Argument: it is obviously valid; are you more confident in its premise (The infliction of horrible pain on random victims is morally wrong), or in the denial of its conclusion (error theory)? If, like me, you are more confident in the former, it seems like you are entitled to conclude to the denial of error theory.[61]

I cannot see what is wrong with this way of vindicating the relevant arguments, even the more problematic-sounding Simple Moorean Argument. And yet, I do not quite find myself believing this vindication. Let me try and do more, then. This will not be so much a solution, as it will be an attempt at placing the discussion here in the context of broader epistemological discussions. Once seen in this context, I will argue, we should be reasonably confident that the arguments in previous chapters do not objectionably beg the question (or commit some other hideous logical crime) against the error-theorist.

The general epistemological context I have in mind is that of the discussion of bootstrapping and easy knowledge.[62] Aren't we entitled to form beliefs, for instance, by employing perception, without first having an independently justified belief in the reliability of perception?[63] If so, can't we then bootstrap, using something like the following inference:

> This tomato appears red to me (by introspection); This tomato is red (by perception); So my color-perception got it right this time; (Similarly for other things); Therefore, my color perception is reliable.

But there *must* be something wrong with such bootstrapping, the thought goes. Perhaps we can somehow come to know that our color perception is reliable. But if such knowledge is attainable, it surely is not attainable in *this* way. This would render attaining it far too easy. And yet, I am inclined to think that at least some cases of easy knowledge must after all be possible. Indeed, I believe that accepting this problematic result is the only alternative to skepticism.[64] Let us postpone a fuller epistemological discussion for another occasion, then: for now, assume with me that bootstrapping is sometimes legitimate, that some knowledge is easy. I am happy to pay the price of asking you to make this assumption – namely, to acknowledge that the power of my

---

confident in, you should discard *q*). I don't think that these complications are relevant here. For an attempt to utilize these complications in an argument against putting things here in terms of confidence, see McPherson (2009, 5).

[61] If you were convinced by the quick discussion above of the mathematical analogue of the Simple Moorean Argument, what this means is that given a plausible error theory, your comparative confidence in the argument's premise and the denial of its conclusion may change; and then, arguments like the ones developed in the earlier chapters of this book may be more of use than the Simple Moorean Argument.

[62] See, for instance, Cohen (2002), Van Cleve (2003), and Vogel (2008).

[63] Here see also the discussion in Chapter 3, section 3.4.

[64] Again, see Van Cleve (2003).

arguments against an error theory depends (to an extent, at least) on the truth of this most general epistemological assumption.

Now, the case we're talking about – an argument against a metaethical error theory employing a moral premise – is not exactly the case of bootstrapping from the previous paragraph. There, the conclusion we reach by way of bootstrapping is about the reliability of the belief-forming method employed to reach one of the argument's premises. This is not precisely what is going on here. But the two kinds of argument, I now want to suggest, are alike when it comes to question-begging. First, both give rise to a strong feeling that some objectionable question-begging is going on. And second, in both cases, this is probably because if you're not already inclined to accept the argument's conclusion before considering the argument, you are not likely to accept at least one of the premises of the argument (in the moral case: unless you are already inclined to reject an error theory before considering this argument, you won't accept the premise that inflicting horrible pain on random victims is wrong; in the bootstrapping case: unless you are already inclined to accept the reliability of perception before considering the argument, you won't accept the premise that the tomato is in fact red). In the ways that are of epistemological significance, then, the arguments are alike.[65] And this means that – on the assumption that at least sometimes bootstrapping is epistemically legitimate – we cannot rule out all arguments of the kind I'm using either. Perhaps there is, then, a kind of question-begging going on here. But it's not the kind that takes away the argument's force against error theory.[66]

If you are reminded of Moore's "Proof of an External World" (1939), this is no coincidence.[67] The recent interest in the success of Neo-Moorean strategies for coping with skeptical challenges is of course also relevant here (though again, not completely directly, as the error-theorist is no skeptic). And the current

---

[65] In this context, see Wright's (2004) discussion of "I–II–III arguments".

[66] For the uncompromising insistence that this kind of question-begging is always objectionable, and that "Beliefs cannot refute a theory that predicts and explains those very beliefs", see Sinnott-Armstrong (2008, 825). For criticism, suggesting the line of thought in the text, see Copp (2008a, 817).

Olson (2010, section 2) also insists that Moorean (and similar) arguments against error theories cannot succeed. He rightly emphasizes here the fact that error-theorists typically come up with debunking explanations of our relevant beliefs. But this does not suffice to undermine the points in the text. For the same is true of the most general skeptical hypotheses: the believer in a brain-in-a-vat hypothesis also offers a debunking explanation of our perceptual beliefs, etc. Now, as Olson emphasized in correspondence, these debunking explanations may – and probably do – differ in their plausibility. And so once again we need to compare overall plausibility points. Ultimately, the reason debunking explanations of Moorean beliefs about morality are unconvincing is, I think, that so much can be said for Robust Realism, and that so little remains of the objections to it.

Olson also ties the force of such debunking explanations to considerations of parsimony. I agree that something like parsimony must be invoked here if such arguments against realism are to work. And the argument of Chapter 3 is supposed to show that Robust Realism is not threatened by plausible versions of a parsimony requirement.

[67] Nor is it a coincidence, I'm pretty sure, that the robust metaethical realist of *Principia Ethica* (1903) and the author of "Proof of an External World" (1939) is one and the same. But it's not at all clear to me exactly how these two are related philosophically (it isn't even clear to me that they *are* related other than, perhaps, by philosophical temperament).

epistemological controversies over Neo-Mooreanism,[68] easy knowledge, and related epistemological debates are evidence of the complexities of the issues here. So I do not want to pretend that anything is simple or obvious here. But what I want to insist on is, first, that it's not at all clear what if anything is problematic with an argument against a metanormative error theory that employs a normative premise; second, that the epistemological issues here are best seen as instances of some of the most general problems in normative epistemology; and third, that once this is seen, the suggestion that there's obviously something flawed with such arguments loses much of its appeal.[69]

At the end of the day, you have to ask yourself what it is that seems plausible to you, given the entirety of evidence and arguments available to you, and everything else you believe. At the end of the day, then, this will be the test for the error theory as well. If you find this – and the preceding discussion – less than fully satisfactory, this again supports the point I started my discussion of error theory with: the error-theorist, it seems to me, is the robust realist's most respectable opponent.

5.3 Quietism

A number of closely related worries – not so much about realism of whatever kind, as about the debate in which it is one of the competing views – are sometimes grouped together under the heading "quietism".[70] These worries, applied to the discussion of the normative, include doubts about the intelligibility of metanormative discussion; claims that significant metanormative discussion is impossible; assertions that metanormative debates – if at all intelligible – can only be decided by engaging in first-order, normative discourse itself; claims that apparently metanormative debate *just is* normative debate in disguise; the thought that the practice of engaging in normative discourse (perhaps like other practices) needs no justification that is external to it, and that it is anyway impossible to supply one; and so on.

Such worries[71] are expressed by thinkers from very different traditions, and with very different other philosophical commitments, as different as Dworkin and

---

[68] See, for instance, Pryor (2000); Pritchard (2007).

[69] Already Ewing (1947, 33) noted that such arguments may be legitimate. See also Huemer (2006, 115–17). McPherson (2009) argues that Moorean arguments against metaethical error theories are less convincing than Moorean arguments against, for instance, external world skepticism or idealism. His argument is based on his diagnosis of what it is that makes Moorean arguments attractive when indeed they are. For reasons I cannot detail here, I do not accept his diagnosis.

[70] I've heard several of the people whom I group together under this title express unhappiness with the term "quietism" (Tom Nagel and Ronald Dworkin, for instance, friendly threatened to reciprocate by calling the opposition "loudists" or "shoutists"). Let me emphasize, then, that I don't use the word "quietism" as a pejorative, and I don't expect any of the argumentative work needed here to be done by the choice of a name for the family of views about to be criticized. And let me also note that the term "quietism" is sometimes used with somewhat different meanings than the one I give it in the text. See, for instance, Wedgwood (2007, 7).

[71] To an extent, at least, and as will become clearer later on, the natural context of such doubts is similar doubts about metaphysics in general. See, for instance, the discussion of deflationism about metaphysics in Manley (2009) and the references there.

Blackburn, Nagel and Cavell, McDowell and Putnam, the Positivists and Rorty. These philosophers differ not only in what motivates their quietist inclinations, but also in what they think follows from quietism. Dworkin (1996 and forthcoming), for instance – and to an extent also Nagel, Parfit, and Scanlon – think that (what I call) quietist observations serve to vindicate our confidence in our own normative beliefs and in some fairly robust version of realism; Blackburn (e.g. 1993) thinks his quietist observations serve to strengthen the case for his Quasi-Realist Projectivism; McDowell (1985) seems to think that similar points allow for a comfortable middle ground in the realism debate, a metaphysically uncommitted, objectivist yet non-Platonist, laid-back kind of realism.[72] It is unclear to me whether the fact that such a variety of philosophers – disagreeing on just about everything else – nevertheless seem to express the very same quietist worries should count as evidence for the seriousness of the worries, or as reason for suspicions regarding their intelligibility or determinacy.

I cannot, of course, discuss all these related worries in detail here, much less can I do justice to the relevant work of all these philosophers. Let me briefly address, then, just quietist worries that seem to show that there is some confusion in the metaphysical commitments I am willing to take on board on behalf of Robust Realism.

5.3.1 Keeping it internal

Let me start, then, with the "no-vantage-point" intuition. So long as the relevant practice – call the one relevant here "the normative practice" – is itself acknowledged to be contingent, or at least – even if necessary in some way – *rationally* arbitrary, then I reject the thesis that it needs no justification external to it. Indeed, a view according to which *our* normative practice determines the only criteria of correctness there are is subjectivist in exactly the sense rejected in Chapter 2.[73]

A closely related point may be made in a more general ontological context. Thus, Scanlon has recently put forward a more detailed ontological discussion,[74] where he argues that in general – not just in the metanormative context – the answers to existence questions are fully determined by the standards internal to the relevant

---

[72] Here see also McDowell (1987, 218).

[73] For a related criticism of Dworkin's quietism, see Raz (2001, 126).

"Philosophy cannot take refuge in reduced ambitions. It is after eternal and nonlocal truth, even though we know that is not what we are going to get" (Nagel, 1986, 10). Nagel himself at times sounds like a quietist of sorts (see, for instance, Nagel (1986, 139) and (1997, 101)). I suspect there is a genuine tension in Nagel's thought about these matters. For a detailed attempt to read the Nagel of *The View from Nowhere* (1986) as a non-quietist, see Svavarsdóttir (2001). I return to Nagel below.

[74] See Scanlon (2009, lecture 2), where Scanlon develops themes that are already introduced in his (1998, 62–3). The discussion that follows of Scanlon's view greatly benefited from email exchanges with Scanlon himself, and with Tristram McPherson.

Scanlon has informed me that he intends to revise his text, and so it's possible that some of the points in the text will no longer apply as they stand to the published version. I take it, though, that the main features of his view and arguments will not undergo a revolutionary change.

domain, so long as no conflicts are generated[75] with other related domains. Thus, numbers exist, and all that it takes for numbers to exist is that claims quantifying over them are licensed by the internal standards of mathematical discourse, together with the absence of any conflict with some other domain (like the scientific, empirical one). Witches do not exist, because even if claims quantifying over witches are licensed by the standards internal to witch-discourse, conflicts *are* generated with the general empirical, scientific discourse (because witch-discourse licenses causal claims, or claims that have causal implications). Getting back to the normative, then: all that it takes for normative reasons to exist is that claims quantifying over them are licensed by the standards internal to normative discourse, and that no conflicts arise between normative discourse and the standards internal to some other domain, like the empirical, scientific one. These conditions are rather obviously met, and so normative reasons exist. But, on this anti-metaphysical view, putting forward this metaphysically looking claim – that reasons exist – just comes down to claiming that some normative statements are (perhaps non-reductively) true. Nothing more metaphysical needs or indeed can be said or done,[76] and in particular there is no coherent further, more robust sense in which things can (not) exist. Such a view is perhaps not quietist through and through: Scanlon does not deny the coherence or even interest of some metanormative discussions and arguments, and he engages them himself. But it is at least quietist (in a sense) about the more metaphysical parts of metanormative discourse.

To see the problem with this way of doing ontology, notice that very little distinguishes this minimalistically realist view of (say) mathematical discourse from some versions of fictionalism. Start with the error-theoretic version of fictionalism (roughly modeled on Field's fictionalism), according to which mathematical discourse is committed to the existence of sort-of-Platonic abstract objects; such objects do not exist; mathematical discourse is therefore systematically erroneous; but it is nevertheless in perfect order as it is, because it is internally consistent, and has the right kind of relations with other discourses we are interested in (in Field's case, it conservatively extends empirical science, while also being useful in facilitating inferences of empirical use). On such a fictionalist view, then, claims quantifying over numbers are licensed by the standards internal to the mathematical domain; there are no conflicts between mathematical discourse and the empirical sciences; and basically, all is well with mathematics (so that mathematicians need not worry about the ontological debate). What, then, is the difference between such a view and Scanlon's? Well, they differ on the truth-value of the claim "numbers exist" and of claims that entail it. But at this point it is hard to view this as anything but a terminological difference: both views,

[75] Scanlon talks here about implications from one domain to another, or about conclusions in one domain that are licensed by those in another. But I don't think that this is the best way to capture what he's after. I think his thought here is better captured by asking whether a certain domain conservatively extends another, in the sense discussed earlier in this book (in the Appendix to Chapter 2). But this point will not be of significance in my criticism of Scanlon in the text.
[76] In this context, see also Dworkin's (1996) mockery directed at the so-called moron view.

after all, agree that positive existence claims are licensed by the internal standards of mathematics; similarly, both can agree that they do not satisfy some external standard (say, that of causal efficacy). It's just that Scanlon uses "exist" in a way that is not committed to this further standard, and the fictionalist uses "exist" in a more committed kind of way. We can use small-letter "exist" to denote soft, licensed-by-internal-standards existence, and capital-letter "EXIST" to stand for metaphysically heavy, Platonistically friendly existence. We can now say that the fictionalist (of this kind) and Scanlon agree that it's not true that numbers EXIST.[77] They also agree that numbers unproblematically exist. What they disagree about, then, is first, how the natural-language word "exist" is used – roughly, whether it stands for existing or for EXISTING. And second, they disagree on the commitments of mathematical discourse, namely, whether it is committed to the EXISTENCE of numbers (etc.).[78] And if we now consider a non-error-theoretic, hermeneutic kind of fictionalism – perhaps one according to which mathematical statements are preceded by an implicit "in-the-fiction" operator and can thus be literally true – of these two differences only the first one remains, and Scanlon's existence seems equivalent to this fictionalist's in-the-fiction EXISTENCE. Having given up on any metaphysical or other domain-external constraints (except for the ones against conflicting implications), mathematical and normative discourses remain on Scanlon's view as free-floating as they are on fictionalist views.

This should already get us somewhat worried – a supposedly realist view that is (pretty much) a notational variant of a fictionalist view seems not to be very realist at all. But we should not treat classifying isms as of intrinsic importance. The more important point is that philosophical objections are almost always closed under notational variance. So Scanlon's view, we can now confidently predict, is vulnerable to the objections such fictionalist views are vulnerable to.

In the metanormative context, perhaps the most useful way of making this clear is by imagining another discourse (or perhaps another community engaging in it), what may be called the counter-normative discourse.[79] The standards internal to the counter-normative domain license claims quantifying over counter-reasons. Those engaged in that discourse treat counter-reasons much as we treat reasons. For instance, they take them to be relevant to their practical deliberation, or perhaps counter-deliberation, in roughly the same way we take reasons to be relevant to ours: when they judge that there is a counter-reason to φ, they tend to φ, to criticize those who do not φ, and so

---

[77] Though for different reasons. The fictionalist understands this claim, and argues that it's false. Scanlon (as he explained to me) thinks that this claim is unintelligible.

[78] For more detail on this general point, though in a different context, see my "Epistemicism and Nihilism about Vagueness: What's the Difference?" (2007c).

[79] What follows is inspired by discussions of counter-induction, and the use to which counter-induction is sometimes put in criticizing analytic and circular justifications (or "justifications") of induction. Here I also benefited from discussions with Tristram McPherson and from reading his very closely related "Against Quietist Normative Realism" (2011).

on. But their judgments about counter-reasons would sound very weird to us (once translated into reasons-talk). For instance, they think that it is rather obvious that that an action will cause the agent pain is counter-reason *for* performing it.

Do counter-reasons exist? I think that Scanlon is committed to an affirmative answer here.[80] Quantifying over counter-reasons is licensed by the standards internal to the counter-normative domain. That domain is, we may safely assume, as consistent as our normative domain is. Furthermore, just as the normative domain is not in conflict with the empirical, scientific one (or so we here assume), neither is the counter-normative domain in such conflict. And this, after all, exhausts Scanlon's criteria for existence. So counter-reasons, Scanlon seems committed to concluding, are as ontologically respectable as reasons are.[81] Of course, they are not as *normatively* respectable as reasons are. And so those acting on them are to be criticized for not acting on the reasons that apply to them. But then again, reasons aren't as *counter*-normatively respectable as counter-reasons are, and we may be counter-criticizable for failing to act on the counter-reasons that apply to us.

Borrowing from Tristram McPherson (2011), we can put this point another way. The real question is not one of *formal* normativity, the generation of correctness conditions. This is something that reasons and counter-reasons do equally well. The real question is about generating (or reflecting) the *right* criteria of correctness, those to which we owe our allegiance. What we want to say, of course, is that reasons do that, and counter-reasons do not.[82] And indeed, I am insisting that no such symmetry between reasons and counter-reasons is tenable. Reasons, on my view, exist; counter-reasons do not. An error theory about counter-reasons is true, but not about reasons. But Scanlon's view, I argue, lacks the resources to reject the false reasons–counter-reasons symmetry.[83] And so Scanlon's view is false.

This objection can be put in terms of the positive arguments for Robust Realism from previous chapters. Once the symmetry (on such a view) between reasons and counter-reasons has been noticed, this view does not supply the kind of objectivity

---

[80] And in email correspondence, Scanlon was kind enough to confirm this.

[81] Remember, Scanlon could deny the existence of witches because of the conflicts between witch-discourse and scientific discourse, conflicts that arise because of the causal commitments of witch-discourse. The point in the text can be made also by noting that Scanlon lacks the resources needed to deny the existence of *weak*-witches, creatures that are much like witches except that they are causally inert. He can, of course, (quite plausibly) deny our interest in talking about them. But Scanlon does not believe that existence is interest-dependent, and neither should you.

[82] McPherson (2011) speaks here of reasons and shmeasons. And see here also Parfit's (2011, vol. 2, for instance section 88) related distinction between normativity in the rule-implying and the reason-implying senses.

[83] Scanlon is obviously sympathetic to Carnap's famous discussion of internal and external questions (1956), to which he refers (he also draws several distinctions between his own view and Carnap's, but ones that are not as far as I can see relevant here). But I do not think that Scanlon is willing to endorse Carnap's radical conclusions. For Carnap, I take it, would gladly acknowledge the theoretical reasons–counter-reasons symmetry, and proceed to ask merely pragmatic questions about which framework it would be more to our advantage to employ. I take it Scanlon is not willing to accept this conclusion – no realist should.

argued for in Chapter 2. And when deliberating, one of the questions you may ask yourself is whether to "go" with reasons or with counter-reasons. And again, Scanlon's anti-metaphysical view has nothing by way of an adequate reply.

I hope the relation to fictionalism is clear. As has already been argued in the previous section, fictionalist views lack – unless supplemented by other, non-fictionalist elements – the resources to discriminate among fictions: we can tell the normative story, or the counter-normative one. Both are – as far as anything internal to fictionalism is concerned – eligible fictions to be told. Scanlon's view, we just saw, suffers from a similar flaw. And this result confirms the suspicion that Scanlon's view – far from being a fairly robust kind of realism – is very close to being a notational variant of fictionalism.

More needs to be said here, of course. For one thing, more needs to be said about how domains or discourses are to be individuated. Given the centrality to views such as Scanlon's of the distinction between standards that are internal and those that are external to a domain, more could be hoped for by way of elaboration of this crucial point. Perhaps, for instance, Scanlon can try to resist the counter-normative domain by understanding it as a part of the normative domain, or by understanding both as a part of some more general domain, or some such. It is hard for me to see how this can be done – certainly, nothing Scanlon says about how domains are to be understood and individuated suggests the details needed for such a reply.[84] But a fuller critical discussion must await here a fuller presentation of the view criticized.

Or perhaps against the counter-reasons point Scanlon can argue that when I ask (somewhat roughly) whether our allegiance is owed to reasons or to counter-reasons, my question already implicitly asks for reasons rather than counter-reasons, and so can be straightforwardly answered (assuming, perhaps, that there are reasons to act on reasons). Perhaps this point can be strengthened by the further claim that the attempt to ask whether we should go with reasons or counter-reasons from outside, as it were, without being already committed to reasons (or to counter-reasons?) is confused.[85] I don't think that this is so – at least not if we are here in the business of vindicating reasons, showing them to be somehow privileged compared to counter-reasons and the like.[86] But here too further details must await a fuller, more careful development of the quietist worry (though see the discussion of unintelligibility, in the next subsection).

Of course, perhaps I'm wrong, and reasons do not after all exist. The point I want to make here is that the objection to this anti-metaphysical kind of quietism would still survive if that were so. For even if I am wrong in saying that reasons exist and

---

[84] Scanlon says that domains are partly constituted by "a certain number of things taken to be settled truths that employ this concept, and accepted procedures for settling questions employing these concepts"(Scanlon (2009), lecture 2). If so, it seems clear that the normative and the counter-normative are two distinct domains in his sense.

[85] As I see things, this is what at the end of the day Velleman and I disagree about, when it comes to my shmagency challenge to his (and others') constitutivism. See my "Shmagency Revisited" (2010b), and the references there.

[86] Again, see "Shmagency Revisited".

counter-reasons do not, still it seems clear to me that we are *committed* to this being so. In other words, even if the considerations above do not (all by themselves) defeat an error theory, they do defeat something like Scanlon's view, understood as an attempt to flesh out the commitments we already hold dear. In this respect, then, this section ends where it started: the attempt to go metaphysically minimalist, just like the attempt to argue that no external justification for our practices is needed – that it somehow suffices that they are indeed *our* practices – fails to take our normative and metanormative commitments seriously.[87]

5.3.2 Unintelligibility

Perhaps the point, then, is not that external justification or grounding for normative discourse is unnecessary, but that this way of putting things is unintelligible. By asking for such practice-independent justification, the thought seems to be, we are already trying, confused as we are, to step outside ourselves, look at the universe from nowhere, view everything from no point of view. And, as the last formulation perhaps makes clear, this very attempt is deeply confused, perhaps even incoherent. The idea of practice-independent justification – or any other practice-independent discussion, including a metaphysical one – is inherently confused. Applied to our context, this line of thought suggests that metanormative discussion is impossible.[88] Rather, it is a confused attempt to discuss the normative practice from without, from no normative point of view. And this is just as confused here as it is elsewhere.[89]

[87] Parfit (2011, e.g. 480) defends the claim that while normative facts exist, they exist only in a non-ontological sense. This may seem like a view that is importantly different from Scanlon's in a way relevant to my objections to Scanlon's view in the text. But in fact I don't think that this is so. Why does it matter, we can ask, whether normative facts exist in an ontological or a non-ontological sense? In Parfit's texts, I found only two ways in which this is supposed to matter. One is by discharging the worry that I will call in Chapter 6 the Sheer Queerness worry. But I will there reject this worry without assuming a non-ontological sense of existence. The other way in which it matters that – so Parfit claims – normative facts exist non-ontologically is that this makes an a priori epistemology for them acceptable (as it presumably isn't for our knowledge of things that exist more heavily, in the ontological sense). But this sounds very close to (though not identical with) Scanlon's insistence that all that is needed for knowledge of such things is supplied by the standards internal to the relevant domain. And so I think that my objections in the text to this part of Scanlon's view apply – with minor changes, perhaps – to Parfit's view as well.

[88] I've heard people – indeed, some of the people whose views I discuss here under the characterization of quietism – talk in terms such as "there just *is* no further question about the existence of normative properties, or numbers" (some statements along these lines can be found in Scanlon (2009, lecture 2), for instance). It's not clear how to understand this way of talking. After all, what are the criteria for existence of questions that are presupposed here? (Are these people – suspicious as they are of metaphysics in general – seriously putting forward their view in terms of a denial of the *existence* of certain questions?) My only way of making sense of such claims is that what appears to be a question of the kind mentioned here (perhaps external questions, or some such) are semantically defective, or perhaps in some other way unintelligible.

Parfit (2011, vol. 2, section 113) is more careful here. He thinks that the questions about the existence of normative properties are just *ambiguous* as between an ontological sense of "exist" (and then the answer is "no"), and a non-ontological one (and then the answer is "yes").

[89] This, I take it, is one central line of thought leading Dworkin (forthcoming) to his version of quietism: thus, he often asks such rhetorical questions – Well, if these statements and questions aren't understood as first-order normative ones, how else can they be understood? – seemingly implying that they cannot, and so

I want to make three points in response to this line of thought. First, to the extent that I understand the considerations that tempt philosophers in this direction, I find them unconvincing. But I cannot hope to discuss this point seriously here.[90] Let me just note that there is nothing obvious about such claims, that they need to be established, and that I am not sure this can be done (much less am I sure it has already been done). Second, whatever force this quietist intuition has, it has it only in its most global version. Surely, we *can* step outside local, specific practices, and still judge them from within our most general point of view. So local practices can be challenged externally without falling into unintelligibility. And our normative practice may be local in this way; at least, it remains to be shown that it is not. So perhaps the metanormative debate can be saved consistently with this most general quietism.[91] Third, I suspect that Fine is right when he writes: "the fact that a notion appears to make sense is strong *prima facie* evidence that it does make sense" (2001, 13).[92] Consider, for instance, the arguments for and against Robust Realism throughout this essay. Are they all confused pseudo-issues?[93] Surely, they *seem* to make sense.[94] And this is strong evidence, I think, that they *do* make sense.[95] At the very least – and here I return to the first point above – some strong argument is needed if we are to be convinced otherwise.

are (as attempts at doing metaethics, not ethics) unintelligible. Dworkin also mentions another line of thought leading him to his quietism – something starting from Hume's Principle (no implications from an *is* to an *ought*). I think that his attempt at reconstructing an argument for quietism from Hume's Principle is multiply flawed, but I will not give the details here. I do, however, think that the most charitable reading of this attempt at an argument takes us back to the unintelligibility point criticized in the text.

[90] Nevertheless, a point I cannot resist making: suppose it's true that practices neither need nor have external justifications, and that seemingly external questions about them are unintelligible. Doesn't this point apply, then, to the metaphysical or philosophical practice itself, and in particular to the practice metaethicists engage in? Wouldn't it be an instance of philosophical discrimination to subject the practice of metaphysicians to the very kind of criticism one denies is either possible or, even if possible, legitimate elsewhere? A generalized version of this objection can be raised against Carnap's (1956) claim that external questions are unintelligible (unless understood pragmatically) and that this undermines metaphysics. Why can't there be – even on Carnap's general view – a metaphysical framework, just as (un)respectable theoretically as other frameworks? For a related objection to (general) quietism, put in terms of self-defeat, see Cassam (1986, 455). Scanlon (2009) mentions this objection, but I do not fully understand his reply to it: he seems to say either that there is no metaphysical domain, or that all that can be said in that discourse is the kind of things that he says, namely, that the truth-value of ontological claims is entirely determined by standards internal to the relevant domains; and he suggests that these two ways of putting things come down to the same thing.

[91] Joyce (2001, 47) makes this point against Carnap, and Leiter (2001b, 70–1) against Dworkin.

[92] For a similar point, see Zangwill (1992, 160).

[93] For similar points, see Shafer-Landau (2010).

[94] A possible claim here is that they *do* make sense, but that they are misunderstood by their proponents as *meta*ethical. I return to this line of thought below.

[95] Here is how Nagel expresses doubts about claims regarding the unintelligibility of apparently intelligible questions: "... if a demonstration that some question is unreal leaves us still wanting to ask it, then something is wrong with the argument, and more work needs to be done" (Nagel, 1979, x). On the other hand, arguments like those in the text may not convince unintelligibility-thinkers, for, as David Lewis (1986, 203 n. 5) once put it, "any competent philosopher who does not understand something will take care not to understand anything else whereby it might be explained".

5.3.3 Undecidability

Perhaps quietism is best understood, then, as a claim not about the unintelligibility of apparently intelligible debates, but rather about the impossibility of deciding them.[96] If this is a point about the impossibility of conclusive proof, perhaps it is well-taken (though this too remains to be shown; certainly, it remains to be conclusively proven). But in the normative case as elsewhere we have learned to settle for less. And it seems highly implausible that these matters – now admitted to be intelligible – do not admit even of good arguments, arguments that give at least some reason to believe, say, Robust Realism or its denial. Again consider some of the arguments for Robust Realism in this book, and some of the objections to Robust Realism: do all of these arguments fail completely, in that they do not provide even the faintest support for their respective conclusions? This seems to me highly implausible, and very strong argument is needed in order to convince us that this is indeed so. (Needless to say, such argument is going to have to be much stronger than any supposed metanormative one, or else the latter's putative impotence is going to convict the former as well.)

5.3.4 It's all first-order after all

So maybe quietism is best understood not so much as the denial of the intelligibility of metanormative debates or as the claim that no metanormative argument carries any force, but rather as a claim about the nature of such arguments. Perhaps what is crucial here is that apparently metanormative arguments are really normative themselves.[97] What is apparently a detached, normatively neutral meta-discourse is thus folded back into the normative discourse itself. And such claims are supported mostly, I think, by examples of supposedly metanormative issues that can be shown to be normative, or at least to have normative implications.[98]

---

[96] This is what Fine (2001, 13) calls methodological quietism. And Prichard's (1912) worry about moral philosophy may be rather similar. Perhaps this is why he is sometimes thought of as a quietist.

[97] This, I think, is the intuition most strongly influencing Dworkin, Scanlon, Kramer, and perhaps also Nagel (when in a quietist mood). In a very different (not robustly realist) way, it is also very central for Blackburn, and perhaps also for Gibbard (after his conversion to quasi-realism). Sometimes quietist positions are really the combination of several points mentioned in the text. They can state that metanormative questions are good ones when they are understood internally, but that they are confused – resting on a false presupposition perhaps, or maybe even unintelligible or semantically defective – if understood (or "understood") otherwise. Though in certain respects more complicated and subtle, such combined positions are still vulnerable to the objections in the text.

[98] As I read Dworkin's (1996), his discussion systematically conflates these two: he repeatedly shows (or attempts to show) that a metaethical issue or controversy has ethical implications, and he then takes himself to have shown that metaethics just is a part of first-order moral discourse. But this, of course, is a mistake: where I come from (and not only there), religious discourse has political implications, but this doesn't show that religion and politics are one. For this point see McPherson (2008, 5). (I think that Kramer's (2009) recent elaboration of this general Dworkinian theme suffers from a similar flaw.) In conversation, though, Dworkin insisted that he doesn't take such implications to entail identity of discourses or domains. Rather, what he takes to entail this is if there are implications from one putative discourse *all by itself* to another. This is an improvement, of course. But it is still not good enough, because, first, this too is just not how we

It would not suffice for this kind of quietism that *some* apparently metanormative arguments and issues turn out to be normative ones. Rather, it is necessary that *all* so turn out. So consider all the arguments in this book, or indeed any other argument you've come across when reading metaethics (or "metaethics"). Are *all* of them plausibly considered normative arguments?[99] In the absence of a general argument to the universal conclusion that all apparently metanormative arguments can be nicely folded back into first-order normative discourse, what needs to be done here in order to fully evaluate this line of thought is to go through all of the possible examples, one by one, and see whether they do collapse back into first-order discourse. And clearly, in each case the answer may depend on how liberal one is willing to be with one's understanding of "normative".

Rather than going through this tiring procedure, let me note that merely labeling apparently metanormative issues as themselves normative is of little interest.[100] Nothing in the arguments themselves – either for or against realism, robust or otherwise – seems to depend on us using the word "metanormative" rather than "normative" to describe them. And yet, quietists of this type take themselves to have established something of importance when they (take themselves to) have shown that apparently metanormative discourse is itself normative. Why?

I can think of three ways in which it might be thought to matter whether apparently metanormative arguments are really themselves normative, and I want to briefly review them here.

First, such an observation may be thought to support doubts about the intelligibility or possibility of genuinely metanormative discourse. If what seems to be metanormative discussion really is just normative discussion, then, this thought goes, genuine metanormative discussion, one that is not really normative, is not possible. This may be so, but it is important to note that this point does not take us beyond the merely terminological debate: for the soundness of (apparently) metanormative arguments does not depend on their classification as normative or as (now genuinely) metanormative. Perhaps, in other words, no genuinely metanormative discussion is possible (if you choose to use these words in this way), but still there are interesting arguments for and against realism (now considered a normative, not a genuinely metanormative, position), and indeed these are the very same arguments we've been thinking of all along when doing metaethics or metanormativity. But quietists surely mean to do

pre-theoretically individuate discourses, and second, and more importantly, it still fails to show why it matters whether one discourse is or is not a part of another, a point to be emphasized in the text below.

For a view according to which metaethics is not morally neutral, but still the distinction between metaethics and ethics "has, of course, some obvious initial justification" see Gewirth (1960; the quote is from p. 188).

I discuss the issue of metaethics' neutrality in the Appendix to Chapter 2.

[99] There is a trivial sense in which all metanormative arguments are indeed normative – namely, they are attempts at giving reasons to believe their conclusions. But of course, in this sense, *all* arguments – not just all metaethical ones – are normative. This can't be the sense quietists have in mind, then.

[100] See Leiter (2001b, 72–3); McPherson (2008, 6–7).

more than recommend (what they see as) a cleaner terminology. So something else must be thought to be at stake.

A second way in which it may seem to matter if apparently metanormative discussion is really just part of normative reasoning is that this being so undermines, it may be thought, certain skeptical or antirealist worries. For if what seems to be a metanormative challenge is really itself normative, then the skeptic herself makes normative assumptions, and is thus guilty of inconsistency. If apparently metanormative thought is really normative thought then normative thought is unavoidable in a way that seems to undermine any radical challenges to it by rendering them unstable.

This line of thought is mistaken, however.[101] Radical skeptical challenges are best thought of as analogous to *reductio* arguments, employing weapons *we* must concede are powerful against us. The radical skeptic is thus entitled to engage in the very discourse she wants to attack so long as it is a discourse *we* want to defend. By so doing she will have shown, if successful, that normative discourse undermines or defeats itself. The observation that her doubts are themselves normative, then, does nothing to defend normative discourse. If her arguments cannot be shown to fail for reasons independent of the quietist observation, the quietist observation, far from dealing a devastating blow to the skeptic, marks her unqualified victory.

The third reason why this putative quietist observation – that apparently metanormative discourse is itself normative – may seem to be significant is that if it is true, there can be no objection, it seems, to the use of first-order arguments and intuitions in order to fight off skeptical or nihilist attacks. Suppose some metaphysical or epistemological – apparently metaethical – considerations seem to undermine morality altogether, supporting either a nihilist or a skeptical conclusion. Then, it seems, all it takes to refute them is the strength of our convictions that wanton cruelty is wrong, and that we know as much.[102] If metanormative considerations were of a very different type from normative ones, perhaps such a move would be objectionable, because of its conflation of two distinct, perhaps even independent,[103] levels of discourse. But given the quietist observations, this worry can be set aside.

I agree that metanormative discourse may have implications for normative discourse – this, after all, was a part of the point of Chapter 2. And as I explained in section 5.2.2, I think there can be no general objection to the use of first-order

---

[101] This paragraph summarizes points made in my "Agency, Shmagency" (2006), and then, in greater detail, in my "Shmagency Revisited" (2010b).

[102] "The situation here [in ethics] is like that in any other basic domain. First-order thoughts about its content – thoughts expressed in the object language – rise up again as the decisive response to all second-order thoughts about their psychological character....That is why we can defend moral reason only by abandoning metatheory for substantive ethics. Only the intrinsic weight of first-order moral thinking can counter the doubts of subjectivism." Nagel (1997, 125). For similar points, see Dworkin (throughout his 1996), Scanlon (1998, 63–4), and Kramer (2009, throughout).

[103] Perhaps this is the line of thought Mackie had in mind when writing: "These first and second order views are not merely distinct but completely independent" (1977, 16). It is, however, unclear whether Mackie consistently accepts this point throughout his *Ethics* (1977).

arguments and intuitions in metanormative contexts. But nothing like the quietist observation follows. Even if normative arguments are metanormatively relevant, this in no way shows that they are the *only* metanormatively relevant arguments, or that once the normative discussion has been conducted nothing further remains to be said.[104]

Perhaps there is after all some significance to the classification of apparently metanormative arguments as normative, though I cannot think of one. Or perhaps something else can be saved from the general (and vague) quietist intuitions, something that survives the discussion above while still constituting a general challenge to my Robust Realism or to the metanormative debate in which it is one of the competing views. Or perhaps – most relevant to the context of this chapter – there is some other way of using quietist observations to show that the realist, even the robust realist, can get what she wants without any heavy metaphysical commitments.[105] But the suspicion now arises that quietist worries are first and foremost expressions of impatience. In the normative context, if they are not merely the shadows of doubts about metaphysics in general they are expressions of impatience with semantic, metaphysical, and epistemological discussions that are perceived as merely hindering the real, practically important, first-order discussion. There may even be good historical reasons for such impatience.[106] As the common story goes (I am not competent to evaluate its historical credentials), in the first two-thirds of the twentieth century there was little philosophical interest in substantive moral questions, because (no doubt among other reasons) moral philosophers were busy doing metaethics, which was perceived as prior to – and independent of[107] – morality. Morality was perceived as either lacking intellectual respectability, or at least as needing metaethical defense. An overreaction to such thoughts may be what is fueling quietist intuitions in the metaethical context, at least the quietist intuitions expressed by the friends of morality. But this is indeed an overreaction. One need not deny the intelligibility or distinctness of metanormativity (or metaethics) in order to acknowledge the legitimacy and intellectual respectability – already here and now, before the metanormative discussion has reached conclusions that enjoy unanimous support – of first-order normative (or moral) discussion.

---

[104]   Have another look at the quote from Nagel in footnote 102 above. Notice that the two appearances of "only" are entirely unsupported by what precedes them.

[105]   On this issue, then, I am with Quine (1960, 242): "I deplore the philosophical double talk, which would repudiate an ontology while simultaneously enjoying its benefits."

[106]   For a related point in the context of the pretensions for the general power of philosophy, see Fine (2001, 2–3).

[107]   Thus, there is a significant volume of literature on the question of the ethical neutrality of metaethics. For a characteristic discussion, and for references to many others, see Sumner (1967). Sumner repeatedly considers the possibility that such a neutrality thesis is analytically true of metaethics, so that by showing that any purportedly metaethical theory has normative implications one will have shown that metaethics is impossible. Perhaps this too is an intuition fueling some quietists' worries. But it should not. As the word "metaethics" is used today, nothing like the neutrality thesis is plausibly considered analytically true, and probably not even as merely true. And once again, here as elsewhere, we should not replace philosophy with terminology.

If I am right, then, there are no metaphysically light ways of getting the robust realist what he wants (namely, what is needed, according to the arguments in previous chapters). Quietism cannot do this, and neither can attempts at a naturalist reduction, or different kinds of error theory and fictionalism. And so, we can now proceed in one of two ways – accepting the ontological commitment that is a part of Robust Realism, or else taking that very commitment as a reason to reject Robust Realism. So it is time for some more metaphysics, this time in the context of defending Robust Realism from the claim that its metaphysical commitments render it unacceptable.

6

Metaphysics

Having presented my positive arguments for Robust Realism, it is now time to address the main objections to this kind of view. Of these objections – which, just like Robust Realism and its relatives, have been with us for a while – the first family of worries I will discuss is metaphysical in nature. Robust Realism, it is sometimes said, is committed to a metaphysics that we scientifically-minded folk should find offensive. It is, after all, explicitly non-naturalist. This all by itself, it is sometimes argued, is sufficient reason to reject it.

In section 6.1, I address the raw version of this worry (the one I call "Sheer Queerness"), concluding that we should not be much impressed with it. I concede, though, that a theory that is naturalist but as good as Robust Realism in other respects (including primarily the ones highlighted by the arguments of the previous four chapters) *would* be, on account of its naturalism, preferable to Robust Realism. In this respect, then, Robust Realism does lose plausibility points merely for not being naturalist, but not many, or so I argue in section 6.1. Even if we can set aside sheer-queerness worries, there are still more specific and focused metaphysical worries that need to be dealt with. Here I discuss – in section 6.2 – two worries having to do with the supervenience of the normative: the worry that supervenience entails (via the purported identity of necessarily co-extensive properties) naturalism, and the worry that supervenience without reduction is objectionably mysterious. I reject the former worry, and do what I can to minimize the harm done by the latter (here, I concede, Robust Realism may lose some plausibility points).

6.1 Sheer queerness

The general worry here is still best captured by the following quote from Mackie (1977, 38), who also coined this use of the term "queerness":

> If there were objective values, then they would be entities or qualities or relations of a very strange sort, utterly different from anything else in the universe.

We seem to have a general view of what there is in the world. These days, this view seems to be, roughly speaking, the scientific world view. What there is in the world, the thought seems to be, is pretty much the kind of stuff our best science says (or will shortly say) that there is in the world. Without pretending that this is the only use of the term, we can call this loose ontological thesis Naturalism. And Mackie's point – the one I call Sheer Queerness – seems to come down to the fact that objective values of the kind he discusses are not the kind of stuff likely to appear on the list of what our best science says or is likely to say exists. Naturalism is inconsistent with Robust Realism, and we should opt for Naturalism. So much the worse for Robust Realism.

But this Sheer Queerness thought – if it is not to be understood as shorthand for some other worry (more on this shortly) – can be rather quickly dismissed, for the obvious reason that Platts (1980, 72) put best:

The queerest thing about this as it stands is the claim that it is an *argument*.... The world *is* a queer place. I find neutrinos, aardvarks, infinite sequences of objects, and (most pertinently) impressionist paintings peculiar kinds of entities; but I do not expect nuclear physics, zoology, formal semantics or art history to pay much regard to that.

Now, this may sound too quick, and as a reply to Mackie it certainly is (for there is much more even in these pages in Mackie than the *Sheer* Queerness point). But as a response to the Sheer Queerness point, it seems to me to stand. This, of course, may put pressure not so much on queerness-related thoughts, as on their interpretation along the lines of the Sheer Queerness point. What else may be going on here, then?

Even the Sheer Queerness point I mentioned above refers to science. So it may be thought that what does the work here is the scientific-sounding claim that we should only believe in the entities of the kind that our best science does (or will) quantify over. But it is important to note that this claim – though scientific-sounding – is in no way itself a part of science. As far as I know, nowhere does science include an "and-that's-it" clause.[1] Nor is it likely to include one any time soon. So merely invoking some further, non-scientifically-grounded queer entities is not *itself* inconsistent with science. Science itself, then, will not save the Sheer Queerness thought.

A more plausible suggestion is that what underlies the Sheer Queerness point is a naturalist kind of a parsimony requirement. Sure, science does not itself rule out queer entities, but we have general (perhaps methodological) reasons not to unnecessarily multiply entities. Given that moral values (or facts, truths, properties, etc.) are not needed for science, we should not believe in them. This, I think, *is* a genuine argument, and one that needs to be addressed by the robust realist. But of course, it *has already* been addressed at some length, under the heading "Harman's Challenge", in Chapter 3 (where I accept the Minimal Parsimony Requirement, refuse to infer from it the Explanatory Requirement, and argue that irreducibly normative truths satisfy the Minimal Parsimony Requirement in virtue of their role in deliberation). So we do not need to spend more time on this here.

Another possible – and somewhat plausible – reading of the Sheer Queerness thought is not as an independent argument against objective values (or some such), but rather as a summary of all the other arguments. The thought that objective values

---

[1] See here also Shafer-Landau (2003, 81).

(or irreducibly normative truths, or some such) are just too queer to exist may just be the thought that given all of the difficulties with them, the payoffs of accepting them into our ontology are outweighed by the costs. This may be so, but we will be better able to evaluate this claim after I complete the discussion of the objections to Robust Realism. Indeed, it will be the job of Chapter 10 to tally the plausibility points and reach a final evaluation of Robust Realism. So we are better off not discussing this further here.

Or perhaps the Sheer Queerness thought is best understood as really shorthand for some more complicated argument – perhaps a metaphysical one about supervenience, or perhaps an epistemological one about epistemic access, or perhaps a motivational one. These may all be important worries, and I discuss them elsewhere in this book.

For now, though, we can safely conclude that unless the Sheer Queerness thought is shorthand for some other kind of argument[2] (in which case it is discussed elsewhere in this book), it can be set aside for Platts-like reasons.

6.2 Supervenience

The Sheer Queerness worry, I argued in section 6.1, is not very threatening. But this doesn't mean that there's no serious metaphysical worry for Robust Realism to deal with. And in fact there is – a family of issues having to do with the supervenience of the normative.

There are, of course, many different kinds of supervenience in the literature. I'm going to bypass the vast majority of this literature, by immediately accepting a supervenience thesis that is probably the least convenient for the robust realist to accommodate: strong individual supervenience, according to which it is impossible for there to be two things – inhabiting the same world *or* two distinct possible worlds – that are indistinguishable in their natural properties but are distinguishable in their normative ones (whether moral or otherwise).[3] If the robust realist can accommodate even this kind of supervenience, she is practically guaranteed to be able to accommodate other, (perhaps loosely speaking) weaker ones. Furthermore, for

---

[2] Or perhaps it can be understood – as Ragnar Francén and Jonas Olson pressed me to acknowledge – as merely insisting that there is just something pre-theoretically implausible, perhaps even unbelievable, about the thought that there are objective facts that, as it were, tell us what to do, that categorically demand behavior irrespective of people's aims, desires, roles, and so on. My ability to respond to this challenge is somewhat burdened by the fact that I don't share this intuition at all. (I know – you must be shocked.) My argument against it consists in the entirety of this book.

[3] For more on strong individual supervenience, for comparisons with many other kinds of supervenience, and for many references, see McLaughlin and Bennett (2005, section 4). For sacrilegious doubts about the supervenience of the normative, see Dancy (1996b), Raz (2000), and Sturgeon (2007). I remain unconvinced – but let me note that if we should not after all accept a supervenience claim, this makes things easier for Robust Realism. Sturgeon (2007, 59) also notes that it is strong supervenience that is the more relevant one to the metaethical debates.

reasons that will be briefly discussed below it seems to me that moral properties and other normative properties do indeed strongly individually supervene on natural ones. So focusing on strong individual supervenience is justified on methodological as well as substantive grounds.[4] Focusing on strong individual supervenience still leaves some disambiguation to be done, though, as the relevant modality has to be determined: are normatively distinguishable but naturally indistinguishable things a *logical* impossibility? A *metaphysical* one? Some other modality? This is an important question, for, as McLaughlin and Bennett (2005, section 3.1) note, "Sometimes there is widespread agreement that a certain supervenience relation holds, but dispute over what its modal force is." But this matter is best left to the discussion in section 6.2.2, below.

I am going to discuss two objections to Robust Realism that use the supervenience of the normative as a premise. The first, often associated in the metaethical context with Frank Jackson,[5] is the claim that a (sufficiently strong) supervenience thesis entails – together with a plausible thesis in the metaphysics of properties in general – that normative properties just are natural properties, thus condemning Robust Realism to incoherence. The second, often associated with Simon Blackburn, is the claim that supervenience calls for explanation, and that robust realists cannot supply a plausible explanation of supervenience.

6.2.1 The supposed identity of necessarily co-extensive properties

Let's assume, then, strong individual supervenience. If two things are naturally indistinguishable, then, it follows that they are also normatively indistinguishable. From this it follows that for any normative property, we can define a set of things in purely naturalist terms, so that, necessarily, something is in that set if and only if it has that normative property. This naturalist way of picking up the set may be long, cumbersome, ugly; it may contain a large number of conjunctions and disjunctions, for instance; it need not present a unified or in any other way simple or theoretically attractive characterization of the set. Still, a naturalistically respectable way of picking out a set it most certainly is.

---

[4] McLaughlin and Bennett (2005, section 4.1) understand Blackburn's supervenience-based objection to moral realism to be based on the premise that moral properties weakly supervene on natural ones (so that any naturally indistinguishable same-world things are guaranteed to also be normatively indistinguishable), but that they do *not* strongly supervene on them (so that two naturally indistinguishable things in two distinct worlds *may* be normatively distinguishable); they then attribute to Blackburn the claim that if weak supervenience holds and strong supervenience does not this calls for explanation; and that realism is not in a good position (say, compared to expressivism) to deliver such an explanation. This is not how the supervenience challenge is usually understood in the metaethical literature (though it does seem to be what Blackburn has in mind, at least in Blackburn (1985)), or how I will understand it in what follows. Let me just note, then, that to this challenge I respond by rejecting its premise – I think that normative properties do strongly supervene on natural ones. For this point see also Wedgwood (2007, 148).

[5] Jackson is obviously influenced here by somewhat similar claims Kim had put forward in the philosophy of mind.

Next step: assume that the set of properties is closed under Boolean operations, in the obvious way – so that if P is a property, and Q is a property, and R is a property, then so are P-and-Q, P-or-R, P-and-Q-or-not-R, and so on.[6]

Almost last step: Assume further that necessarily co-extensive properties are identical.

Then we're done, and Robust Realism has been refuted: for given the assumption that the set of properties is closed under Boolean operations, there is a property that corresponds to the naturalistically picked-out set above – whichever ugly way was used to pick out the set *just is*, given this assumption, a way of picking out a property too. And it seems *very* plausible that it is a natural property.[7] Furthermore, it is necessarily co-extensive with the normative property we started with. If so, it follows that the normative property and the (perhaps ugly) natural one are one and the same. But given supervenience, we are guaranteed to be able to generate such a little argument for any normative property. So any normative property is identical with a natural one. So there are no normative properties that are not identical with natural ones. So Robust Realism is false.[8]

If you're into that kind of stuff, you may want to question the premise about the set of properties being closed under Boolean operations. There is some controversy on this and related issues in the metaphysics-of-properties literature.[9] I won't do this here, though, and not only because such a discussion is a touch too metaphysical even for my philosophical taste. My main reason for not engaging this discussion is that it is very hard for me to believe that the fate of Robust Realism should depend on this debate. And indeed, regardless of whether an ugly sort-of-property counts as a genuine property, if having a normative property just is having that ugly natural sort-of-property, this would suffice, I think, for it to be the case that the normative is nothing over and above the natural. And this, in turn, would suffice for a refutation of Robust Realism. So I am going to grant this premise, and what follows from it. In other words, I am going to grant that every normative property is necessarily co-extensive with a natural one.

What I am not going to grant, then, is the identity of necessarily co-extensive properties. The common examples that are used as (purported) counterexamples are

---

[6] Here and throughout the presentation of this argument I am being somewhat loose – for instance, making the argument fully explicit may require a detour through a discussion of predicates and their relation to properties – after all, Boolean operators are defined primarily on predicates, not on properties. (This is Streumer's (2008) way of presenting the argument, possibly closely following Jackson (1998).) Or there may be a way of formulating an at least somewhat similar argument that is purely ontological, without any semantic detour. This is Brown's (forthcoming) project. And there may be ways of formulating the argument with other premises instead of the supervenience one, and so on. I can afford this nonchalance about the details here, because my way of rejecting the argument works against any precisification thereof.

[7] Though see Majors (2005, 483).

[8] For this argument, see Jackson (1998, 113–29), Jackson and Pettit (1995, 22). For a comprehensive critical overview of the literature here, see Streumer (2008). I thank Bart Streumer also for comments on a previous version of this section, and for very helpful discussion.

[9] There are some references in Streumer (2008).

things like triangularity (having three angles) and trilaterality (having three sides), or the property of being the number 2 and the property of being an even prime,[10] or – more closely to our context – the property of being an obligatory action and the property of being such that it is an essential property of God to command all persons to perform it (assuming some suitable version of a divine command theory).[11] Intuitively, it seems that these are distinct properties, even though they are necessarily coextensive. Of course, proponents of the argument above may just dig in their heels, and insist that in these cases too the seemingly distinct properties are actually identical (though the relevant concepts may be distinct, of course). And so we find ourselves at a frustrating impasse.

Notice that in our context an impasse is not neutral in its dialectical effect.[12] We are now considering an objection to Robust Realism. If one of the objection's premises is at best optional – because of the above described impasse – then we don't have here a strong objection to Robust Realism. In order to have a more serious threat here, the naturalist owes us a reason to accept the identity of necessarily co-extensive properties (in general, or in the normative–natural context in particular).

And here, I think, Campbell Brown's recent discussion (forthcoming) is helpful. For he rightly classifies what is at issue here as a matter of ontological parsimony. The deep reason the naturalist has for objecting to distinct necessarily co-extensive properties has to do not so much with intuitive judgments about some examples, but with parsimony, with the methodological requirement not to multiply entities (including properties) unnecessarily.[13] Brown works hard to define a precise notion of redundancy, and to prove that distinct necessarily co-extensive properties are redundant. But we don't need to spend time here on the precise details of his account. The important part for my purposes is that Brown seems to be right when it comes to his diagnosis: it's all about parsimony. It seems, for instance, that multiplying distinct necessarily co-extensive properties does not add explanatory power. So we have no reason to accept

[10] For discussion along these lines, see van Roojen (1996), Shafer-Landau (2003, 90–2), Majors (2005), Fitzpatrick (2010, 24–7), Parfit (2011, vol. 2, section 87). For criticism, see Streumer (2008, 541–5).

[11] Plantinga (2010).

[12] At times Streumer (2008) sounds like he's missing this dialectical point (though in correspondence he explained to me that he just differs on whether or not there is an impasse here).

[13] Streumer (2008, 542 and on) presents what looks like a *reductio* argument against those positing distinct but necessarily co-extensive properties, saying things like that if we accept triangularity and trilaterality as distinct properties, "there would be no reason why the predicate 'is a triangle' would not ascribe a third property...", a claim he considers absurd. But this, of course, is false. If we accept triangularity and trilaterality as distinct properties it doesn't follow that there is *no* reason to rule out being a triangle as a third property. All that follows is that we don't have *this* reason (namely, the one assuming the identity of necessarily co-extensive properties) for denying a third property here. But there may be others – like, perhaps, a general parsimony requirement as in the text here. Or perhaps it makes sense to think of the property of being a triangle as identical by definition to one of the other two (say, that of having three angles), and then we only have here two properties after all.

distinct necessarily co-extensive properties into our ontology. This, it seems, is the underlying naturalist thought here.

But in the context of this book, Brown's diagnosis is of course good news for Robust Realism.[14] For the parsimony requirement has been extensively discussed in Chapter 3 above. As you may recall, I distinguish between the General Parsimony Requirement (which I accept) and the Explanatory Requirement (which I reject), and I show that normative facts (truths, properties) satisfy the parsimony requirement by being deliberatively indispensable. If my arguments there fail, Robust Realism is in serious trouble even independently of the specific objection discussed in this subsection. If, on the other hand, my arguments there work, and if (as I think) Brown is right in diagnosing the argument here as really resting on a parsimony requirement, then the argument discussed in this subsection does not pose a further threat to Robust Realism. On the assumption that Chapter 3 adequately deals with the parsimony requirement, then, we can safely conclude that there is no further problem here that has to be dealt with.

This means that in a way, the case of normative properties and "their" naturalist counterparts (that is, the natural properties that are necessarily co-extensive with them) is even easier than that of triangularity and trilaterality (and the like). For it remains to be seen if accepting two properties in the latter case can survive a parsimony requirement. But it has already been shown – if the argument in Chapter 3 is successful, that is – that accepting into our ontology necessarily co-extensive natural and normative properties does survive the parsimony requirement. Perhaps this is (partly) why the claim that necessarily co-extensive properties are identical sounds more plausible when discussing just natural properties (where presumably all properties earn their place in our ontology by the kind of explanatory work they're doing) than when discussing normative ones as well (which earn their place in our ontology because of the non-explanatory, deliberative work they're doing).[15]

6.2.2 Explaining supervenience without reduction

As you may recall, I accept the (strong) supervenience of the normative on the natural. But – as is widely acknowledged today[16] – such supervenience is a part of the problem, not a part of the solution. It does not make it any easier for a robust realist to find "room" for her normative facts in the natural world. Rather, it constitutes a closely related problem, to which I get shortly. In the philosophy of mind, there is a discussion

[14] Which is not to suggest that this is how he intends it.
[15] Streumer (2008, 557) anticipates an objection to Jackson's argument that accepts the identity of necessarily co-extensive properties in general, but makes an exception in the normative case. He rightly notes that those offering this objection owe us an explanation, one answering the question: What's so special about the normative case? Streumer then says, "It is hard to see how they could explain this." The point in the text can be seen as supplying the explanation Streumer thinks is not forthcoming.
[16] This point is very widely acknowledged in the philosophy of mind, perhaps mostly following the influential work of Jaegwon Kim. In the normative context, see, for instance, Blackburn (1985, 415) and Railton (1993, 298 n. 2).

concerning the relation between (different kinds of) supervenience claims and "onto-logical innocence":[17] whether, in particular, the (purported) fact that the mental supervenes on the physical suffices to make the mental ontologically respectable. An affirmative answer here may be motivated by Kripke's (1972, 153–4) metaphor, according to which once God fixes the subvening facts, he is done – there is nothing further he needs to do in order to fix the supervening facts as well. I am suspicious of such suggestions in general, but I'm going to focus just on the case of the normative now: whether, with regard to the normative, God has any work left having created the natural facts probably depends on some interesting theological and metanormative questions – for instance, whether God has the power to change basic normative truths, and perhaps whether God can defeat metaphysical necessity more generally. More importantly, if you find normative facts metaphysically problematic (queer, perhaps), there is no reason to think that supervenience could allay your worries. Rather, it adds yet another mystery in need of explanation.

Had accepting the supervenience of the normative on the natural made the normative facts ontologically more respectable, this would have been one possible motivation for accepting supervenience. Having rejected this possible motivation, though, what *can* be said for supervenience? Viewed from the other direction, how high is the price in plausibility points of rejecting the supervenience of the normative? I don't think that much can be said for supervenience. I don't know of any compelling argument with this supervenience claim as its conclusion (though some of the following thoughts can, I guess, be put in a form more resembling an argument). Nevertheless, I think that the price of rejecting supervenience is un-acceptably high.[18] The thought that there could be two naturally indistinguishable things[19] where one of them is good (or a good something-or-other) and the other isn't, is just so highly implausible, that if it were implied by a metaethical view, this would qualify, I think, as an adequate *reductio* of that view. This is also why I go all the way in endorsing *strong* supervenience:[20] the thought that a mere difference in modal location – in which possible world something is – can all alone, without a natural difference, make (or indicate) a normative difference seems utterly implausible to me, barely intelligible even. I may be wrong about all this, of course. If so, things go even more easily for Robust Realism (as the explanatory challenge soon to be discussed does not arise, or arises in a weaker version). But in what follows I assume that the normative supervenes – indeed, strongly supervenes – on the natural. If Robust

[17] See McLaughlin and Bennett (2005, section 3.4) and the references there.
[18] Sturgeon (2007) argues that reasons to accept different supervenience claims here are always parochial – they depend on a prior endorsement of a specific and controversial metaethical theory. As I note in the text, Sturgeon may be right when it comes to *arguments* (though see McPherson (manuscript)), but not when it comes to *reasons* to accept supervenience.
[19] This would require, of course, that the two things are indistinguishable also in the relevant parts of their histories, their relevant relations to other things, etc. At the limit, the relevant supervenience claim may be global rather than local. See also Wedgwood (2007, 148 n. 19).
[20] Wedgwood (2007, 148) also thinks that it is strong supervenience that is intuitively compelling.

Realism is committed to the denial of this claim, I am willing to assume, this would amount to a devastating loss of plausibility points.[21]

And so, the following challenge[22] threatens Robust Realism: as I've just conceded, and as the supervenience slogan goes, there can be no normative difference without a natural one. Well then, isn't this surprising? Doesn't this fact seem like an amazing modal fluke? It seems to call for explanation. And it's hard to see how the robust realist can come up with one. If you need convincing – either that there is something here that needs explaining, or that there is at the very least an initial difficulty in seeing how the robust realist can meet this explanatory challenge – it may help to see how easy everything here is for the naturalist, reductionist realist. For if normative properties are nothing over and above natural ones, then *of course* there can be no normative difference without a natural one. The problem is that nothing as easy as this can be offered by the robust realist. If normative properties are utterly distinct from natural ones, isn't it quite surprising indeed that their possession always satisfies the rather strong conditions of strong supervenience?

There are here really two explananda that are sometimes conflated in the literature, and that should be clearly distinguished.[23] The first is the supervenience of the normative properties on the natural ones *that they do in fact supervene on*. If, for instance, the normative property *being morally wrong* supervenes on the natural property *failing to maximize utility*, then the first explanatory challenge here is to explain this very super-venience, the supervenience of *being wrong* on *failing to maximize utility*. This I call *specific* supervenience.[24] But there is another explanandum in the vicinity here, namely, the supervenience of normative properties on *whatever natural properties they supervene on*. This is a supervenience claim you can be committed to even if you haven't yet settled on a first-order normative theory you're happy with. You may think that you don't yet know what natural property, for instance, *being morally wrong* supervenes on, but that you know that it supervenes on *some* natural property. I call this *general* supervenience.

---

[21] I am really not sure about this, but there may be the beginning of an argument for supervenience in the indispensability argument in Chapter 3 above. Certainly, the way in which we do in fact deliberate seems to assume or presuppose that once all natural facts have been determined, so have the normative ones (even if we are still not sure what they are). Perhaps, then, we can fill in the details here in a way that will make plausible the suggestion that supervenience (perhaps even strong supervenience) is deliberatively indispensable. I thank Mark van Roojen for the suggestion that this is how an indispensability argument for supervenience might go.

[22] Simon Blackburn (1973) gets credit for introducing this challenge into the metaethical literature. I am not, however, invested in this or that reading of Blackburn's text. The challenge in the text seems to me the important one for robust realists to face, and this regardless of what Blackburn has or may have had in mind. Also, that this is the challenge *robust* realists should face does not mean it's the most interesting challenge for other realist views. My discussion will be limited to just Robust Realism. For a helpful sustained attempt at making sense of Blackburn's own arguments here, and evaluating their merits against different kinds of realism, see Dreier (1992, 15–22).

[23] For making me see this – and this required patience and insistence – I thank Dan Baras, Russ Shafer-Landau, and especially Jonas Olson.

[24] See Horgan and Timmons (1992, 226) and Wedgwood's (2007, 203) related (but not quite identical) "specific supervenience facts".

Specific and general supervenience claims are distinct, and logically independent.[25] They should be discussed separately. This is what I do in the next two subsections.

6.2.2.1 Specific supervenience.

Without pretending, then, that anything about supervenience can guarantee ontological innocence for Robust Realism,[26] let us address specific supervenience: what if anything can a robust realist say to explain the supervenience of normative properties on the natural properties they do in fact supervene on?

One possible response, of course, would be to accept this supervenience as brute. But this response is not satisfying. There does seem to be something here that calls for explanation, and so if Robust Realism has nothing to offer by way of explanation, then for this very reason it loses significant plausibility points. This is especially so if some of its main metaethical and metanormative competitors do a much better job of explaining supervenience. At the very least, then, Robust Realism will be much better off if it can offer something by way of an explanation of the supervenience of the normative. And this is what I intend to do in the rest of this section.

So consider the relation between someone's legal drinking status (that is, whether she is legally allowed to purchase alcohol) and her age.[27] And for now, let's restrict our attention to the relation between these two kinds of properties (drinking-status properties, that come in a simple yes-or-no way, and age properties, that come in a much wider variety) just *within a jurisdiction*. Within a jurisdiction, there cannot be a drinking-status difference without an age difference.[28] If two people are of the same age, they are either both legally allowed to purchase alcohol, or none are, so that either way there is no difference between them when it comes to legal drinking status. And notice also that though the restriction to a jurisdiction is important, and the modality relevant here is rather weak (we will shortly return to both of these), still the relation between drinking-status and age is not merely coincidental. Rather, what we want to say is that (given the laws of the jurisdiction) there *can*not be a difference in drinking-status without a difference in age. In other words, drinking-status supervenes on age (within a jurisdiction).

---

[25] Clearly, specific supervenience is stronger than general supervenience. But it is also weaker, because – as I am about to argue – general supervenience is plausibly considered a matter of conceptual necessity, whereas specific supervenience is only necessary in some weaker way.

[26] This is one important difference between the discussion here and the discussion of superdupervenience – robustly explained supervenience – in the philosophy of mind, where clearly what is at issue is the hope of rendering the mental materialistically respectable. See, for instance, Horgan (1993).

[27] The explanation of specific supervenience that follows emerged from a conversation I had a long time ago with Masahiro Yamada. Though the details here are mine, I gratefully acknowledge that the initial idea that got me thinking in this direction came from him.

[28] I am making some simplifying assumptions here – namely, that the relevant legal rules set a simple age-limit for purchasing alcohol, that they are not more sensitive than that (say, saying that one is allowed to purchase beer on one's own only if one is at least 21, but that if one is in the company of one's parents, one is entitled to purchase beer even at 19). Nothing important will depend on such simplifying (though realistic, in many Western jurisdictions) assumptions.

But it's not as if we are here tempted by a reduction. We do not think – nor should we think – that drinking-status properties are reducible to age properties, that being legally allowed to drink (say) is nothing over and above being at least 21 years old. First lesson, then: sometimes, we're happy with specific supervenience without reduction. But let's not stop here. It's not just that we don't here go for a reductionist view. More than that, the supervenience relation doesn't even seriously tempt us in the direction of a reduction. Second lesson, then: sometimes, specific supervenience doesn't even (significantly) count in favor of a reductionist view.

However, given that we have here supervenience without reduction, doesn't it call for explanation? I think that it does, but that the explanation is pretty obvious. If someone arrives at our jurisdiction, notices that people have drinking-status properties, that they also have age properties, and that the former supervene on the latter, and proceeds to ask for an explanation of this (perhaps surprising) fact, all we need to do is direct her attention to *the relevant legal norm*. We can tell her things like "Oh, the law here says that so-and-so", or "you must understand, the relevant legal norms here view gender as irrelevant to drinking-status, and determine only the age as a relevant factor", and so on. What explains the supervenience of legal drinking-status on age is simply the content of the relevant legal norms.

OK, OK – this is all just within a jurisdiction. And we haven't even started to talk about the modality of the relevant supervenience claim (we will shortly). But none of this, I think, prevents us from concluding with the following, third lesson: sometimes, the content of norms suffices to explain a genuine specific supervenience phenomenon (without reduction).

And this – as I'm sure you've already understood – is how I suggest that we explain the specific supervenience of (e.g.) the moral on the natural: what explains, for instance, the supervenience of wrongness (including, perhaps, degree of wrongness) on natural properties is the content of the moral norms or principles of right and wrong.[29] Suppose that some fairly basic version of utilitarianism is true. Then the relevant moral norm states, roughly, that an action is wrong if and only if there is an alternative action (or inaction) that could be opted for, and that had a larger (perhaps expected) utility value. Given that this is the content of the norm, no mystery remains about the supervenience of wrongness on the (perhaps expected) utility values of the relevant action and its alternatives. If someone notices that actions have utility-value properties, and also wrongness properties, and that the latter supervene on the former, and wonders what explains this supervenience, all we need to do is to direct her

---

[29] I don't know of anyone developing this solution in the literature. But for suggestive remarks in this general direction, see Johnston (1989, 154); Hurley (1989, 197–8) (in the context of discussing epistemic rather than moral norms); Shafer-Landau (2003, 85–6, 96–7); Kramer (2009, 352–3); Scanlon (2009, lecture 2).
  Ridge (2007, 330) insists that "strategies which may work well for explaining supervenience in the philosophy of mind and other areas cannot be assumed to carry over successfully to the metaethical context". So it is worth mentioning here that the strategy in the text is actually quite peculiar to the supervenience of the normative.

attention to the relevant moral norm. What explains the supervenience of wrongness on utility-values is the content of utilitarianism (assuming, that is, that it is the true morality).[30]

We will get to possible disanalogies in a moment. But if at this stage you're not even convinced that there is here an initial analogy, think of the possibility of a moral legislator. If there is a moral legislator – a Moral Legislator, perhaps – then, I take it, the analogy with the legal case is *extremely* close (perhaps to the point of making it misleading to describe it as an analogy). If that were a true picture of morality, then, the content of the moral norms would unproblematically explain the supervenience of the normative on the natural (within the Moral Legislator's jurisdiction). And whatever the failings of such a metaethical view, they are not, I think, relevant to the acceptability of such an explanation of supervenience. So the analogy initially holds even if other, more plausible metaethical views are correct.

But in the legal case, the supervenience may be called ultra-weak. Not only doesn't the no-drinking-status-difference-without-age-difference apply across possible worlds, it doesn't even apply across jurisdictions within a world: if in the United States the drinking age is 21, and in Israel it's 18, then there *can* be a difference in the (local) drinking-status of two persons even if there is no age-difference between them, if, for instance, they are both 19, and one of them lives in the States and the other in Israel. And clearly, had the law in Texas (say) been different, the drinking-status of certain people would have been different. So across possible worlds, *of course* drinking-status differences are possible without age differences. But this constitutes an important disanalogy between the legal and the moral cases. For in the moral case, we certainly believe in stronger supervenience than that.

True, there *is* this disanalogy. But it does not, I now want to argue, undermine the force of the analogy in motivating my way of explaining the supervenience of the normative. To see this, we should just think about increasingly larger jurisdictions. As the jurisdiction rises in size, the scope of the supervenience thesis in the legal cases also increases. If there are norms with maximal jurisdiction, for instance, then the scope of the resulting supervenience claim will be maximal as well. And if there are norms with *modally* maximal jurisdiction, then their content will suffice to explain strong supervenience as well. But this, according to Robust Realism, is precisely the nature of the (basic) moral and other normative norms – they are norms with maximal, and even modally maximal, jurisdiction.[31] So all the robust realist has to do in order to explain

---

[30] If you're a particularist, this explanation of supervenience may not be available to you. And if you're also a robust realist, this may mean that you still have some unfinished business to deal with in explaining supervenience, and this even if the explanation in the text here is entirely successful for universalists. It is not clear, in other words, that anything I say here can help Dancy deal with the supervenience of the normative. But see Dancy (1996a) for what seems like a similar thought about supervenience, and Dancy (1996b) for thoughts about thick concepts as motivating a denial of supervenience.

[31] Wait a minute – am I not here begging the question against non-robust-realists by assuming that this is indeed the status of basic norms? No, I am not. Remember that the supervenience challenge is supposed to be a fairly independent objection to Robust Realism (and perhaps to other views as well). If the

the (strong) specific supervenience of the normative is to point at the content of the basic or ultimate[32] norms.

So far I have said nothing at all about the modality of the relevant specific supervenience claim. What *is* the right modality here? And can the supervenience thesis thus understood be explained by the content of the relevant norms? The explanation above can work for a supervenience thesis whose modal status is no stronger than that of the basic (for instance moral) norms themselves. If the (basic) moral norms are only, say, nomologically necessary, then their content can at most explain a nomic supervenience relation. But this is not a problem, I think, for it is anyway highly implausible to think that there is a true *specific* supervenience thesis whose modal status is stronger (in the obvious sense) than that of the basic norms themselves. (General supervenience is different in this regard, as I explain below shortly.) If, for instance, the ultimate moral norms are nomologically necessary but metaphysically contingent, then the supervenience of normative properties on the natural ones they do in fact supervene on must also be metaphysically contingent.[33] Thus, though the strength of the explanation offered here is constrained to just specific supervenience theses whose modal status is not stronger than that of the basic norms, still this is not a significant restriction – we are highly unlikely to have stronger explananda anyway.

But still, you may insist, *what is* the precise modal status of the basic moral (and other) norms, and with them of the strongest plausible supervenience claim? I am not sure what to say here. I think it should be at least metaphysical necessity – so that there is no metaphysically possible world where the basic norms are different. But perhaps it is even stronger than that. I am just not sure here. Perhaps there is a *sui generis* modality which we can call normative necessity.[34] But luckily, I don't think I need an answer to this (interesting) question for my purposes here. The crucial thing for my purposes here is just that whatever the modal status of the basic norms, it suffices for the explanation above to work as an explanation of the strongest plausible specific supervenience claim.

robust realist – utilizing whatever dialectical means at her disposal – can deflect this objection, she is off the hook (this hook, that is). If the view of the status of moral (and other) norms in the text here is problematic, then this must be shown, presumably on grounds independent of the supervenience challenge (though the discussion below of Hume's Dictum may be relevant here).

[32] There may be some problems in making the idea of a basic or an ultimate norm fully explicit. But the idea is, I take it, intuitive enough – we just backtrack, so to speak, practical syllogisms to their major premises, until we reach such a major premise that is not itself the conclusion of a practical syllogism, or that is (roughly speaking) free of empirical content. And the problems in making this idea fully precise and explicit are not, I think, ones that undermine the limited use to which I put the notion of basic or ultimate norms in the text.

[33] Because the modal status of the relevant legal norms is rather fragile, the supervenience claim it is reasonable to apply to the legal example above is also rather weak – exactly as modally weak as that of the relevant legal norms.

[34] For an attempt at an argument showing that normative necessity cannot be defined in terms of metaphysical and nomological necessity, see Fine (2002). This need not be, of course, the same "normative necessity" employed in discussions in deontic logic, according to which "normatively necessary" is roughly equivalent to "obligatory".

A problem remains, though: haven't we learned from Hume that we should not accept necessary relations between distinct existences? And on Robust Realism, aren't normative and natural properties distinct existences? And isn't the specific supervenience thesis itself a statement of such relation? Perhaps the content of the norms can help somewhat in explaining the supervenience. But it does not undermine the conflict with Hume here. In fact, with this lesson from Hume in mind, all the explanation in terms of the content of the norms does is push the mystery one step back. If the basic moral (or other) norms call for necessary relations between distinct existences, doesn't this itself count strongly against accepting such norms?

At long last, it is time to bite (what some may think of as) a bullet. (Surprised?) Hume's Dictum is false. There *can* be necessary relations between distinct existences, at least when the distinct existences are normative on one side, and natural on the other. Asking how this could be is another way of asking how there could be moral (and other) norms that are of maximal jurisdiction. I do not have an answer to this question, but I do not feel the need to give one. Notice that unlike the extremely plausible specific supervenience thesis, the no-necessary-relations-between-distinct-existences principle is a highly theoretical metaphysical doctrine. The price in plausibility points of rejecting it is – if there even is a price here – completely affordable.[35] Now, the objection can be improved, and put in terms of a more modest Humean thesis. McPherson, for instance, puts things thus: "Commitment to brute necessary connections between distinct properties counts significantly against a view." Now, I think I am willing to accept this modestly Humean thesis (though I may have doubts about the "significantly" here). But it is not clear what it would take for a necessary connection between distinct existences to be *brute*. Is the necessary connection between Socrates and the singleton set whose only member is Socrates brute? Presumably we can explain it (to the extent that an explanation is necessary) by saying something about the nature of the membership relation or some such. And this, we usually seem to think, is quite enough. So perhaps we should settle for saying something about the nature of the normative properties – that it is in their nature to be determined in the right kind of way by natural ones – as an explanation of the necessary relation between

---

[35] For a general critical discussion of Hume's Dictum and the reasons for believing it, see Wilson (2010). Among other things, Wilson places pressure on the relevant understanding of distinctness, noticing that it is very hard to fill in the details here so that Hume's Dictum remains non-trivial and also at least somewhat plausible. Thus, for instance, if distinctness is understood as non-identity, then Hume's Dictum is arguably refuted by the purported necessary relations between sets and their members, or wholes and their parts, or determinables and their determinates. The version of Hume's Dictum that would be a problem for Robust Realism would be one that employs a "not-merely-nothing-over-and-above" understanding of distinctness. It is this version of Hume's Dictum that I reject in the text. I thank Josh DiPaolo for relevant discussion.

Some say that the supervenience challenge itself *just is* the problem for Robust Realism having to do with necessary relations between distinct existences (Dreier (1992, 18); Ridge (2007, 335); McPherson (manuscript)). As the text makes clear, I do not think that this is so. The initial problem is that of explaining supervenience. I think my drinking-age example shows that we can gain explanatory ground here *before* we get, as it were, to Hume's Dictum. But I agree that at that stage too a challenge remains, and so we need to reject Hume's Dictum.

distinct existences here.[36] Or perhaps we can again refer to the drinking-age analogy, extrapolating it to the case of necessary norms, and offering that as the needed explanation. I don't know if any of this suffices to show that in our case the necessary connection is not brute, but if not, this just shows how small the loss in plausibility points can be that is involved in violating Hume's Dictum.

It's important to notice here that it's one thing to accept *specific supervenience* as brute and quite another to accept *some* bruteness in the vicinity here.[37] I rejected earlier on as unsatisfying the strategy of accepting the supervenience itself as brute. And I offered something by way of explanation of it – the reference to the content of the relevant norms. So long as you agree that this does at least *some* explanatory work (and it seems you have to, unless you are willing to reject as worthless also the analogous explanation in the legal case), you have to concede that my line on specific supervenience does not amount to accepting it as brute. But my line on specific supervenience does require that I accept *some* brute (or pretty brute – see the previous paragraph) relation here between distinct existences, and so that Robust Realism stand in violation of Hume's Dictum. It is *this* result that, I argue, is not intuitively damaging. And if what remains of the venerable supervenience challenge to Robust Realism (after the explanation of specific supervenience in terms of the content of the relevant norms) is just the need to reject this piece of metaphysical dogma, progress has been made.

6.2.2.2 *General supervenience.*

So much, then, for specific supervenience, the supervenience of normative properties on the natural properties they do in fact supervene on. But what about general supervenience? The general supervenience thesis states that normative properties supervene on *some* natural ones. Unlike specific supervenience, general supervenience is independent of the true first-order theory. The intuitive thought here is that regardless of the true first-order theory, there can be no normative difference without a natural one, and it is a thought that can be (and usually is) accepted by people with radically different first-order views. Obviously, then, *general* supervenience cannot be explained by references to the content of specific norms.[38] But general supervenience too is highly plausible. Can it be explained consistently with Robust Realism? If not, isn't this a devastating problem for Robust Realism?

The modality relevant to the general supervenience of the normative is, it seems safe to say, conceptual.[39] It is conceptually impossible for there to be a normative difference

---

[36] Wedgwood (2007, 207 and on) offers something along these lines. But I have my doubts about the details of his suggestion. For some such doubts, see Schmitt and Schroeder (forthcoming).

[37] Dreier (1992, 28) and McPherson (manuscript) do not notice the significance of this distinction.

[38] Unsurprisingly, then, nothing like general supervenience straightforwardly applies in the legal case. It's not as if you can be confident before checking the content of the valid legal norms that drinking-status supervenes, say, on *some* age properties, even though you still don't know which. Whether something like global supervenience (on the natural, perhaps) applies to the legal case depends on jurisprudential issues (for instance, whether legal validity may be a matter of moral content) which I cannot discuss here.

[39] Notice how much less plausible the analogous claim about the purported supervenience of the mental on the physical sounds.

without a natural one. We can support this claim by reflecting on our responses to a hypothetical speaker who professed to reject general supervenience, or whose specific judgments seemed to constantly violate general supervenience – we would be inclined to treat her as using the relevant terms in some non-standard way.[40] This may seem to make things worse for the robust realist, for the stronger the explanandum, the stronger the needed explanans. But the truth lies in precisely the opposite direction.[41] For once general supervenience is seen as a conceptual thesis, it is harder to see what by way of explanation is called for here.

True, some conceptual truths can presumably be explained by other conceptually necessary truths. But some – perhaps the most basic ones – cannot. And it is quite plausible that it is a fairly basic feature of the way in which we use normative words that we take normative facts to be determined by non-normative, natural ones. It is not more mysterious, then, why general supervenience holds than it is that a word stipulated to have a certain meaning has that meaning.[42]

Notice that thus understood, there is nothing *metaphysical* about the (general) supervenience challenge (this will have to be qualified below).[43] In particular, the general supervenience worry has nothing directly to do with Hume's Dictum, or more generally with the need to accommodate some relation between two very different kinds of facts or properties. In particular, there is no parallel regarding general supervenience to the obvious advantage that the naturalist realist has over the robust realist in explaining *specific* supervenience (for on naturalist realism, normative properties are nothing over and above natural ones). When discussing general supervenience, metaphysics has by and large been left behind.

But there may be other challenges in the vicinity. Thus, Michael Ridge argues (2007, 339; perhaps following Blackburn (1985)) that what the realist still has to explain is why it is that we possess normative concepts (of which it is a conceptual truth that what falls under them supervenes on the natural). And he thinks that in explaining *this* the expressivist has a distinct advantage over the realist, because of the expressivist emphasis on the *function* of normative talk. But talk of function is something realists – even robust realists – can easily help themselves to. True, because we realists believe in normative properties that do not in any way depend on our conceptions of them, we would still need to explain how it is that concepts referring to these properties are also the ones that can serve helpful functions (say, recommending actions). But first, this is a different challenge from traditional ones about supervenience, and second, and more

---

[40] See, for instance, Dreier (1992, 15), and the references there.

[41] Here again I am indebted to comments from Jonas Olson.

[42] See here Ridge's (2007, 338) "shmong" example. Dreier (1992, 20) uses "cosmite" in a somewhat similar context, and on the following page discusses bachelor-related examples (though in the context of discussing Cornell, not Robust, Realism).

[43] See here Klagge's (1988) related distinction between ontological and ascriptive supervenience, and Darwall, Gibbard, and Railton's (1992, 36 n. 11) claim that the expressivist understands supervenience as "a normative constraint upon admissible moral argumentation rather than as a principle of metaphysics".

importantly, I believe it is a *very* close relative of the best understanding of the epistemological challenge to Robust Realism. My suggested solution to this latter challenge (in Chapter 7) can apply rather straightforwardly here too.[44] Relatedly, one can ask (as McPherson (manuscript) does): what reason do we have to believe that our stipulated concept is not incoherent, or that it is instantiated? The relevant conceptual knowledge, one may insist, is that normative properties supervene on natural ones *if the former exist*. But why believe the antecedent? Stipulation can't help with that. But again, if we have some general reason to believe that there is some correspondence between our relevant concepts and the relevant part of reality, then all is well. And as I argue in Chapter 7, we do have such reasons. So all is well.

Perhaps at the end of the day, the supervenience challenge – whether in the form of the call to explain specific *or* general supervenience – comes down merely to an expression of disbelief in the very possibility of norms, robustly realistically understood. If so, we find ourselves pretty much back at the initial challenge, the one I called Sheer Queerness. The thought that norms that satisfy general supervenience and that guarantee necessary relations between distinct existences are – for this very reason – unacceptable amounts to little more than the thought that objective values (or some such) are just too queer to be admitted into our ontology. And so at this point we should return also to Platts's impatient response: The queerest thing about the argument from queerness (understood as explicating the Sheer Queerness worry) is that it is called an argument.

---

[44] In Chapter 7 I suggest that we understand the epistemological challenge as a request for an explanation of the (purported) correlation between our normative beliefs and the normative truths, robustly realistically understood. The problem that emerges here in the text is, perhaps roughly, that of explaining the (purported) correlation between our normative concepts and normative properties. Once put this way, I take it the similarity is rather clear.

7

Epistemology

Even if Robust Realism is rather safe metaphysically – as I've tried to show in the previous chapter – it may be thought to be on shaky grounds epistemologically. For a common worry[1] runs – very roughly, and in a way to be refined later on – as follows: realists owe us an account of how it is that we can have epistemic access to the normative truths about which they are realists. If normative beliefs are about an independent order of normative facts, how is it that we know anything about them? How are these beliefs even justified, when they are? If realists resort to the highly suspicious faculty of rational intuition, how do they suggest to best understand its nature? What evidence can they present that it exists?

That Robust Realism faces this challenge is, it seems, uncontroversial among metaethicists, myself included. But this is as far as the agreement goes, for it is neither clear nor uncontroversial how best to understand the challenge, what the best realist attempt of coping with it is, and how successful this attempt is. In this chapter, I present the challenge in what I take to be its strongest version. Then, I show how robust realists can cope with it. I start by criticizing (in section 7.1) ways of articulating the epistemological challenge to realism that are found in the literature, claiming that they do not present the best – most challenging, and most challenging specifically for robust realists – version of the epistemological challenge. This purely negative discussion will result in a better grasp of the conditions a characterization of the epistemological challenge has to meet if it is to be theoretically useful in this way. With these desiderata in mind, I then present (in section 7.2) a *very* strong version of the epistemological challenge to realism, a version which has not, I believe, been adequately addressed in the literature, and which is the one I proceed to clarify and – eventually – respond to. I then argue that realists need a solution to the epistemological challenge *thus understood*. We realists shouldn't kid ourselves – it is a solution to this version of the challenge that we should be after. Before proceeding to suggest a solution to the epistemological challenge, I dedicate a section (7.3) to a discussion of Sharon Street's recent "Darwinian Dilemma" challenge to realism. I argue that at least as against *Robust* Realism it is a particular instance of the epistemological challenge as articulated in the preceding section, and that noticing this fact is the first step towards adequately addressing it.

---

[1] For one *locus classicus*, see Mackie (1977, 38).

In section 7.4 I finally present my suggested solution to the epistemological challenge properly understood. In the spirit of the methodology throughout this book, my suggested solution is somewhat modest in its ambition: I argue that the explanatory problem robust realists face is at least manageable, and that the theoretical price realists may end up paying because of the epistemological challenge is much lower than it may initially be thought. Here too, then, there may be a small price in plausibility points involved. But it is entirely affordable. In section (7.5) I briefly comment on the generality of the epistemological challenge (properly understood) and of my solution to it. In the final section (7.6) I address – in a *very* preliminary way – a worry about semantic access that is in some ways similar to the epistemological challenge addressed in the other sections of this chapter.

7.1 How not to understand the epistemological challenge

In this section I argue that the epistemological challenge to realism is not most helpfully put in terms of epistemic access, or epistemic justification of normative beliefs, or their reliability, or normative knowledge, or a particular instance of general skeptical worries, thus preparing the ground for the next section, where I present the version of this challenge that I will be most interested in.

7.1.1 Access

The worry is sometimes put in terms of epistemic access.[2] If there are normative truths that are independent of us – of our motivations, our responses, our social practices, indeed our normative judgments themselves – how can we gain epistemic access to them? Indeed, even assuming for the sake of argument that we do have normative knowledge, *how* is it that we do? By what *means* can we gain such knowledge? And the thought is, of course, that if the robust realist has nothing to say about the *means* by which some privileged epistemic status (like perhaps knowledge) is secured for normative beliefs, she has to conclude that normative beliefs do not after all enjoy this privileged epistemic status.

I think we can rather safely postpone discussion of these worries to the following subsections, without saying much more on epistemic access. This is not just because one way of understanding talk of epistemic access is as an unofficial introduction to one of the other ways of stating the challenge, or because as they stand, worries about epistemic access are too metaphorical to be theoretically helpful (it isn't clear, after all, what "access" exactly means here). The more important reason why we can safely avoid further discussion of the worry put in terms of epistemic access is the following. In the following subsections, I discuss versions of the epistemological worry put in terms of justification, reliability, and knowledge. It is possible, of course, that my arguments there fail. But if they do not, what *remaining* epistemological worry could talk of epistemic access introduce? If in the next subsections

---

[2] See, for instance, Timmons (1990, 114).

I manage to convince you that there are no special problems with the justification of normative beliefs, with the reliability of normative beliefs, or with normative knowledge, it seems to me you should be epistemologically satisfied. I do not see how talk of epistemic access should make you worried again.

However exactly talk of epistemic access is understood, then, it does not pose an epistemological challenge that is independent of those discussed below.

7.1.2 Justification

Many realists (and perhaps others as well) take the epistemological challenge to be one about the possibility – or perhaps actuality – of epistemic justification for our normative beliefs. And they reply in the obvious ways: by developing a theory of epistemic justification that allows for such justification of normative beliefs, or – more commonly – by showing that their favorite theory of epistemic justification in general nicely applies to the case of normative beliefs.[3]

It is, of course, an important metanormative (and also normative) question how normative beliefs (if indeed this is what they are) are to be justified, and so such intellectual endeavors are not without value. But still this is not a promising way of understanding specifically the epistemological challenge to Robust Realism, for the following three reasons.

First, on no theory of epistemic justification I am aware of do normative beliefs constitute an interesting particular instance of beliefs, an especially problematic class of beliefs (I'll have to qualify this point below). Whether you are a coherentist or a foundationalist (or perhaps hoping for some middle ground between them), whether you are an internalist or externalist about epistemic justification (or perhaps hoping for some middle ground between them), whether or not you think that epistemic justification is conceptually tied to epistemic responsibility, whether or not you like working with a conception of epistemic virtue – whatever your theory of epistemic justification, it is hard to see any *special* difficulties applying it to normative beliefs. Surely, for instance, the relations between beliefs that coherentists emphasize – consistency, explanatory coherence, etc. – can have as their relata normative beliefs as well.[4] Similarly, though perhaps there are no attractive candidates for indubitable normative foundations, we have pretty much given up on foundations thus under-stood elsewhere as well, and once foundationalism is made appropriately modest in its requirements – settling, perhaps, for defeasible justificatory status for the foundations – there are after all attractive candidates for such foundations among our normative beliefs as well.[5] Furthermore, it seems one can be as epistemically responsible (or

---

[3] See, for instance, Brink (1989, ch. 5), Sayre-McCord (1995), Scanlon (1998, 64–72), Shafer-Landau (2003, chs. 10–12), Tännsjö (2010, 60). For an antirealist presentation of the challenge in terms of justification (and also in terms of knowledge), see, for instance, Waldron (1992, 175). For a skepticism-friendly discussion of moral epistemology that focuses primarily on moral knowledge and justification see Sinnott-Armstrong (2006).

[4] See, for instance, Brink (1989, ch. 5) and Sayre-McCord (1995).

[5] See Audi (1995) and Shafer-Landau (2003, 258).

irresponsible) in one's normative beliefs as in any other, it seems one can hold a normative belief – just like any other – against one's epistemic duties (if there are such duties), it seems one can exercise – or fail to exercise – any intellectual virtue in the forming, revising, or holding of normative beliefs, and so on. If the problem is that of allowing for the epistemic justification of normative beliefs, then – given an acceptable general theory of epistemic justification – it seems too easy to solve, at least in outline.[6] And this suggests that the epistemological challenge to realism should not be understood as one about justification at all. Things would have been different, of course, had there been any reason to believe that some feature of normative beliefs made them an *especially* problematic class of beliefs when it comes to justification. But I know of no reason to believe that this is so.[7]

To see my second reason for thinking that the epistemological challenge to realism is not best thought of as a challenge about justification, remember that we are trying to articulate an epistemological challenge *to Robust Realism*, and so one that highlights a difficulty that metanormative robust realists face but that others do not, or at least a difficulty that is especially acute for realists. But the problem of accommodating epistemic justification for normative beliefs does not seem to be of this sort. Notice that nothing in the previous paragraph seemed to depend on a realist (much less a robust realist) view of normativity or morality. Of course, perhaps some metanormative views work better with some theories of justification – everything here depends on the details. And so perhaps it can after all be shown that the problem of accommodating the epistemic justification of normative beliefs is somewhat more acute for Robust Realism than in general. But I don't know of any way of filling in the details here that has this as a consequence. Until one is presented, there is no *specific* problem here for Robust Realism.

Third, let us not pretend that we have a theory of epistemic justification we are all happy with. Given this unhappy state of affairs, if a theory of epistemic justification rules out all normative beliefs as epistemically unjustified, this counts at least as heavily against that theory of justification as it does against the justificatory status of normative beliefs. For is there really a theory of epistemic justification in the truth of which you are (and should be) more confident than in the truth of such sentences as "I justifiably believe that torture is prima facie wrong"? When we try to determine which theory of epistemic justification to accept, it seems to me it counts rather heavily against a proposed theory if according to it no normative belief is justified.[8] (It counts even more heavily against such a theory if according to it no a priori belief is justified, a point

---

[6] At least with regard to justification, then, I agree with Sayre-McCord (1995, 138) when he says: "there is no distinctive epistemology of moral belief".

[7] It may be thought that the fact that normative beliefs are *controversial* in some fairly robust way could do the job here. But it is not at all clear that they *are* controversial in a way that many other beliefs aren't, nor is it clear what follows from such disagreement that we do find here. I discuss disagreement at length in the next chapter.

[8] Compare: If the causal theory of knowledge entails that we have no mathematical knowledge, this counts heavily against that theory, perhaps *more* heavily against it than against mathematical knowledge.

to which I return.) Now, perhaps given a theory of epistemic justification that entailed this surprising result, but otherwise scored sufficiently highly on the list of theoretical virtues, we would be justified in biting the bullet and acknowledging that no normative belief is ever justified.[9] But it seems to me highly unlikely that we have such a theory at hand or that one is likely to emerge. And this poses yet another difficulty for the attempt to understand the epistemological challenge to realism as one about epistemic justification.

Important questions about the justification of normative beliefs remain, of course, and I am not suggesting that there are no interesting philosophical challenges in filling in the details of a theory of justification and a metanormative theory so that the two cohere nicely with each other in a non-skeptical way. But for the reasons just specified, I suggest that we not understand the epistemological challenge to Robust Realism as one about justification.

7.1.3 Reliability

Reliability may be thought necessary for justification, or for knowledge, or perhaps epistemically relevant in some other way. So if there is a special problem about the reliability of normative beliefs, perhaps it is in terms of reliability that the epistemological challenge to realism is best understood.

I think there is something right in this suggestion, and I get back to it in section 7.2. But let me here set aside what is *not* a good way of understanding the challenge. The problem cannot be that normative beliefs *cannot* be reliable, or that classifying them either as reliable or as unreliable constitutes a category mistake, or something of that sort.

A class of beliefs is reliable, I take it, if and only if a sufficiently large portion of it is true.[10] If so, wherever there is truth, there is the possibility of reliability. Now, it is not obvious, of course, that there *is* truth in ethics and in normativity, and some

---

[9] Compare: If the causal theory of knowledge entails that we have no mathematical knowledge, but otherwise scores sufficiently highly on the list of theoretical virtues, perhaps we would be justified in biting the bullet and acknowledging that we never have mathematical knowledge, indeed that such knowledge is impossible.

Of course, we need to be careful here. Perhaps, for instance, the causal theory of knowledge only entails that we have no mathematical knowledge *when conjoined with mathematical Platonism*. If so, we should reject (at least) one of the *three* propositions: the causal theory of knowledge, mathematical Platonism, and that we have some mathematical knowledge. Analogously, a given theory of justification may entail that we have no justified normative beliefs *only when conjoined with a specific metanormative theory*, say, Robust Realism. In such a case, one way out would be to discard Robust Realism (while continuing to accept both the relevant theory of justification and the justificatory status of some normative beliefs). And this significantly weakens the point in the text – that such a theory of justification (together with Robust Realism) rule out justified normative beliefs counts against that theory of justification only if we're (justifiably!) less confident in it than in *each* of the two propositions (i) Robust Realism, and (ii) that we have some justified normative beliefs. I thank Stephen Finlay for pressing me on this and related points.

[10] You may think that more is needed for reliability, and in particular that reliability contains some modal feature, so that a set of beliefs is reliable only if, roughly speaking, it is not an accident that sufficiently many of them are true. At least one natural way of understanding such a requirement leads to what I take to be the proper understanding of the epistemological challenge, in section 7.2.

metaethicists think no such truth is to be had. But such a claim can certainly not be used as a premise in what is supposed to be an independent challenge to Robust Realism. If there are no normative truths, then realism is indeed defeated, but not by the epistemological challenge, but rather by whatever argument is supposed to support the claim that there are no normative truths. In our context, then, the antirealist cannot help himself to anything like the denial of normative truths. And if so, nor can he establish this worry about the reliability of normative beliefs.

There is no objection to the very attribution of reliability to some sets of normative beliefs, then, at least not one that is not question-begging in our context.

7.1.4 Knowledge

Isn't the epistemological worry, though, primarily about knowledge? Isn't the worry that robust realists have no plausible way of accounting for moral or more broadly normative knowledge? Isn't the worry that in order to allow for the kind of access or relation to the purportedly independent truths the realist is going to have to resort to that awful trick, the mysterious faculty of rational intuition? If she does, it seems her realism should be rejected for this very reason, and if she does not, she cannot accommodate normative knowledge, and so must settle for a very skeptical kind of realism. The epistemological challenge thus comes down to one about the impossibility of knowledge on robustly realist assumptions.

But this too is not, I think, a promising way of stating the challenge. To see why, let me assume (for now) that knowledge is justified true belief of a special kind (the qualification needed in order to deal with Gettier cases). If this is so, all that the realist has to do in order to accommodate normative knowledge is to account for normative truths, normative beliefs, justification of normative beliefs, and that extra bit needed to deal with Gettier. Very well, then, let's see: for the reason mentioned in the previous subsection, in the context of an attempt to articulate an independent challenge to Robust Realism, we are to assume that there are normative truths, and furthermore that at least some normative judgments express beliefs (rather than, say, some conative attitudes). And we already dealt with justification in section 7.1.2. All that remains, then, is to accommodate with regard to normative beliefs the necessary anti-Gettier clause, whatever it is. But then surely the realist is entitled at least to a wait-and-see attitude. "Given that I've given you already so much, what reason do we have to believe that I won't be able to give you *that* too? When you epistemologists have settled on an anti-Gettier clause, let me know, and we'll take it from there." Things would have been different had we had some reason to think that any plausible anti-Gettier clause is going to disallow normative knowledge. But I see no reason so to think. Indeed, we can draw the distinction between Gettier cases and non-Gettier cases *within* the set of normative beliefs. Furthermore, the anti-luck intuition with which Gettier is often identified – that what is needed for knowledge is a non-luckily justified true belief – seems to apply in the normative realm as it does anywhere else (compare a sophisticated true normative conclusion reached by a sloppy thinker and by a careful one).

True, some suggested anti-Gettier clauses are hard to apply with regard to normative beliefs (I have in mind causal and counterfactual ones,[11] which – assuming that normative truths are causally inert and that some of them are necessary – raise problems for normative knowledge). And indeed, it is no longer uncontroversial that knowledge can be analyzed as justified true belief together with some anti-Gettier clause or another. But here I want to rely again on a point already made with regard to justification: given the unhappy situation of our understanding of the nature of knowledge, if an account of knowledge entails that we can never know that racist discrimination is unjust (and the like), this should be taken as a strong reason to reject that account of knowledge, rather than to reject normative knowledge.[12]

7.1.5 Particular instances of skeptical worries

But perhaps all of this has been misguided, as I have been assuming that *some* of our beliefs are justified, that some of our beliefs constitute knowledge, etc. In an epistemological discussion, it may be thought, such assumptions cannot be taken for granted. Perhaps, in other words, the epistemological challenge to metanormative realism should be understood as a particular instance of a general skeptical worry, or perhaps a family of particular instances of general skeptical worries?

It is, of course, a worthwhile epistemological project to find ways of coping even with the most general of skeptical worries. But at least absent some further story, it is hard to see why worries about evil demons, or brains in vats, or criteria, or regresses, or fallibility, should prove to be especially problematic with regard to *normative* knowledge (or justification, or warrant, or whatever), or indeed why – if they cannot be satisfactorily addressed – such worries are especially problematic for Robust Realism compared to competing metanormative views.[13] And though I think we should take

---

[11] Roughly speaking: a causal anti-Gettier clause requires, as a necessary condition for knowledge, that the relevant justified true belief be caused by the relevant fact (or its constituents). A counterfactual anti-Getttier clause requires, as a necessary condition for knowledge, that the relevant justified true belief "track the truth", so that had the believed proposition been false, it would not have been believed by the relevant thinker. This requirement is sometimes called *sensitivity*; and there are other suggestions for modal requirements on knowledge in the vicinity here.

[12] This is especially true if the scope for which the relevant account of knowledge causes trouble is even wider than the normative – if it includes, for instance, the apriori in general. For this dialectical point, mostly in the context of discussing the causal theory of knowledge, see Liggins (2006), and somewhat more generally, Lewis (1986, 109).

[13] Much of Shafer-Landau's (2003, e.g. 235) epistemological discussion in the context of a general defense of metaethical realism is really an attempt to deal with particular instances of general skeptical worries. And he repeatedly emphasizes this very point – that the challenge to realism is a particular instance of general skeptical worries – as a part of his defense of realism (see e.g. 239). But I take this not as evidence that realism can cope with the epistemological challenge, but rather as evidence that this is not the best way to put the epistemological challenge.

Sinnott-Armstrong's (2006) elaborate discussion of moral epistemology is almost entirely a discussion of general skeptical arguments as applied to morality. Indeed, in a recent symposium about this book (in *Philosophy and Phenomenological Research* 77(3)), the entire discussion – both by the commentators (Railton, Copp, and Timmons) and by Sinnott-Armstrong himself – is purely epistemological. Morality has by and large dropped out of the picture.

such skeptical worries very seriously, they do not give the robust realist any reason to worry that is not shared by everyone else. They do not, in other words, increase the plausibility of any competing metanormative theory, and so are not even the beginning of an objection to Robust Realism.

If it could be shown that some general skeptical argument is *especially* worrying when it comes to normative beliefs, or perhaps with regard to normative beliefs realistically understood, this would of course be of interest in our context. But I don't know of any attempt – let alone successful attempt – to show any such thing.

7.1.6 What we want from the epistemological challenge

Here, then, are the desiderata for a suggested understanding of the epistemological challenge to Robust Realism: we want it to be peculiar to *normative* beliefs; we want it to pose a special, or at least especially hard, problem *for Robust Realism*; we do not want it to beg the question against the robust realist (by, for instance, assuming that there are no normative truths); and we want to avoid as much as possible relying on a highly contested epistemological notion (like that of knowledge or justification). Let me turn to the challenge that does, I think, satisfy all these desiderata.

7.2 How to understand the epistemological challenge: explaining correlations

It will prove helpful, I think, to introduce the challenge with a couple of analogies. After presenting the challenge, I then comment on some implications of understanding the epistemological challenge along these lines.

7.2.1 The challenge

Suppose that Josh has many beliefs about a distant village in Nepal. And suppose that very often his beliefs about the village are true. Indeed, a very high proportion of his beliefs about this village are true, and he believes many of the truths about this village. In other words, there is a striking correlation between Josh's beliefs about that village and the truths about that village. Such a striking correlation calls for explanation. And in such a case there is no mystery about how such an explanation would go – we would probably look for a causal route from the Nepalese village to Josh (he was there, saw all there is to see and remembers all there is to remember, or maybe he read texts that were written by people who were there, etc.). The reason we are so confident that there is such an explanation is precisely that the striking correlation is so striking – absent some such explanation, the correlation would be just too miraculous to believe.

Utilizing such an example, Hartry Field (1989, 25–30) suggests the following problem for mathematical Platonism. Mathematicians are remarkably good when it comes to their mathematical beliefs. Almost always, when mathematicians believe a mathematical proposition p, it is indeed true that p, and when they disbelieve p (or at least when they believe not-p) it is indeed false that p. There is, in other words, a striking correlation between mathematicians' mathematical beliefs (at least up to a certain level of complexity) and the mathematical truths. Such a striking correlation calls for explanation. But it doesn't seem that mathematical Platonists are in a position to offer any such explanation. The mathematical objects they believe in are abstract, and so causally inert, and so they cannot be causally responsible for mathematicians' beliefs; the mathematical truths Platonists believe in are supposed to be independent of mathematicians and their beliefs, and so mathematicians' beliefs aren't causally (or constitutively) responsible for the mathematical truths. Nor does there seem to be some third factor that is causally responsible for both. What we have here, then, is a striking correlation between two factors that Platonists cannot explain in any of the standard ways of explaining such a correlation – by invoking a causal (or constitutive) connection from the first factor to the second, or from the second to the first, or from some third factor to both. But without such an explanation, the striking correlation may just be too implausible to believe, and, Field concludes, so is mathematical Platonism.

Notice how elegant this way of stating the challenge is. There is no hidden assumption about the nature of knowledge, or of epistemic justification, or anything of the sort. There is just a striking correlation, the need to explain it, and the apparent unavailability of any explanation to the challenged view in the philosophy of mathematics.

Returning to normativity, then, here is the version of the epistemological challenge I suggest that we focus on: very often, when we accept a normative judgment j, it is indeed true that j; and very often when we do not accept a normative judgment j (or at least when we reject it), it is indeed false that j. So there is a correlation between (what the realist takes to be) normative truths and our normative judgments. What explains this correlation? On a robustly realist view of normativity, it can't be that our normative judgments are causally or constitutively responsible for the normative truths, because the normative truths are supposed to be independent of our normative judgments. And given that (at least basic) normative truths are causally inert,[14] they are not causally responsible for our normative beliefs. Nor does there seem to be some third-factor explanation available to the robust realist. And so the robust realist is committed to an unexplained striking correlation, and this may just be too much to believe.[15]

This way of understanding the epistemological challenge to metanormative realism nicely satisfies the desiderata mentioned in section 7.1.6 above: it is not an instance of

[14] If you think that normative truths are causally efficacious, and in particular cause (perhaps indirectly) our normative judgments, you are off the hook (this is one advantage of Oddie's version of Robust Realism). But presumably then there are other problems you have to deal with.
[15] I think – but I am not sure – that Nagel (1997, 76 and 131) flirts with the claim that such correlations are to be taken as brute, and perhaps necessarily so.

the most general skeptical worries, because in many other domains, most notably with regard to beliefs about middle-sized physical objects, this challenge can be coped with rather easily (what explains the correlation between these truths and our beliefs about them is presumably the causal-perceptual relations between us and the physical objects around us); it poses a special problem to Robust Realism, because other metanormative views are arguably immune to it (a point I return to below); it does not beg any question against the realist; and it elegantly avoids relying on contestable accounts of knowledge, justification, or any other epistemological notion.

7.2.2 Some implications

When thus understood, to which metanormative views does the epistemological challenge apply? The initial challenge – the need to explain the supposed correlation between normative truths and our normative beliefs – seems to me to be perfectly general. But some metanormative views can explain such correlation with relative ease. In particular, views according to which normative truths are causally efficacious – perhaps because reducible to or identical with natural facts[16] – can (in principle, at least) explain the correlation in the obvious way, by claiming that the normative truths (facts, properties, objects) are causally responsible for our normative beliefs. I say that naturalist versions of realism can *in principle* explain the correlation between the normative truths and our normative beliefs, because whether or not such an explanation can be supplied depends on the details of the relevant naturalist account, and nothing here is obvious. It's just that there is no general reason to suspect that a naturalist realist can*not* come up with such an explanation, whereas there does seem to be such a reason in the case of the robust realist.

In a very different way, response-dependence views of normativity are also not threatened by the challenge above, because they can explain the correlation by invoking a causal or constitutive connection from our relevant dispositions or judgments to the normative truths.[17]

This suggested understanding of the epistemological challenge, then, is primarily about reliability. But it's not about the possibility of reliable normative beliefs. Rather, it starts from the claim that such reliability is highly unlikely to be brute, unexplainable. Given the apparent unavailability of any such explanation to the robust metanormative realist, then, the challenge concludes that such realism is highly implausible. Now, this way of putting things may give rise to the suspicion that the challenge misses its target. Perhaps, it may be conceded, the realist has a problem with the *reliability* of our normative beliefs. But their epistemic *justification* can survive, because reliability is not

---

[16] Oddie is not a reductionist or a naturalist, but he thinks values are causally efficacious, and indeed his motivation for this (surprising, I think) claim is that this is his way of coping with some version of the epistemological challenge. See Oddie (2005, 181).

[17] *Ideal*-response-dependence views may not be in a better shape regarding the epistemological challenge compared to robustly realist views. See Dancy (1986, 178–9).

necessary for justification. The suggested challenge, in other words, is externalist in the sense of the internalist–externalist debate with regard to epistemic justification, it is about matters of fact in the objective world. But justification, so the thought goes, is internal, supervening on what is cognitively accessible to the thinker by reflection alone.[18] And so perhaps the robust realist should just acknowledge the loss of reliability while insisting that she can account for justified normative beliefs, and perhaps also for normative knowledge.

True, the challenge does start from an externalist perspective, asking about the explanation of our reliability in normative matters or of the correlation between the normative truths and our normative beliefs. But in order to appreciate its full strength it is important to see that the challenge can be "internalized", and this even assuming that internalists are right about epistemic justification.[19] It can, in other words, be shown to defeat (or perhaps undermine) even justification internalistically understood. Perhaps, if internalists are right about epistemic justification, I can justifiably form a belief using an unreliable belief-forming method. But even if this is so, I can't justifiably form a belief using what *I know* is an unreliable method. Perhaps, for instance, I can be justified in forming color-beliefs based on color-perception even in circumstances in which my color-perception is not reliable, and without having any beliefs *about* the reliability of color-perception in general or in these circumstances in particular. But in circumstances in which I *know* (or *justifiably believe*) that my color-perception is unreliable (say, because of misleading lighting) surely I lose whatever justification I may have had for my color-perception-based beliefs. Perhaps, in other words, reliability is not necessary for initial justification, but any such justification is at the very least defeated (or perhaps even undermined) when one *knows* (or justifiably believes) that one's belief or the method that formed it is in fact unreliable. Getting back to our challenge, then: if a brute correlation is too much to believe, and if no explanation is available to the robust realist, then she must conclude that there is after all no correlation between her normative beliefs and the normative truths. And knowing that, any (internalistically understood) justification she may have had for her normative beliefs is defeated (or undermined).[20] In other words, even if our robust realist has a general internalist account of epistemic justification she's entirely happy with, and even if this account

[18] This characterization of internalism comes from Pryor (2001, section 3). There are others, of course.

[19] For a closely related point, see Joyce (2006, 179–82).

[20] As a conversation with John Bengson made me see, the reasoning in the text here is in a number of ways imprecise. First, things have to be put in terms of degree of justification – so that if the robust realist does not have an explanation for the correlation, she is *less* justified in believing that it is there than she otherwise would have been. Second, there is a non-obvious (but clearly highly plausible) transition assumed here from being less justified in believing that the correlation is there to being more justified in believing that the correlation is not there. Third, there is a final transition from being more justified in believing that the correlation is not there to being less justified in having the relevant moral beliefs themselves. Each of these two transitions may, I guess, be questioned. But they are – if not in general, at least as applied here – highly plausible, and it would be a very inadvisable dialectical move on behalf of the robust realist to let her Robust Realism depend on rejecting the legitimacy of any of these transitions.

unproblematically applies to normative beliefs as well, and even if it doesn't require anything about reliability, she should *still* be worried about the epistemological challenge as presented above. For given the (purported) unexplainability of her reliability of our normative beliefs, she should come to believe that they are unreliable. And their unreliability would defeat whatever initial justification she may have had for them.[21] If so, the realist can then maintain her commitment to realism only at the price of a rather thoroughgoing skepticism about the normative.[22] And while this is a possible position to have, stakes have certainly been raised: if the only way to be a realist is to deny epistemic justification for any normative belief (at least of the epistemologically informed, those who can run the argument in this paragraph in their heads), then Robust Realism loses significant plausibility points.

This is also the reason why the robust realist cannot avoid the need to explain the correlation by denying that it exists: knowing that there is no correlation between even his own normative beliefs and the normative truths, he can no longer hold these normative beliefs justifiably (and so, perhaps nor can he hold them as beliefs at all). The price of denying the correlation is skepticism. And it is without a doubt a serious price.

This version of the epistemological challenge also nicely explains the role of the resort to the faculty of rational intuition in this context – both the need for it, and why it will not help. A robust realist may feel that her only way of explaining the correlation between the normative truths and her normative judgments depends on there being some quasi-perceptual faculty that puts us in touch with the normative truths in roughly the same way our perceptual faculties put us in touch with empirical truths about nearby mid-sized objects. But a resort to such a faculty won't help the robust realist: For either this quasi-perceptual faculty is causal (like perception), putting us in causal relations with the normative truths, or it isn't. If it is, then the normative truths cannot be causally inert, as on Robust Realism they must be. And if this faculty is not causal, then for everything thus far said it is very hard to see how it can help in explaining the correlation that needs explaining.

Until very, very recently, no realist (to the best of my knowledge) has ever addressed the challenge thus understood.[23] For instance, in Brink's (1989, ch. 5), Scanlon's (1998,

---

[21] Bedke (2009, for instance 200) emphasizes the distinction between the initial justification and the availability of a defeater here.

[22] "Skepticism about the normative" is here meant to denote a view that is skeptical in the general epistemological sense, that is, roughly, the view according to which knowledge or justification or warrant of normative propositions is impossible. Of course, such terms are often used in other ways (as denoting some nihilist, or error-theoretic views of the normative).

[23] The very recent contributions (following Street (2006), perhaps some of the recently fashionable scientifically minded discussions of moral epistemology, and to a small extent also following my paper on which this chapter is based (Enoch 2010a)) include Skarsaune (2011), Wielenberg (2010), and Parfit (2011, vol. 2, section 114 (mostly the Massive Coincidence Argument, starting on page 492)).

Wedgwood (2006) mentions something very close to this challenge, but by the time he gets to his solution, it is no longer, I think, this challenge he is addressing, and in conversation he has made it clear that he is indeed interested in a different challenge (that of explaining how it is that we are justified in our moral beliefs).

64–72), and Shafer-Landau's (2003, chs. 10–12) rather elaborate epistemological discussions – all conducted in the general context of defending some kind of moral realism – nothing like this challenge is even mentioned, let alone addressed.[24] And the same is true of a fairly recent collection of papers on moral epistemology.[25] This may give rise to the worry that "my" epistemological challenge is simply a *different* epistemological challenge from more traditional ones, that it does not capture the traditional worry(ies). But I don't think that this is so, for the following reason. My version of the epistemological challenge to realism makes other versions redundant: if a realist can cope with my version of the challenge, it's not clear that she needs to worry about others; and if she cannot deal with my version of the challenge, she should find no comfort in her ability to cope with the other versions. The first of these conditionals is partly supported by the arguments in section 7.1, showing the limited force of other ways of understanding the epistemological challenge to Robust Realism. Furthermore, given a plausible explanation of the correlation between our normative beliefs and the normative truths, it seems we are justified in believing that *there is* such a correlation, and this seems to suffice for our being justified in holding on to many of our normative beliefs, regardless of whatever else we can say about their justification. In the other direction, the second conditional – if the robust realist cannot cope with this challenge, she is not off the epistemological hook – has been established by the earlier point in this section, namely, that without a solution to this epistemological worry realism entails skepticism, and this regardless of what else the relevant realist can say about knowledge, or justification, or some such. But if an epistemological challenge is such that without solving it the realist is still in epistemological trouble (regardless of her replies to other epistemological worries), and that after solving it the realist is (almost completely) off the epistemological hook, then, I submit, it is a very good understanding of what underlies traditional epistemological challenges to Robust Realism.

For these reasons, then, the challenge as stated in section 7.2.1 is how I suggest that we understand the epistemological challenge to Robust Realism. And we realists should not kid ourselves: without a solution to this *strongest* version of the epistemological challenge we are not off the epistemological hook.

7.3 Interlude: Street's Darwinian Dilemma

As already mentioned, no one (as far as I know) has articulated the epistemological challenge to Robust Realism in quite this (strongest) way. But in a recent paper Sharon

For anti- (or non-) realist hints at this challenge, see Wright (1988, 25 n. 36), Timmons (1990) (though Timmons raises it as a worry only for the combination of (naturalist, new-wave) realism and a coherentist theory of justification), Gibbard (2003, 258) (though Gibbard raises it as a worry for his quasi-realism rather than for realism), and Bedke (2009) (though Bedke thinks of his "cosmic coincidence" challenge only as a challenge to the conjunction of non-naturalist realism and an intuitionist epistemology).

[24] For a similar accusation against (fellow) realists, see Wedgwood (2006, 62, especially footnote 2).
[25] Sinnott-Armstrong and Timmons (1995).

Street (2006) comes very close. And it will prove useful, I think, to discuss some of her claims in detail.[26]

Realists, Street argues, are committed to the response-independence of some normative truths. And if they are to avoid large-scale skepticism about our normative judgments, realists must think that often enough we get things right, that our normative judgments are at least often enough in line with the independent normative truths. But our normative judgments have been shaped to a large extent by evolutionary pressures. So realists are committed to a rather strong correlation between the independent normative truths and the normative judgments you can expect evolutionarily successful creatures to make, the normative judgments that were (roughly speaking) selected for. But how can the realist explain such a correlation? In answering this question, realists face a dilemma. If the realist fails to supply such an explanation, she is committed to what looks as unbelievable as a miracle – the fact that as sheer coincidence evolutionary forces pushed us in the direction of the independent normative truths. A commitment to such an amazing fluke is unacceptable. On the other horn of the dilemma, the only realist-friendly explanation of the correlation seems to be a tracking account of some sort, according to which our normative judgments and the evolutionary pressures shaping them causally track the independent normative truths. And Street rejects such an explanation on scientific grounds (alternative explanations of the emergence of our normative judgments are simply much better). Either way, then, the realist is in deep trouble.

Let me not pause here to attempt an evaluation of the scientific claims and evolutionary speculations[27] Street relies on, for – as Street herself concedes (2006, 155) – there is nothing essentially Darwinian about her Darwinian Dilemma. Replace any other (non-tracking) causal explanation of why we make the normative judgments that we do in fact make, and the realist will again find herself up against the problem of explaining strong correlations analogous to the one Street draws attention to. So any such causal story will do in order to raise the challenge of explaining a correlation of this kind, and the realist still needs a way out.[28]

Once this is noticed, it is clear, I think, that Street's Darwinian Dilemma can be seen as a particular instance of the most general epistemological challenge to Robust Realism, properly understood. The general challenge – so I suggested above – is that of coming up with an explanation of a correlation between our relevant beliefs and the relevant truths. If we plug in the further premise that what explains our having the

---

[26] For a precursor, see Gibbard (2003, 263–5). And for a related argument, see Joyce (2006, ch. 6).

[27] For Street's own characterization using this term, see Street (2006, 112–13).

[28] Perhaps this is why Thomas Nagel – a robust realist (in some moods, at least) – suspects (1986, 145) that realism is incompatible with the availability of a purely naturalistic explanation of our normative judgments. And the full generality of this way of understanding the challenge – its independence of any specific story about how our moral and other normative judgments come about – is why I can afford my nonchalance regarding the recently fashionable more empirically minded evolutionary and neuroscientific literature here: The details just aren't important either for the best statement of the challenge, or for my suggested way of coping with it. For a discussion of this recent literature in a closely related context, see Wielenberg (2010).

normative beliefs we do in fact have is broadly speaking evolutionary explanations, we get, in essence, Street's *Darwinian* Dilemma. For *naturalist* realist views, Street's dilemma may very well be an especially interesting or problematic particular instance of the general epistemological challenge.[29] For *robust* realists, though, it is quite safe to assume that Street's dilemma is *merely* a particular instance of the general epistemological challenge.

Noting the relation between Street's Darwinian Dilemma and the epistemological challenge in its strongest version is, I want next to argue, more than just an interesting observation. Street's way of thinking about the epistemological challenge is also a good way to think about how to solve it. I move, then, to the presentation of my suggested solution to the epistemological challenge (and Street's Darwinian Dilemma along with it).

7.4 How to cope with the epistemological challenge

In order to present my realist way of coping with the epistemological challenge, I start with two methodological remarks (in 7.4.1 and 7.4.2). I then proceed to present the solution (in 7.4.3).

7.4.1 *Scoring points in an explanatory game*

The challenge, it should be clear, is an explanatory one. Brute, unexplained and even unexplainable, correlations are not, after all, impossible, and so even if the realist has nothing to offer by way of an explanation of the correlation between the normative truths and our normative beliefs (or – in Street's version – the normative truths and the normative beliefs which are likely to have been selected for) realism is not yet *refuted*. It's just that we should opt for the best metaethical theory, the one that – perhaps among other desiderata – best explains whatever needs explaining. And so, if the robust realist cannot explain a striking correlation such as the one the epistemological challenge focuses on, realism loses plausibility points, perhaps to the point of un-acceptability.

But then, once it is kept in mind that here too it's all about plausibility points, and furthermore about *overall* plausibility points,[30] the following three points are worth making.

First, the correlation that calls for explanation is not *all that* striking. We are not, after all, *that* good in forming and revising our normative beliefs.[31] Furthermore, how strong the correlation is between the normative truths and our normative judgments depends

---

[29]   I think that it is in this spirit that Copp (2008b) replies to Street.

[30]   This is a point Shafer-Landau (2003, 234) emphasizes in our context.

[31]   Or, in Street's version – the correlation between (what we take to be) the normative truths and normative judgments that are likely to have been selected for is not that strong. Consider the false but seemingly evolutionarily useful "The interests of others with whom we have no privileged genetic or reciprocal relations do not count at all", and "The interests of non-human animals do not count at all".

on – among other factors – who "we" are. All humans who ever existed? All humans now existing? All well-educated, adult, humans? All those living in liberal democracies? All those with a college education? All philosophers? Just you and me? Just me?[32]

The reason the robust realist could not plausibly deny the correlation to be explained, remember, was that doing so would result in skepticism. But then the correlation the realist must acknowledge – and the one it seems independently plausible to believe in – can be fairly weak, so long as it is strong enough to block the inference to skepticism. In other words, so long as the realist accepts that she and the like of her are at least somewhat more likely to get things right rather than wrong with regard to normative issues (or a specified subset of them), she can rationally and wholeheartedly if modestly hold on to her normative beliefs (or to those in the specified subset) and not deteriorate to skepticism. And here as elsewhere, the weaker the correlation to be explained, the less impressive the explanans has to be in order to shoulder the explanatory burden. I return to this point shortly.

Second, the explanandum is weaker also in another respect. Given a starting point of normative beliefs that are not too far-off, presumably some reasoning mechanisms (and perhaps some other mechanisms as well) can get us increasingly closer to the truth by eliminating inconsistencies, increasing overall coherence, eliminating arbitrary distinctions, drawing analogies, ruling out initially justified beliefs whose justificatory status has been defeated later on, etc. Now, it may of course be asked what explains the reliability of these reasoning mechanisms themselves.[33] But first, this question is much more general, because such reasoning processes occur everywhere, not just in revising and shaping our *normative* beliefs, so that this is not especially a problem for the metanormative realist. And second, evolutionary answers to this question – what explains the reliability of our reasoning processes – can rather easily (if speculatively) be thought of here. Precisely because they are applied everywhere, including in revising beliefs that are more transparently evolutionarily beneficial, the ability to employ reliable reasoning mechanisms may very well be itself evolutionarily beneficial, or the upshot of more basic reasoning abilities that are themselves evolutionarily helpful. It seems, then, that in our context we are entitled to assume that given good enough starting points our reasoning processes will in general get us closer to rather than further from the normative truths. So what remains to be explained is not the full scope of the correlation between our normative beliefs and the normative truths, but just the correlation in starting points,[34] why, in other words, we are not too far off from the start, so that even reasonably good reasoning mechanisms can't get us to the kind of correlation between beliefs and truths we do in fact see.[35] Of course, the details depend

---

[32] For sometimes "'we' means: 'you and I, and I'm none too sure about you'" (Lewis, 1989, 84).

[33] What I say in section 7.5 can be seen as a partial answer to this question.

[34] A point acknowledged by Street (2006, 123), and emphasized also by Copp (2008b).

[35] Wedgwood (2007, 79–80) mentions the starting-point problem for his reflective-equilibrium-like theory of justification, noticing that his suggested solution of (his version of) the epistemological challenge does not solve it.

on the details of the relevant empirical science. My point here is then a rather modest one: it seems plausible to speculate that some reasoning (and perhaps other) mechanisms can get our normative beliefs closer to the normative truths, so long as the starting points are not too far off. To the extent that this speculation can be supported, what the epistemological challenge requires that realists explain is this weaker explanandum, namely, that the relevant starting points are not too far off.

Finally, what I must do in order to vindicate Robust Realism is to show that it beats competing theories in overall plausibility points. I do *not* have to show that Robust Realism does better than competing metanormative theories *in every respect, with regard to every problem*. Given the positive arguments for Robust Realism in Chapters 2–5, then, the task of this chapter is to show that Robust Realism doesn't lose *too many* plausibility points in responding to the epistemological challenge as presented above. And this means that flukes are not as theoretically frightening as Street, for instance, seems to think they are – so long, that is, as belief in them is well-motivated by the advantages of Robust Realism elsewhere. Of course, it is still important to show that the flukes realists are committed to are not all that fluky – and this, indeed, is what I am about to do. But that some flukes remain should not be a cause for too much distress.

7.4.2 How correlations get explained

That said, I agree that the (somewhat) striking correlation between the purported independent normative truths and our normative beliefs does call for explanation, and that declaring it a fluke is something we realists should avoid if at all we can. How, then, can the robust realist explain this correlation? Indeed, how can correlations *in general* be explained?

The obvious ways (and the ones Street focuses on) are two: if the correlated factors are A and B, then (roughly speaking) either A-facts are somehow (causally, constitutively, or both) responsible for the B-facts, or the B-facts are responsible for the A-facts. And applied to our case: the correlation would be explained if either the normative truths were responsible for our normative beliefs, or our normative beliefs were responsible for the normative truths. But, as argued in section 7.2.1 above, it is exactly these two kinds of explanation that are unavailable to the robust realist. So the realist has to look for another way of explaining correlations in general, and the one the epistemological challenge focuses on in particular.

The thing to look for is a third-factor explanation. For it is possible that the explanation of a correlation between the two factors A and B is in terms of a third factor, C, that is (roughly speaking) responsible both for A-facts and for B-facts.[36]

---

[36] Street (2006, 134) is explicit about there being only two types of possible explanations of such correlations – the two mentioned earlier in the text. But in her discussion of pain (section 9) she may be implicitly flirting with a third-factor kind of explanation. I briefly return to this part of her discussion below.

Throughout Copp's (2008b) discussion of Street's Darwinian Dilemma, he speaks of "the tracking thesis" as something realists must endorse if they are to avoid the skeptical horn of the dilemma. But talk of tracking here is misleading. "Tracking" is naturally understood as a causal term. If so, the availability of third-factor

Pre-established-harmony explanations, for instance, are always of this sort. And the realist-friendly explanation of the correlation I am about to offer is exactly such a third-factor explanation, or indeed a (Godless) pre-established-harmony type of explanation.

7.4.3 Survival is good – an evolutionary speculation

Here, finally, thinking about Street's Darwinian Dilemma can help in coping with the epistemological challenge to Robust Realism more generally.

Assume that survival or reproductive success (or whatever else evolution "aims" at) is at least somewhat good. Not, of course, that it is always good, or that its positive value is never outweighed by other considerations, or even that it is of ultimate or of intrinsic value, or anything of the sort. Furthermore, I am not asking you to assume that the evolutionary "aim" is of value *because* it is the evolutionary "aim". All I will be relying on is the assumption that survival (or whatever) is actually by and large better than the alternative.[37]

Selective forces have shaped our normative judgments and beliefs, with the "aim" of survival or reproductive success in mind (so to speak).[38] But given that these are by and large good aims – aims that normative truths recommend – our normative beliefs have developed to be at least somewhat in line with the normative truths. Perhaps somewhat ironically – because Street thinks evolutionary considerations serve to ground the epistemological challenge to realism – evolutionary considerations can help the realist cope with the challenge. Given that the evolutionary "aim" is good, the fact that our normative beliefs have been shaped by selective forces renders it far *less* mysterious that our normative beliefs are somewhat in line with the normative truths. This is so, then, neither because the normative truths are a function of our normative beliefs, nor because our normative beliefs causally track the normative truths, but because our normative beliefs have been shaped by selective pressures towards ends that are in fact – and quite independently – of value. The connection between evolutionary forces and value – the fact that survival is good – is what explains the correlation between the response-independent normative truths and our selected-for normative beliefs. The fact that (roughly speaking) survival is good pre-establishes the harmony between the normative truths and our normative beliefs.

---

explanations shows that the skeptical horn can be avoided without endorsing a tracking account. If "tracking" is understood as not necessarily causal (perhaps merely indicating some counterfactual relations), then Copp may be including under the same term causally-tracking and third-factor explanations. Indeed, at the end of the day it is not entirely clear to me whether Copp's own way out – that relies on his society-centered version of moral realism – is an instance of the former or the latter. His talk of "a close relative of the tracking account" seems to suggest that perhaps his solution too can be understood as a third-factor explanation of sorts, though of course not the one I am about to offer.

[37] These clarifications should make it clear that the assumption I will be relying on is significantly weaker than those considered by Gibbard (2003, 264) and Timmons (1990, 107–8). If I am right in what follows, the weaker assumption suffices for my purposes.

[38] Of course, evolution has neither a mind, nor an aim in mind. Talk of the evolutionary "aim" in the text is meant as shorthand for the usual respectable, non-teleological, evolutionary way of putting things.

The causal influence of selective forces only directly "pushes" us in the direction of having *evolutionarily beneficial* beliefs, not necessarily true ones. But here as elsewhere, the two may be systematically related.[39] For we are the kind of creatures whose actions seem to be closely related to their normative beliefs about how they should act, or how it would be good to act, or what consequences it would be good to bring about. That is, our mental and motivational set-up seems to include a mechanism roughly like Gibbard's (1990, ch. 4) "normative governance" mechanism. And this completes the explanatory story needed here: survival (or whatever) is good; so behaving in ways that promote it is (pro-tanto) good; but one efficient way of pushing us in the direction of acting in those ways is by pushing us to believe that it is good to act in those ways. And in fact, as we have just seen, it *is* good so to act. So the normative beliefs this mechanism pushes us to have will tend to be true.

Now, unlike the paradigmatic pre-established-harmony kind of explanation – of the mind–body harmony, for instance – my explanation of the correlation between the normative truths and our normative beliefs is not causal in both directions. Perhaps the evolutionary "aim" – whatever exactly it is – causally shapes our normative beliefs, but the fact that the evolutionary "aim" is of value does not *causally* shape the normative truths. It seems more appropriate to say that it is related to them in some constitutive way, a way the details of which depend on the details of your favorite first-order, normative theory. For instance, the fact that survival is good is plausibly related in coherence relations to many (though perhaps not all) other normative truths, like that pain is pro-tanto bad, that some close relationships are good to have, etc. Relations of this nature between that survival is good and many other normative truths – though not causal – still allow me, I think, to explain the correlation between the normative truths and our normative beliefs in a way that resembles pre-established accounts sufficiently to merit the name.

To see this more clearly, think about the following example: What explains the correlation (if indeed there is one) between giving rise to strongly affectionate feelings and having a poor sense of time? Here's one possible answer: Young children are cute. Being a young child explains – indeed, perhaps causes – having a poor sense of time. And of course, being cute is closely though perhaps not causally related to giving rise to strongly affectionate feelings. The fact that young children are cute, then, pre-establishes the harmony between giving rise to strongly affectionate feelings and having a poor sense of time.

Needless to say, I have no idea whether this explanation actually works (or whether the phenomenon it is supposed to explain is actually a real phenomenon). All that is crucial for me is that it *could* work, and that its *structure* is exactly similar to that of the explanation I am really after. Selective forces have causally shaped our normative beliefs; that survival is good is (non-causally but closely) related to many normative

[39] Discussions with Pete Graham and Sigrún Svavarsdóttir helped me with this paragraph.

truths; and so that survival (or whatever the evolutionary "aim" is) is good explains the correlation between our normative beliefs and the normative truths. Similarly, being a young child causally inclines one to have a poor sense of time; cuteness is (perhaps non-causally but closely) related to giving rise to strong affectionate feelings; and so that young children are cute explains the correlation between giving rise to strong affectionate feelings and having a poor sense of time.

Now, given how qualified we should be about attributing goodness (or perhaps some other value) to survival and reproductive success, this explanation could not explain a very strong correlation between the normative truths and our normative beliefs. But as noted above the correlation in need of explanation is not that strong anyway. And given the effect of reasonably reliable reasoning mechanisms starting from reasonably good starting points, there is even less that calls for explanation.[40] With these points in mind, it becomes clear that the fact that survival is good can play its role in this explanatory story even when it is understood rather loosely, as indeed it should be. Notice, for instance, that the children-are-cute explanation works well even if not *all* young children are cute, even if puppies are cuter than young children, and so on. In other words, the claim that children are cute can be understood rather loosely and still play its role in the explanation of the relevant correlation. Similarly, then, the fact that the assumption I relied on – that the evolutionary "aim" is good – is weak in the ways described above does not prevent it from playing an analogous role in explaining the correlation that the epistemological challenge calls upon the realist to explain.

How satisfactory, then, is this explanation of the correlation between the normative truths and our normative beliefs?[41]

One natural worry is that the normative assumption my explanation relies on – that the evolutionary "aim" is good – may be false. I have already partly answered this concern, by emphasizing how loosely this normative assumption can be understood while still successfully playing its role in the relevant explanation. But I want to note here two further points.[42] First, all the explanation really requires is that *our* survival or reproductive success is good, or that those of our ancestors are. After all, it is only the selective forces that acted on us and them that have played a role in shaping our normative beliefs, about whose reliability we are asking. Even if there are some

---

[40] In particular, perhaps such reasoning mechanisms can explain – given reasonably good starting points – how "beings like us would be good judges of ultimate worth, even in those cases where ultimate worth comes apart from maximizing the long-run reproduction of one's genes" (Gibbard, 2003, 265), as indeed Gibbard himself suggests later on (2003, 266).

[41] Notice that the use to which I put (speculative) evolutionary considerations is not that of (directly) justifying our normative beliefs. Rather, it is that of explaining the correlation between the normative truths and our beliefs, thereby possibly defeating a defeater of the justification of our normative beliefs. To an extent, then, I need not disagree with Nagel when he (1997, 136) says: "This means that the evolutionary hypothesis is acceptable only if reason does not need its support. At most it may show why the existence of reason need not be biologically mysterious."

[42] For the first, I am indebted to comments from Ralph Wedgwood and Sigrún Svavarsdóttir. For the second, I thank Jonas Olson.

organisms whose survival or reproductive success (or whatever) is of no even pro-tanto value, then, this is consistent with the normative assumption my explanation relies on. And when it comes to creatures like us and our fairly close ancestors, the claim that their survival and reproductive success is of value gains much plausibility, I think, from the observation that survival (or some such) is at the very least good *for* the creature surviving, or *for* a close group of relatives, or something of this kind. Again, this may not be true of creatures in general (some creatures just do not have interests, and so presumably nothing is good for them). But when it comes to us and to creatures like us, this claim seems very hard to deny. Furthermore, it seems almost undeniable that there are close (if not obvious) connections between being good *for* someone and being good. So it's very hard to deny that the survival (or some such) of creatures like us is good in the very loose sense needed for my explanation of the correlation between the normative truths and our normative beliefs to go through.

Second, even if the selected-for "aim" is of no value at all, the suggested explanation for the correlation between the normative truths and our normative beliefs can succeed almost unchanged, if many of the things that are conducive to this aim are of value (even if they are of value independently of their being conducive to the selected-for "aim"). If, for instance, well-being and feelings of interpersonal trust tend to promote reproductive success, and if *they* are good (and if there are no bad things that tend to promote reproductive success more effectively), then this suffices for the explanation above to go through.[43]

My normative assumption, then, is quite plausible. Let me make two further points here, though, in case you are still not convinced. First, I am much more confident in the general strategy of my response to the epistemological challenge – the pre-established-harmony strategy – than of my specific way of pursuing this strategy. And perhaps there are other ways of pursuing this strategy, ones that rely on other normative assumptions.[44] Second, we can make the response to the epistemo-logical challenge even stronger by borrowing a point from Skarsaune (2011):[45] for either this (quite plausible) assumption is true, or it isn't. If it is, the suggested explanation of the correlation works. If it is not, then the suggested explanation fails, and then Robust Realism may be committed to skepticism. But if such a highly plausible normative premise is false, perhaps skepticism is precisely the way to go here – as Skarsaune puts the point, if we don't know, then we don't know. Either way,

---

[43] This is a point I failed to appreciate in the paper this chapter is based on (2010a). Again, I thank Jonas Olson for making me see this.

[44] Thus, Skarsaune (2011) pursues a similar strategy with a normative assumption about the value of pain and pleasure, and Wielenberg (2010) pursues a similar strategy utilizing an assumption about the value of certain cognitive faculties. And though many of the details in Parfit's relevant discussion (2011, vol. 2, section 114) differ from my line in the text, still his solution too seems to me to be an instance of the general pre-established-harmony way of coping with the epistemological challenge.

[45] Except he puts things in terms of the value of pleasure and pain, not that of survival. Though this may be an important difference, it is not a difference that matters for the point I am borrowing from Skarsaune in the text.

then, the suggested way of coping with the epistemological challenge gives the right result.

Another obvious challenge is that this explanation itself seems to invoke what may be thought of as a miracle. For isn't it an amazing fluke that whatever evolution "aims" at happens to also be good? And isn't this itself something that calls for explanation, an explanation that the realist is not in a position to offer?[46] One way of putting the point – following Copp (2008b) – is in terms of counterfactual robustness: on the story just told, had evolution "aimed" at something else, something that is not of value or perhaps is even of negative value, our normative beliefs would have been systematically mistaken. So doesn't it follow that the story just told, far from showing how the realist can avoid commitment to miraculous correlations, *relies* on a miracle?

It is not completely clear that the thought that a miracle remains here can be made fully coherent.[47] For what would have to be the case for this "miracle" not to occur? The evolutionary "aim" would have had to not be of any value.[48] And how could that be? Fundamental normative truths are presumably necessary in a fairly strong sense, or at the very least so we are entitled to assume in the context of critically evaluating the epistemological challenge to Robust Realism. So the main way in which the evolutionary "aim" (which is actually of value) could have failed to be of value is if evolution had a very different "aim". But it's not clear what to make of this suggestion: for surely, it's not contingent that evolution has something to do, for instance, with survival and reproductive success rather than their opposites.[49]

It is not immediately obvious, then, how to state the remaining miracle. Still, I believe that a miracle remains. Even if as a conceptual matter, *evolution* could not have had a very different "aim" in "mind", still our normative beliefs could have been (I think) shaped by forces with a different "aim" in "mind" (forces that for this reason would not merit the name "evolutionary forces"). *Some* miracle, it seems to me, does

---

[46] Street (2006, 150) makes an analogous claim against the pain-explanation of the correlation she is interested in. And Copp (2008b) is explicit about his attempt to avoid a commitment to any such remaining miracles.

[47] I thank Ralph Wedgwood for relevant discussion here. For the claim in a very close context that an explanatory challenge remains, see Huemer (2006, 123).

[48] Another small remaining miracle is that we are the kinds of creatures equipped with normative governance, for had we not been – had endowing us with certain normative beliefs been not at all efficient in bringing us to the actions recommended by the normative propositions thus believed – we would presumably not have been at all reliable in our normative judgments. But this is not, I take it, a remaining miracle we should be too worried about, at least not *more* worried than we are about the analogous miracle elsewhere (had endowing us with perceptual beliefs not been at all effective in allowing us to escape tigers, we would not have been at all reliable in our beliefs about nearby mid-sized objects).

[49] Wielenberg (2010) offers a response to Street (and related challenges) that is in certain respects closely related to my own (though he seems to assume a reliabilist account of epistemic warrant; see here also his relevant qualification, in footnote 27). But he adds the following point: our very having of moral beliefs guarantees their (in-general) truth, because as a matter of moral truth, the having of moral beliefs suffices for the possession of moral rights, and the content of our moral beliefs is to a large extent related to the having of moral rights. Now, I am not sure about the details of this suggestion. But the important part for our purposes is that Wielenberg's is another possible way of arguing that there is not in fact a remaining miracle.

remain.[50] But this remaining miracle does not place a particularly heavy burden on Robust Realism. For first, of the striking correlation we started with (between numerous normative truths and numerous normative beliefs) we are now left only with the one-time "correlation" between whatever evolution "aims" at and the good. Given the rules of the explanatory game and how we can score points in it, it is hard to deny that significant progress has been made. Think about the analogous explanation again. That young children are cute may be considered a miracle. Perhaps it isn't – perhaps, in other words, we can come up with explanations of this fact (if it is a fact). And if we can, this will make the explanation of the correlation between giving rise to strongly affectionate feelings and having a poor sense of time even better. The important thing to note here, though, is that *even in the absence of such a further story*, even while still treating the cuteness of young children as a miracle, *still* explanatory progress has been made. Analogously, then, even if we have to think of the goodness of the evolutionary "aim" as a miracle, still explanatory progress has been made.

Second, how surprising is the miracle that remains? It is indeed true that had the causal forces shaping our intellectual and other normative faculties been very different, had they "aimed" at things that are of no value at all or that are of disvalue, we would have been systematically mistaken in our normative beliefs. And we are indeed epistemically lucky that this (presumably) isn't the case, just as we are epistemically lucky that our other intellectual (and perceptual) faculties have been shaped to be reasonably reliable. We are, after all, epistemically lucky to have evolved in an environment in which having by-and-large true beliefs is presumably conducive to survival and reproductive success. So yes, some brute luck may remain. But it is the same kind of luck that is present everywhere else. And though in some moods I too feel the call to explain it, still the pressure to supply such an explanation is not particularly strong, nor does it pose a particular problem for robust realists.

As already noted, then, the explanation suggested is not fully counterfactually robust. Still, it would be a mistake to suggest that it lacks *any* counterfactual robustness. For the explanation still works in a large number of fairly close possible worlds. Had the selective forces worked only somewhat differently, or had the evolutionary "aim" been different but still of value, still the starting points of our normative beliefs would have been close enough to the truth for our normative

---

[50] There are some important similarities between my suggested solution of the epistemological challenge to Robust Realism and Bloomfield's (2001, ch. 2) epistemological discussion. In particular, and as became clearer to me in correspondence with him (for which I am grateful), he explains the correlations between the truths about which foods are healthy for us and our beliefs about these matters in a way that is somewhat similar to the one I employ for normative beliefs in the text. But there is an important difference: Bloomfield, let me remind you, is a naturalist. This means that the epistemological challenge is not as hard for him as it is for me from the very start. For one thing, the mechanism he needs to do the work that normative governance is doing in my account is more simple and straightforward (and perhaps less evolutionarily speculative). And of course – and this is the point relevant to the text here – for his view, there does not seem to be any remaining miracle. But I take it is not surprising that naturalists are prima facie better placed compared to non-naturalists to deal with the epistemological challenge.

beliefs to be (somewhat) correlated with the normative truths. The possible worlds in which – on the suggested story – there is no correlation between our normative beliefs and the normative truths are quite far: these are worlds in which, for instance, evolution "aims" (only or mostly) at suffering or humiliation, or worlds in which survival (or whatever) has absolutely no value. And though we can think about the fact that none of these worlds is the actual one as a miracle, it seems like a rather small miracle. Counterfactual robustness, then, comes in degrees. Perhaps more by way of counterfactual robustness can be hoped for. But *some* significant counterfactual robustness is satisfied by the suggested explanation of the correlation between the normative truths and our normative beliefs.

We can now address two remaining worries about knowledge and access. First, Gettier's insight about knowledge is often presented as highlighting that knowledge is *non-luckily* justified true belief. If so, you may wonder whether the reliability of our normative judgments is sufficiently counterfactually robust on the suggested account to accommodate the anti-luck condition presumably necessary for knowledge.[51] Now, it's not completely clear how best to understand the anti-luck intuition, nor is it clear just *how much* counterfactual robustness is needed in order to satisfy it. Seeing that the remaining miracle on my account is not significantly more miraculous than the one involved in the "miracle" of (for instance) our perception being largely reliable, then, it does not seem to me that there is enough luck here to make knowledge impossible. And, of course, even if there is here a problem for knowledge, there need be no problem here for justification or warrant.

Second, the discussion in this chapter – and perhaps in section 7.1 particularly – may have left you somewhat frustrated. You may want to ask[52] how *is* epistemic access secured on this account? It's not as if on this account we are in touch (in some sense of "touch") with the normative facts, after all. The response, then, is that there is no access of this kind, but that access of this kind is necessary neither for justification nor for knowledge (and so the term "epistemic access" is misleading). The kind of non-accidental, significantly (though not completely) counterfactually robust relation between our normative truths and the normative facts is – together with the more internalist features presumably needed for justification – epistemically sufficient. Insisting that it is not amounts to a dogmatic acceptance of the causal theory of knowledge or something too close to it for comfort.[53]

---

[51] I thank Mark van Roojen and Stephen Finlay for this objection.

[52] As Stephen Finlay did.

[53] Mark van Roojen insisted on the intuitive plausibility of the requirement that someone believe *p because p* as a necessary condition for knowledge (and also for reference, so this is relevant also to section 7.6, below). Of course, it's not entirely clear how this "because" is to be understood. And so I want to insist that the story in the text suffices for *some* ways of understanding this "because"; for other ways of understanding this "because" I suggest that we reject the requirement that someone believes *p* because *p* as a necessary condition for knowledge.

What is the scope of the normative truths such that the correlation between them and our relevant normative beliefs is explained by the suggested story? All those normative truths that are closely enough related to the goodness of whatever it is evolution "aims" at. In order to say more about this scope, then, we need a first-order normative theory, a theory of (among other things) the relations between different normative concepts and judgments. But even without presenting such a theory, it seems to me clear that coherence relations between normative beliefs will take us quite far, and so that it is rather safe to speculate that the scope of the correlation is rather wide. And once the effect of reasoning mechanisms – including reasoning by analogy from other parts of the normative domain – is taken into account, the scope of the explained correlation becomes wider still, indeed perhaps maximally so.[54]

In his closely related discussion, Gibbard (2003, 263) puts forward another, related, requirement for the sought-after explanation – it must explain "why, in such matters, I would tend to be *correct as such*", that is, without relying in this explanation on the substantive truths with regard to which our reliability is to be explained (for instance, that survival is good). But this requirement is either too strong to be plausible, or weak enough to be satisfied by the suggested explanation. If Gibbard requires that our reliability be explained completely independently of the relevant substantive truths, the requirement cannot be defended. Even with regard to perceptual beliefs, for instance, if facts about middle-sized objects were very different, we would not have been reliable.[55] So the requirement must be understood in a weaker way, as saying (roughly) that the explanation shouldn't rely on too many, too specific substantive truths of the relevant domain. But thus understood, it seems to me the explanation suggested here passes the test.

Let me not give the impression that this suggested way of coping with the epistemological challenge is ideal. Indeed, because of the (perhaps) remaining small miracle, perhaps Robust Realism does lose some plausibility points here. But not, it seems to me, too many, and certainly not as many as you may have thought.

---

[54] In a follow-up paper, Street (forthcoming) puts forward a similar challenge to her original Darwinian Dilemma as a challenge to realism about *epistemic* norms. So it is worth pointing out that a perfectly analogous solution to the one suggested above applies in the epistemic case as well. And here, in outline, is how it would go: start with an evolutionary story of why it is useful to have by-and-large true beliefs about many non-normative matters; plug in a normative premise – roughly, that we have epistemic reason to believe the truth (this is the analogue of the claim that survival is good); add a premise about something like epistemic-normative governance (so that one good way of influencing what we believe about many non-normative matters is by influencing what we believe about our reasons for belief); and together you have a pre-established-harmony explanation of the correlation between the independent epistemic normative truths and our beliefs about them. (See Parfit (2011, vol. 2, section 114) for a story along these lines.)

That an analogue solution to the one in the text applies in the epistemic case as well further supports the plausibility of my suggested solution.

[55] Here see also the discussion of easy knowledge in Chapter 5 (section 5.2.2) and the references there, and the discussion of the justification of basic belief-forming methods in Chapter 3 (section 3.4), and the references there.

7.5 Generalizing

How general is the epistemological challenge discussed in this chapter? And how general is my suggested way of coping with it?

As already noted, the need to explain the correlation between a specified class of truths and our relevant beliefs is quite global, since if we cannot explain this correlation in a given domain, we may conclude that no such correlation is likely to exist in that domain, and so that we are completely unreliable in our relevant beliefs, a conclusion that will defeat – and perhaps even undermine – any justification for the relevant beliefs, and therefore also knowledge in the relevant domain.

The abstract challenge, then, is quite general, but it is not equally difficult to cope with across contexts. First, perhaps with regard to some classes of truths and beliefs, a brute correlation will not be too much to believe. If there are such cases, the problem with regard to them is, of course, solved. Second, and more importantly, the available explanations differ across contexts. In the paradigmatic case of, say, everyday beliefs about nearby middle-sized objects, the correlation gets explained in a rather obvious causal way: there are causal (perceptual) relations between the relevant truths (or facts, or properties, or whatever you think the causal relata are) and our (perceptual and other) beliefs. And there may, of course, be cases where the explanation goes the other way, that is, where the relevant truths are determined by us and our responses.

This suggests the following conclusion: the epistemological challenge as understood in this chapter is at its strongest when applied to discourses purportedly consisting of response-independent truths that are knowable – if at all – a priori.[56] In these cases, a causal explanation from truths to beliefs presumably can't work (because of the apriority), and a causal or constitutive explanation from beliefs to truths cannot work (because of the response-independence). Perhaps this generalization should not come as a surprise, our discussion having started with the epistemological challenge to mathematical Platonists and metanormative realists.

Does my suggested solution, then, generalize to all such discourses? The answer, I suspect, depends on the details. The suggestion my explanation utilized – that the evolutionary "aim" is good – may not have plausible analogues in other cases. And perhaps there are other third-factor explanations that are available in other domains, ones the analogues of which I could not think of with regard to normativity. So let me tentatively conclude with the following remark: a priori, response-independent domains for which something analogous to the explanation given in this chapter can be made to work are off the epistemological hook. Those – if there are any[57] – for which nothing

---

[56] Schechter (2006) notices this point. McGinn (1997, 58) notices that the epistemological challenge to realism is a particular instance of the general problem of a priori knowledge (but he thinks it cannot be solved by creatures like ourselves).

[57] If there are domains for which nothing like the story in this chapter can work, then this counts somewhat against this very story. The problem, it may plausibly be thought, is a general one (at least for a

like this story can explain the (supposed) correlation between the relevant truths and the relevant beliefs are still in trouble. Whether they can cope with it in some other way is not something that should worry us in the context of defending (or evaluating) Robust Realism.

7.6 A quick and unsatisfying thought about semantic access

There is a problem for Robust Realism that comes from the philosophy of language, which is in certain ways related to the epistemological problem discussed in this chapter. It is a problem of metaphysical rather than linguistic semantics[58] (or, in a different terminology, of metasemantics rather than semantics), and may be thought of as a problem of semantic access. For on Robust Realism the word "good" (to pick one example) refers – at least in some of its occurrences – to the property *goodness*. And this property is, on Robust Realism, causally inert and response-independent. How is it, then, that our word manages to latch onto that property – rather than some other property, or perhaps no property at all? Is it some kind of referential magic? If Robust Realism is committed to some such magic, this seems to count rather heavily against it, especially if alternative metanormative theories can avoid this commitment. And it seems they can – for if, for instance, naturalists are right and *goodness* is a natural property (even if "good" is not equivalent to any natural term), then presumably there are non-magical stories we can tell about how it is that the word "good" refers to *goodness*;[59] and if some response-dependence theory is right, presumably it should be no harder to explain how "good" refers to *goodness* than it is to explain how the words "my desires" refer to *my desires*; and so on.[60]

   This problem does not, as far as I can see, depend on any problematic or controversial assumptions about how reference works. In particular, the problem need not be based on a causal theory of reference – though it certainly *can* be based on it. Indeed,

---

priori, response-independent domains) and so there's something to be said for looking for a similarly general solution. And I concede that other things being equal, a solution that is general in this way would for this very reason be better than one which isn't. (I thank Jens Johansson for making me see this.) Still, it's always possible that even though the hope for a general solution is quite reasonable, it is not in the end realistic. We should then settle for piecemeal solutions. In other words, it is quite possible that the solution to the epistemological challenge for Robust Realism developed in this chapter is not a general solution that is equally good in all other respects, except there is no such general solution that is equally good in all other respects.

   [58] In the terms introduced by Block (1998).

   [59] See, for instance, Boyd (1988).

   [60] Old-fashioned emotivists avoid this difficulty altogether, by denying the existence of normative properties to which normative words refer. But it is entirely unclear what the situation is with their contemporary heirs, quasi-realist expressivists. Here as everywhere else, they seem to want to have it both ways – normative properties sufficiently exist to avoid some obvious objections, but are sufficiently unreal to avoid the semantic-access problem. Here as everywhere else, I don't see that they can get what they want. But I digress.

even if you are a minimalist or deflationist of sorts,[61] believing that no substantive theory of reference is either possible or needed, you can still be made to see the worry. For here, in our world, we have all these words and patterns of use; and all the way out there in Plato's heaven, there is a plethora of normative (and presumably other) properties and relations. In virtue of what, then, does the word "good" manage to find the property *goodness* and not some other property? This seems like a question that robust realists should at least have something to say about. (Notice the analogy between this naive way of putting the semantic-access worry while remaining as neutral as possible about theories of reference and my suggested way of understanding the epistemological challenge to Robust Realism while remaining as neutral as possible about theories of knowledge and epistemic justification. This analogy will be important later on.)

Let me not engage in pretense: I am not a philosopher of language. I believe that my ability to contribute to the literature here is rather limited, and so I won't try (this is also why I do not dedicate a full chapter to this challenge). But what I nevertheless want to do, in order to complete my defense of Robust Realism, is give you some reasons to believe that this challenge is not one it is impossible to cope with. And this is what I plan to do in this section. I do this by first placing the discussion here in a broader philosophical context, then by borrowing a page from Ralph Wedgwood's (2007) book, and finally by drawing on the lessons of previous sections in this chapter in order to solve a remaining problem.

The problem – I am sure this won't surprise you – is much more general, and seems to apply wherever apriority seems plausible. For instance, if Platonism about numbers is a plausible view to take, then we can ask a similar question about the miracle of the word "eight" referring to the number *eight* rather than to *seven*, or to *the empty set*, or to nothing at all. Depending on what else you believe, you may take this either as reason for optimism about the possibility of solving this problem, or as reason for pessimism about mathematical Platonism. But think of the logical case. "If . . . then . . . " constructions manage to pick out *material implication*, or some such. And the semantic-access problem seems to arise again: How is it, we can ask, that our locution manages to find the material implication out there in Plato's heaven and latch onto it? And even if you're not a Platonist about such things as the material implication, it seems like there is an initial problem here.

Logical words manage to pick out arguably abstract truth-functions (for instance). And this means that there must be *some* way of solving the semantic-access problem, at least for logical words. And if this is so, then it seems plausible – though by no means

---

[61] See, for instance, Horwich (1998), and Schiffer (2003). I am not at all confident in my understanding of these currently fashionable deflationist views of reference (and meaning, and truth, and so on). Perhaps on such theories (or perhaps on some versions of such theories) the semantic access challenge to Robust Realism collapses. While such a result will surprise me, I obviously do not need to worry about it – if this result follows from a plausible account of reference, things are going even better than planned for Robust Realism.

necessary – that a similar solution will be applicable to the normative case as well. This, at least, is the hope.

The point of the analogy with logic here is, then, that even without a solution to the semantic-access problem, there is rather strong reason to believe that it *can* be solved. But we can say more, for there is at least one rather natural thing to say in the logic case the analogue of which has recently been developed in the normative case as well.

In the logic case it seems like a promising starting point to focus on our use of "if . . . then . . ." locutions, perhaps especially on the rules of introduction and elimination for such locutions. And when we have these rules in mind, it seems *very* plausible to say that there is a relation between the fact that "if . . . then . . ." refers to *material implication* and the fact that we use "if . . . then . . ." locutions roughly according to the rules of implication-introduction and implication-elimination (or *modus ponens*). Indeed, it seems plausible that our words "If . . . then . . ." manage to refer to *material implication* precisely *in virtue of* the fact that such reference will render our use of the relevant introduction and elimination rules rational, or valid, or justified, or truth-preserving, or in some other way OK. This is the kind of view I will be talking about when using the term "conceptual role semantics" (or CRS) – a view according to which what explains or grounds the fact that a certain linguistic expression has a certain referent is that this is the referent that will render the use of the linguistic expression largely OK.

Nothing here is obvious, and it's not as if CRS is uncontroversial, even when constrained in the ways just mentioned. But I think that with these constraints in mind, it is hard to deny its appeal.[62]

Can we employ an analogous CRS strategy to solve the semantic-access problem for normative language? To do that, we would need a conceptual or inferential role for the target normative word or expression (say, "good", or "ought", or "reason", or some such). Presumably, this can be done partly by noting inferential relations within the normative-evaluative domain. But it is not clear that this will pick out a sufficiently determinate conceptual role: for instance, this strategy seems vulnerable to "inverted normative spectrum" counterexamples.[63] And so a more promising – and certainly more interesting – proposal is to focus on the inferential role of normative expressions also in *practical* inferences. And it is here that Ralph Wedgwood is helpful.

Wedgwood defends (first in his 2001, and in more detail in his 2007, mostly in chapter 4) a conceptual role semantics for normative terms. The one he focuses on (in his (2007)) is "ought". And here's his suggestion for a conceptual role for "ought":

---

[62] For more both on the appeal of and on the objections to CRS, and for references, see Block (1998).

[63] It is hard to see, in other words, that inferential relations within the normative-evaluative domain will suffice to distinguish between an assignment of *good* to "good", *bad* to "bad", *right* to "right", and so on, and the mirror-assignment of *bad* to "good", *good* to "bad", *wrong* to "right", etc.

Acceptance of the first-person proposition 'O<me, *t*> (*p*)' – where '*t*' refers to some time in the present or near future – commits one to making *p* part of one's ideal plan about what to do at *t*. (2007, 97)

The "committing" here is thought of as analogous to the commitment to believe *q* that is arguably involved in believing *p* and *if p then q*. And Wedgwood's suggestion captures the role of (some) ought judgments in *practical* inferences, inferences the conclusions of which are, perhaps somewhat roughly, intentions or plans.

In a minute I will have to say more on the background theory Wedgwood is here assuming and on the parts of it I cannot accept. But I want to emphasize first that nothing in the CRS strategy sketched above prevents it from being employed with regard to inferential role in *practical* inferences as well. Just like assigning *material implication* as the reference of "If...then..." renders our use of "If... then..." in accordance with the relevant introduction and elimination rules largely OK, and just like this fact is a part of the answer to the question in virtue of what does "If... then..." refer to *material implication*, so too (to pick one plausible example) assigning *has the strongest undefeated reason to* as the reference of "has the strongest undefeated reason to" renders our proceeding from the judgment that we have the strongest undefeated reason to ϕ to an intention to ϕ largely OK[64], and this fact is a part of the answer to the question in virtue of what does "has the strongest undefeated reason to" refer to *has the strongest undefeated reason to*.

This is the main insight I am taking from Wedgwood. But it's important to note that I reject many of the details in Wedgwood's specific account. Thus, Wedgwood (2007, 25–8) endorses some kind of (mitigated) judgment-internalism, of the kind that I will reject (as either false or uninteresting in our context) in Chapter 9 (section 9.4). Perhaps more fundamentally, Wedgwood (2007, ch. 7) accepts some version of the claim that "the intentional is normative", and he believes (2007, 2) this to be the key to metaethics. To the extent that I understand this idea, though, I reject it, and anyway would not want my Robust Realism to depend on it. But Wedgwood, it seems rather clear, thinks that the availability of the CRS strategy depends on this idea. So there may be a problem here for me.

In fact, I think that the availability of the CRS strategy for dealing with the semantic-access problem does not depend in (almost) any way on the other details of Wedgwood's theory. (I explain the "almost" qualifier shortly.) To see this, it is important to note the differences between Wedgwood's ambitions and mine here. Wedgwood wants to offer a full semantic theory for normative words. I, on the other

---

[64] I am using the highly scientific phrase "largely OK" so as to remain neutral on what more precisely this property has to be – rational, perhaps, or some such. But there is a suspicion that is relevant here: if the relevant property in the case of "If...then..." is *truth-preservation*, then the case of practical reasoning is after all not exactly like the case of "If...then..." (for practical inferences are not in the business of preserving truth). If so, we must think about the application of the CRS strategy to practical inferences as a natural *extension* of the CRS strategy for logical words. For some discussion, see Wedgwood (2007, 100).

hand, just want to indicate a general way in which the semantic-access problem for Robust Realism may be solved. In fact, Wedgwood's ambition is even greater – for he thinks that his semantic theory for normative words has also a crucial role to play in allowing his kind of Platonist to dodge the relevant metaphysical and epistemological bullets. And here too I do not share Wedgwood's ambitions. Indeed, I have offered ways of dodging these bullets that do not depend on the supposed "normativity of the intentional". So even if Wedgwood's rather heavy background theory is needed in order for the CRS strategy to achieve all Wedgwood wants it to achieve, it doesn't follow that this heavy background theory is needed for my much more limited use of that strategy.

Have a look again at the paragraph following the quote from Wedgwood – nothing there seems to depend on the more problematic (or anyway more idiosyncratic) parts of Wedgwood's book. A CRS strategy for solving the semantic-access problem for Robust Realism partly by utilizing the role normative words have in practical inferences (leading to actions, or intentions, for instance) is thus available to the robust realist (who does not accept Wedgwood's version of judgment-internalism,[65] or his version of the normativity of the intentional). So there is still reason here for cautious optimism.

Notice that this optimism must indeed be cautious, for everything here depends on the details which I have not supplied. First, it is, of course, neither obvious nor uncontroversial that CRS is the way to go even with regard to logical connectives. Furthermore, in order to make good on the promise of a CRS strategy we need to specify a conceptual role for the target normative words and expressions. This will presumably involve laying down in detail the conceptual relations among all the normative words and expressions, an intra-normative task which I completely avoid in this book. And there may be other difficulties too: for instance, a detailed analysis may find out that for some normative terms – perhaps unlike most logical ones – there just *is* no conceptual role that enjoys enough by way of consensus in the relevant linguistic community to ground an application of the CRS strategy.[66] Such a result may give rise to a semantic-access version of worries about disagreement (provisionally discussed in Chapter 8, section 8.4). For instance, such a result may give rise to very serious problems of global referential indeterminacy.[67] So nothing here is obvious. But I think enough has been said to establish the very limited conclusion I set out to establish here: namely, that it's not as if the robust realist can have nothing at all to say

---

[65] In Chapter 9 (section 9.4) I will emphasize that rejecting a *necessary* connection between the making of a moral judgment and motivation is consistent with accepting both *normative* connections between them (say, that in some circumstances being motivated accordingly is rationally called for) and *empirical* connections (say, that very often, when someone judges that she ought to ɸ she is at least somewhat motivated to ɸ). Such connections suffice for the employment of the CRS strategy, as described in the text.

[66] Wedgwood nowhere discusses this worry, but in conversation he agreed that his account is at least potentially vulnerable here.

[67] I thank Ray Buchanan for making me see that this is a very serious worry here.

here, that it's not as if the semantic-access challenge is in principle one Robust Realism cannot cope with.

But a major problem remains. For on Robust Realism, isn't it a miraculous fluke that the inferential roles we do in fact employ correspond in the appropriate way to existing properties out there in Plato's heaven? On a view that renders the normative properties dependent on our inferential (including practical inferential) practices, there is, of course, no mystery here. Indeed, this is where Wedgwood's endorsement of the normativity of the intentional is supposed to do some work. For Wedgwood (2007, 163) endorses a no-priority mutual-dependence view between the normative and the mental. And so, he thinks that the very essence of the relevant mental, intentional states is given by their role in inferences such as the ones employed in his version of the CRS strategy, or by their being subject to norms that license these inferences (2007, 158). The details here are complicated, and not sufficiently clear to me, and objections may certainly be raised to all of this (though I won't do so here). But what *is* clear is that if all of this can be made to work, no mystery remains. The normative properties and the intentional states that pick them out are so intimately interrelated, that there is nothing surprising about there being normative properties that correspond in the appropriate way to our (practical) inferential practices. It could not have failed to be this way.[68]

But what can I – unwilling as I am to accept the normativity of the intentional – say here? On Robust Realism, doesn't there remain an unexplained miracle even after employing the CRS strategy sketched above?[69]

We should be careful in stating the problem. If the problem is just that we don't have reason to believe that such normative properties and relations exist out there in Plato's heaven, then my reply consists in the entirety of this book (and mostly, Chapters 2–5). But even if those arguments succeed, a problem remains. The best way to see this here is to draw on an analogy with the discussion of the epistemological challenge to Robust Realism earlier in this chapter. The best understanding of this epistemological challenge, I argued, is as a request for an explanation of a correlation between something down here in our world (our normative beliefs) and something all the way out there in

---

[68] I thank Ralph Wedgwood for a conversation that helped me pinpoint the way in which his commitment to the normativity of the intentional is supposed to make a difference here. On this see Wedgwood (2007, 102). And see also the next footnote.

[69] Here's a related worry (for which I thank Ralph Wedgwood): the guiding idea of CRS is that what explains or grounds the fact that a certain linguistic expression has a certain referent is that this is the referent that will render the use of the linguistic expression largely OK. This "OK" is, of course, normative. So by using CRS in my metanormative theory, haven't I *already* bought into the normativity of the intentional? Isn't the nature of the relevant mental states – those that are a part of the inferences that consist of the relevant conceptual role – now partly determined by this normative "OK-ness" of the relevant inferences? The answer is that on my theory, it is not. The nature of the relevant mental states does not in any way depend on the relevant normative condition. Rather, this normative condition is something that is true *of* them. You may find this reply frustrating (as Ralph Wedgwood did) – for what, on my account, *explains why* this normative condition is true of the relevant mental states? The answer is, I suspect, that nothing does. But I don't see this as a problem, at least not a significant one. This is especially so given the solution I am about to offer to the problem in the text.

Plato's heaven (the normative truths). That problem remains, I've argued, even if we have sufficient independent reason to believe in normative truths, or indeed to be robust realists. And the problem we're up against now is that of explaining a correlation between something else down here in our world (our relevant inferential practices) and some other things in Plato's heaven (normative properties and relations). And *this* problem remains, I think, even if we already have sufficient reason to believe in the existence of such normative properties and relations, or indeed to accept Robust Realism.

And so, a problem remains. But noticing the close analogy with the epistemological discussion also points us in the direction of its solution. For there, as you may recall, I defended a (Godless) pre-established-harmony solution to the epistemological challenge, utilizing the fact that survival (or whatever else is the evolutionary "aim") is good as pre-establishing a harmony between our normative beliefs, which are presumably shaped to a large extent by evolutionary forces, and the normative truths, which presumably stand in coherence relations to the goodness of survival. I do not have to get into all the details of this suggestion here. The point I want to make now is that if that story works as a way of dealing with the (best version of the) epistemological challenge to Robust Realism, something very much like it should also work for the semantic-access challenge.

One thing achieved by the CRS strategy is that the seemingly intractable problem of explaining semantic access was reduced to the problem of explaining a correlation between our relevant inferential practices and the relevant parts of (to return to this metaphor) Plato's heaven. But this is precisely the kind of problem which the pre-established harmony story can – if successful – solve. There is a problem here, then, but equipped with the lessons of earlier sections in this chapter, it is not a problem that it should be too hard to deal with.

You may have your doubts about my suggested solution to the epistemological challenge. This – though somewhat saddening – is quite legitimate, of course. But I now want to emphasize that if you do, you have rather strong reasons to be suspicious of Robust Realism even before considering the semantic-access problem. But even if Robust Realism loses plausibility points on account of its reliance on the above way of dealing with the epistemological challenge, it does not lose *further* plausibility points because it relies on that story *again* in order to deal with the semantic-access challenge.[70] At this stage of the project this should come as good news for the robust realist.

---

[70] And this annihilates, I think, Wedgwood's dialectical advantage here. As explained earlier in the text, by relying on the "normativity of the intentional" Wedgwood avoids the need for something like my pre-established harmony here. But if he needs that story *anyway* in order to deal with epistemological problems for his kind of realism or Platonism, then the mere fact that he doesn't rely on this story *here* doesn't bolster the comparative plausibility of his theory compared to, say, my own. And in fact – though you wouldn't know it just from reading the chapters in his book dealing with the epistemological challenges to his view – I suspect that at the end of the day Wedgwood too needs something like my pre-established-harmony story to deal with the epistemological challenge (a suspicion that Wedgwood graciously confirmed in conversation).

Let me again emphasize how preliminary the discussion in this section is. The details have to be filled in: some of the details have to be filled in by offering rich and detailed accounts of the relations among different normative concepts. And some further details probably have to be filled in by people with philosophy-of-language competence that I do not have. But I hope enough has been said to convince you that in all likelihood the details *can* be filled in, and to indicate how. And so I tentatively conclude that Robust Realism is not after all in serious trouble because of the need to account for semantic access.

8

Disagreement

The next challenge or family of objections to Robust Realism I want to discuss is the one focusing on the phenomenon of moral disagreement. Moral disagreement is widely held – in philosophical literature as well as in the general culture – to pose a threat for metaethical realism and objectivity,[1] yet it is surprisingly hard to find careful statements of arguments that start with moral disagreement and end with a conclusion that is in tension with realism – robust or otherwise. Much of the discussion in this chapter, then, is going to be an attempt to understand "the" argument from disagreement. Thus, I will be going through several distinct (though often related) arguments from disagreement, responding to each as I go. There is, then, something tiring about this chapter – and indeed, if you have a rather focused disagreement-concern about Robust Realism in mind please feel free to skip other parts, and proceed directly to the section that deals with your favorite argument from disagreement (the titles of the sections are meant to be sufficiently informative, and the sections are meant to be largely self-contained).

My conclusions are going to be very encouraging to fellow robust realists (and to other realists as well, presumably).[2] Some of the arguments from disagreement I discuss can, I think, be rather clearly dismissed. Others should be seen not so much as refutations of, but rather as challenges to, realism, and furthermore as challenges that it does not seem like realists should have at all a hard time addressing. Some of the arguments from disagreement do, I think, pose a serious challenge to realism, but the phenomenon of moral disagreement plays a relatively minor role in them (and so they are addressed elsewhere in this book). Of course, there may be other ways – ways I do not consider below – in which disagreement is supposed to pose a problem for Robust Realism, but I cannot think of such ways, and so I tentatively conclude that moral disagreement does not pose a very serious challenge to Robust Realism. I confess that there is something puzzling about this conclusion: if moral disagreement is not the enemy of metaethical realism it is often thought to be,

---

[1] For a helpful survey, see Gowans (2000).

[2] Let me remind you that Robust Realism is an existential, not a universal, thesis. It asserts that *there are* perfectly objective, irreducibly normative moral and other normative truths, not that *all* moral or normative truths are of this nature. If there are some values, then, that are somehow available only locally, in a culture-dependent way, this is not inconsistent with Robust Realism. Such values are discussed – in the context of a discussion of objectivity – by Raz (2001).

why are thoughts to the contrary so widespread, even among good philosophers? Some of the popularity and apparent plausibility of the claim that disagreement counts against realism stems, I think, from conflating the different arguments to be considered below, equivocating between them.[3] And in what follows I hint at other possible explanations as well. Nevertheless, the popularity of the thought that moral disagreement undermines realism surprises me, and I do not have a fully satisfactory explanation of this fact.[4]

Before proceeding, let me note three ways in which the discussion that follows is wider than it may seem. First, while for the most part I discuss *moral* disagreement, the issue is really that of *normative* disagreement more widely. I focus on moral disagreement because this is the context in which most relevant discussions can be found. Second, while the discussion that follows is of moral disagreement as a challenge to *Robust* Realism, for the most part the robustness does little work here – the different challenges from disagreement are (for the most part) just as effective against other kinds of realism as they are against Robust Realism. Third, I suspect that the discussion below applies much more generally than merely to metaethical or metanormative realism, or is at least easily so generalizable. Disagreement is thought to be a problem for realism in many other contexts as well, and there too it is not clear exactly how.[5] Nevertheless, in what follows I directly discuss only the metanormative context, leaving the generalization for another occasion. It is, however, important to note that sometimes arguments from disagreement are supposed to apply more forcefully against metanormative realism than against realisms in other domains, and in what follows I comment on which of the arguments considered satisfies this condition.

How, then, is disagreement supposed to undermine, or even challenge, Robust Realism?

8.1 Worries we can dispense with rather quickly

In order not to tire you, let me be *very* quick with three ways of fleshing out a disagreement problem for Robust Realism.[6]

In a case of moral disagreement, robust realists are committed to pronouncing (at least) one of the parties simply wrong. And this may sound intolerant (or some such). But it is hard to think of this as a serious problem for Robust Realism. First, it is a problem for any view that refuses to accept seemingly contradictory moral judgments

[3] Tersman (2006, xiii) also notes that many different arguments go by the name "the argument from disagreement".

[4] Nagel (1986, 147) expresses similar surprise.

[5] For a discussion of disagreement in a more general context, see Bonjour (1988, 138–42). For an attempt to marshal an argument from reasonable disagreement in the context of the ontological debate over abstract objects, see Rosen (2001).

[6] In the paper on which this chapter is based (Enoch 2009a) I am not as considerate of my reader's patience – so that is where you can find a more detailed discussion of these ways of understanding the disagreement worry, as well as relevant references.

(namely, almost any plausible metaethical view at all). Second, if this challenge assumes a general, universal moral principle of tolerance, then it is hard to save it from self-defeat. And third, the importance of tolerance (if indeed it is important) may give rise to *practical* reasons to avoid acting in certain ways, perhaps even to avoid saying certain things (like "We are right and you are wrong and that's that"). But it cannot give *epistemic* reasons to believe that a certain metaethical view is false.

Another popular understanding of the problem of moral disagreement – though much more popular in the classroom than in the literature – is as a deductive argument, starting with a premise about actual (perhaps inter-social, or inter-generational) disagreement, and ending with some conclusion that is inconsistent with Robust Realism. But as is often noted, no such argument is valid. In order to restore validity, we would have to assume, perhaps roughly, that none of the disagreeing parties is mistaken in their relevant moral belief. But making such an assumption amounts to begging the question against Robust Realism.

Another way of making a deductive argument from actual disagreement a little more respectable is by plugging in an epistemological premise – say, that fundamental moral truths have to be self-evident (if any moral truth is knowable at all, at least). Disagreement is then taken to undermine self-evidence. But it is not completely clear what "self-evidence" comes to. For the argument to go through, there must be a sense of "self-evidence" that makes it true both that the only hope for realist moral epistemology has to assume self-evidence, and that disagreement undermines self-evidence. And I don't know of any such sense. So this argument too fails, though it may be seen as an introduction to better arguments that take disagreement to be a part of an epistemological problem – and I discuss this line in more detail below.

So much, then, for these ways of understanding disagreement as a problem for Robust Realism, ways that can be rejected quickly and without remainder. We are back, then, with the original question – how is disagreement supposed to be a problem for Robust Realism?

8.2 From actual disagreement, by inference to the best explanation, to the denial of Robust Realism

In philosophical discussions of moral disagreement and its relevance to the metaethical debate over realism disagreement is perhaps most often taken as an *explanatory* challenge. The argument implicit in such suggestions is, I think, the following:

(1) There is deep, wide-ranging disagreement in moral matters (across cultures and historical eras, as well as within them).

(2) What best explains such disagreement is that moral opinions do not reflect (with different success) an objective, independent moral reality, but rather perspectives, cultures, ways of life, or something of the sort.

(3) Therefore, moral opinions do not reflect (with differing success) an objective, independent moral reality, but rather perspectives, cultures, ways of life, or something of the sort. (From (1) and (2), by inference to the best explanation.)[7]

Premise (1) is often thought to be (empirically) obvious, apparent to anyone without a realist axe to grind. And the intuitive thought behind premise (2) is that it is harder for the realist to explain moral disagreement than it is for those rejecting realism. Assuming some version of subjectivism, or relativism, or perhaps noncognitivism, such wide-ranging disagreement is just what one would expect, but if there is an objective, universal, moral truth, why is it hidden from so many people in so many matters? It is hard to see, so the thought goes, how robust realists can come up with a satisfactory answer to this question, and this, the intuitive thought concludes, is a powerful reason to reject realism.

This line of thought, like the more explicit argument attempting to capture it, arguably distinguishes in an intuitively plausible way between morality and other discourses, where disagreement seems a much less serious worry for realism. This is so because of the apparent difference in the scope and nature of the disagreement in ethics on one side, and (say) mathematics and physics on the other,[8] a difference which puts the metaethical realist in a tougher spot (compared to the mathematical or scientific realist) in terms of the explanatory challenges she must face.[9]

Notice, however, that it is not clear how exactly this line of thought can be made reasonably precise. The argument above, for instance, is in our context problematic first and foremost because its conclusion as it stands is consistent with Robust Realism. Robust Realism, remember, is not an epistemological thesis — it makes claims about what truths there are, not about our relevant opinions or beliefs or judgments reflecting these truths. Faced with the above argument, then, a sufficiently resilient robust realist can retort: very well then, perhaps our moral opinions do not reflect the objective moral reality. But this does not show that there is no such reality to be reflected. The argument, the realist may conclude, fails to engage her realism.[10]

---

[7] I take this to be at least one plausible way of understanding Mackie's (1977) so-called argument from relativity. A similar argument pervades Wong (1984); and Gowans (2000, 4) presents a similar argument as *the* argument from disagreement. Shafer-Landau (2003, ch. 9) understands the argument from disagreement as an explanatory one, but he combines the argument in the text here with the argument from rationally irresolvable disagreement, discussed below. Some version of this argument was already put forward by Price; see Schneewind (1998, 382). And at least at times Wiggins (1990, 67 and 75) seems to have a similar argument in mind (though at other times he seems to think of other arguments from disagreement, and it seems that he thinks of the most important problem disagreement poses ("the real challenge of relativity") as a challenge specifically to his subjectivism, not to Robust Realism or even to plain old realism).

[8] As Shafer-Landau (2003, 220) notes, however, it is not at all clear whether this line of thought can distinguish between ethics and philosophy more generally (metaethics, of course, included) or economics. See also Railton (1993, 283). I return to metaethical (as opposed to moral) disagreement and its significance in the concluding section of this chapter.

[9] A point emphasized by Shafer-Landau (2003, ch. 9).

[10] For a related point, see Tersman (2006, 46). And for discussion, see Sinnott-Armstrong (2006, 39–40).

But this would be too quick. If the best way out for the robust realist is to concede that moral beliefs – hers included, of course – do not reflect the moral facts, then she may perhaps have her realism, but only at the price of the most radical of skepticisms. A realm of moral facts that are not in any way reflected by even the best of our moral beliefs is, I think, a very small comfort for the realist. Such realism may, at most, serve as a last resort, but it is to be avoided if at all possible. Perhaps this is why metaethical realism and related theses are sometimes (including in the context of discussions of moral disagreement) understood as incorporating an epistemological requirement that the moral facts not be too radically inaccessible.[11] Let me postpone, then, discussion of the relevance of disagreement to the most general epistemological worries about realism until section 8.8, and proceed here to see how the realist can avoid the conclusion (3).

The argument leading to (3) is an inference to the best explanation (IBE), and I can think of three general ways of rejecting such arguments:[12] one can deny the need to explain the relevant phenomenon, one can deny the existence of the relevant phenomenon, or one can come up with alternative explanations for the phenomenon. Let me discuss these strategies in turn.

8.2.1 Does disagreement call for explanation?

Not every phenomenon calls for explanation – we are inclined to take some facts as brute, as things that just are the way they are, and that is an end to it. And IBE can only work as a rule of inference, it seems, when applied to phenomena that call for explanation.

Does moral disagreement call for explanation? In order to present a full answer to this question, we would have to determine first what makes a phenomenon explanatorily interesting, what it is, in other words, that distinguishes between phenomena that do and those that do not call for explanation. And I am afraid I know of no satisfactory answer to

[11] See Tolhurst (1987, 610–11). And see also Thomson's (1996, 68) characterization of the thesis of moral objectivity.

There is another line of thought showing that (3) poses a serious threat for the realist: if our moral beliefs are radically disassociated from a supposed realm of moral facts, it becomes hard to see how our beliefs could be *about* these moral facts. Indeed, if moral beliefs systematically reflect ways of lives, or social conventions, or something of the sort, is this not at least some strong reason to think that *this* is what they are about? This conclusion *is*, of course, inconsistent with realism. See the preliminary discussion in section 7.6.

[12] Assuming, that is, that in general IBE is a good rule of ampliative inference. This assumption is not uncontroversial. For the best-known critique, see van Fraassen (1980 and 1989). In the text I avoid this complication for four reasons. First, I believe that IBE is a good rule of inference, but arguing the point will take me too far afield (but see Enoch and Schechter (2008) and the discussion in Chapter 3, section 3.4). Second, if the IBE version of the argument from disagreement can be rejected because IBE is not a good rule of inference, this makes things easier, not harder, for the realist, so there is no dialectical flaw in assuming, in our context, that IBE is a good rule of inference. Third, I believe the argument can be rephrased without using IBE, instead using other inferential mechanisms allowed by critiques of IBE (such as probabilistic reasoning). Doing so will require very minor changes in the argument and in the realist responses to it. And fourth, realists – or at least scientific realists – typically rely on IBE in arguing for their realism. So a realist who rejects IBE would be, at the very least, a dialectical oddity.

this question. Let me settle, then, for the following very tentative point: perhaps the realist is not entitled to just assume that disagreement does not call for explanation, but nor is the antirealist entitled to assume that it does. And the point can be made quite plausibly that given our cognitive shortcomings agreement rather than disagreement is what calls for explanation, that quite generally disagreement is what you should expect, and agreement the surprising exception that cannot be accepted as brute.

Perhaps this is not so, or perhaps both agreement and disagreement call for explanation,[13] or perhaps there is some other way in which it can be shown that disagreement calls for explanation. In what follows I do not rely on this possible way to reject the IBE version of the argument from disagreement. But I nevertheless want to note that there is some unfinished business here for the antirealist if he is to employ this argument.

Now I agree that declaring all cases of moral disagreement as explanatorily uninteresting is a rather desperate (and dogmatic) move. But declaring *some* such cases as brute or explanatorily uninteresting seems not at all implausible. I return to this point shortly.

8.2.2 Denying moral disagreement

It is often noted that premise (1) – that moral disagreement is widespread – is not in fact as obvious as some seem to think.

The by-now familiar line (on which I can thus afford to be quick) goes something like this:[14] Yes, there is widespread disagreement on specific moral judgments, but this disagreement need not be a genuinely *moral* disagreement, or even any disagreement at all. Perhaps, for instance, cross-cultural disagreements about the morally appropriate way of treating the dead (or their corpses) should be attributed to metaphysical disagreements about their fate after death rather than to genuinely moral disagreement – disagreement, that is, about fundamental or ultimate moral principles or values.[15] If this is so, there is a disagreement involved, but it is not a moral disagreement in the intended sense: it is not more of a moral disagreement than if you and I disagree about which switch to press simply because you think pressing the first one will save more lives and I think pressing the second one will (and both of us agree that we should save as many lives as possible). Or perhaps some apparently moral disagreements about the morally proper way of treating the elderly are best seen as the adaptation of the very same general moral principles to radically different circumstances.[16] In such a case there may be no genuine disagreement involved at all. In both kinds of cases the disagreement about specific moral judgments is attributable not to a genuinely moral disagreement – one stemming from disagreement about moral

---

[13] Bernard Williams (1985, 132–3) suggests – after having noticed that disagreement need not be surprising – that in some contexts agreement calls for explanation and in others disagreement does.

[14] Writing over thirty years ago, Mackie (1977, 37) already treated this line of thought as well known.

[15] See, for instance, Rachels (1999, 23). For a critique of the empirical – anthropological and historical – evidence purportedly supporting the claim that there is widespread, genuinely moral disagreement see Moody-Adams (1997).

[16] Again see Rachels (1999, 27–9).

fundamentals – but to different factual beliefs (in the second case, both true because about different circumstances) that are relevant to the applications of the presumably agreed-upon moral principles. And disagreement of *this* kind clearly does not support antirealism.[17]

It cannot be denied, I think, that this line of thought demonstrates that there is less moral disagreement than may otherwise be thought. Surely, at least some disagreements in specific moral judgments are attributable to differences in (true or false, justified or unjustified) non-moral beliefs rather than to deep, genuinely moral disagreements. But like Mackie (1977, 37–8) I find it exceedingly hard to believe that this is the whole story of moral disagreement. It seems to me overwhelmingly unlikely that if we only get all our (non-moral) facts right (or even just uniformly wrong), all moral disagreement will disappear.[18] Just teach the principled violent tyrant about the physiology of pain and the psychology of humiliation, the thought seems to be, and that both apply to his subjects as well, and he will become a member of the human rights community, or at least will acknowledge that he ought to become one; all we need is a better understanding of the biology of fetuses (and perhaps the metaphysics of the mind or the soul) and the moral status of abortions will become the subject of a happy consensus. These may be caricatures, but not, I think, unfair ones. And it seems to me overwhelmingly unlikely that anything like this is true. It is very hard, of course, to establish this empirically, because of difficulties in interpreting observed cases of moral disagreements and in deciding whether they are grounded in factual disagreements. Still, it seems to me the realist will be well advised not to let her realism hinge on as strong a claim as that all cases of moral disagreement are attributable to factual, non-moral disagreements.

8.2.3 Alternative explanations

Assuming, then, that enough of the phenomenon of moral disagreement remains to be explained after differences in factual beliefs have been accounted for, is premise (2) true? Is it true that what best explains such disagreement that is genuinely moral is that moral judgments reflect not an independent moral reality but rather social conventions, ways of life, and the like?

If I am to reject this as the best explanation, I must come up with better alternative explanations. And the striking fact about the IBE version of the argument from disagreement is that such alternative explanations are so easy to come by:[19] many

---

[17] In the text I describe this line of thought as rejecting the phenomenon to be explained. But there is an alternative description: no one, it seems, denies that *superficially* moral disagreement, disagreement about specific moral judgments, is widespread. With *this* phenomenon as the explanandum, the thought in the text should be seen not as denying the phenomenon, but as suggesting an alternative explanation of the phenomenon – the claim is that what best explains superficially moral disagreement is not genuinely moral disagreement (and so not the denial of Robust Realism) but rather disagreement in factual beliefs.

[18] For a similar point, see Sinnott-Armstrong (2006, 38).

[19] One can find such explanations already in Aquinas: see the excerpts from *Summa Theologiae* in Gowans (2000, 55–63). For contemporary discussions, see, for instance, Boyd (1988, 212–13), Brink (1989, 204–8),

moral matters are complex and not at all straightforward; people are the victims of any number of cognitive shortcomings (we are not all as intelligent as may be hoped, we do not reason carefully enough, we discount prior probabilities, . . .), and to different degrees, so that some may be more likely to make moral mistakes than others; many find it hard – or do not want – to sympathize and imagine what it is like to occupy a different position in the relevant interaction, and different people are sensitive to the feelings of others to different degrees; we let our interests influence our beliefs (moral and otherwise), and given that our interests differ this accounts for differences in our beliefs (moral and otherwise); we are subject to the manipulation of others, and so to the distorting effects also of their self-interests; and perhaps there are cases of moral disagreement in which there really is no fact of the matter as to who is right, because the issue in dispute is just indeterminate.[20] These and many other facts can help to explain moral disagreement consistently with Robust Realism.

Let me draw special attention to one of these kinds of alternative explanation: that in terms of the distorting effects of self-interest. This kind of explanation is especially important for at least two reasons: it is extremely powerful, and it helps explain the difference in the scope of disagreement in morality and in other discourses.[21] Consider the following example: Peter Singer (1972) and Peter Unger (1996) believe that we should give almost all our money to famine relief, that unless we do so we are morally

Hurley (1989, 292), Darwall, Gibbard, and Railton (1992, 30) (though they think these alternative explanations do not seem entirely satisfying), Railton (1993, 282–3), Loeb (1998, 283), and Shafer-Landau (2003, ch. 9). Wong (1984, 117–20) also mentions many possible alternative explanations of disagreement, though he ultimately thinks that they do not suffice to explain at least some important cases of such disagreement.

[20] Some writers suggest that indeterminacy is the key to the explanation of moral disagreement (see, for instance, Shafer-Landau (1994), and Parfit (2011, vol. 2, 560 and on); Parfit here discusses indeterminacy alongside imprecision – I think what I am about to say about indeterminacy applies to imprecision as well). For relevant discussions see also Brink (1989, 202); Wiggins (1990, 77); Gert (2002, 298 n. 9). But I am suspicious of such suggestions, for two related reasons. First, if it is genuinely indeterminate whether abortions are morally permissible then *both* Pro-Choice activists (believing abortions are determinately permissible) *and* Pro-Life activists (believing abortions are determinately impermissible) are morally mistaken. Instead of having to attribute a mistake to one party to the debate, we now have to attribute a mistake to both. It is hard to see this as explanatory progress. (Schiffer (2003, 259) notices that such indeterminacy will make both parties to the disagreement epistemically at fault, but he fails to notice that this undermines whatever motivation we may have had for the claim that there is no relevant epistemic difference between the disagreeing parties. But see Shafer-Landau's (1994, 336) attempt to deal with this worry.) Second, if indeterminacy is to play a key role in the explanation of moral disagreement, it follows that most cases of (genuinely) moral controversies – or the most important ones – must be indeterminate (for otherwise indeterminacy is not as central a factor in the explanation of disagreement as it is thought by some to be). And given the scope of (what seems to me like) genuine moral disagreement, this would leave very little – if anything – as determinate moral truths (or falsehoods). And this is certainly not a victory a robust realist should be happy with. (For instance, Schiffer's (2003, ch. 6) version of antirealism asserts that there are no (or hardly any) determinate moral truths.) Thus, indeterminacy can perhaps play *some* role in accounting for moral disagreement, but not the key role some thinkers attribute to it.

[21] Brandt (1944, 487) quotes a passage from Thomas Reid (*Essays in the Intellectual Powers of Man*, s. VI, ch. VIII), where Reid already notices this point. Brandt himself is critical of explaining moral mistake and disagreement by resorting to the distorting effect of interests, but only when such explanations are offered by someone claiming the self-evidence of ethical truth.

corrupt, that our behavior is (almost) as morally objectionable as that of murderers. Perhaps they are wrong (though I do not know of any convincing argument to that effect). But even assuming they are right, there is no mystery about the common – almost universal – belief that morality does not require all that Singer and Unger believe it does. Acknowledging that they are right would exert a high price: it would involve exposing "our illusion of innocence",[22] leading us either to give up almost all of our belongings or to the horrible acknowledgment that we and our loved ones are morally horrendous persons. Refusing to see the (purported) truth of Singer's and Unger's claims thus has tremendous psychological payoffs. Now, this is an extreme case, but it illustrates what is typical, I think, of many cases of moral debates – very much is at stake, and so false moral beliefs can rather easily be explained in terms of their psychological payoffs. And where mistakes can easily be explained, disagreement can easily be explained without resort to antirealism. Furthermore, given a standing interest in not revolutionizing one's way of life, in not coming to view oneself and one's loved ones as morally horrendous people, explanations in terms of the distorting effect of self-interest can explain the phenomenon Mackie was so impressed with – that our moral convictions seem to reflect our ways of life, and not the other way around.

Notice that moral beliefs are susceptible to such effects much more than many other discourses. In controversies over, say, the theoremhood of a mathematical conjecture, typically not much is at stake in terms of the interests of those taking part in the debate. Similarly for controversies about the nature of sub-particles. The effect of self-interest can thus serve to explain not just the scope of moral disagreement, but also the difference between the scope of moral and other disagreement.[23] (Sometimes interests *are* affected rather strongly by controversies in other areas as well. What then? Well, in such cases – where the promotion of mathematicians, the religious convictions and institutional interests of some Creationists, or, say, the economical interests of social classes are deeply affected by controversies in mathematics, physics, and economics – in such cases we *do* see much more disagreement. And this is just as the explanation in terms of interests predicts.[24])

And notice also how powerful the explanation in terms of interests is. For given explanations in terms of the distorting effect of interests on moral beliefs, what would be *really* surprising is if we found moral disagreement *against* interests. What would be surprising, for instance, is if the South thought slavery was wrong and the North thought it morally unobjectionable, or if the rich believed in Socialism and the poor in Libertarianism.[25] But this is not typically the case. There is a striking correlation between the moral views people take on controversial moral matters and the views

[22] This is the subtitle of Unger's book.
[23] For similar points see Nagel (1986, 148), and Shafer-Landau (2006, 219).
[24] Again see Nagel (1986, 148), and Shafer-Landau (2003, 219).
[25] Tersman (2006, 27).

that would – if realized – serve them better. And what best explains *this* phenomenon? Surely, the distorting effect of interests on moral beliefs.

These alternative explanations – those in terms of interests as well as others – are of course not full explanations. They are the mere sketches of explanations, the details of which are to be completed by more detailed philosophical as well as empirical work. So this way of addressing the IBE version of the argument from disagreement is importantly incomplete. But, first, so is the IBE version of the argument from disagreement itself, for in order to establish its second premise (that the denial of realism is the best explanation of moral disagreement), the proponent of that argument has to reject alternative explanations, those suggested here included.[26] And second, I hope enough has been said to make it at least a plausible hypothesis that moral disagreement or much of it can be explained by doing psychology, sociology, and politics, not metaethics.

Let me mention just one more point here regarding competing explanations of moral disagreement. Competing explanations are evaluated holistically and against a background of prior beliefs. A theory that explains a certain phenomenon in terms of a kind of entity, for instance, is better as an explanation if we already have previous reason to believe in that kind of entity, one that does not depend on this very explanandum, and worse if the ontological commitment is a new one introduced by this very theory.[27] But this means that when the time comes to compare competing explanations of moral disagreements – some of them compatible with Robust Realism, some not so – the result of the comparison is going to be heavily influenced by the beliefs we come to this task already equipped with. And this is true of our metaethical beliefs as well. So how good psychological explanations of disagreement are compared to metaethical, antirealist, ones will partly depend on whether we were metaethical realists to begin with, on what independent reasons – independent, that is, of this version of the argument from disagreement – we have for endorsing or for rejecting Robust Realism, and on how they interact. It follows that it is not just that whether we should accept Robust Realism depends (among other things) on what the best explanation of moral disagreement is. What the best explanation of moral disagreement is also depends (among other things) on whether we should antecedently accept Robust Realism. And this limits the strength of the IBE version of the argument from disagreement – standing alone – as an objection to Robust Realism.[28] If there are reasonably strong arguments for Robust Realism, and no (other) reasonably strong objections to it, then this version of the argument from disagreement does not pose a serious threat to realism, because in such circumstances we are virtually guaranteed not to have any reason to accept antirealist explanations of moral disagreement as the best

---

[26] Loeb (1998, 289–92) notes that the IBE version of the argument from disagreement is very much up for empirical grabs. See also Gowans (2000, 11). And a similar claim is the main point in Gowans (2004).

[27] Ontological parsimony is often mentioned as one feature that makes one explanation better than another. See, for instance, Thagard (1978).

[28] Shafer-Landau (2003, 219; 2006, 219) notices this point.

explanations. This does not mean, of course, that the IBE version of the argument from disagreement has no force at all, or that it necessarily begs the question against the robust realist (failing, as it does, if we have strong antecedent reason to believe in realism). Where there are many considerations both for and against Robust Realism, this argument may enhance the plausibility of some and not of others, thus making a legitimate difference in the metaethical debate. And it may have some force on its own as well. But it should be remembered that this argument – all on its own – can have at most limited force against Robust Realism (and this even independently of the specifics of alternative explanations of the sort discussed above).

8.2.4 Conclusion, and the combined strategy of dealing with the explanatory challenge

Let me sum up the discussion of the IBE version of the argument from disagreement. The intuitive thought that the argument attempts to capture is that it is going to be exceedingly hard for the realist to explain – consistently with her Robust Realism and without falling into the most radical of skepticisms – the widespread moral disagreement we obviously encounter. I mentioned three possible lines of reply: I argued that it is not completely clear that all cases of moral disagreement call for explanation; that there may be less moral disagreement than there seems to be, but that it is highly implausible that there is none; and that there is no reason to expect that the realist is going to have a hard time explaining such disagreements in alternative ways, ones that are perfectly consistent with realism, perhaps most commonly by referring to the distorting effects interests have on moral beliefs. I want to conclude the discussion of this version of the argument from disagreement by making two further points.

First, we may of course combine some of these strategies to offer a complex reply to the argument. We may, for instance, argue that there is less moral disagreement than there seems to be, that much of what is left can easily be explained consistently with Robust Realism, and that whatever disagreement – if any – remains unexplained does not in fact call for explanation. Some such combined strategy seems to me the most promising one for the realist to take.[29]

Second, the IBE version of the argument from disagreement may be thought of as a particular instance of a family of IBE arguments, each one beginning with a slightly different explanandum. The antirealist may argue that it is not moral disagreement itself that is best explained by the denial of realism, but rather its scope, or perhaps its intractability,[30] or the absence of a method to decide such disagreement (I consider this

---

[29] Gowans (2000, 24) mentions that such a combined strategy may be possible, and Brink (1989, 204–9) – I think – employs a version of some such combined strategy.

[30] Intractability may be understood in more than one way. It may be understood descriptively, as just noting that no party to the debate is likely to convince the other. This is the sense intended in the text. But it may be understood normatively, as applying to a disagreement when it is rationally irresolvable. I discuss this kind of intractability below, in section 8.7. Gowans (2004, 143) suggests an argument from disagreement that is a version of the IBE argument, with the explanandum being apparently rationally irresolvable disagreement.

to be a particularly important instance, and so I discuss it separately in section 8.6), or the absence of a gradual elimination of such disagreement, or some such. For any such explanandum, the moves discussed in this section may be re-employed, but there is no guarantee of the same success. Perhaps, for instance, moral disagreement does not itself call for explanation, but its intractability does. And perhaps denying the phenomenon of intractable moral disagreement is highly implausible, but denying the (perhaps slow) gradual elimination of disagreement is much more plausible. Most importantly, with each different explanandum, alternative explanations have to be re-evaluated. It cannot be ruled out in advance, for instance, that though the best explanation of actual moral disagreement is in terms of the distorting effect of interests on our moral beliefs, a similar explanation is not satisfactory as an explanation of the absence of a method to decide controversial moral issues. Of course, I cannot hope to discuss all possible disagreement-related explananda here. Let me just say, then, that I see no reason to think that there is a version of this argument regarding which no combined strategy (of the kind mentioned in the previous paragraph) can work. If the antirealist thinks otherwise, let him fill in the details (what *exactly* is the relevant explanandum?) and argue his case.

8.3 Undermining the support agreement would have lent to realism

The next way of taking moral disagreement to undermine metaethical realism starts from an argument that proceeds in the opposite direction:

8.3.1 From agreement, by inference to the best explanation, to realism

Consider, then, the following argument:

(1) In many discourses there is wide-ranging agreement about the truths central to the relevant discourse.
(2) What best explains such wide-ranging agreement is that there are objective truths the discourse answers to, truths on which opinions gradually converge.
(3) Therefore, there are objective truths the relevant discourse answers to. (From (1) and (2), by inference to the best explanation.)[31]

You may have doubts about this argument. For one thing, the argument might be stronger with a slightly different explanandum – perhaps, for instance, the phenomenon the explanation of which lends support to realism is not mere agreement, but agreement of a special kind; or perhaps it is not just agreement but the progress towards more and more agreement, the gradual elimination of disagreement; or perhaps what is crucial here is not so much agreement regarding specific judgments as it is agreement

---

[31] A hint at this argument can be found in Gowans (2000, 17).

about methods, about what it would take to settle disagreements about judgments. Furthermore, you may doubt whether the conclusion really *is* what best explains the explanandum (whatever exactly it is).[32] But let me assume for the sake of argument that the argument from agreement to realism does have at least some force.

As it stands, the argument is an argument from agreement to realism, not from disagreement to the denial of realism. But there is in the vicinity an argument of this latter kind.

8.3.2 From disagreement to the denial of realism

(4) We are justified in believing realism about a given discourse only if it can be supported by (an instance of) the argument from agreement to realism.

(5) There is no wide-ranging agreement in moral matters.

(6) Therefore, the argument from agreement to realism does not support metaethical realism. (From (4) and (5).)

(7) Therefore, we are not justified in believing metaethical realism. (From (4) and (6).)[33]

This argument too promises to distinguish between moral and other discourses, where realism is allegedly more plausible and disagreement allegedly less of a problem.

The argument is valid, and so if it is to be rejected at least one of its premises must be rejected. Some of the issues discussed in section 8.2 above – in particular in section 8.2.2 – can be raised again, perhaps in order to doubt premise (5). Instead of returning to these matters, though, let me grant premise (5) for the sake of argument, and address the distinctive feature of this argument – premise (4). It is hard to see what could possibly support it.[34] Even accepting – for the sake of argument – a broad epistemology in which only explanatory need could justify a commitment to a realism about a discourse, still we have no reason to accept that agreement (or some fact about it) is the only phenomenon explanation of which can ground such a commitment. And furthermore, as you may recall, I think that we have strong reasons to reject such an epistemology in general, and with regard to the metaethical and the metanormative in particular. The upshot of Chapter 3 was that our main reason to believe in Robust Realism is not based on the role that normative truths, facts, and properties may have in explaining agreement (or, for that matter, any other phenomenon), but rather on the role they play in our deliberation about what to do. Even if such facts and properties are

---

[32] Street (2003, ch. 2), for instance, argues that much of the agreement we see on basic normative matters is more readily explained by evolutionary considerations than by the hypothesis that there are objective normative truths. Tersman (2006, 52) also mentions the possibility that agreement can be explained by things other than convergence on the truth.

[33] I think – but I am not sure – that something like this argument underlies Williams's (1985, ch. 8) disanalogy between ethics and the empirical sciences. And Tersman (2006, 46–7, 53, 104–5) argues, in different contexts, that perhaps disagreement can be taken not so much to refute realism as to undermine one major way of arguing for realism.

[34] For a related point, see Shafer-Landau (2003, 223).

explanatorily dispensable, I argued in Chapter 3, they are *deliberatively* indispensable, and there is no non-question-begging reason to take explanatory but not deliberative indispensability seriously. If the argument of Chapter 3 is successful, then, it delivers – among other things – a refutation of premise (4), and with it a collapse of the argument based on it.[35]

Nevertheless, let me make here two related concessions. First, some metaethical realists seem to concede premise (4) or something very much like it. At least, one of the ways in which they argue for their realism is by employing the argument from agreement to realism.[36] As an ad hominem argument with these realists as the relevant homini, then, the argument above does have some force.

Second, even if premise (4) as it stands is false (or at least unsupported), still there may be in the vicinity here a problem – though a weaker one – for realists. For even if the argument from agreement to realism is just *one* way of lending support to realism, then the unavailability of this argument in the case of metaethical realism, though it neither refutes this view nor renders it philosophically unmotivated, still takes away from its plausibility. Because we are here in the business of collecting plausibility points, Robust Realism is better off the more support it can mobilize. Robust Realism would have been somewhat better off, then, had it been able to enlist to its cause also the argument from agreement to realism, and is thus somewhat worse off for not being able to do so. (In the terminology I have been using, this does not amount exactly to a loss of plausibility points, but to the observation that an avenue of gaining plausibility points that is available elsewhere is not available to the robust realist.)

8.4 From disagreement, via the absence of semantic access, to the denial of Robust Realism

Imagine two communities, both of which seemingly speaking English, both seemingly engaging in moral discourse. And suppose that the moral standards common in each society are radically different from each other. But then, if the range of actions which are pronounced "wrong" by members of one society is radically different from the range of actions pronounced "wrong" by members of the other, why think that the two societies assign the same meaning to "wrong"? Why not believe, rather, that the two communities speak two different idiolects of English, with "wrong" meaning one thing in one, quite another in the other? And if the two communities' "wrong"s are not semantically equivalent – if they do not have the same meaning – then it is

---

[35] This may be one place where the argumentation is not straightforwardly generalizable to other, non-normative, discourses. The argument in Chapter 3 is specific to normative discourse. Perhaps for other discourses explanatory indispensability *is* the only consideration that can justify a commitment to realism. If this is so – and I have yet to see an argument with this as its conclusion – then the point in the text does not carry over to other discourses.

[36] See Nagel (1986, 145–9). Sturgeon (1992, 108) – a naturalist realist – also seems to rely on agreement in one of his attempts to support his realism. For a critical discussion of such arguments see Seabright (1988).

possible for a member of one society to say "Abortions are wrong," for a member of the other society to say "It is not the case that abortions are wrong," and for both of them to be right. And is this not inconsistent with Robust Realism?[37]

Much work needs to be done if this is to be made into a fully explicit objection to realism: it is necessary to distinguish between the claim that such different uses *give reason to believe* that the meanings of the relevant words are different in the two societies and the more ambitious claim that they *make it the case* that the meanings are different;[38] it needs to be shown why the problem is a problem for realism in general (and so also for Robust Realism) rather than just for contemporary versions of naturalist realism, which make themselves especially vulnerable to such problems because of the semantic theory they typically endorse;[39] and the point has to be argued that the conclusion of this semantic argument really is incompatible with Robust Realism or its underlying philosophical motivations. Why, in other words, can't the robust realist happily concede that "wrong" has different meanings in the two communities' languages, but insist that abortions are universally, objectively, wrong? Of course, perhaps this is not best translated as "Abortions are wrong" to languages of other communities, but so what?[40]

These are all interesting and important matters which I cannot hope to engage in satisfactorily here. Instead of trying to do that, then, let me make the following point: true, robust realists have to come up with a meta-semantic theory for moral language, one that will explain (roughly speaking) how it is that moral words gain their meaning, what they refer to, what it is – if anything – in virtue of which the word "wrong" refers to the (objective, abstract) property *wrongness* rather than to other properties or to nothing at all, and so on. The argument above seems to highlight the need to address this challenge. But notice that with the challenge understood as the general one of coming up with a satisfactory meta-semantic theory for moral language, moral disagreement no longer has the central role it is presumably supposed (by proponents of arguments from disagreement) to have as a problem for Robust Realism. The challenge of accounting for the semantic access to moral properties realistically understood is thus a genuine one, but it has nothing essentially to do, I conclude, with moral disagreement.[41] And I hint at a way of addressing it in

---

[37] As it stands the objection is constrained in scope to just inter-social or inter-cultural disagreement. It may be possible to apply a similar line of thought also to intra-social disagreement, but doing this will complicate matters because of the need to take into account also the social aspect of meaning, division of linguistic labor, and so on.

[38] Tersman's (2006) discussion is – following Davidson in this respect – not sensitive to this distinction.

[39] For powerful presentations of this and related objections to naturalist realism, see Horgan and Timmons (1991), and Loeb (1998, 292–9). For an attempt at a reply, see Brink (2001). Tersman (2006, 85) claims that his related points apply to non-naturalist as well as naturalist realist views. But it seems to me that Tersman's characterization of realism – and in particular, his emphasis on the continuity of moral and natural facts (2006, e.g. 98) – in fact shows otherwise.

[40] At times, Tersman's (2006, e.g. 130) characterization of realism seems to understand it as inconsistent with such a reply. But it is not clear to me why this should be so.

[41] For a similar point, see Tersman (2006, 131).

Chapter 7, section 7.6. It is possible, of course, that the phenomenon of moral disagreement is relevant to an adequate account of semantic access here: perhaps, for instance, some attempts at a meta-semantic theory consistent with Robust Realism yield the result that the two communities from a few paragraphs back are talking past each other, and perhaps this result is unacceptable. If so, an understanding of this disagreement refutes the suggested meta-semantic theory.[42] So if a realist view responds to the meta-semantic challenge (or any other challenge, for that matter) in a way that commits it to some problematic claims about the scope and persistence of moral disagreement, this may render the view vulnerable to relevant arguments from disagreement.[43] Moral disagreement, then, may very well be metaethically relevant here, but only to the extent that it sets adequacy constraints on solutions to the more general problem of coming up with a meta-semantic theory consistent with realism.

8.5 From disagreement, via internalism, to the denial of Robust Realism

Assume that someone morally ought to Φ only if they are, or under suitable conditions would be, motivated to Φ, and call this assumption "Internalism".[44] Assume further that agents' motivations (or motivational sets)[45] diverge fairly radically, so that there is no type of action that all are, or under suitable conditions would be, motivated to perform. It then follows that there is no moral ought-judgment that is true of everyone. And this means, it seems, that Robust Realism is false. This line of thought – associated perhaps most clearly with Gilbert Harman's case for relativism[46] – starts from a claim about disagreement *in motivation*, and proceeds to conclude that Robust

---

[42] This is the gist of much of Tersman's (2006, ch. 5) argumentation (though he thinks that such reasoning does not refute realism – it merely serves to undermine the support realism could have mobilized from the objective feel of moral disagreement (2006, 104–5)) Tersman thinks that just about any semantic theory consistent with realism (and indeed cognitivism) falls prey to this objection, which he calls "the argument from ambiguity". At least with regard to Wedgwood's (2007) suggestion (which I utilize in Chapter 7, section 7.6), though, I remain unconvinced.

[43] This is the case, it seems to me, with regard to the metaethical theories of Boyd, Sturgeon, and (in a different way) Michael Smith. For a criticism along these lines of Boyd's and Sturgeon's optimism regarding the nature of moral disagreement, see Tersman (2006, 99–100) and the references there. For a criticism of Smith's optimism regarding the convergence in desires of all rational creatures, see my (2007b). For Smith's reply, see his (2007).

[44] The literature distinguishes between many different kinds of internalism. The one in the text is the one Darwall (1983) calls existence-internalism (distinguished from judgment-internalism). In this chapter, this is the only kind of internalism I will be talking about, and so I will just refer to it using the term "internalism". For more discussion of this and related issues, see Chapter 9.

[45] This is of course Williams's (1981) term.

[46] See, for instance, Harman (1984). The distinction is sometimes drawn between agent- and speaker- or appraiser-relativism (see, for instance, Sturgeon (1984)). In these terms, the relativism that the line of thought in the text seems to support is agent-relativism – relativity in the applicability of moral judgments to the actions of different agents (rather than relativity in the truth-values of a moral statement uttered by different speakers). This distinction mirrors the distinction between existence- and judgment-internalism.

Realism is false. Granted, it may be a bit of a stretch to call such divergence in motivations disagreement, but it does seem to qualify as disagreement in a naturally generalizable sense, sufficiently so in order to justify discussing it here.

The argument above is deductively valid, so only two realist strategies are available here: rejecting internalism, or arguing that agents' motivations are not – or under suitable conditions wouldn't be – radically diverse (or, of course, both).

Notice that a mere empirical finding according to which the motivational sets of all humans share certain features would not be enough. The blow for Robust Realism, it seems, would be just as serious if the argument were to be reformulated in terms of *possible* agents to whom the relevant moral judgments do not apply. So if the argument is to be rejected without rejecting internalism, it must be argued that some motivations are *necessarily* found (or would be found, under suitable conditions) in all agents. And some thinkers have indeed taken this line, usually in its constitutivist version, claiming that some motivations or dispositions are constitutive of agency.[47] Now, for reasons that I cannot discuss here I find the attempt to ground normativity in what is constitutive of agency unconvincing.[48] Let me proceed, then, to discuss the internalist premise.

Now, I think that this internalist premise is rather clearly false, and that it entails even more clearly false propositions (like Harman's (1977, 107) famous claim that it is not true to say of Hitler that he ought not to have done what he did). But in our context there is not even a need to establish this claim. For our purposes it is sufficient to note that unless one is already highly suspicious of Robust Realism one has no reason to accept the internalist premise.[49] So assuming internalism would be begging the question against the realist. What is really needed if there is going to be an argument here against realism is *an argument* for this internalist premise. And this means, first, that the argument as presented is importantly – indeed, crucially – incomplete, and second, that the premise about disagreement (in motivations) has no part to play in the real work that needs to be done, that of establishing the internalist premise.

Of course, the relation between Robust Realism and plausible theories of motivation and action has to be given considerable attention, and it is the main topic of the next chapter of this book. But there is not in the vicinity here, I think it is safe to conclude, a serious disagreement challenge to Robust Realism.

---

[47] David Velleman's (1996) discussion of what may be called quasi-externalism – giving the externalist all she wants consistently with internalism – is the most explicit discussion I know of that fits the pattern in the text. For the attempt to find motivations that are constitutive of agency (motivated also by considerations different than the one in the text), see Korsgaard (2009) and Rosati (2003).

[48] See my "Agency, Shmagency" (2006). For constitutivist responses, see Velleman (2009) and Ferrero (2009). For my response, see "Shmagency Revisited" (2010b).

[49] This should be qualified – perhaps a constitutivist who is agnostic (to the extent possible) about Robust Realism can find reason to accept internalism. But again see the references in the previous footnote.

8.6 From the absence of a method, deductively or by inference to the best explanation, to the denial of Robust Realism

The thought is sometimes expressed that the problem with moral disagreement is not the disagreement itself, but rather that it seems not to be resolvable in anything like the ways scientific or other disagreement often is. In this section I start my attempt to understand this thought, an attempt I continue to pursue in the next two sections.

When two physicists disagree – sometimes rather strongly – about the truth (or acceptability) of a scientific theory, they typically agree at least about what would settle their disagreement. They agree, for instance, that if such-and-such an experiment were to yield this-and-that result, or if some observation were to reveal certain data, this would settle the controversy, and they agree *how* such further evidence would settle it. So although there is often disagreement in physics it is somewhat superficial, and underneath it lies a deeper agreement, if not about the truth of theories, at least about what findings support what theories and (roughly) to what extent. But it is exactly this feature, the thought goes, that is missing in cases of moral disagreement. Moral disagreement runs much deeper than disagreement in the sciences, because typically, or at least often, in cases of moral disagreement there is no deeper agreement underlying it, no agreement about how to settle the more superficial disagreement. And it is this fact – not merely the disagreement itself – that is supposed both to pose a problem for Robust Realism and to distinguish between morality and discourses about which realism is presumably a more natural view. So the general form of the argument looks something like:

(1) There is no method for deciding cases of moral disagreement.
(2) Therefore, at least in cases of moral disagreement, there is no objective moral truth.[50]

Notice that the conclusion is rather limited in scope. Some versions of the argument from disagreement – most notably the IBE version discussed in section 8.2 – hope to support a conclusion about morality as a whole, not just about those parts of morality that are controversial. This argument has no such aspiration. But let me assume, for the sake of argument, that just about any moral claim (or at least any interesting moral claim) is controversial, so that we can safely ignore the restriction on the scope of the conclusion.

---

[50] A version of this argument can be found already in Ayer (1946, 106). For a fairly explicit contemporary discussion of this argument see Sturgeon (1984, 49) (though he also presents the IBE version of the argument from disagreement), and Sturgeon (2006, 107). In general, and for reasons to be discussed below, often writers put forward the IBE version of the argument from disagreement together with some version of the argument from the absence of method. This, I think, is the case with Mackie (1977, 36–8).

As it stands, though, the argument is clear neither on how the conclusion follows from the premise, nor on what the premise exactly means. Let me discuss these points in turn.

The conclusion (2) does not follow deductively from (1). What would be needed for the argument to regain deductive respectability is a further premise to the effect, roughly, that objective moral truth (or perhaps objective truth more generally) is necessarily decidable, that there can be no (moral) truth at which we have no method of arriving. But I see no reason why anyone should accept such a verificationist premise in general,[51] and I see no reason why anyone should accept it about morality unless they are already prepared – for independent reasons, presumably – to reject Robust Realism (and just about any other view worth calling "realism"). This, however, is a controversial point even among philosophers sympathetic to realism,[52] and so I will place most of the weight of the rejection of this argument on the discussion of premise (1), to which I get shortly.

Let me just add here that even if (2) does not follow from (1) deductively, it may follow from it by inference to the best explanation. For it may be argued that the unique feature of moral disagreement that realists cannot explain is the fact that it goes all the way down, that there is no agreement on method underlying specific disagreements. Now, I will not again discuss the three general ways of rejecting an inference to the best explanation. Rather, I want to argue that depending on how premise (1) is to be understood, it can be either safely denied or satisfactorily explained in a realist-friendly way, and that the argument from absence of method thus does not pose a serious threat to Robust Realism.

What is meant, then, by the claim that there is no method to decide cases of moral disagreement? It seems to me that four different thoughts may be – and often are – expressed by such claims. The point may be, first, that we just have no method of proceeding in cases of moral disagreement, that facing disagreement we are, as it were, at a loss for words, knowing not what we can possibly say or do next; or second, that though we do proceed in any number of ways, none of them is justified; or third, that there is no method that is guaranteed to lead to agreement, to make at least one party to the debate see her or his error; or fourth, that there is no method of settling the disagreement that is itself accepted as the proper method by all parties to the original disagreement.

8.6.1 Literally no method

It would perhaps be alarming for Robust Realism if in the face of moral disagreement – which is, we may assume, widespread – we just did not have a clue how to proceed (though it is not completely clear what would follow from this; in particular, it is not clear that such a hypothetical is more friendly to alternative, antirealist metaethical

---

[51] For a related point, see Chang (1997, 21).

[52] See Bond (1983, 65); Nagel (1986, 139); Kim (1998, 78–81); and Dancy (2000, 65–6). And see Tersman's (2006, 70) useful distinction between different kinds of inaccessibility, and its relevance to the point in the text.

positions). But this is nothing to worry about, because thus understood premise (1) is clearly false.

We do proceed in any number of ways in conversation, deliberation, and action, even facing moral disagreement. We try to reason, to convince, to draw analogies and make comparisons, to reduce *ad absurdum*, to draw conceptual distinctions, to imagine what it would be like to be on the other side, to engage each others' emotions and desires, to rely on authority, and so on. Perhaps we are mistaken in employing such methods, or perhaps there are too many methods and none enjoys a consensus about its status. I discuss these possibilities in the next subsections. But it cannot seriously be suggested that we literally have no method of proceeding in moral thought and action once faced with moral disagreement.[53]

So charity requires that we not read premise (1) literally. How else can it be read?

8.6.2 No justified method

Perhaps the point is, then, that facing moral disagreement we have no *justified* method of proceeding, and that this fact entails, or is best explained by, the denial of Robust Realism.

Now if moral disagreement is widespread, and if it undermines the justification of moral beliefs (because facing moral disagreement we have no justified method of proceeding to form or revise our moral beliefs), this is indeed a troubling result (though it does not entail the rejection of Robust Realism; rather, it raises the stakes by allowing the robust realist to maintain her realism only at the price of a rather extreme skepticism). But as a premise in an argument against realism the denial of a justified method in the face of disagreement will just not do. Why should we accept it, unless we already lean rather heavily in antirealist directions? Perhaps some argument can be given, but then it will be this *other* argument – the one supporting premise (1) – that does the real work. So the argument from the absence of a justified method cannot stand as an objection to metaethical realism unless it stands on the shoulders of another objection to that view, and so it can be safely set aside here.

But perhaps this is too quick. Perhaps the worry underlying the thought that disagreement somehow undermines justification is really best seen as a general worry about disagreement and epistemological access, a worry to which metaethical realism is purportedly especially vulnerable. This may be so. I discuss this worry in section 8.8, below.

---

[53] If one wants, one may earn respectability for the claim that there is no method in such cases by introducing a tendentious definition of "method", one that rules out methods that are not unified enough, or the status of which is not in consensus, or something of the sort. But such redefinition – here as elsewhere – achieves nothing. Thus understood, premise (1) may be true, but it becomes much harder to justify the transition from it to the conclusion (2).

8.6.3 *No method guaranteed to convince*

Getting closer to the intuition I started this section with – that in other discourses disagreement typically rests on a deeper agreement, but not so in morality – the thought may be that in physics, for instance, the scientific method is (perhaps eventually) guaranteed to generate convergence, indeed consensus; that there are at least possible results of possible experiments that are guaranteed to convince the erring party that she was indeed mistaken. But this does not seem to be the case with moral disagreements. True, we have methods of proceeding in cases of disagreement, and perhaps even some of them are justified. But justified or not, they do not succeed in generating agreement. And it is this feature of moral discourse that either entails or is best explained by the denial of metaethical realism.

Here again, one may deny that this is indeed a feature of moral discourse. It may be argued that some method – perhaps some version of the method often referred to as Reflective Equilibrium – *is* guaranteed to generate (perhaps eventually) agreement, or at least that the claim that this is not the case needs to be argued for. But here again, this is not the way I will go. Yes, some disagreement may very well disappear if methods such as Reflective Equilibrium were to be carefully employed, but I find it highly implausible that all disagreement will disappear in this way. I tend to agree that moral disagreement goes – in this way too – all the way down.

Thus understood, then, I accept the premise. But thus understood, it is very hard to see how it can support the conclusion. Certainly, the absence of a method guaranteed to eliminate disagreement does not deductively entail the denial of realism. To do that we would need to add another premise, to the effect that though they may be morally mistaken, people cannot be *too* mistaken, they cannot be such as to resist the moral truth when presented to them via a justified method. But I see no reason to accept this further premise, at least not unless one is already committed to the denial of realism. Neither is the absence of guaranteed dialectical success best explained by the denial of realism. The morally mistaken may be unconvinced by justified methods for any number of reasons – they may be too stupid, or may have epistemological beliefs (about which methods justify which beliefs) that are too crazy, or may not be willing to listen open-mindedly, or may again be subject to the distorting effects of interests – all of which are perfectly compatible with Robust Realism.

The absence of guaranteed dialectical success does not, then, support the denial of metaethical realism.

8.6.4 *No agreed method*

The intuitive thought about what distinguishes disagreement in morality from disagreement in, say, physics, seems to support another reading of the argument from the absence of a method. For in physics not only is there a justified method of settling disagreements, but also this method is universally accepted by physicists. And it is exactly this feature that is absent in moral disagreements, and that suggests that metaethical realism is false.[54]

Again, let me accept that there is no agreed method of settling moral disagreement,[55] though I should say that I have doubts with regard to the availability of such a method in physics or anywhere else.[56] But how is this fact supposed to support the denial of realism?

In an important sense, we are back at step one. For in this chapter we are looking for a way in which disagreement supports the denial of realism. And now we have in front of us an argument that *presupposes* that disagreement (about a method, this time) counts heavily against Robust Realism. But surely, this is not something the antirealist is entitled to take for granted in the context of an honest attempt to find out whether and how disagreement is a problem for realism. So the situation seems to be this: if there is some *other* way of showing that disagreement is a serious problem for realism then the argument from the absence of agreed method can perhaps have some force, parasitically, as it were, on the force of that other argument. And if there is no other version of an argument from disagreement that can be made to work, then neither can this one (because it has no way of supporting the move from disagreement on method to the denial of realism). And this means that we can safely set aside the argument from absence of agreed method, and just proceed to discuss all other versions of the argument from disagreement. The argument from absence of agreed method poses no independent threat for the realist.

But perhaps none of the suggestions above is the best understanding of the thought that the argument from the absence of method attempts to capture. Perhaps the worry is not just that no method is guaranteed to convince everyone or to itself enjoy consensus, but rather that no method is guaranteed to convince – or enjoy consensus among – even all those who are perfectly rational. Indeed, perhaps the real worry is that moral disagreement itself persists even among the rational. It is to discussing this worry that I now turn.

---

[54] See, for instance, Waldron (1992, 158–87) (though at times Waldron seems to think of the argument from the absence of a justified method).

[55] What is meant here by "settling" is, roughly, finding out who is right and who is wrong, or who is justified and who is unjustified. Whether or not there is agreement about how to proceed practically when facing a moral disagreement (say, by a majority vote) is beside the point here.

[56] Some Creationists, for instance, do not accept the scientific method. Of course, they are not often thought of as physicists. But utilizing this fact to save the purported disanalogy between physics and morality here would be cheating. One can always guarantee agreement on method by restricting the group of those who count (physicists, say) to just those who already agree on the relevant method. For an attempt to defend the analogy between disagreement in ethics and in the natural sciences (partly) by noting this point, see Sturgeon (2006, 108).

8.7 From possible rationally irresolvable disagreement, deductively or by inference to the best explanation, to the denial of Robust Realism

Perhaps the troubling worry about moral disagreement comes not merely from its being so widespread or from its persistence, but from the (apparent) fact that it persists even among rational, reasonable, sensible people. If someone refuses to take evidence into account, or refuses to eliminate inconsistencies in his beliefs (moral and otherwise), or refuses to acknowledge that others too have interests, or refuses both to take analogies seriously and to offer relevant disanalogies, and so on, then perhaps a persistent moral disagreement with him is not so much of a problem for the realist. After all, what reason do we have to expect *this* guy to see the moral truth? The situation is much more problematic, so the thought goes, when moral disagreement persists with perfectly sensible people on both sides. It is this kind of disagreement that is deeply surprising, indeed perhaps inconsistent with or at least not plausibly explained consistently with Robust Realism. The thought seems to be captured by the following argument:

(1)   There are possible cases of rationally irresolvable moral disagreement, where both parties are equally rational, guilty of no flaw of reasoning or some such.

(2)   Therefore, at least in cases where such disagreement is possible, there is no objective fact of the matter.[57]

Notice that unlike previous arguments, this one starts not with actual but rather with possible disagreement. If rationally irresolvable, no-fault disagreement is possible, but just happens not to be actual, this may make things politically simpler, but it does not seem to alleviate whatever worry about realism rationally irresolvable disagreement gives rise to. And the fact that the argument starts from possible and not actual disagreement has immediate effects on both its generalizability and its vulnerabilities. For it applies even to discourses that do not exemplify wide-ranging no-fault disagreements, so long as it is possible for them to do so.[58] And the argument is not vulnerable to the worries (mentioned in section 8.2.2 above) about whether actual moral disagreement should best be seen as genuinely moral or rather as stemming from differences in non-moral beliefs. This does not mean that actual moral disagreement is irrelevant to the assessment of this argument. Indeed, beliefs about actual moral disagreement and its nature may be used to support premise (1) (a point I return to below). But though actual disagreement may very well be relevant in this indirect way,

---

[57] Something like this argument can be found, for instance, in Blackburn (1981, 177); Shafer-Landau (1994, 332); Schiffer (2003, ch. 6); Lillehammer (2004, 97); Parfit (2011, vol. 2, 545), Goldman (1990); and Bennigson (1996) (though Goldman and to an extent also Bennigson at times conflate the argument with other arguments from disagreement).

[58] Railton (1993, 281) takes this as reason not to interpret "the" argument from disagreement along these lines.

it is not strictly speaking assumed or required by the argument from possible no-fault disagreement. A similar point holds with regard to the persistence or intractability of moral disagreement, with these understood descriptively: the fact (if indeed it is a fact) that disagreement actually persists may lend some support to premise (1), but there may be other ways of supporting it, and anyway the argument does not strictly speaking require that moral disagreement be actually intractable in this descriptive sense.

In these ways, then, the argument from the possibility of rationally irresolvable disagreement requires less than arguments that start with empirical claims about actual moral disagreement and its special features. But in another way the argument requires more, for its premise incorporates a normative judgment not assumed by previous arguments, one about the rational permissibility of conflicting views in moral matters: if there can be a moral disagreement – say between Pro-Choice and Pro-Life activists with regard to the moral permissibility of abortion – where both parties share all relevant evidence and no party is being irrational in the intended sense, this means that neither a Pro-Choice nor a Pro-Life view on the permissibility of abortion is in violation of any requirements of rationality. And this means that both views are rationally permissible. The proponent of the argument from rationally irresolvable disagreement, then, trades the need to establish an empirical claim for the need to establish this normative one.

The first thing to note here is that if this argument is generalized from the metaethical to the metanormative level, it dangerously flirts with self-defeat. This is so, because the argument has a paradigmatically normative premise (about what it is rationally permissible to believe) and its conclusion (once generalized) – some kind of metanormative antirealism – is inconsistent with at least the most natural way of accepting this premise (that is, as a full-fledged, truth-directed belief). Now, this is not exactly self-defeat just yet, because depending on the details of the relevant antirealist view there may be a way of accepting the premise that is consistent with the argument's conclusion. Furthermore, the proponent of this argument may resist its generalization – perhaps, for instance, she can somehow claim that while no-fault moral disagreement is possible, no-fault epistemological disagreement (or other normative disagreement) is not possible. So I do not claim that we have here an insurmountable problem for the proponent of this argument. But it does not seem premature to conclude already at this stage that if this argument is to pose a serious problem for Robust Realism, its proponent owes us an antirealist view according to which the generalized argument does not self-defeat, or a rationale for resisting the generalization (or both).[59] In what follows I proceed on the assumption that the proponent of the argument can do that.

Notice further that the conclusion of this argument – like that of the argument from the absence of method – is restricted in scope to just those cases where rationally irresolvable disagreement is indeed possible. For this argument to pose a serious threat

---

[59] Another way the argument could work is as an ad hominem *reductio* argument against a realist who accepted the argument's normative premise.

to metaethical realism, then, it must be shown that rationally irresolvable disagreement is possible with regard to every moral judgment, or at the very least with regard to sufficiently many, sufficiently important cases.

Now, the proponent of the argument owes us also an account of what "rationally irresolvable disagreement" (or "no-fault disagreement") comes to, as these terms can be understood in more than one way. And in giving such an account it is possible to get for free either the premise (1) or the transition from it to the conclusion (2), but not both. If, for instance, one employs a very liberal understanding of "rationally irresolvable" according to which a disagreement is rationally resolvable only if one of the parties can be shown to be inconsistent, then (1) seems highly plausible, but it is exceedingly hard to see how it supports (2). After all, there are many crazy, yet internally consistent, views in physics, mathematics, philosophy, and so on, and this fact may be important in many ways, but it is hard to take it as refuting realism about any of these discourses. To take the opposite extreme, if one packs too much into one's understanding of rational resolvability, so that, for instance, any mistake counts as a rational flaw, then the move from (1) to (2) seems on firmer grounds, but then (1) itself cannot be supported without begging the question against the robust realist by assuming – not establishing – that neither of a pair of contradictory moral claims need be false. The challenge, then, is to come up with an understanding of rational irresolvability or rational fault that avoids both extremes. (Indeed, perhaps the argument owes some of its appeal to the temptation to equivocate on "rationally irresolvable," thus making both (1) and its support for (2) apparently attractive.)

Let me put the intuitive idea here – without pretending that this way of putting things is satisfactorily precise – by saying that moral disagreement need not involve anything worth calling a cognitive shortcoming,[60] where the paradigmatic cognitive shortcomings are failures of logic (in a perhaps wide enough sense), and the absence of (relevant) evidence. Premise (1) asserts, then, that moral disagreement is possible even in the absence of anything worth calling a cognitive shortcoming, and the argument moves from this claim to the denial of Robust Realism.

Before proceeding to reject premise (1), let me make two points regarding the transition from (1) to (2). First, it is tempting to think that the argument fails because it proceeds from an epistemological premise to a metaphysical conclusion, ignoring the gap between justification and truth. The possibility of a rationally irresolvable disagreement shows at most, so the thought goes, that no moral belief (in matters about which such disagreement is possible) is justified, but this does not show that none is true. Now, the argument does, I think, proceed in a suspicious way from an epistemological premise to a metaphysical conclusion, and a supporter of this argument is going to have to tell a story legitimizing such a transition.[61] But if this is the only reply that the realist

[60] I take this phrase from Wright's (1992) characterization of Cognitive Command, to which I also briefly return in footnote 70 below.
[61] For an attempt at such a story see Bennigson (1996, 428–9).

can give to the argument, she faces a problem that has already been mentioned: for it would follow that none of our moral beliefs (regarding which such disagreement is possible) is justified, and this conclusion – though strictly speaking compatible with Robust Realism – is nevertheless so unwelcome to the realist, that it should be avoided if at all possible.

But – and this is the second point regarding the legitimacy of the transition from (1) to (2) – it remains unclear whether the epistemic justification of our beliefs should be held hostage to the necessary agreement of all who are not guilty of a cognitive shortcoming. In the general context of discussions of skepticism, for instance, the point is sometimes made that we need to distinguish between the justificatory status of our beliefs and the dialectical effectiveness we can hope to achieve in convincing the skeptic (who, it seems rather safe to assume, suffers from nothing worth calling a cognitive shortcoming).[62] And if this is true in the most general of epistemological contexts, it is hard to see why it does not apply in ours.[63] Perhaps, then, there can be cases of rationally irresolvable moral disagreement that nevertheless do not undermine the justificatory status of our relevant moral beliefs.[64] If so, the argument from rationally irresolvable disagreement poses no threat to realism, even assuming the truth of its premise.[65]

But should we accept premise (1)? What can the proponent of the argument from rationally irresolvable disagreement offer us by way of support for its premise? What reason is there for believing that moral disagreements are possible where no party is guilty of anything worth calling a cognitive shortcoming?[66] It seems to me that – as mentioned above – here again empirical observations about actual disagreements enter the picture. For we know of many cases, the thought presumably goes, where two parties to a moral disagreement are equally smart, are both careful thinkers, are both attentive to evidence either way, to arguments and counterarguments, and yet none is convinced. In such cases, the thought proceeds, both parties *seem* to be rational in the relevant sense, and so it would be at least implausible to attribute to them a relevant cognitive shortcoming. The support for the claim that rationally irresolvable

---

[62] See, for instance, Boghossian (2000, 251–3). Moody-Adams (1997, ch. 3) argues that there is no sufficient reason to believe even that such dialectical ineffectiveness is an essential feature of moral experience.

[63] Brink (1989, 199), Scanlon (1995, 353), and Shafer-Landau (2003, 221–7) make similar points.

[64] Interestingly, Rosen (2001, 83) thinks this may be true of rationally irresolvable moral disagreements but not of rationally irresolvable epistemic disagreements. He does not supply a rationale for this distinction.

[65] Here is David Lewis (1982, 101) making what I think is a similar point, in the context of defending the law of non-contradiction: "No truth does have, and no truth could have, a true negation. . . . That may seem dogmatic. And it is: I am affirming the very thesis that Routley and Priest have called into question, and – contrary to the rules of debate – I decline to defend it. Further, I concede that it is indefensible against their challenge. They have called so much into question, that I have no foothold on undisputed ground. So much the worse for the demand that philosophers always must be ready to defend their theses under the rules of debate."

[66] Shafer-Landau (2003, 223) notes that we may have no good reason either to affirm or to deny (his version of) the claim in the text, and if so the argument from irresolvable disagreement fails to give a reason to reject realism.

disagreement is possible seems to come, then, in the form of an inference to the best explanation from actual disagreements that do not appear to depend on cognitive shortcomings of (at least) one of the parties.[67]

But now consider the following case. You have had conversations on many topics with both Joan and John, though you have never before observed their mathematical talents in action. Based on your acquaintance with them you have a very high opinion of their intellectual abilities. As it turns out, they are now engaged – separately – in the very same fairly complex arithmetical calculation. Observing them you notice that they are both being very careful, doing what they can to avoid mistaken reasoning and slippages. You know that neither of them lacks any relevant information or evidence (it is just a calculation, after all), neither of them seems over-tired or drunk, and so on. And suppose that – as is surely possible – when they are done they get different results. Here in front of you is an *apparently* rationally irresolvable mathematical disagreement, and yet it seems clear that you should not conclude that the disagreement *really is* rationally irresolvable, you should not conclude that neither Joan nor John is guilty of anything worth calling a cognitive shortcoming. Why?

The answer, it seems to me, lies in your prior commitment to a kind of realism about arithmetical calculations. We come to this case already equipped with the (presumably justified) conviction that arithmetical calculations admit of one result. Seeing that Joan and John got different results, at most one of them can be right. And according to our antecedent beliefs about the nature of such calculations, you can only get the wrong result if you are guilty of something worth calling a cognitive shortcoming. What prevents the transition from a belief in an *apparently* no-fault disagreement to a belief in a no-fault disagreement in this case is, then, your commitment to some version of realism about arithmetic.[68] Of course, typically in cases such as Joan's and John's the disagreement is not very persistent – Joan and John can check each other's calculations, and usually come to an agreement about who made the original mistake. But even if this is not so – even if in our case they do not manage to reach agreement – still your commitment to some version of realism about arithmetic prevents you from taking the apparent rational irresolvability of the disagreement as reason to think it *is* rationally irresolvable.

The same applies, I think, in other discourses where we are intuitively comfortable with a realist view of some kind, one not allowing for rationally irresolvable disagreement. If John sees an object as square-shaped and Joan sees it as rectangular, then this alone is reason enough for us to conclude that one of them is guilty of something worth calling a cognitive shortcoming (has poor eyesight, stands too far from the relevant object, sees it in poor lighting, and so on). We are not even initially tempted to reassess

---

[67] See Lillehammer (2004). Attfield (1979, 519–20) mentions this way of supporting claims about rationally irresolvable disagreements, and finds it unconvincing. And I think that much of Parfit's (2011, vol. 2, 545 and on) relevant discussion is implicitly devoted precisely to rejecting this way of supporting claims about disagreement in ideal conditions (a close relative, presumably, of rationally irresolvable disagreement).

[68] Nothing like mathematical Platonism need be implied here, of course.

our view of shapes (whatever it is), and this even without any independent evidence – independent, that is, of this very disagreement in Joan's and John's shape-judgments – that one of them is guilty of something worth calling a cognitive shortcoming.

Getting back to moral disagreement, then, suppose Dan and Dana disagree about whether the state should criminalize the use of certain drugs, Dana claiming it should and Dan that it should not. And suppose further that we have no independent evidence – independent, that is, of this very moral disagreement – that either one of them is guilty of anything worth calling a cognitive shortcoming. Why should we not take this very disagreement as all the reason we need to believe that at least one of them *is* guilty of such a shortcoming? In the mathematical and shape cases, our (roughly speaking) realist commitments seem to justify such an attitude. And this means that the analogous metaethical views would license the analogous attitude in the moral case. Assuming metaethical realism, then, we are perfectly entitled to take this very disagreement as reason to attribute to at least one of them a cognitive shortcoming, even if at this point we have no further story to tell about this shortcoming.[69] Of course, if we should not start off as metaethical realists this line of thought is not available to us. But this does not save the argument from rationally irresolvable disagreement. Remember, the argument is supposed to present an objection to metaethical realism. But now we have found that it poses a problem for realism only if we come to this argument already rejecting (or at least not accepting) realism. If we start off as antirealists, the argument may have force on us, but not so if we start off as realists.[70] And this means that it fails as an independent objection to metaethical realism. The obvious way to support premise (1) thus simply begs the question against the realist.

Another way of making what I think is the same point is as follows.[71] There is bound to be *some* difference between Dan's and Dana's psychologies in virtue of which they differ on the moral justifiability of the criminalization of certain drugs, just like there is bound to be a difference between John's and Joan's psychologies in virtue of which they got different results in the arithmetical calculation. Focusing on this difference, then, are we to count it as a defect, as something worth calling a cognitive shortcoming? In both cases, it seems to me that the answer depends primarily – though perhaps not exclusively – on whether we think of moral and arithmetical facts as something out

---

[69] For a similar point see Moore (1992, 2479–80). Tersman (2006, ch. 2) emphasizes the general difficulties in deciding whether a given disagreement is a no-fault disagreement, as well as the specific worry that any such decision will flirt with begging the question (2006, 22, 42).

[70] For somewhat similar points, see Bennigson (1996, 425 and 429), and Gowans (2000, 18). The argument in the text shows that in order to decide what force to give the argument from rationally irresolvable disagreement you have to already have decided (though perhaps provisionally) the debate over realism one way or another. Perhaps this is why Wright (1992) introduces his Cognitive Command (from which I borrow talk of cognitive shortcomings as features of some but not other disagreements) not in the context of *giving an argument* for or against realism, but rather in the context of *characterizing* the realist–antirealist debate.

[71] I thank Josh Schechter for discussions on this point.

there to be noticed or missed. The answer depends, in other words, on whether or not we already accept realism about morality (and arithmetic).

Assuming realism, then, we have reason to believe of any specific disagreement that it does involve something worth calling a cognitive shortcoming, and so that premise (1) itself begs the question against the realist.[72] And this point becomes even stronger when we remember that in order to pose a challenge to metaethical realism premise (1) must apply to sufficiently many, sufficiently important moral disagreements.

This does not mean that moral disagreements that are apparently rationally irresolvable are irrelevant to the debate over metaethical realism. First, if we come to this argument unbiased either for or against realism, and if it does seem implausible – pre-theoretically – to attribute a cognitive shortcoming to one of the disagreeing parties, then the argument from (apparently) rationally irresolvable disagreement does have some weight against realism. Notice, by the way, that here the availability at this point in the discussion of my positive arguments for Robust Realism makes a difference – given these arguments, I can now insist, we should no longer come to the discussion of disagreement "unbiased" one way or another. Rather, we are entitled at least to a presumption in favor of realism, indeed of Robust Realism. Second, and relatedly, after having rejected the characterization of such disagreements as genuinely rationally irresolvable in the way discussed above, the realist may still need to explain the appearance that the disagreement was a no-fault one. She owes an account, in other words, of what it is that leads smart, sensitive, well-reasoning, sober persons to disagree on such matters. And how well the realist faces this explanatory challenge may have an effect on the plausibility of her realism.[73] In these ways, then, and depending on the conditions above, the argument from rationally irresolvable disagreement may cost Robust Realism some plausibility points. But, first, I see no reason to suspect that the kind of considerations discussed in section 8.2.4 above cannot do the explanatory work needed here in a realist-friendly way, and second, and perhaps more importantly in the context of the argument from rationally irresolvable disagreement, nothing in the realist's reply to *this* argument hinges on her doing this extra explanatory work (just like we should not believe that Joan's and John's disagreement is a non-fault one even without a further story to tell about either Joan's or John's arithmetical error).

8.8 From disagreement, via the absence of epistemic access, to the denial of realism

Perhaps the problem moral disagreement points to is that in cases of moral disagreement – or perhaps just in cases where the disagreement involves no apparent cognitive

[72] Brink (2001) thinks there is just no good reason to believe either that irresolvable disagreement is possible or that it is not.

[73] I therefore concede here a point central to Gowans's (2000, 16) version of the argument from disagreement – that an apparently rationally irresolvable disagreement is at least some prima facie evidence against realism.

shortcoming of any of the parties – we have no way of knowing, of finding out who is right and who is wrong.[74] The problem, it may be thought, is that at least on realist grounds there is no plausible way of giving an account of moral knowledge, indeed of justified moral belief. How is it, the thought goes, that our moral beliefs track reasonably reliably these supposed objective moral facts? And if they do not, does it not follow – assuming this is what our moral beliefs have to track to be true, that is, assuming realism – that moral knowledge is impossible, and that therefore there is no way of deciding moral disagreement? And is this not a *reductio ad absurdum* of realism?[75]

I hope that all of this sounds familiar to you, for this was precisely the topic of Chapter 7. And the most important thing to note about this in our context is that the general epistemic challenge to Robust Realism need not be put in terms of disagreement at all. Disagreement may be *relevant* to it, by placing adequacy constraints on possible ways of addressing the epistemic challenge. But as you may recall, nothing in my suggested way of coping with the epistemic challenge depended in any objectionable way on assumptions about agreement, consensus, convergence, or the like. Nor did my discussion in Chapter 7 have (as far as I can see) any disagreement-related implications. If the argument in the previous chapter fails, then, so much the worse for Robust Realism, though for reasons that have nothing to do with the phenomenon of moral disagreement. If it succeeds, however, there isn't here another, new challenge robust realists have to respond to.

8.9 Conclusion, and a note on higher-order arguments from disagreement

Where does the discussion leave us, then? Some of the arguments from disagreement I have considered above are rather clearly confused, some can be seen to beg the question against the robust realist (the argument from rationally irresolvable disagreement (to an extent), some versions of the argument from the absence of method, and to an extent also the IBE version of the argument from actual disagreement), or at least rely on a premise that from a realist-friendly perspective is highly implausible (one version of the argument from the absence of method, and the argument from

---

[74] Seeing that others disagree, should we not at least take back some of our confidence in our moral judgments? Perhaps so, but this has nothing to do with an argument from disagreement to antirealism. What this thought shows is that we should – in morality as elsewhere – update our beliefs in accordance with the evidence, and that the evidence sometimes includes the fact that others have different beliefs. Perhaps more importantly, in this regard there is nothing special about moral beliefs – what we have here is just a particular instance of the general epistemological problem now known as the problem of peer disagreement. For my own view here, and for many references, see my "Not Just a Truthometer" (2011).

[75] Loeb (1998, 285) understands "the traditional argument from disagreement" as something along the lines in the text, though he ties it also to the IBE version of the argument from disagreement. Brandt's (1944) discussion is very similar in these respects. And Schiffer's (2003, 245–52) discussion of the "argument from irresolubility" eventually boils down to the general epistemic challenge of accounting for a priori moral knowledge.

internalism), some manage to point at genuine problems for Robust Realism, but problems that are not after all essentially related to moral disagreement (the argument from semantic access, the argument from epistemic access, and one version of the argument from the absence of method), and that are therefore discussed in detail elsewhere in this book. Some of the arguments do have some force, presenting a prima facie challenge realists must face, but not, I've argued, a challenge we have any reason to believe realists cannot face successfully – though perhaps at a certain price in plausibility points (the IBE version of the argument from actual disagreement, and perhaps also the argument from rationally irresolvable disagreement and the argument undermining the support agreement would – some realists think – have lent to realism). And the phenomenon of moral disagreement can cause problems for realism also in another way – by setting adequacy constraints on realist ways of addressing the most general semantic and epistemological challenges.

Perhaps some of these arguments can be amended in a way that renders moral disagreement more problematic for the realist. Perhaps some auxiliary premises (such as some version of internalism) can be defended in a non-question-begging way, such that together with them some claim about moral disagreement would entail, or at least support, a conclusion incompatible with Robust Realism. But I do not now see how any such line can be convincingly pursued. Nor can I think of other ways in which disagreement may be thought of as a problem for Robust Realism, though, of course, I have not given any argument supporting the exhaustiveness of the list of arguments discussed above. I leave it to antirealists to present better versions of arguments from disagreement.[76]

Let me conclude by emphasizing a fact that will make this an exceedingly hard task. Disagreement is widespread not just *in* morality, but also *about* morality, in metaethics, and indeed in philosophy in general.[77] Here too, one comes across widespread disagreement among those who do not appear to be guilty of anything worth calling a cognitive shortcoming, here too this disagreement seems to call for explanation,[78] here too it is not clear that there is some underlying agreement, say about the method to settle superficial disagreements. But this means that it is not going to be easy to present an argument from moral disagreement that does not defeat itself.[79] If, for

---

[76] Notice that the discussion above – if successful – also casts doubt on the availability of antirealist arguments that are based on combining the effect of more than one of the arguments from disagreement.

[77] Dworkin (1996, 114) argues that there is *more* disagreement in philosophy than in morality.

[78] Indeed, it seems to me easier to come up with explanations of moral disagreement in terms that do not in any way entail antirealism, than it is to come up with alternative explanation of this kind for metaethical disagreement. Think, for instance, about explanations in terms of self-interest.

[79] For a somewhat similar point see Swinburne (1976). Shafer-Landau (2003, 220; 2006, 218–21) notices that arguments from disagreement can be applied in philosophy in general, and in metaethics in particular, so that there is something self-defeating about the antirealist's employment of this argument from disagreement. But Shafer-Landau does not notice that this may render the arguments from disagreement *themselves* self-defeating in the way described in the text. Tersman (2006, 112) notices that a key premise in his favorite argument from disagreement – the one he calls "the latitude idea" – applies to much in philosophy as well as to ethics. But he does not proceed to discuss the self-defeat worry this fact may give rise to.

instance, the argument takes actual disagreement as a reason to be suspicious of realism, then given actual disagreement about metaethical realism (robust or otherwise) and indeed about arguments from disagreement (this one included), the proponent of the argument seems to be committing himself also to a denial of realism *about* the realism debate in metaethics and so about his very argument. If an argument is constructed with the conclusion that apparently rationally irresolvable disagreement gives rise to a denial of a unique truth-value, then given apparently rationally irresolvable disagreement about this very argument and its conclusion, the proponent of the argument cannot consistently defend the truth of his conclusion.[80] (Does it seem plausible that one need not be guilty of anything worth calling a cognitive shortcoming in order to reject, say, ideas about gender equality, but that rejecting the antirealist's favorite argument from disagreement must involve a cognitive shortcoming?) And so on.

Thus, in order to present an argument from moral disagreement that poses a serious problem for Robust Realism it is necessary that the relevant argument should avoid not only the kinds of flaws discussed throughout this chapter, but also this kind of self-defeat. And given the similarities between the purportedly relevant features of moral and metaethical disagreement,[81] it is hard to see how such an argument can be constructed.

---

[80] Schiffer's (2003, ch. 6) version of an argument from irresolvable disagreement is an especially clear case, except the conclusion is the denial of *determinate* truth. But an argument that undermines the *determinate* truth of its premises or conclusion seems just as disturbingly self-defeating as one that undermines their truth.

[81] This is perhaps clearest with regard to the IBE arguments from disagreements. Disagreement about which explanation is *best* is, of course, a normative disagreement, and it is hard to see what features distinguish between it and paradigmatic moral disagreements.

9

Motivation

If the arguments of the last three chapters are even just roughly right, then the price in plausibility points that Robust Realism has to pay because of traditional objections having to do with its metaphysical and epistemological commitments and with the phenomenon of moral (and perhaps more broadly normative) disagreement is not sufficiently high to cause problems for the robust realist. But now we need to address another family of worries, worries that can imprecisely be put as worries about the *distance*, according to Robust Realism, between the normative truths and what brings us to action.

According to Robust Realism, after all, the normative truths are out there, as it were, in Plato's heaven, utterly independent of us and our motivations. And when we are successful in our normative inquiries, we discover these normative truths. But then isn't this picture all too theoretical to be at all practically relevant, perhaps a piece of practical reasoning? What is the relation between these normative truths (robustly realistically understood) and how we are to guide our actions? How do they engage, perhaps even bind, our will? How can a robust realist account for the intimate relations between normative truths and judgments on one side, and our motivations on the other? If she cannot, isn't this reason enough to reject Robust Realism?

I take it this is not the first time you've heard (or read) such worries. But it's one thing to voice inchoate worries, and quite another to present a serious philosophical objection (this even if the inchoate worries are voiced in a rhetorically effective way). And so one natural way to proceed here would have been to show how some of the things people say in this context thinking that they are thereby putting forward a profound objection to Robust Realism or to some related view can be rather easily debunked. And I will not resist the temptation to do just that, in some of the later sections in this chapter. But I think it will prove more useful – and perhaps more pleasing to the somewhat impatient reader – to start with what seems to me to be the genuinely interesting issue in this vicinity. This is the thought that – now put in reason-talk – surely it is at least possible, and indeed often plausible, that we act for reasons. And it may be thought that Robust Realism cannot accommodate this highly natural thought. If this is so, let me concede already here, this does count strongly against Robust Realism – perhaps especially so given the emphasis on deliberation in my arguments for Robust Realism.[1] So it is important to show that Robust Realism is in fact compatible with action for reasons. But of course, the idea of acting for a (specific) reason is anything but philosophically transparent. So in section 9.1 I offer an analysis of this idea, one that I hope you will find attractive independently of what you happen to think of Robust Realism. I then proceed to show that Robust Realism can accommodate action for a reason, thus understood. The discussion of acting for a (specific) reason is needed here not only (perhaps not even primarily) in order to allay the worry that Robust Realism cannot accommodate action for a reason, but also in order to better prepare the robust realist for *other* motivational challenges. In the sections that follow, then, I discuss some of the more common ways in the literature of raising motivational concerns for Robust Realism. These include thoughts about practicality (in section 9.2); about the kind of moral skeptic who asks why-be-moral and related questions (9.3); about judgment-internalism (9.4); and about existence-internalism (9.5). As will become clear as this chapter unfolds, my responses to these related worries will rely (to different degrees) on the results of section 9.1, and in particular on the possibility of Robust Realism accommodating action for a reason. With this weapon in the robust realist's hands, we can rather easily see the problems with the challenges discussed in following sections.

Interestingly, my discussion will assume *very* little in the theory of motivation. Robust Realism is compatible, I will argue, with all the things we should want to say about the relation between normativity and motivation, however precisely we think of the latter, and in particular even if we are (perhaps broadly speaking) Humeans in the theory of motivation – accepting the claim, roughly, that desires are always necessary for motivation. Of course, Robust Realism is *not* compatible with Humeanism as a theory of *normative reasons* (more on this in section 9.5) – roughly, the claim that all your normative reasons are grounded in your desires or motivational set. Nor is it compatible with all the things philosophers *do* say about the relation between normativity and motivation. But it *is* compatible with all the *plausible* things that can be said in this vicinity. Or so, at least, I will argue in this chapter.

A final preliminary: let me remind you that in this chapter (as in the last three) I am merely playing defense. The question, then, is not whether Robust Realism can shed interesting light on theories of motivation (or some such). The question, rather, is whether it is (reasonably) immune to objections from motivation, and so whether it is compatible with plausible claims in the vicinity. I do not pretend that the discussion in this chapter earns Robust Realism positive plausibility points. It merely shows that Robust Realism doesn't lose (too many, if any) plausibility points because of thoughts having to do with motivation.

---

[1] Heuer (2004, 46) emphasizes the thought (which she emphasized to me even more in several conversations) that unless we can act for (specific) reasons, deliberation is a sham. And here's Dancy (2000, 171) making what I think is a similar point: "If we said to the agent: 'You can tell us as often as you like what your reason was for doing what you did, but we know in advance that that reason can never be the reason why you did it', I think he would feel rightly insulted – and this even though we are not disputing the *truth* of what he tells us."

9.1 Acting for a (specific) reason

My three-year-old son sometimes acts for reasons. Sometimes, for instance, he goes to his room because I tell him to go to his room. Describing such cases, we find it natural to say things like that he went to his room for the reason that I told him to do so, or that his reason for going to his room was that I told him to, or that he went to his room because I told him, or perhaps even that part of what explains why he went to his room is that I told him to. So action for a reason is a phenomenon that seems to tie talk of reasons – presumably,[2] normative talk – to talk about the explanation of actions.

9.1.1 Why there's a suspicion that Robust Realism is incompatible with action for a (specific) reason

On Robust Realism, normative truths are response-independent. In particular, they do not constitutively depend on the relevant agent's (or anyone else's) desires. Of course, desires may be, consistently with Robust Realism, normatively relevant: it may be the case, for instance, that we have a reason to satisfy our desires, or perhaps our loved ones' desires, or some such. But nothing about desires plays a role in making the basic normative truths true, or anything of the sort. And in particular, Robust Realism seems compatible with a normative truth applying to someone, whatever mental states (including desires) she's in. Furthermore, on Robust Realism normative truths are abstract, causally inert. But now it can seem mysterious how Robust Realism can accommodate action for a reason. For even before we have an explicit account of action for a reason, it seems like a plausible starting point that whether or not someone counts as having acted for a reason R, depends on the causal story leading to the action, and presumably in particular on the motivations of the agent. But then, if whatever reasons – *normative* reasons, that is – that justify my son's going to his room are out there, as it were, in Plato's heaven, then how can his actually going to his room be *for* those reasons? If the story explaining his going to his room is in terms of desires and motivations, and anyway in causal terms, how can this story be closely related to the normative truths that apply to my son, as it would have to be for the action to count as having been performed *for* those reasons?

Now, we need to be clearer on a related topic. My son's reason for going to his room, we're assuming, is *that I told him to*. This is not – it certainly need not be – itself a normative truth or fact. The reasons for which we act – that it contains vitamin C, that she needs help, that he's charming, that it's so expensive, that I really want to – these can be perfectly ordinary, naturalistically respectable things.[3] So Robust Realism – and any other metanormative theory, really – need have nothing interesting to say about them. In particular, even if normative truths are desire-independent, causally inert, and out there in Plato's heaven, this is consistent with the reasons for which we act (that I told him to, that it contains vitamin C, that she needs help, . . .) being causally

---

[2] But not obviously. More to follow.

[3] This is a point often noted in the literature. For an example in a closely related context, see Dancy (1995, 6).

efficacious right here in our concrete world, and perhaps also playing a suitable motivational role in leading agents to actions. So we still do not have here a clear understanding of the initial suspicion, of why it may be thought that Robust Realism cannot accommodate action for a reason.

But two other considerations – independent of one another, as far as I can see – lead to this suspicion. The first is that though the reasons we act on *need* not be themselves normative, it seems like they *can* be normative. For it seems possible – anyway, not something we would want to rule out as an impossibility from the start – that my seven-year-old daughter won't hit her little brother back because that would be wrong. And in such cases it would be just as natural to say things like that she leaves him alone for the reason that hitting him would be wrong, that her reason for leaving him alone is that hitting him would be wrong, that she left him alone because hitting him would be wrong, that part of what explains why she left him alone is that to hit him would be wrong. Now I understand, of course, that this is all controversial, and that you may have a view – perhaps some hyper-buck-passing view of wrongness – according to which the wrongness is never a reason itself (perhaps it merely indicates that there are other reasons). But even if wrongness is not a reason in itself, it may be treated as one by my daughter, and anyway robust realists would be well advised not to have their Robust Realism decide such controversies as whether that an action is wrong is or can be a reason. Now, that hitting her brother back is wrong is, of course, a normative truth. It is also, as we've just seen, my daughter's reason for (not) performing an action. Sometimes, then, normative truths (or facts, or properties) are themselves the reasons for which we act. And this makes the initial suspicion about Robust Realism more serious, for it may be hard to see how the purportedly mind-independent, causally inert normative truth can be something *for* which my daughter acts.[4]

The second, and perhaps more important (because more general) reason for the suspicion that Robust Realism cannot accommodate action for a reason is that when we attribute to someone action for a reason, what we attribute to them is not just a response to the reason, but also a response, perhaps roughly speaking, to *it being* a reason.[5] If we want to say that my son went to his room for the reason that I told him to, we do not want it to merely be the case that his going to the room was a response to my telling him to do so. There are many ways in which the action could qualify as a response *to that* without amounting to acting *for* that reason (I take it, for instance, that when a dog responds to a command – say, to sit – it doesn't thereby act for the reason that it was told to sit[6]). What is missing is for the relevant action to be a response not

---

[4] Some parallel issues – about which I do not know enough – come up in discussions of the causal (and perhaps other) work naturalistically respectable *universals* are supposed to be doing. I take this analogy to be reason for cautious optimism that the problem for Robust Realism in the text here can be dealt with. But I do not think of this analogy (even if the details of the discussion in the case of universals end up being Robust-Realism-friendly) as showing that the problem for Robust Realism *has already* been adequately dealt with.

[5] See, for instance, Velleman (1989, 191).

[6] Here see Korsgaard's (2008, 213) similar lioness example.

just to the reason, but to *its being a reason*, or to the fact that it is a reason, or to the relevant reason's property of being, precisely, a reason, or some such (the differences between these ways of putting things may be important in some contexts, but not in mine). But the reason's reason-ness, or its being a reason, or the fact that it is a reason, are precisely the kind of things robust realists are robust realists about. How can it be, then, that my son's going to his room can be a response not just to my telling him to do so, but also to (perhaps roughly speaking) the fact that my telling him to do so is a reason for him to so act, if this fact is desire-independent, causally inert, and all the way out there in Plato's heaven?

9.1.2 A Φ-s for reason R if and only if:

I will answer this question in section 9.1.3. Before doing that, though, we need to unpack the idea of acting for a (specific) reason. In particular, we need an account of – or at least necessary and sufficient conditions for – someone doing something for some specific reason.

Talk of reasons is multiply ambiguous, and so we need to draw some distinctions. A common distinction in the literature is that between normative reasons and motivating reasons. Normative reasons are the things that count in favor of certain actions, that justify or make certain actions rational. Motivating reasons are the things that – unless defeated by stronger causal forces – motivate, that causally bring agents to actions (in the special way in which actions are motivated[7]). I do not want to beg any controversial questions here about the relations between the two. In particular, I want to remain neutral at this early stage on whether there are any necessary connections between normative and motivating reasons. I even want to remain open-minded about the possibility that motivating reasons just are normative reasons, or the other way around, or some such – that, in other words, the very same thing can play both roles, and perhaps even must play both roles (if it plays either). All I am assuming here is that the conceptual distinction holds, that it's one thing *to say* that R is a normative reason for agent A for φ-ing, and another *to say* that it was the motivating reason why A φ-ed. This much, I think, should be pretty uncontroversial.

In addition to normative and motivating reasons, we can also talk of the consideration in light of which the agent acted, the feature of the situation that made the relevant action one the agent thought worth performing. We can designate this as *the agent's reason*.[8] The agent's reason can't be simply understood as the relevant normative reason, because, after all, the agent may be mistaken in taking a feature of the situation to make an action worth performing. In such a case, the agent's reason is not (also) a normative reason. And the agent's reason can't simply be the motivating reason,

---

[7] This qualification is needed, because not any causal explanation of an action – certainly, not any causal explanation of a bodily movement – qualifies as a motivating reason. See, for instance, Schroeder (2007, 12).

[8] For this terminology, see, for instance, Rawls (2000, 166), Setiya (2007, 30).

because, for instance, the agent may be mistaken about the causal origins of her action. In such a case, the agent's reason and the motivating reason can be distinguished.

Not convinced? Think of the following example, then. Glenn voted to ban gay marriage. His reason – the one he cites in discussions of such things, and sincerely believes led him to action – is that gay relationships are unnatural. Assume, as seems likely, that the fact that gay relationships are unnatural (if it is a fact) does not at all count for voting to ban gay marriage, so that this isn't a normative reason so to vote. Assume further that it's not the case that the unnaturalness of gay relationships is what moved Glenn to action, because, well, there is nothing unnatural about gay relationships. Motivation is partly causal, and causation is factive – so that gay relationships are unnatural can't motivate unless it is true that gay relationships are unnatural, which for now we're assuming is not the case. What *really* motivates Glenn to so vote – what causally leads him to this action – is something quite different. Perhaps it is his *belief* that gay relationships are unnatural. In this case, then, that gay relations are unnatural is neither a normative reason for voting to ban gay marriage, nor is it Glenn's motivating reason so to vote. But still, there is *a* sense in which it is a reason, indeed *his* reason, for his action. It is his reason, then, in the sense specified above, of the agent's reason. It is the consideration in light of which he acted.

Notice that the agent's reason is not reducible to his motivating reason. Suppose that Glenn's motivating reason – the thing that played the appropriate causal role in bringing him to vote for the ban on gay marriage – is his belief (false though it may be) that gay relationships are unnatural. Still, this is highly unlikely to be his (agent's) reason for so voting. This is so, because the consideration in light of which he acted was not *that I believe that gay relationships are unnatural*. The consideration in light of which he acted was *that gay relationships are unnatural*. His own beliefs are not a part of what, in his mind, makes voting to ban gay marriage the thing to do. We can see this by employing a simple counterfactual test. If we ask Glenn to contemplate a possible world in which gay relationships are unnatural, but he (in that world) has come to falsely believe that there's nothing unnatural about gay relationships, Glenn will still be in the actual world opposed to gay marriage in that other possible world. The feature of the situation that is normatively relevant, Glenn thinks, is the unnaturalness of gay relationships, not his belief about it. This is a point I emphasized in Chapter 2 (section 2.1) – typically, our reasons for action, the thing we take to be the normatively relevant feature of the situation, is not our beliefs (or desires, or our other mental states), but other things, perhaps things that occupy some role in the content of our beliefs (or other mental states).[9]

---

[9] This is a central point in Jonathan Dancy's work, in his *Practical Reality* (2000) and elsewhere. But this point is also made by people more sympathetic to the Humean tradition here, for instance Darwall (1983, 37), Pettit and Smith (1990). Moran (1994, 169) employs a counterfactual test similar to the one in the text. For a similar point in the political context, see Raz (1998, 27). And for the analogous point in the epistemic case, see my "Not Just a Truthometer" (2011) and Schroeder's "Having Reasons" (2008a).

Now, many things in the vicinity here are controversial and hotly debated in the relevant literature. But I don't think anything I said so far should be. Interesting questions do arise, of course, about the relations between motivating, normative, and the agent's reasons. For instance, is there a recognizable class of actions – perhaps *successful* actions, in some sense – for which all three coincide? Is the motivating reason *ever* the normative one? Is the motivating reason *ever* the agent's reason? These are indeed interesting questions, and later on I will have something to say about some of them. But they have nothing to do, I think, with the very limited points I've been emphasizing – namely, the conceptual distinction between the three kinds of reasons. To establish this three-way distinction all that is needed is that a Glenn of the kind I described be conceptually possible. And such a conceptual possibility is, I think, very hard to deny.

Things are complicated here, as often elsewhere as well, by terminological issues. Thus, I think that Dancy (2000) understands motivating reasons as (what I call) the agent's reasons, and this understanding plays a crucial role in leading him to equate motivating and normative reasons. But the apparent disagreement between us here is a combination of a different use of words, and Dancy's commitment to a substantive thesis that I want at this stage to remain neutral on. Thus, if I understand him correctly, it is no part of Dancy's understanding of motivating reasons that they play an appropriate *causal* role in leading the agent to action. This, I take it, is why Dancy (1995, 17–18; 2000, ch. 8) spends time arguing for the compatibility of causal explanations with other explanations, explanations in terms of (what he calls) motivating reasons. But this means that we can translate whatever Dancy says about motivating reasons to my talk of the agent's reasons. What I call motivating reasons are just a particular instance of Dancy's causal explanations of actions. And Dancy's insistence on the identity of (what he calls) motivating reasons and normative reasons is, once translated into my terms, the interesting substantive claim that the agent's reason for action just is the normative one (at least in success cases). I have not taken a stand on this question, though I get back to it later on. Presumably, other writers use these and related terms in different ways still. But we should not let terminology confuse us. The points I've been making can be put in fairly neutral terms, and should, I think, be quite uncontroversial: the consideration in light of which the agent acts (which I stipulatively, but following some of the literature here, denote by "the agent's reason") need not be something (like perhaps her own beliefs or desires) that plays an appropriate causal role in bringing her to action (which I stipulatively, but in line with much of the literature, denote by "the motivating reason"); nor need it be a consideration that does in fact justify the action in any way (which I stipulatively, though again in line with the literature, denote by "the normative reason" for performing the action).[10]

This rather long detour about different kinds of reasons was needed just in order to make the following point: When we say that an agent A φ-ed for a reason R, our claim

---

[10] For a similar taxonomy, see Hieronymi (manuscript), and for a similar taxonomy utilizing different terminology, see Olson and Svensson (2005).

is about the agent's reason, not (necessarily) about the relevant normative or motivating reasons. When you say that my son went to his room for the reason that I told him to, you are not committing yourself to the legitimacy of parental authority (in general, or in my case). What you're saying is consistent, I think, with your also believing that this is no reason at all for him to go to his room, that is, that that I told him to doesn't in any way count in favor of him going to his room. And it would be true (if awkward) to say that my son went to his room for the reason that I told him to even if in fact I said no such thing, and my son merely misheard – so long, that is, as the consideration in light of which he acted when going to his room was that (as he believed) I told him to do so. So the reason for which someone acts is not – as a matter of conceptual necessity – her motivating reason either. It is precisely the agent's reason, in the sense sketched above.

If so, I think that an analysis of "A ϕ-s for R" should allow for – and hopefully explain – three kinds of mistakes A may be making, all of which have already been briefly mentioned. The first is a normative mistake, so that A's ϕ-ing for R is consistent with R not counting in favor of A's ϕ-ing at all. Thus, Glenn can vote to ban gay marriage for the reason that gay relationships are unnatural even if that is no (normative) reason at all for anyone to vote to ban gay marriage. The second kind of mistake is factual, so that A's ϕ-ing for R is consistent with R not being the case.[11] Acting for a reason, in other words, is not factive in this way. Thus, Glenn can vote to ban gay marriage for the reason that gay relationships are unnatural even if it's not the case that gay relationships are unnatural. The third kind of mistake an analysis of acting for a reason must allow for is introspective mistake (and ignorance), so that A's ϕ-ing for R is consistent with A not believing that she is ϕ-ing for R, and indeed with her believing that she is not ϕ-ing for R (but for some other reason); and her believing that she is ϕ-ing for R does not guarantee that in fact she is. That this kind of mistake is possible seems to follow from commonsensical observations about our fallibility regarding our own mental states and the causal origins of our actions. Thus, even if Glenn believes that he's voting to ban gay marriage for the reason that gay relationships are unnatural, it's quite possible that the causal origins of his action do not respond to the (real or supposed) unnaturalness of gay relationships in the way needed for his action to be *for* that reason. Perhaps, for instance, the causal origins of his voting to ban gay marriage stem from his being somewhat unconfident about his own sexual orientation, and his suspicion that seeing married gay couples around may thus cause him considerable unease. (Notice that this story is not *just* a causal story, it is a *motivational* story, it is a causal story of the right kind to play a motivational role.

---

[11] I am not one of the people who get all excited about whether agents' reasons are propositions, or facts, or states of affairs, or properties, or perhaps something else. In the text I write as if reasons are at the very least something that can be true or false, as would clearly be legitimate if they are propositions. If they are not, though, everything I say here can rather straightforwardly be translated to talk of (real or purported) facts, or states of affairs (that do or don't obtain), or some such.

If, for instance, you like belief–desire models of motivation, note that this little story can easily be put in such terms.)

Before I put forward my suggested account of action for a reason, let me note just one more complication I want to avoid here. The suggested account is rather unambitious: I do not think of it as an account of what it is to act for a reason, much less of what it is to act, or of what action consists in. It is merely an account of what it is for an agent to perform an action for a *specific* reason.[12] Of course, there may be interesting relations – perhaps even implication relations – between these different phenomena. It is tempting, for instance, to think that an event (or perhaps a bodily movement) can only count as an action if it is done for a reason, and it may be at least as tempting to think that an action is performed for a reason if and only if there is some reason such that the action is done for *it*. But whether we should succumb to these temptations is something I think we should remain open-minded about. After all, nothing here is obvious. It seems to me, for instance, that many animals perform actions (this is certainly true if we employ Wittgenstein's (1953, §621) subtraction as a test for action, for surely *something* is left if we subtract from the fact that a dog moves its leg the fact that its leg moves, and pre-theoretically it seems like the very same thing remains here that remains when we employ a similar subtraction about human action). But it seems to me rather clear that animals never act for some reason R. So something in the transition above (any action is done for a reason, and for any action done for a reason there is some reason R such that the action is done for R) must have gone wrong. This needn't be anything especially deep. Perhaps, for instance, the acting-for-a-reason that seems necessary for action is acting for a *motivating* reason, but when we talk about acting for a specific reason R we usually talk of the agent's reasons, so that the transition above equivocates. Be that as it may, I want to suggest an account of what it is for an agent A to φ for a reason R, and that's it.

Here, then, is my suggestion. A φ-s for R just in case:[13]

(1) A intentionally φ-s; and
(2) A believes that R; and
(3) The belief *that R is a (normative) reason for A to φ (in the circumstances)* plays an appropriate causal role in bringing about A's φ-ing.[14]

---

[12] For this reason, I can afford not to engage the recent guise-of-the-good literature. See, for instance, Velleman (1992), Setiya (2007), and Raz (2010).

[13] In what follows I will sometimes refer to this suggestion as my account or analysis of acting for a reason. But I do not want to commit myself to these stronger claims (perhaps – a suggestion that was powerfully pressed on me by Jonathan Dancy – acting for a specific reason is not analyzable at all). All that is needed for showing that Robust Realism can accommodate action for a reason is that the conditions that follow in the text are sufficient for action for a reason. I use these other locutions simply to get shorter, more manageable wording.

[14] I don't know of anyone putting forward precisely this analysis. But I do not claim originality for the general idea here. See, for instance, Velleman (1989, 191). Schroeder (2007, 152) characterizes the requirement that an agent take the relevant considerations to be a reason as "a now more-or-less standard way of" characterizing the further, interesting condition needed for action for a (specific) reason. But he rightly notes

Depending on how exactly we unpack "an appropriate causal role" – more on this shortly – clause (2) and the "intentionally" in clause (1) may be redundant.

On this suggestion, then, a normative belief – or anyway judgment[15] – that *R is a reason for φ-ing* is a necessary condition for φ-ing for R. You may be worried that this makes the suggested account of acting for a (specific) reason over-intellectual. I don't think this is so. To make it clear that the account doesn't over-intellectualize *action*, let me re-emphasize that none of this is meant as a necessary condition for actions or intentional actions in general. So the over-intellectualization worry only applies to the idea of action for a (specific) reason. But this may still be bad enough. So let me resort to what may seem to be a dirty trick, and then explain why it isn't a dirty trick after all. The normative belief cited in (3) may be an implicit one. It's not as if in order to count as φ-ing for R, A has to think to herself something like "Oh, R counts in favor of my φ-ing now" (much less does she have to think "Oh, R is a normative reason for me to φ"). She needn't even think to herself in explicitly normative terms, or even have a rather clear understanding of what R precisely is. Still, if we are to describe her as having φ-ed for R, we must be willing to attribute to her the belief that R counts in favor of her φ-ing (in the circumstances).[16]

The reason a resort to implicit beliefs may look like a mere theory-saving trick is that it may seem as though implicit beliefs – unlike more explicit ones, perhaps – pose no restrictions on a theory invoking them, and so can serve as an artificial plug-in for any theory invoking beliefs, meant to deal with any possible counterexample: to any claim of the form "Here the phenomenon we are after is present, but no belief is", the theorist can reply with "Ah, no *explicit* belief is present, but an implicit belief is indeed present", and sometimes it's hard to see how such insistence amounts to anything more than just insisting that one's favorite theory must be true, so that an implicit belief comes to whatever it is that is needed in order to save the theory. But that this move is often suspicious should not convince us that it is *never* kosher. Invoking implicit beliefs may be legitimate if it is not empty, if there are substantive criteria for when an implicit belief is in place. And I think there are such criteria, criteria that we can capture in a dual functional-phenomenological test for implicit beliefs. The thought is quite simple, then: first, implicit beliefs should be able to play roughly the explanatory role more explicit beliefs routinely play. And second, if an implicit belief is made explicit (perhaps by asking the relevant person whether he indeed believes it), this should feel to the

that this "taking to be a reason" has to be unpacked. Setiya (2007), for instance, accepts this condition, but unpacks it in terms of a self-referential belief-desire about the *motivating* reasons explaining one's behavior. In the text I understand this "taking" as a straightforward normative belief. In this respect, I am following suggestions by Scanlon (1998) and Quinn (1993), and maybe also Parfit (1997, 113).

[15] Given Robust Realism, of course, this is a belief. But as you may recall, the discussion in this section is supposed to be motivated in a way that's completely independent of Robust Realism. Nothing in this section has to change if you replace "belief" with "judgment", remaining non-committed on whether or not it is a belief.

[16] Notice that this belief is entirely normative, not metanormative. I am not suggesting that we need to attribute to A the belief that R is a normative reason for her to φ, *with this belief robustly realistically understood*.

thinker as the articulation of a belief that he has already had before the articulation, not as some new belief that he has just acquired, something he has just found out (though, of course, the belief *that* he has this belief may be a novelty).[17] Thus, a driver's implicit belief about certain features of the road in front of her (say, that it veers slightly to the left) explains the driver's action in the same way more explicit beliefs do[18] (for instance, this is why she turned the steering wheel slightly to the left), and if we ask her (soon enough) "So, you noticed the road veering to the left?" she will answer "Yes", and it will feel like bringing to full awareness what was there all along, rather than like the acquisition of a new belief. I do not know whether it's a matter of necessity that all and only implicit beliefs pass this dual test. But passing this test does seem at least good evidence for the presence of an implicit belief. And it certainly isn't empty. If we require that any implicit belief pass this dual functional-phenomenological test, then invoking implicit beliefs can't be the theory-saving blank check it is sometimes (rightly) suspected to be.[19]

Getting back, then, to my suggested necessary and sufficient conditions for acting for a (specific) reason: I claimed that it's a necessary condition for A's φ-ing for R that A believe that R counts in favor of her φ-ing (in the circumstances). To the charge that this would over-intellectualize action for a reason, I replied with the retreat to an implicit belief. Does this (purported) implicit belief pass the dual test just described, then? The functional, explanatory one is rather easy here, because of the "appropriate causal role" in clause (3). If this condition is satisfied, then we already know that the (purported) implicit belief passes this part of the dual test, because if it doesn't play the explanatory role beliefs typically do play, whatever role it does have won't be an *appropriate* causal role. (This is not, of course, a way of showing that the relevant purported implicit belief passes this part of the dual test. It just shows that passing this part of the test doesn't pose an additional problem over the one posed by the need to play an appropriate causal role.) How about the phenomenological test, though? Here it seems to me we can again do best by thinking of examples. Suppose, then, that I walk home from work for the reason that walking is good for one's health. And assume that this is a case in which I do not have an explicit belief, one that I'm aware of, that is in front of my mind's eye at the moment (or pick your favorite metaphor

---

[17] For one account of implicit beliefs that vindicates the dual test for them in the text, see Crimmins (1992). Though Crimmins's account seems to me plausible, I don't think I need to rely on its details. The other views Crimmins critically surveys also seem to suffice for my purposes in the text. See the references in Crimmins (1992).

[18] I described this part of the dual test as functional, and so you may want to employ a broader functional test, one that includes not just what the belief explains, but also what tends to bring about the belief (say, in this example, perception), what tends to make it go away (some countervailing evidence), etc.

[19] I am perfectly happy calling states that pass this test "beliefs". If you don't like this way of using the term, feel free to call states that pass this test by some other term, perhaps "beliefish-sort-of-things". If you replace uniformly "belief" with "beliefish-sort-of-thing" throughout, nothing will have to be changed. In other words, nowhere in this chapter do I rely on the attitude required in (3) being anything more than what I call an implicit belief, or what you call a beliefish-sort-of-thing.

here) to the effect that that walking is good for my health is a reason for me to walk home from work. Indeed, assume that I did not in this case engage in anything worth calling deliberation. But make sure you hold constant the starting point – I did, in this case, walk home (rather than take a taxi, say) *for the reason that walking is good for one's health*. In such a case, then, what do you think my answer will be if you ask me: "Oh, so you think of the health-value of walking as a reason to walk home from work?" It seems to me that the answer we would expect is something like "Of course!" Indeed, it seems to me rather clear that if we get a very different answer (such as "No", or "The health-value? Really? I hadn't even noticed that") we would take that as strong reason to take back the description of the action as walking home *for the reason* that this would be healthy. And this, I think, is strong evidence that the relevant normative (often implicit) belief is indeed a necessary condition for acting for a (specific) reason.

Notice that insisting that a normative belief (that R is a reason for A to φ) is a necessary condition for A to φ for R is consistent with the possibility that A also have the normative belief that it's *not* the case that R is a reason for her to φ (in the circumstances).[20] This will be so, if the agent is inconsistent in her relevant normative beliefs.[21] True, typically, if we have strong evidence that A believes that R is not a good reason for her to φ, we may take this as rather strong reason to take back our commitment to her having φ-ed for R. This makes sense, because typically that an agent believes some proposition is strong evidence that she does not believe its negation, and so if she believes that R is not a reason for her to φ, this is strong evidence that she does not believe that R *is* a reason for her to φ. So our inclination to take back the judgment that A φ-ed for R in the face of evidence that she believes that R is not a reason for her to φ is nicely explained by the account I'm suggesting here – which should again strengthen your confidence in it. But the relation between an agent believing some *p* and her not believing *not-p* is not one of necessity, so that – to repeat – it's not impossible for A to φ for R while believing that R is not a reason for φ-ing. Of course, implicit beliefs that are inconsistent with other things the relevant person believes can be rather hard to observe – the other beliefs may interfere with the explanatory role played by the implicit belief, and it's entirely unclear how the conflicted agent will respond when asked whether he does have that belief (or how he will feel about that response). So things are complicated here. Still, the possibility of acting for R while believing that R is not a reason for the relevant action should not, I think, be excluded. And this possibility is important also for the

---

[20] This normative belief is certainly consistent with the belief that one has other, even stronger, reasons not-to-φ. The account suggested here thus has no problem with accommodating weakness of will. And the account can accommodate in similar ways over-determined actions (actions done for more than one reason). And if causal influence comes in degrees (as seems likely), it can also straightforwardly accommodate asymmetrical over-determination, where an action is performed for (say) two reasons, but more for one than for the other. I thank Stephen Davey for some related discussion.

[21] This is a possibility Setiya (2007, 36 and on) completely ignores.

account's ability to accommodate another kind of case.[22] Think, then, of an instrumentally resourceful unwilling alcoholic, who feels alienated from his craving for
rum, but who still drives across town in the middle of the night to get to the one
liquor store that sells rum that late at night. Pre-theoretically, it seems he's driving
there for the reason that that's where he can get rum. So an account of action for a
specific reason should accommodate this result. And this means that I am committed
to attributing to the unwilling alcoholic the normative belief that the fact that that's
where he can get rum is a reason to go there. And this may seem like an odd result,
seeing that he's an *unwilling* alcoholic. The thing to say here, I think, is that he *does*
have that belief, but he also has the belief that that there's rum there is no reason at all
for him to go there. Plausibly, he also has other relevant normative beliefs – like that
he has reason to rid himself of the alcohol cravings and addiction, etc. But I do not
think it too implausible to attribute to him the belief that *given* the craving, that
there's rum in that liquor store is a reason for him to go there.[23]

It is a consequence of my suggested account of acting for a (specific) reason that
creatures who cannot have (even implicit) normative beliefs cannot act for a (specific)
reason.[24] In the case of animals, I've claimed, this gives the desired result. How about
my three-year-old son? It does seem possible that he went to his room for the reason
that I told him to. So if it is implausible to attribute to him the (implicit) normative
belief that my telling him to is a reason for him to go to his room, this would be a
problem for my account. But I don't think that such an attribution would be at all
implausible. He does (sometimes) take that I tell him to go to his room to count in
favor of going to his room, and he is capable of at least rudimentary normative
judgments. Indeed, when I think back of his intellectual development, as my willingness to attribute to him normative beliefs decreases, so does my willingness to attribute
to him actions for (specific) reasons.[25] This too, it seems to me, should strengthen our

---

[22] It comes from Wallace (2001, 8), where Wallace uses it to criticize some related points in Korsgaard.
I thank John Deigh for showing me the relevance of this kind of case to my project here.

[23] But I am not confident about this. So let me add that if the suggestion in the text fails, the unwilling-
alcoholic example is a counterexample only to the account's necessity for action for a reason, not to its
sufficiency. And the defense of Robust Realism (in the next sections) relies only on the account's sufficiency.

[24] This is consistent, let me remind you one more time, with them acting, acting intentionally, and indeed
perhaps also with them acting for a reason in general, perhaps for a motivating reason.

[25] My son doesn't, I think, have beliefs – not even implicit ones – about the explanations of his own
actions, or about the appropriateness of his own motivations in action. If so, the fact that he can act for specific
reasons counts seriously against Setiya's (2007, 46) and Korsgaard's (2008, 214–15) accounts of action for a
reason. Of course, these writers try to *support* their accounts. A fuller discussion of action for a (specific)
reason – fuller, I believe, than is needed here – would have to include a critical discussion of their
argumentation. With regard to Setiya, then, let me just say the following. Setiya's main support for his
analysis – certainly for his rejection of something along the lines of the analysis in the text – is based on the
need to explain *Belief*, namely, "When someone is acting intentionally, there must be something he is doing
intentionally, not merely trying to do, in the belief that he is doing it" (2007, 26; for employing this to rule
out normative belief as necessary for action for a reason, see 41). This does seem to me like a plausible thing to
say, and explaining it does seem important to me. But I don't see why we should think that the only way to
explain Setiya's *Belief* is by endorsing anything like his (implausible) account of action for a reason.
Presumably, our theory of practical reasoning (and related phenomena) can include much more than just

confidence that a (perhaps implicit) normative belief is needed for action for a (specific) reason.

But so far I've been allowing myself the luxury of talk of "an appropriate causal role", without saying anything about what it is. I don't think it can be denied that something like this condition is indeed necessary for acting for R. If my son believes that my telling him to go to his room is reason to go to his room, but this belief is entirely epiphenomenal – it plays no causal role at all in bringing him to action; perhaps he goes to his room simply (causally) because he wants to play with his favorite toy, and believes that that's where it is – then we would not be willing to say that he went to his room for the reason that I told him to. Similarly if the normative belief does play a causal role, but only a deviant-causal-chain kind of role (for instance, if my son has a general urge to go to his room whenever a normative thought pops into his little head).[26] So we do need, as a necessary condition for A to have ϕ-ed for R, to require that A's belief that R is a reason for her to ϕ has played an appropriate causal role in bringing about her ϕ-ing. But still, what is it here for a causal role to be appropriate?

The natural thing to say here is that whatever reply we give in general to the problem of deviant causal chains we should be able to employ here as well. There is a problem here, alright, but it's not an *especially* serious one for me or my account of acting for a reason, and so I am entitled to use "an appropriate causal role" as a place-holder for whatever general solution we end up settling on. But there is a complication here. Some may argue, for instance, that the appropriate causal role beliefs play in bringing about actions is one that always requires also the presence of a desire, or at least of a disposition to act in a certain way given the certain belief. Others, on the other hand, think that normative beliefs can motivate all by themselves, without the causal help from a desire. Yet others agree that desires are necessary for motivation, but insist that desires may themselves be caused and brought into existence by beliefs alone, or indeed that having a desire sometimes just amounts to being motivated by a belief. This controversy – precisely the kind of controversy in the theory of motivation I was hoping to remain neutral on – is likely to have implications for what constitutes "an appropriate role" for a belief to play in the bringing about of action. Nevertheless, I think I can (still) afford to remain neutral on these issues. Let us simply say, then, that in order to be appropriate the causal role played by the (perhaps implicit) belief that R is a reason for A to ϕ has to be roughly that role – whatever exactly it is – that normative beliefs (or judgments) typically play in motivation. Eventually, I am going to have to say a little more on these controversies in the theory of motivation. But I think it's best to do as much as we can without deciding these controversial issues. And in fact

---

an analysis of action for a reason. So perhaps an explanation of *Belief* is to be found elsewhere, in a way that is compatible with – but not entailed by – an adequate analysis of action for a (specific) reason.

[26] In some contexts we may need to distinguish between right and wrong kinds of reasons. Where there is room for such a distinction, it seems reasonable to suppose that even though A may believe that she has a wrong-kind-of-reason to ϕ, this belief of hers cannot play the appropriate causal role in bringing about her ϕ-ing.

I think that the conditions listed above do indeed succeed as necessary and sufficient conditions for acting on a (specific) reason, with the "appropriate role" proviso understood as a place-holder for the general mechanisms of avoiding deviant causal chains and incorporating whatever it is we end up saying about the role of normative beliefs (or judgments) in motivation. And note that for a belief – normative or otherwise – to play an appropriate causal role in motivating action it is not necessary that it play a *necessitating* role in creating such a motivation (nor, even more clearly, in bringing the agent to act in the relevant way). This point will be important below.

Another advantage of the account suggested here is that it straightforwardly accommodates – and sheds light on – the three kinds of mistakes mentioned above. The normative mistake – where A φ-s for R even though R is no (normative, good) reason for her to φ – occurs when A believes that R is a reason for her to φ, this belief plays an appropriate role in bringing about her action, but this belief is nevertheless false. The factual mistake – where A φ-s for R even though R is false (or doesn't hold, or doesn't obtain, etc.) occurs when A falsely believes that R is true, and also (truly or falsely) believes that R is a reason for her to φ, and this belief plays an appropriate causal role in bringing about her action. And the introspective mistake – where A believes that she's φ-ing for R but in fact she isn't – occurs where A (truly or falsely) believes R, (truly or falsely) believes that R is a reason for her to φ, this belief does not play an appropriate causal role in bringing her to action, but A nevertheless believes that it does (or perhaps more simply that she is φ-ing for R).

Note also that the suggested account of action for a (specific) reason nicely accommodates another desideratum mentioned above. For according to this account, there is a straightforward sense in which when A φ-s for R A's φ-ing is a response not just to R, but also to R's being a reason.[27] Often an action can count as a response to something if a belief in that something plays an appropriate causal role in bringing the action about. Thus, if the belief *that a piece of cake is fattening* plays an appropriate causal role in bringing about my skipping dessert, this suffices for my skipping dessert to be (among other things) a response to *the cake's being fattening*. And so, if the belief *that the cake's fatteningness is a reason to skip dessert* plays an appropriate causal role in bringing about my skipping dessert, then this suffices for my skipping dessert to qualify as a response to *the cake's fatteningness's being a reason for skipping dessert*. There is no further need for a mysterious responding-relation between the reason (or its being a reason) and my action – the responding relation simply consists in (sometimes, and here) the relevant belief playing an appropriate causal role.[28] Now, perhaps "response" is a success term, so that an action cannot respond to something that is false (or doesn't exist). So perhaps the relevant belief has to be true for the action to count as a response

---

[27] Schroeder (2007, 154) cites a similar point as a reason to accept what he calls "the Attitude-Content view", namely, the view he finds in Quinn and Scanlon which takes a belief in a normative reason to be a necessary condition for acting on a (specific) reason.

[28] For a somewhat similar suggestion, see Lenman (2009, final paragraph).

to the relevant feature. But this complication doesn't break the symmetry between the case of the response to the natural fact (that the cake is fattening) and the normative one (that the cake's fatteningness counts in favor of skipping dessert), and so – in the successful cases, where the cake is indeed fattening, and its fatteningness is indeed a reason to skip dessert – just as the causal role played by the belief in the cake's fatteningness makes the action a response to the cake's fatteningness, so too the causal role played by the belief in the fatteningness's being a reason makes the action a response to the fatteningness's reason-ness.

Let me end this section with a few thoughts on how what has been said about action for a specific reason can serve to shed light on some relevant considerations emphasized by Jonathan Dancy. Dancy introduces (2000, 103) "the normative constraint", which "... requires that a motivating reason, that in the light of which one acts, must be the sort of thing that is capable of being among the reasons in favour of so acting; it must, in this sense, be possible to act for a good reason". Let me remind you that when Dancy uses the locution "motivating reasons" he seems to have in mind what I've been calling here the agent's reason. Dancy's normative constraint thus comes down to the requirement that it at least be possible for the agent's reason *to just be* the relevant normative reason.[29] Thus understood, the suggested account of acting for a (specific) reason satisfies this constraint. In cases in which A's belief (that R is a reason for her to ϕ) is true, her reason – the agent's reason – for ϕ-ing is R. And in those cases, R is indeed a normative reason for A to ϕ. So in these cases, the agent's reason for ϕ-ing is indeed a normative, good reason for ϕ-ing. Of course, where A's belief that R is a reason for her to ϕ is false, there is no such overlap between the agent's reason and normative reasons. But this is precisely as it should be, and Dancy is unlikely to differ – presumably, this is why Dancy only requires that the agent's reason be "*the sort of thing capable* of being among the reasons in favour of so acting"; when the agent's reason is bad, it can't be a good reason. No big surprise there.

Dancy also introduces (2000, 101) the explanatory constraint: "Now there is a constraint on any theory about the relation between normative and motivating reasons. This is that the theory show that and how any normative reason is capable of contributing to the explanation of an action that is done for that reason. Call this the 'explanatory constraint'." We should again take care not to be confused by terminology. What Dancy means by "motivating reason" is that in light of which the agent acts, or in the terms I am using here, the agent's reason. So Dancy's explanatory requirement comes down to the requirement that normative reasons be of the kind that can be

---

[29] Heuer (2004, 45) puts forward "the identity thesis": "when an agent acts for a (specific) reason that very reason is also the explanation (or at least part of the explanation) of why she did what she did. Normative or justificatory reasons and explanatory reasons are the same reasons in such a case . . . ." If the reference to "*the* explanation" is supposed to rule out other (e.g. causal) explanations, then I reject this claim. Similarly if the reference to explanatory reasons is supposed to pick out motivating reasons in the sense given to them in the text. But the account of acting for a (specific) reason in the text can accommodate the crux of Heuer's identity thesis: for on it it is possible that the agent's reason and the normative reason be one and the same.

agents' reasons. And it seems to me that (with one qualification I mention in a footnote[30]) my account of action for a specific reason explains this. For R to be the sort of thing that can be an agent's reason for φ-ing, all that is necessary on my account is that R be the sort of thing about which agents can have beliefs (normative and otherwise) which can play an appropriate role in motivation. And this is a fairly easy requirement to meet. In particular, even if normative facts themselves are causally inert (as on Robust Realism they are), still normative reasons can meet this requirement (more on this in the next section). This is so, because the way in which normative facts – such as that R is a reason for A to φ (in the circumstances) – explain action is not by *causing* action, but rather by being that in the light of which an agent acts – in terms of the account here, by being the content of a belief that plays an appropriate causal role in bringing about the action.[31]

9.1.3 *Robust Realism and acting for a reason*

Let me remind you where the discussion of acting for a (specific) reason is located in the larger context of this chapter (and indeed, this book). I hope to show that Robust Realism can rather unproblematically allow for action on a (specific) reason. And I promised – but this promise has yet to be made good on in the next sections – that equipped with this lesson it will be relatively easy to respond to other objections to Robust Realism that are grounded in thoughts about motivation. This is why there was need, in our context, for an analysis of (or at least necessary and sufficient conditions for) A's φ-ing for R. (In fact, all that is necessary for what follows is that the conditions listed are sufficient for acting for a specific reason.[32]) But this is also why it was important not to assume anything like Robust Realism in the defense of the

---

[30] Are all reasons for actions necessarily actable-on? In particular, and perhaps somewhat more strongly, is it a necessary condition for R qualifying as a reason for A to φ, that it be in some sense possible for A to φ for R? I seriously doubt it. Think here about the things Jon Elster (1983) calls "essential by-products" – good things that cannot be achieved by direct action intended to achieve them, but only by engaging in actions with other intentions and aims. It seems reasonable to say that agents have reasons to act in ways that will achieve these (good) essential by-products, but it does not seem possible for them to act on these reasons. (See here also Schroeder's (2007, 165) example of the reason someone who loves surprise parties in his honor and hates all other parties has to go to the living room, where a surprise party awaits him.) If this is the right thing to say about such examples – and let me not pretend that I am sure it is – then perhaps it is not a constraint on practical reasons that they be actable-on. And if so, Dancy's explanatory constraint may very well be false (perhaps depending on how exactly the capability invoked by the explanatory constraint is to be understood). But if this is so, it is false for reasons that have nothing to do with the suggested account of action for a (specific) reason. And then it should be noted that this account can still satisfy the suitably qualified version of the explanatory constraint that can adequately deal with the complication discussed in this footnote.

[31] For his insistence that this is the kind of explanation relevant here, that not all explanations are causal, and that this explanation of an action is consistent also with there being a complete causal explanation of the action, see Dancy (2000, ch. 8).

[32] My *motivation* for attempting an analysis of action for a specific reason was the need to show that Robust Realism can accommodate such action. But the previous section is to be judged, of course, largely independently of this motivation. Hopefully, it offers an interesting and plausible account of action for a specific reason. Let me note, though, that if that account fails, we need another one, and it's still quite possible (but not guaranteed) that the other one too will allow Robust Realism to accommodate action for a reason.

suggested analysis.[33] The challenge, after all, is not to show that Robust Realism can accommodate some cooked-up understanding of action for a reason, one tailor-made for Robust Realism. Rather, the challenge is to show that Robust Realism can accommodate action for a reason, when this is understood rather naturally, and independently of Robust Realism or even its underlying motivations. So let me state here that so far as I can see, nothing in the discussion in the previous section depended on Robust Realism or on anything too close to it. The necessary and sufficient conditions for action for a reason suggested in the previous section seem to me to be plausible whatever your metaethical or metanormative view is. If it can now be shown that Robust Realism can accommodate them, then, this will be a genuine achievement (rather than a trick of linguistic legislation).

Well then, can Robust Realism accommodate action for a reason, thus understood? Can it accommodate, in other words, the three necessary – and together sufficient – conditions for action on a specific reason suggested in the previous section? The first two seem rather unproblematic here. The more interesting condition is, of course, (3), which states, to repeat:

(3)   The belief *that R is a (normative) reason for A to φ (in the circumstances)* plays an appropriate causal role in bringing about A's φ-ing.

Clearly, on Robust Realism there are normative beliefs, and so there is no problem with A having the belief that R is a normative reason for her to φ.

The challenge, then, is to show that Robust Realism can accommodate an appropriate causal role for the normative belief (that R is a reason to φ) in bringing about A's φ-ing. But here again it is important to see that we are not (not yet, anyway) in the context where really controversial issues in the theory of motivation have to be decided. The question relevant here is not whether on Robust Realism normative beliefs can motivate all on their own, without the assistance of an independent desire (or some such). The question is the more limited one, whether on Robust Realism normative beliefs can play an appropriate causal role in motivating action. And though my partial silence on what it takes for a causal role to be appropriate makes answering this question harder, it does not make it impossible: for it seems to me there are *several* ways in which a normative belief – robustly realistically understood – can play a causal role that is *paradigmatically* appropriate. Thus, if A has a general desire to do as she has (normative) reason to do, her belief that she has (normative) reason to φ can play a paradigmatically appropriate causal role in bringing her to φ-ing. Now, there are controversies regarding such a desire, which is a generalization of Michael Smith's (1994, 73) desire to do the good, understood de dicto (more on which later in this chapter). But the way I'm invoking it here is very unambitious, so that these controversies are not, I think, relevant: I am not saying that everyone always has this desire, only that

---

[33] In particular, the normative belief my account of acting for a specific reason invokes need not be robustly-realistically understood, certainly not at this stage of the analysis.

some people sometimes may. And I'm not saying that only when this desire is present can the belief that R is a reason to φ play an appropriate causal role. I'm only saying that this is *one* possible way of playing such a role. There are others. One other possibility is that though we do not (necessarily) have a desire to follow reasons, we have other desires that a general policy of following reasons is instrumental to. In such cases too, presumably, the normative belief (that one has a normative reason) can unproblematically play an appropriate causal role in motivating. Another possibility is for this belief to bring about a desire that will itself play an appropriate causal role in bringing about A's φ-ing. Another possibility is if the belief – all by itself, or in cooperation with other mental states – brings about a change in the *strength* of a relevant desire. Yet another is if the normative belief plays some suitable causal role in the acquisition, retention, or revision of other *non*-normative beliefs, themselves playing an appropriate causal role here. Perhaps, for instance, the belief that R is or would be a reason for her to φ can play an appropriate causal role in leading A to check whether R, and perhaps this role sometimes suffices for this belief to also play an appropriate causal role in motivating A to φ (when, say, she believes that R partly because of the inquiry motivated by the normative belief, and she φ-es partly because she believes that R). And there may be other ways in which the normative belief that R is a reason for her to φ can play an appropriate causal role in motivating A to φ.[34] Notice that all of the ways sketched here

[34] Think about Schroeder's (2007, 165) case of Nate, who loves successful surprise parties held in his honor, but hates all other parties, and is told by someone who knows that that he has a reason to go to the living room (where unbeknownst to Nate a surprise party in his honor awaits). When Nate proceeds to the living room, what is his reason for doing so? Pre-theoretically, it does not sound like his reason can be that a surprise party awaits him there, for he doesn't know that this is so (and had he known, he would no longer have had a reason to go there). One plausible thing to say, then, is that Nate went to the living room for the reason that he has a reason to go there. This is his reason – that he has a reason. Assume that this is the right thing to say here. Then I am committed also to saying that Nate must have the belief that *that I have a reason to go to the living room is a reason to go to the living room*. Furthermore, I am committed to saying that this belief must play an appropriate causal role in bringing about Nate's going to the living room. But it's not clear that I can accommodate this result, for it seems like the causal roles specified in the text (which are consistent with Robust Realism) are ones for which the belief *that I have a reason to go to the living room* is quite sufficient. If so, there is no room for an appropriate causal role for the more complicated belief that *that I have a reason to go to the living room is a reason to go to the living room*. (I thank Mark Schroeder for pressing this objection on me.) I can think of two responses. The first is to insist that Nate's reason for going to the living room is not *that he has a reason* but rather *that he's told that he has a reason*, and then to find an appropriate causal role that the belief that that he was so told is a reason can play, consistently with Robust Realism. Finding an appropriate role for this belief will not be hard, I think, but I am not sure how plausible it is to say that Nate's reason to go to the living room is that he's told that he has a reason (perhaps this is just his evidence that he has a reason, not the reason that he has). The second response is to find – consistently with Robust Realism – a causal role for Nate's belief *that that I have a reason is a reason*. This, I think, is the way to go. This can be done if at times appropriate causal role can over-determine an action, as seems likely. If so, it can be the case that both of Nate's beliefs – *that I have a reason*, and *that that I have a reason is a reason* – can play an appropriate causal role along the lines suggested in the text (so that, for instance, both can interact with the general de dicto desire to follow reasons; the resulting motivation to go to the living room may differ in its strength from the one that would have resulted from the simpler belief alone). And there may be causal roles that only the more sophisticated belief plays. For instance, perhaps only the belief *that that I have a reason is a reason* can motivate (perhaps together with some desires) an inquiry into what reasons one has (as when Nate can ask, "Are you sure I have a reason to go to the living room?").

in which the normative belief can play an appropriate causal role in motivating A are available to the robust realist. In other words, nothing at all here depended on, say, that normative belief being anything but a Humeanly kosher, intrinsically motivationally inert, fully representational, straightforward belief about things that are out there in Plato's heaven.

Of course, it's not enough, in order to show that Robust Realism can adequately accommodate action for a reason, to show that there is no contradiction between Robust Realism and the mere possibility of action for a (specific) reason. Rather, what has to be shown is that Robust Realism can accommodate action for a reason in roughly all and only the circumstances in which pre-theoretically it seems to us that action for a (specific) reason occurs. But I think that the previous paragraph makes this claim too very plausible. What would be needed in order to show that this is not so is a case that we are pre-theoretically inclined to classify as a case of action for a specific reason, but where there is no plausible robustly-realistically-acceptable way of allowing the relevant normative belief to play an appropriate causal role. And I can't think of one. When I try to imagine a case in which such normative belief (robustly realistically understood) does not play an appropriate causal role – even a *paradigmatically* appropriate causal role – I am just not at all inclined to classify it as a case of an action for a specific reason.

Now, you may be worried that even if the belief that R is a reason for her to φ does play an appropriate causal role in bringing A to φ-ing, still this is not enough. For on Robust Realism, normative truths are response-independent. In particular, they are judgment-independent. And so the fact (if it is a fact) that R is a reason for A to φ (in the circumstances) is independent of A's belief that it is. And so you may think that even if A's belief that R is a reason for her to φ plays an appropriate causal role in bringing about her φ-ing, still this only suffices for her φ-ing to be a response to *this belief*. But we wanted an action for a reason to be not just a response to the belief, but a response to the reason itself, and to the fact that it is a reason.

A partial response to this concern has already been given: often, being (partly) caused in the appropriate way by a belief that p is *just what it is* for an action to be responsive to p's being the case. This is true for many different possible propositions p, not just for normative ones. So there's nothing ad-hoc-ish about employing a similar line for normative beliefs as well. All it takes, in other words, for A's φ-ing to count as a response to R's being a reason is that A's belief that R is a reason for her to φ play an appropriate causal role in bringing about her φ-ing. But you may be still worried. In particular, you may think that sometimes an appropriate causal role for the belief that p suffices for the action to be a response to p's being the case *in virtue of the fact that the belief that p is itself responsive to, well, p*. And so, perhaps by the transitivity of "is responsive to", the action can be a response to p via its being responsive to the belief that p, this belief itself being responsive to p. But then, if on Robust Realism there is no way of accommodating the thought that normative beliefs are responsive to the normative truths, the transitivity move is blocked. So you may think that even though there are many cases in which the causal role of the belief that p suffices for the action to qualify as responsive to p, still in the normative case this isn't the case, at least if we're assuming Robust Realism.

I don't know whether a causal role for the belief that p can only secure for the action the status of being responsive to p if the belief itself is responsive to p. If not, then, obviously, this objection fails. Let's grant for the sake of argument, then, that this is so. Even then, though, the robust realist – armed with the lessons of Chapter 7 – has an available reply. After all, it is not completely clear what it would take for a belief to be *responsive* to a fact (or truth, or proposition, or state of affairs). Presumably, anything here that would suffice to make the belief epistemologically legitimate would suffice to render it responsive to the relevant fact in the sense of "responsive" relevant to the objection. And in Chapter 7 I've argued at some length that Robust Realism can account for the reliability of normative beliefs. As I've also argued in that chapter, once Robust Realism accounts for the reliability of normative beliefs, there is no *further* epistemological worry it is especially vulnerable to. There is no further consideration, so I've argued, that prevents Robust Realism from acknowledging the justification of (some) normative beliefs, the fact that some of them amount to knowledge, etc. If this is so, then it becomes hard to see why we should believe that on Robust Realism normative beliefs can't be responsive to the normative facts in whatever sense is necessary (if there is such a sense) for an action to count as a response to a normative fact, simply in virtue of the normative belief (that that fact is indeed a reason) playing an appropriate causal role in bringing about the action.

9.2 Practicality

According to Robust Realism, normative truths are out there to be discovered. They are utterly independent of us – our desires, our attitudes, our will. But this may give rise to a puzzle. After all, some normative truths – the ones we've been mostly concerned with throughout this book – are supposed to be practically relevant, they are supposed to matter when we come to form intentions and perform actions. But if normative truths are independent of us, how can that be so? And if what we do when successful in our normative inquiries is *discover* these normative truths, haven't we left behind all hope of vindicating anything worth calling *practical* reason? In what sense is this employment of reason at all practical, if it's just the discovery of some metaphysical truths of a peculiar kind? How are these truths at all relevant to what we should do? And how should discovering them – a paradigmatic operation of *theoretical* reason, presumably – engage our *will*?[35]

As already noted in the introductory paragraphs of this chapter, it's not at all clear what these worries precisely mean. The mere classification of operations into those of theoretical reason and those of practical reason cannot be what is at stake here, because

---

[35] See, for instance, Korsgaard (1997, 240 and on).

both these notions are technical philosophical terms, not ones that all by themselves capture something we pre-theoretically find important or plausible. The question, then, is not whether on Robust Realism practical reason turns out to be an instance of theoretical reason, but rather whether it matters if this is so. And indeed, once we are clearer about why this is supposed to matter, we can drop all talk of theoretical and practical reason and just proceed to discuss the objection to Robust Realism put directly in terms of what it is that matters to us about that distinction. Here as elsewhere, then, we shouldn't let terminology do the work philosophy is supposed to do.

It is very rare to find a not-merely-verbal, non-question-begging explanation of the sense in which practical reason on the robust realist picture is not *really* practical (or perhaps is just an instance of theoretical reason).[36] The explanation I was able to find comes from Rawls's (2000, 74–5) discussion of rational intuitionism. There, Rawls says that on rational intuitionism (a close cousin of Robust Realism, certainly) practical reason is a form of theoretical reason, because according to it the fitness of actions is determined by the essences of things, known presumably by theoretical reason; acting wrongly is as absurd as refusing to recognize a true statement; and obligations are independent of God's commands. This at least gives some content to the claim that (on the target view) practical reason is an instance of theoretical reason. But of course, it falls well short of a criticism of the relevant target view, because so far nothing has been said to support the claim that this result is at all implausible[37] (and nothing in Rawls's discussion here suggests that he thinks of this as a criticism of rational intuitionism). In particular, reason may be theoretical in something like this sense while *also* being practical in whatever sense in which it seems plausible that it is practical (by, say, being relevant to what we do, or to the reasons we act for, or by engaging our will, or whatever – more on this shortly).

What, then, do people have in mind when they say that normative truths must be able to "engage our will"? And why do so many people seemingly think both that this is so, and that Robust Realism and related views cannot accommodate this result? Myself, I don't know of any way of unpacking the idea of "engaging our will" such that both these claims (normative truths must be able to engage our will; on Robust Realism they lack this ability) come out as at all plausible. And so things are going to become pretty negative for a while.[38] Here it goes.

A crucial distinction to be made here, of course, is that between a *normative* and a *motivational* understanding of talk of engaging the will, or of practicality, or of practical significance, and so on.[39] It is one thing to insist – quite plausibly, if somewhat

---

[36] Brink (1997b, 30–2) registers a similar complaint.

[37] Broome (1997) gives another, different criterion: practical reason is essentially first-personal. I don't know if this is so, but in this sense too – as Broome proceeds to argue – there is no reason to believe that theoretical reason can't also be practical.

[38] Parfit (2011, vol. 2, section 104) also makes some of the points I am about to make here.

[39] The relevance of this distinction in our context is acknowledged by many (see, for instance, Frankena (1958)), but is perhaps most forcefully employed by Parfit (1997; 2011, vol. 2, section 104).

trivially – that normative truths must be able to bear *normatively* on our action, they should be relevant to what we *should* do, or what we *have (normative) reason* to do, or some such. It's quite another to insist that normative truths must be able to bear *motivationally* on our actions. And the point to note here is that Robust Realism has absolutely no problem with the first of these two claims. *Of course* the normative truths bear on what we have (normative) reason to do – after all, many of them *just are* truths about what we have reason to do. It is utterly misleading to suggest that these truths out there in Plato's heaven cannot have any bearing on what we down here should do. For on Robust Realism these truths out there in Plato's heaven *just are* truths about what we down here should do. Indeed, they are the truths that ultimately explain (together with non-normative facts) *all* truths about what we should do. Of course, perhaps Robust Realism should be rejected. But if it should, this must presumably be for different reasons, reasons that are independent of this version of the practicality worry. If there are no sufficient other reasons to reject Robust Realism, then the need to accommodate the normative significance of normative truths can't give such reasons. The rhetoric of the critics thus should not confuse us: if what is at issue is *normative* significance, then Robust Realism can accommodate it quite easily – trivially, indeed, much like any other view of normativity.

If there is to be a serious objection here, then, it must be based on the thought that the normative truths must be *motivationally* relevant, they must engage our will in some motivational, non-normative (or perhaps not-merely-normative) way. And so our question becomes – in what sense is it plausible to say that the normative truths must be motivationally relevant to us and our actions?

One exceptionally strong way of filling in the details here would be to insist – as some writers seemingly do[40] – that what normative truths are supposed to do is to *make* people behave according to them. Normative truths robustly realistically understood do not satisfy this requirement, but neither do normative truths according to any other even remotely plausible way of understanding them. In particular, even if your view of normative truths ties them much more closely to the motivations of actual agents than Robust Realism does, still the normative truths all by themselves cannot win the war against ill-will.[41] Here too, then, "philosophy [cannot] replace the hangman" (Lewis, 1996, 60).[42]

There may be other, more plausible ways of understanding the requirement that normative truths be practical in some motivational way. Perhaps the best way to make sense of this requirement is via a commitment to judgment-internalism, or perhaps existence-internalism. I discuss these in following sections. Or perhaps there is some

---

[40] Mackie (1977, 40).
[41] For a similar claim in the context of a discussion of Korsgaard's criticisms of realism, see Fitzpatrick (2005, 689).
[42] Korsgaard sometimes writes as if she thinks that philosophy – presumably, her philosophy – can after all replace the hangman. For discussion and references, see my "Agency, Shmagency" (2006).

altogether other way – one that is neither exactly normative, nor exactly motivational – in which we should understand the practicality objection (and related ones). But I can't think of a remotely plausible way of filling in the details here (I briefly discuss two suggestions in a footnote).[43] Indeed, typically the practicality worry is put forward in a way that blatantly equivocates between normative and motivational relevance (a point emphasized by Parfit (1997)): the claim is presented as the kind of truism it can only be if understood normatively, and conclusions are drawn from it as if it is understood motivationally. Such equivocation may be due simply to failure to distinguish normativity and motivation. But it needn't be – it may be due to a *refusal* to acknowledge this distinction, or perhaps due to a principled insistence on normativity and motivation being much more intimately related than they are on Robust Realism. Perhaps the latter is the more charitable interpretation of at least some writers. But note that on this more charitable reading, the thought about practicality does not function as a *premise* in an argument against Robust Realism and related views. Rather, it serves as an *interim conclusion* in an argument that starts with some other reasons to think that the

---

[43] The word "autonomy" is sometimes used in contexts such as this, as if it can bridge the normative–motivational divide. See, for instance, Darwall (1995, 20). I am not sure I understand talk of autonomy here – presumably, not autonomy as the political ideal of (roughly) living one's life according to one's own choices and judgments about how one should live one's life, but the Kantian idea of being subject only to laws one legislates oneself, or some such. To the extent that I do understand this idea, I don't understand why anyone would find it attractive. (Yes, I have read the *Groundwork*.) And on top of this, even granting something about autonomy of this kind, I don't see how it would help here. But this may be because of my limited understanding of this and related topics.

Notice also that the argument of Chapter 3 – the argument from the deliberative indispensability of normative truths – can be thought of as in a way grounding normative truths in the will of autonomous beings. It's just that the relevant grounding here is epistemological, not metaphysical. Roughly, what depends on our deliberative nature is not the metaphysical status of the normative truths, but our reasons for believing in them. To an extent, then, perhaps this accommodates some of the intuitive force (if there is one) underlying thoughts about autonomy and grounding normative facts in the will of autonomous beings. I think – but I'm not entirely sure – that the way in which Fitzpatrick (2005, 686) is willing to concede some way of grounding normative truths in our will is this epistemological way, not the metaphysical one. If this is so, he's less close to Korsgaard than these paragraphs (but not others) seem to suggest, as he seems to have in mind something closer to the indispensability argument of Chapter 3.

Another suggested way of understanding the practicality point is by analogy to a lesson we've all learned from Lewis Carroll's "What the Tortoise Said to Achilles" (1895). Carroll has shown that the role rules of inference play in an inference cannot be reduced to that of premises – however many premises we add, we still need rules of inference to license a transition to any conclusion. And the point is sometimes made (Korsgaard, 2009, 65–7; for some reason Korsgaard does not refer to Carroll, but makes the Carroll point as "a now familiar argument", 67) that the role of practical reason is analogous to that of rules of inference. And just as premises can't replace inference rules, more theoretical truths (normative or not) can't suffice for the transition to action – we would still need something else to justify *doing* anything. Practical reason, then, cannot be replaced by theoretical reason.

Upon reflection, though, nothing at all remains from this argument by analogy. First, it is plausible to think that in the practical case too we need more than just premises, that some practical analogue of rules of inference is called for. Perhaps these would be norms or some such. But this is perfectly consistent, of course, with understanding these norms robustly-realistically. Second, and relatedly, the Lewis Carroll point works in precisely the opposite direction from that apparently intended by Korsgaard. After all, it's not as if we are tempted – either in general, or because of the lesson we've learned from Lewis Carroll – to be constructivists about *modus ponens*, or to think that either logical validity or the rationality of following a *modus-ponens* inference in any way constitutively depend on our motivation or our (or anyone else's) will.

normative and the motivational are intimately related. If so, we can bypass talk of practicality altogether, and assess these other reasons to tie normativity so close with motivation (as I do later in this chapter). Be that as it may, and whatever explains the normativity–motivation equivocation in thought about practicality, this equivocation should be resisted.

Let me nevertheless say something more positive here, utilizing the lesson of the previous section. There I presented an analysis of what it is to act on a (specific) reason, and argued that Robust Realism has no problem accommodating such action. Furthermore, the suggested analysis accommodated the intuitive thought that when an agent A ф-es for R, her ф-ing is not just a response to R, but also to R's status as a normative reason, and it accommodated this thought even assuming Robust Realism. The way in which A's ф-ing can be responsive to R's being a normative reason, I suggested, was by being caused (in the appropriate way) by A's belief that R is a normative reason for her to ф. But if all this is right, it is *very* hard to see what remains of the practicality worry about Robust Realism. If, in other words, even on Robust Realism agents can act for reasons, and when they do their actions can be responsive to the relevant normative truths *in the same sense* in which actions are responsive to other, non-normative truths or facts (when in fact they are), what by way of practicality is supposed to be missing here? With all this accounted for, any understanding of practicality – or perhaps of what it takes to engage the will – that will imply that practicality is still not fully present here is bound to be both tendentious and implausible.

We can put this point in terms of the distinction between theoretical and practical reason (though I am doing this somewhat tentatively, because I am not confident of my understanding of this distinction or why it is supposed to be important). Because of the point made in the previous paragraph, Robust Realism has no problem accommodating a genuine practical role for reason. But the way in which it does this is by securing an appropriate role for normative beliefs. And presumably it is theoretical reason that is at work in forming and revising those. So it is by employing theoretical reason that we discover normative truths out there in Plato's heaven and form beliefs accordingly, and it is in virtue of having those beliefs that we can act in ways that are responsive to the relevant normative truths. To the extent that I understand these terms, then, reason here is both theoretical and practical,[44] at least in whatever sense of "practical" in which it is important to secure such a role for reason.[45]

---

[44] See Broome (1997) for a similar suggestion of how reason can be practical via its (theoretically, presumably) leading us to true normative beliefs. And for a similar claim made in the context of a sympathetic critical discussion of Korsgaard, see Fitzpatrick (2005, 691).

[45] And notice that on the general epistemological picture of Chapter 3, there is something deeply practical about theoretical reason as well.

9.3 Why be moral? And why do what I have reason to do?

But it may be thought that this way of putting things avoids the most pressing issue in the vicinity: the need to have something by way of a convincing reply to a special kind of moral or normative skeptic. This is the person who asks the frightening why-be-moral question, or some (meta?)normative analogue thereof. And if we cannot show that the normative force of morality (or rationality, or whatever) is grounded in her own will, how can we even hope to answer this kind of skeptic? So doesn't Robust Realism entail that we cannot cope with this kind of practical skeptical challenge? In terms made popular – but nowhere nearly clear enough – by Korsgaard (1996), doesn't it follow that robust realists cannot answer "the normative question"?

Once again, though, we need to draw distinctions. First, we need to distinguish different possible understandings of the relevant "why" in the why-be-moral challenge. And second, we should distinguish between the question about morality and the question about the most general practical norms – perhaps about the ought *sans phrase*, or perhaps about reasons in general.

The first distinction is not going to surprise you. For we need to distinguish between the kind of why-question to which a response in terms of normative reasons is an appropriate reply, and the kind of why-question to which a motivational reply – perhaps somewhat roughly, an *incentive* – is appropriate. Is the dreaded skeptic, in other words, someone who doesn't believe or judge that he should be moral? Or is he someone whose problem is not one of belief (or its absence) in moral or normative truths, but rather that he just doesn't care (or doesn't think that he cares) about them? If the latter, the challenge presumably calls upon us to make it the case that he does care, or perhaps to show (him) that he already cares and indeed has cared all along. If the former, we are presumably asked to give him reasons to believe that he should be moral, or perhaps to convince him to be moral (I am going to return to this further distinction shortly).

Any of these challenges may be raised specifically with regard to morality, or more generally with regard to what we have (most) reason to do. And so we have (at least) four options: there is a request for normative reasons to be moral, or for normative reasons for doing what we have (most) reason to do, or for an incentive to be moral, or for an incentive to do what we have (most) reason to do. Let me discuss these four challenges in this order (though I am going to discuss the last two together).

9.3.1 Why (normatively) be moral?

If nothing else, a request for a general normative vindication of morality at least makes sense. (Spoiler alert: This is *not* going to be a suitable way of starting the next subsection.) Presumably, morality makes all sorts of demands on us, and these often have a price in other things we care and should care about. So it makes sense to ask whether we have reasons to do as morality requires that we do. And importantly, this is an entirely *intra-normative* question.

To an extent, then, I can remain neutral on this question. Robust Realism is a metanormative theory, and is arguably consistent with many different intra-normative stories (though not with all of them; let me remind you that several times already in this book (especially in Chapter 2) it turned out that there are interesting relations between the normative and the metanormative). Indeed, had Robust Realism *only* been a metanormative theory, I think this would have been an adequate response. In particular, nothing about Robust Realism as a metanormative theory is in any way inconsistent with there being no reason to be moral, or with any number of ways of showing that (necessarily, or at least often) we do have reasons to be moral.

But Robust Realism is also a meta*ethical* theory, and so a little more has to be said here. Indeed, a little more *has* been said, in Chapter 4, section 4.3, where I argue for a very moderate kind of moral rationalism, according to which morality has at least pretty good normative credentials, so that it's not entirely contingent that often, when we have moral reason to do something we also have (good, real) reason to do it. I will not rehearse these arguments here. I just want to note the relevance of that discussion to the point here.

But the crucial point remains that there are many possible ways of showing that we (at least often, perhaps even necessarily) have reasons to be moral – or have (real) reasons to do what we have moral reasons to do – that are perfectly consistent with Robust Realism. What we need here is a general first-order theory of what we have reason to do, and a general first-order theory of morality. Robust Realism is a theory about what such theories will come to – they will come to a true representation of the mind-independent normative and moral truths – but has little to say about their content. So it may turn out, for instance, that though the necessary connections between moral reasons and real reasons are not very strict (not stricter, that is, than those called for by the argument in Chapter 4), still as a matter of contingent fact almost always when we have moral reason to do something we also have reason to do it. Or it may turn out that the relations between morality and what we have reason to do are much stricter than that. Perhaps, for instance, nothing can be a moral reason for one to φ without it – that very same thing – also qualifying as a reason for one to φ. Or perhaps it turns out that very often we do not have reasons to be moral. And there are presumably other options as well, all of which, as far as I can see, perfectly compatible with Robust Realism as a metanormative and metaethical theory. As far as I can see, then, all of this (with the exception of the constraints of the argument of Chapter 4, section 4.3) is up for first-order-theory grabs.

Even if this is so, you may insist, all that I've shown is that Robust Realism can *accommodate* many different possible answers to the (normative) why-be-moral challenge. But is this enough? Didn't we want not just the *possibility* of an answer, but an *answer*? Wasn't a metaethical theory supposed to *generate* such an answer, rather than merely not rule out answers generated by other resources? The answer, I think, is that it wasn't. If the challenge is understood as a normative one – and this is how we understand it in this subsection – then coping with it is a matter for first-order, normative theories. Thus put, I take it there is nothing surprising about this result.

Let me emphasize just one more thing here. It is one thing to ask whether we have reason to be moral, quite another to ask whether we (always) have *most* reason to be moral, or to do what we have most moral reason to do. I suggested that Robust Realism can remain largely neutral about the former question. And now I want to emphasize that it can remain *entirely* neutral on the latter. The minimal rationalist claim I defended in Chapter 4 was motivated by the thought that morality is not a system of rules like etiquette – where it's quite possible that the relevant rules come with no genuine normative force. This, I argued, is not a plausible thing to say of morality. But that moral reasons and norms come with genuine normative force says nothing at all about *how much* such force they come with, and whether it is always more force than any other consideration. The question of morality's overridingness, then, is most clearly one for first-order normative theory to deal with. Robust Realism has nothing interesting to say about it (nor, I'm afraid, does this robust realist). But this does not count at all against Robust Realism.

9.3.2 Why (normatively) do what we have (most) reason to do?

If the skeptic we are concerned with asks a normative question about not morality but the whole normative domain, though, then (as many have noted[46]) it is *very* hard to even read the challenge as a coherent and substantive one. For once unpacked the question just comes down to something like "What reason do I have to do what I have reason to do?" or perhaps "*Do* I have reason to do what I have reason to do?" And on a simple understanding, such questions barely make sense, and anyway can be answered rather trivially. Suppose we're talking about a specific action, ϕ. Then the question "Do I have reason to ϕ, given that I have reason to ϕ?" is not a very interesting one. The answer is a trivial "yes". Nothing more can or should be said here. That Robust Realism has nothing more to say here is, then, not to its discredit.

There are other ways of understanding such questions that render them more intelligible, but they are not ones that are problematic for Robust Realism. Thus, the question "What reason do I have to do what I have reason to do?" can be understood simply as asking what the reason (which one acknowledges is there) is. This, of course, is a perfectly legitimate question, but not one that is any cause for concern for Robust Realism.

Or, the question "What reason do I have to do what I have rason to do?" can be understood as asking about non-specific actions one has some reason to do. The question then becomes the (interesting!) question whether there is some reason – some one and the same reason – to perform all reason-supported actions. And it just doesn't follow from the fact that *for any action we have reason to perform we have a reason to*

---

[46] See, for instance, Shafer-Landau (2003, 179–80), Parfit (2011, vol. 2, section 104).

perform it, that *we have a general reason to perform all reason-supported actions*. And so this last claim may be coherently questioned. I am not sure what to say about it,[47] but I am sure that Robust Realism is not committed here one way or another, nor should it be.

Another possible way of making sense of these questions is by understanding them as highlighting a suspicion about self-defeat. Thus, if it follows from your favorite first-order theory of what we have reason to do that sometimes we don't have a reason to do what we have reason to do, this is a serious problem for your theory. But this worry – though perfectly legitimate – is a worry about first-order theories, not about Robust Realism. And I can't see any reason to believe that Robust Realism is going to somehow end up committed to a first-order theory that suffers from this problem.

Notice that by insisting that these questions – on their most natural understanding – are simply bad questions (in the sense explicated above, namely, that a simple and trivial "yes" is all that is needed in order to answer them) I am not pretending that some profound skepticism has been defeated. Some people are in the business of defeating skeptics (of different sorts) by showing that these skeptics defeat themselves, in something like the following way: by, say, offering arguments for her skepticism, the epistemological skeptic commits herself to some beliefs being justified, thereby defeating her most radical skepticism about justification; or, by asking for reasons the practical skeptic shows himself to be an agent and to care about the constitutive aim of agency, thereby defeating his most radical practical skepticism. As I explain in detail elsewhere,[48] I think that such attempts at defeating skeptical and related challenges are bound to fail. So it's important to see that this is not what I am attempting here. My point is *not* that by asking for normative reasons (and this is how we understand the "why", for now) the skeptic makes it impossible for him to also argue against normative reasons or some such. My point, rather, is that the skeptic who asks whether we have reason to do what (he acknowledges) we have reason to do is not a very challenging skeptic at all.

There is one other legitimate challenge in the vicinity here. For the challenge may be understood as *epistemic* in nature. It may be understood, in other words, as a request for epistemic reasons to believe that we sometimes have practical reasons. Thus understood, of course, the challenge is perfectly legitimate. But thus understood, the way to respond to it is to offer arguments for some kind of realist metanormative view. And this is what I do, after all, throughout this book. Perhaps I fail – but this will have to be shown. There is no independent challenge here.

Let me conclude this section with another way of understanding the challenge, one that is not, I think, very interesting, but that seems to be quite influential (a version of this will reappear in the next subsection as well). This is the thought that an adequate argument to the conclusion that we have reasons to perform actions in general, or

---

[47] If having a reason is a reason, then it seems to follow that there is a reason to perform all reason-supported actions – namely, that there is a reason to perform them.

[48] See my "Agency, Shmagency" (2006) and "Shmagency Revisited" (2010b).

perhaps some specific action, must be such as to *necessarily convince* all interlocutors. It can then be pointed out that on Robust Realism this cannot be done. As Korsgaard (1996, 40–2) emphasizes, there will come a time in the debate in which the realist will just insist that you have a reason to ϕ, and that's the end of the matter; and you should acknowledge that this is so, simply because, well, this is so. Korsgaard seems to think that this exposes some great flaw in the realist's position. But she is mistaken, of course. Here as everywhere else, it is one thing to offer an adequate justification, quite another to convince all interlocutors. And after all, it's not as if other metanormative views – alternatives to Robust Realism – score better on this impossible standard. In particular, it's not as if we have any reason to believe that Korsgaard's view is more dialectically effective in the relevant way than Robust Realism is (nor, to repeat the previous point, would it matter if it were).

Robust Realism, then, has nothing interesting to say in reply to the question "Why do what I have reason to do?" Nor should it. No view should.[49]

9.3.3 Why (motivationally) be moral, or do what we have (most) reason to do?

But perhaps the why-be-moral or why-act-as-I-have-reason-to-act challenges are to be understood motivationally. Perhaps, the person putting forward the challenge is thought of as someone who just doesn't care (or thinks that he doesn't care) about these things, and the challenge is thought of as the need to make it the case that he cares, or perhaps to show him that he already does. Perhaps the relevant skeptic is, somewhat roughly, someone asking not whether it's the case that (say) he should be kind to others, but rather "What's in it for me?"[50]

Once again we may be up against the thought that philosophy should replace the hangman. The fact (if it is a fact) that some people do not care about morality or (more importantly) about those things that morality requires that they care about is indeed a problem. But it is a political one, not a metaethical one. It is not a flaw in a metaethical or metanormative theory that it doesn't adequately address this problem, and of course, no metanormative theory (robust realist or otherwise) addresses it adequately. And the happy thought that we can show everyone that they *already* care just seems utterly implausible on its face.[51]

---

[49] Fitzpatrick (2005, 656) writes: "... realism implies neither a refusal to answer the normative question nor the view that this needn't be done". He may be right that (robust) realism does not imply these claims. But at least if "normative question" is understood as it is understood in this subsection in the text, then these claims are still very much true.

[50] Notice, by the way, the interesting ambiguity in "Why should I care?" This question seems normative. But I take it often it is asked by someone who knows that he *should* care, but just doesn't. Pragmatically, then, it is often used equivalently to "What's in it for me?".

[51] For the claim that there's just not enough content to whatever it is that is plausibly constitutive of action to vindicate morality, see Setiya (2003). And for the claim that even if there is, no constitutivist line can achieve what it is supposed to achieve (most relevantly in our context, to defeat the skeptic), again see my "Agency, Shmagency" (2006) and "Shmagency Revisited" (2010b).

Things would have been different, perhaps, if we had some *independent* reason to believe that there is a close, necessary connection between normativity and motivation. If, say, we had some independent reason to believe that no one can have a normative reason to φ unless they already care about φ-ing or about something that φ-ing would promote, then that some (possible) agents don't care about their moral obligations would entail that they don't have a normative reason to do as morality requires that they do, and this *would* be a problematic result. But what would do the work here, of course, is the independent reason to think that normativity and motivation are so intimately related. And so far we have seen no argument to this effect. We will evaluate some such arguments in the following sections.

To conclude, then: Whether we understand "the" why-be-moral challenge as normative or motivational, and whether we understand it as about morality or about normative reasons in general, there is no serious challenge here for Robust Realism. This is so because understood motivationally the challenge turns out to completely rely on *other* reasons to believe that normativity and motivation are intimately related, and understood normatively the challenge is either real but irrelevant to Robust Realism (if it is understood as one of a set of intra-normative questions about the normative force of morality), or it is not real (if it is understood as a doubt about whether we have reason to do what we have reason to do). And the suspicion again arises that the thought that there is here a serious challenge to Robust Realism comes from the failure to distinguish between the normative and motivational questions that may be asked here.

Perhaps there is some other way of understanding "the" why-be-moral challenge. Or perhaps the challenge is meant to be neither solely normative nor solely motivational, but somehow a combination of the two. If so, what we need is a clear presentation of this challenge that will be guilty neither of equivocating between normative and motivational readings of its relevant claims nor of taking for granted a suspicious claim about the relation between normativity and motivation (one that itself needs support in an argument against Robust Realism). I can't think of such a challenge in the vicinity here.

Let me emphasize again that none of this goes any way at all towards showing that on Robust Realism normative or moral truths are somehow practically irrelevant. For Robust Realism is – as I argued above – perfectly consistent with us often acting for the specific reasons that apply to us. And this is all the practical relevance that needs accommodating.

9.4 Judgment-internalism

"Internalism" and "externalism" are two of the most widely abused terms in philosophy. They come up in many different sub-disciplines bearing different meanings. And even just within the same sub-discipline they often have multiple meanings. This is the case when it comes to metaethics and practical reasoning. And so we again need some distinctions (the ones that follow are not at all original[52]).

The term "internalism" is sometimes used to denote, perhaps roughly, the view I called earlier in this chapter (and in Chapter 4) moral rationalism, namely a claim about necessary relations between moral requirements on one side and (real, genuine) reasons on the other. This is not a sense of "internalism" that I will use.

The literature now rather routinely distinguishes between judgment-internalism and existence-internalism (for instance, about morality, or about reasons). Judgment-internalist views endorse some necessary connection between sincerely making a relevant *judgment* and being *motivated* in some way. Thus, the view that one cannot sincerely judge that ϕ-ing is morally required without being at least somewhat motivated to ϕ is an example of a judgment-internalist view (about moral requirements). Existence-internalist views endorse some necessary connection between the *truth* of some kind of normative claim and something about the motivations of the agent to which it applies. Thus, the view according to which it can't be true of you that you have a reason to ϕ (or – no reason for you to ϕ exists) unless there is a sound deliberative route from your motivational set to ϕ-ing[53] is an instance of existence-internalism (about reasons). Judgment-internalism and existence-internalism are thus very different theses, with different implications and different arguments supporting (or challenging) them. They should be discussed separately. And so I discuss existence-internalism in the next section (9.5). Judgment-internalism is the business of this section.

The reason judgment-internalism is supposed to be a problem for Robust Realism can be stated rather simply. On Robust Realism, normative judgments express beliefs about response-independent (and so in particular desire-independent) entities, properties, facts. Whether such beliefs can motivate you – bring you to action in an appropriate way – seems to be something that should depend on your other psychological states, perhaps your desires. Certainly if we accept the view that beliefs alone cannot motivate – that for motivation there's always a need for some desire, sufficiently broadly understood – then it is hard to see how Robust Realism can accommodate judgment-internalism. So robust realists seem committed either to rejecting judgment-internalism, or to rejecting what is sometimes called Humean psychology (roughly, the claim that beliefs alone cannot motivate).

---

[52] See for instance, Darwall (1983, ch. 5), Brink (1989, 40–1; though Brink uses somewhat different terminology); Parfit (1997, 103–5); Shafer-Landau (2003, 142–5). Darwall (1995, 9) attempts to nevertheless understand what is common to all kinds of internalism here (though note that his suggestion remains disjunctive): "What these [all the different views that go by the name of "internalism"] have in common is the assertion of a necessary connection between either the having or the truth conditions of ethical or normative thought (or language) and *motivation*."

[53] I discuss Williams in section 9.5.

I have some doubts about Humean psychology (perhaps some beliefs can motivate without desires, perhaps some beliefs just are desires,[54] perhaps some beliefs can bring about the desires needed for motivation,[55] perhaps some desires consist epiphenomenally in the state of being motivated by a belief[56]), but I am not confident here one way or another, and so I am going to stick to my policy of remaining as neutral as I can on the theory of motivation. I'm going to do this by assuming for the sake of argument Humean psychology, and proceeding to reject judgment-internalism. My discussion of judgment-internalism will start from the strongest, clearest version of judgment-internalism. This version, I think, can be rejected rather easily. I then proceed to discuss some suspicious ways of weakening it, and then several other attempts at capturing the grain of truth in the vicinity of judgment-internalism. And I will argue that such grains of truth that can be found can be accommodated by Robust Realism (without rejecting Humean psychology).

9.4.1 Really Strong Judgment-Internalism, and Mitigated Internalism

A very strong judgment-internalist thesis about morality would state that necessarily, if agent A judges that she morally ought to ϕ, then A is at least somewhat motivated to ϕ. A similarly strong version of judgment-internalism about reasons would state that necessarily, if agent A judges that she has (normative) reason to ϕ, then A is at least somewhat motivated to ϕ. And the necessity here is supposed to be at least as strong as metaphysical necessity, and indeed perhaps conceptual necessity. I will call such theses "Really Strong Judgment-Internalism". Stronger versions can be thought of – like ones that you get from Really Strong Judgment-Internalism by replacing "is at least somewhat motivated to ϕ" with "ϕ-s". But I take it this (crazily strong) internalism is not of genuine interest.

If true, Really Strong Judgment-Internalism would cause trouble for Robust Realism. For how would the relevant necessity be explained? One could, I guess, opt for a *tracking* internalism,[57] according to which our motivations necessarily track our moral and other normative judgments. Such tracking internalism is consistent with Robust Realism, but this, I think, is its only virtue. Certainly, a robust realist would lose significant plausibility points for endorsing it (and would have to defend substantive commitments in the theory of motivation, commitments of the kind I was hoping to

---

[54] For some discussions relevant here, and for references, see Smith (1994, 111–19) and Shafer-Landau (2003, ch. 6).

[55] See, for instance, Nagel's *The Possibility of Altruism* (1970).

[56] See Dancy (1996a, 174) for such a suggestion, in the context of criticizing Smith's (1994) direction-of-fit argument for Humean psychology.

[57] See Darwall (1995, 10–11), and Sobel (2001, 473), though note that Sobel discusses the tracking version of existence-, not judgment-internalism.

avoid). Let's set the tracking version of Really Strong Judgment-Internalism, then, to one side.[58] But if we rule out tracking internalism, the only thing that could explain, it seems, the necessary connections highlighted by Really Strong Judgment-Internalism is something about the nature of normative judgment. In particular, it would be hard to see how to reconcile in a non-mysterious way a robust realist picture of normative judgments as expressing fully representational beliefs about response-independent pieces of reality with anything like Really Strong Judgment-Internalism.

Fortunately for Robust Realism, though, Really Strong Judgment-Internalism is rather obviously false.[59] One way to see this would be to engage the amoralist wars, where claims are made by externalists of sorts that amoralists of one kind or another – people who do not care about morality, but continue to make moral judgments with the rest of us – are at least possible (in whatever modality that captures the necessity claim in Really Strong Judgment-Internalism); internalists then respond by offering alternative descriptions of such apparent possibilities (perhaps, for instance, these persons do not *really* make moral judgments, but rather express "inverted commas" moral judgments, or some such), and stand their ground about the impossibility of genuine amoralists; externalists can then retort by arguing that such re-descriptions are unmotivated;[60] and the wars go on.[61] Now, for what it is worth it seems to me clear that at least the kind of amoralist needed to refute Really Strong Judgment-Internalism is possible. (But then it *would* so seem to me, wouldn't it?) And there is something frustrating about the amoralist wars: they seem to have reached what is at least dialectically (if not necessarily philosophically) a stalemate, and continuing to engage them certainly doesn't feel to me like a promising way of making philosophical progress. For this reason, then, let me not engage them. Instead, let me note a dialectical point emphasized by Svavarsdóttir (1999, e.g. 182): if nothing else, the stalemate (if it is that) shows that the internalist cannot just *take for granted* something like Really Strong Judgment-Internalism.[62] In the context of defending Robust Realism

---

[58] Perhaps – I am really not competent to make an assertion here – Plato was a tracking internalist of sorts (see Darwall (1995, 10)). But note that arguably the thing that was according to Plato necessarily connected with motivation was not *judgments* about the good, but rather *knowledge* of the good. So even Plato thus understood could have rejected Really Strong Judgment-Internalism. (The claim that normative *knowledge* necessarily motivates may not be much more plausible than the claim that normative *judgment* does, but it is certainly an interestingly different claim.)

And perhaps something like the tracking version of Really Strong Judgment-Internalism is what Rawls (2000, 237) attributes to the rational intuitionists when he writes: "A basic psychological assumption of rational intuitionism is that people can recognize first principles and that the recognition of those principles as true of a prior order of moral values gives rise to a desire to act from them for their own sake."

[59] For an elaborate defense of the analogous claim with regard to aesthetics, and the suggested analogy with the moral case, see Railton (2009, 103 and on).

[60] For the claim that the motivation for such re-description is typically a prior commitment to some not-fully-realist metaethics, and that therefore such re-descriptions cannot be non-question-beggingly used in an argument against realism, see Shafer-Landau (2003, 153–4).

[61] See, for instance, Brink (1989, 45–9) and (1997b, 21–30), Svavarsdóttir (1999, throughout), and the references there; and in the context of defending a fairly robust realism, see Shafer-Landau (2003, ch. 7).

[62] Here's a related and dialectically powerful point that Svavarsdóttir (1999) makes: it seems that among those who are appropriately motivated by their normative judgments, there are (and certainly can be) significant differences in the *degree* of the relevant motivating force. But if such variance is possible, very

(this is not Svavarsdóttir's context), we can say that it remains to be shown that rejecting Really Strong Judgment-Internalism has any price at all in plausibility points.

Things are even better than that, because even among self-proclaimed judgment-internalists Really Strong Judgment-Internalism is no longer fashionable (if it ever was).[63] Perhaps because appreciating the possibility of some kinds of amoralists, or perhaps for some other reasons, judgment-internalists typically go for versions of what we can call (following Sayre-McCord)[64] "Mitigated Internalism". There are many ways of mitigating internalism. Thus, one could settle for a necessary connection between an agent's normative judgments and her motivations only when she's practically rational, or not weak-willed; or one could weaken the relevant necessity (say, to nomological necessity); or one may get rid of the necessity altogether and settle for an empirical regularity; or one may employ a *ceteris paribus* clause; some of these suggestions may be related, and a mitigated internalist may want to employ more than one mitigating device.

But such mitigating moves – while typically successful in rendering the resultant (mitigated) internalism more plausible than Really Strong Judgment-Internalism – are in our context entirely unhelpful. This is so, first, because for each version of Mitigated Internalism the amoralist wars will start anew (in fact, because Really Strong Judgment-Internalism is so unpopular these days, the amoralist wars typically take place with regard to some version or another of Mitigated Internalism[65]). And though the more mitigated the internalism, the less obviously possible is the amoralist needed to refute it, still it is hard to see anything here as the way to philosophical progress, and still the externalists seem to have done enough here to at least make it the case that the internalist cannot rely on her Mitigated Internalism as a reasonably good philosophical starting point.[66] And second, the suspicion arises that what does the real work in Mitigated Internalism is not so much the internalism as it is the mitigation. Thus, if the necessary connection is supposed to hold, say, between an agent's normative judgments and her motivations *in so far as she is rational*, then it is *very* tempting to read the resulting Mitigated Internalism either as a trivial claim (so that the understanding of rationality invoked here is whatever it is that is needed in order to render this Mitigated Internalism true),[67] or else as a substantive, intra-normative thesis, one about

strong argument is needed if we are to believe that the allowed-for variance does not extend also to the limiting case of no motivational force at all.

[63] Gibbard (2003, 154) characterizes something like Really Strong Judgment-Internalism as "the weaker, more usual formulation" of internalism. But the context makes it clear that he thinks of it in comparison with the thesis that I referred to above as crazily strong judgment-internalism.

Interestingly, something like Really Strong Judgment-Internalism does seem rather plausible when it comes to epistemic reasons: it's not clear that it's even conceptually possible to judge that one is justified in believing *p* without being at least somewhat inclined to believe *p*. I don't know how to explain this phenomenon, or the disanalogy with the practical case here.

[64] Sayre-McCord (1997) uses this phrase to characterize Smith's internalism, but we can use it more generally, in the way suggested in the text.

[65] See Brink (1989, 57–62) and Svavarsdóttir (1999).

[66] For many details here, again see Svavarsdóttir (1999).

[67] See Schroeder (2007, 165) for a similar suspicion.

what it takes to be rational.[68] Understood in any of these two ways, of course, Mitigated Internalism is no threat at all to Robust Realism. In our context, then, the challenge for the judgment-internalist is to come up with a non-trivial Mitigated Internalism that is pre-theoretically attractive, Robust-Realism-unfriendly, and reasonably immune to amoralist counterexamples. I don't know of any remotely successful attempt at coping with this challenge.

This, of course, does not mean that there is no genuine challenge in the vicinity here. The next subsections are all attempts at pinpointing and addressing such challenges.

9.4.2 Explaining correlations

Forget necessities, then. Isn't it at least true, as an empirical matter, that people are rarely motivationally indifferent to the things they judge to be good, or reason-supported, or morally required, or some such? If – as seems likely – there is in the vicinity here a fairly strong correlation between, say, people's moral judgments and their motivations, or perhaps between a change in their normative judgments and a change in their motivations,[69] doesn't it call for explanation? And if so, if no plausible explanation of such correlations is consistent with Robust Realism or its underlying philosophical motivations, doesn't this count heavily against Robust Realism?

This, I want to emphasize, is a perfectly legitimate challenge. Such correlations as can be found[70] (and this, of course, is largely an empirical matter) do call for explanation here. But, as I am about to show, there is no reason to think that no such explanation is compatible with Robust Realism.[71]

Now, different explanations will work for different (purported) explananda. Consider Smith's (1994, 71–2) favorite one, namely, that at least among the virtuous and the not-too-weak-willed, a change in motivation will reliably follow a change in normative judgment.[72] Well, nothing here is obvious. For one thing, one may doubt that this is in fact precisely so (for any non-trivial understanding of "virtuous"). Perhaps, for instance, the psychology works the other way around, so that even the virtuous among us resist a change in normative beliefs (even against evidence) until their motivations are roughly in line. This is an empirical speculation, of course, but then so is its negation; and the speculation here is not implausible – it seems to invoke the kind of psychological mechanisms we know are in play elsewhere. If this is a better description of what goes on when virtuous persons change their normative

---

[68]   See Svavarsdóttir (1999, 183) for a similar suspicion.

[69]   This is the explanandum Smith (1994) emphasizes. I return to it below.

[70]   Notice that – as noted by Copp (2001, 12) in the context of a discussion of Smith – such empirical correlation would suffice in order to explain why we doubt the sincerity of someone who pronounces a moral judgment but doesn't show any inclination to act accordingly. And such empirical correlation should also suffice to explain the asymmetry Oddie (2005, ch. 2) emphasizes between first- and third-personal attributions of gaps between value and desire.

[71]   Similar suggestions are made, for instance, by Brink (1997a, 263–4), Railton (1993, 297; and in more detail 2009), Boyd (1988, 215), Shafer-Landau (2003, ch. 7), and Svavarsdóttir (1999, throughout).

[72]   For a similar statement of the explanandum here, see Rawls (2000, 80), and Scanlon (1998, 62).

beliefs, clearly no problem for Robust Realism emerges. Or perhaps the correlation Smith wants to explain is really extremely superficial. Consider the following analogy: what explains the investment success of good stockbrokers? You may start off looking for a *deep* explanation, perhaps in terms of some special properties that good stockbrokers have and that mediocre ones lack. But it may very well be the case that no such explanation is forthcoming. It may be the case that the market just cannot be systematically beaten[73], and that what explains the observed correlation between a stockbroker's classification as a good stockbroker and his success at beating the market is simply that we don't classify a stockbroker as good until we observe his outperforming the market (as a matter of sheer luck, of course). Similarly, then, perhaps what explains the correlation between a change in virtuous people's normative beliefs and a change in their motivations is simply that no one gets labeled virtuous until we observe this very regularity. I take it this is not the phenomenon Smith has in mind, but then he owes us some reason to believe that the phenomenon he wants explained is genuine and deep, not one explained by this superficial kind of selection-effect, analogously to the stockbroker example.[74]

But I am not going to rest with such doubts about the specific explanandum the (seriously mitigated) judgment-internalist wants explained. Let me grant for the sake of argument, then, that there is some correlation here that calls for (deep) explanation, perhaps simply the correlation between people's (or even just some people's) normative judgments and motivations. Can Robust Realism explain such correlation?

Well, Robust Realism does not, I think, have within it the resources to explain such correlation, but nor should it. The thing we are now trying to explain is an empirical, psychological regularity. And so the obvious place to look for explanation is empirical psychology, not metaethics or metanormativity (or indeed philosophy in general). Here's another analogy: There is, I take it, a rather striking correlation (no less striking than in the case of normative judgments and motivations) between being someone's parent and loving them, caring about their well-being, etc.[75] In trying to offer an explanation of this correlation, we are not tempted to look for better philosophical understandings of parenthood. The explanation is to be found elsewhere – in empirical psychology, perhaps, or evolutionary theory, or some combination of the two. The most we can ask from a philosophical theory of parenthood in this context is that it not rule out any of the plausible psychological explanations of this correlation. And so, the crucial question about Robust Realism and the correlation between normative

---

[73] Thus states the efficient market hypothesis. Needless to say, the example is just an example, and I do not know what if anything in the vicinity of the efficient market hypothesis is true.

[74] For somewhat similar doubts about Smith's explanandum, see Copp (1997, 49–51).

[75] As stated in the text, the parent-analogy is more closely analogous to existence- than to judgment-internalism. For a closer analogy with judgment-internalism, we would need to speak of the correlation between someone *believing* that a child is his or her child, and them caring about the child. I don't put things this way in the text merely in order to avoid the awkward wording that would result. Nothing of importance for the use to which I put the analogy – here, and later on – hinges on this, I think.

judgments and motivation then becomes whether Robust Realism somehow makes the otherwise plausible psychological explanations of this correlation unavailable. And I don't see that it does.

I am not going to do empirical psychology here, so let me just hint at some initially promising directions, some possible ways of explaining (if the empirical work is done) the correlation that calls for explanation here (some of them have already been mentioned in section 9.1.3). One way in which we could explain the correlation is if we had some reason to believe that people often have a desire (or some other motivating state, if there are other alternatives here) for the good, or for the reason-supported, or to act in ways that make sense, *under those descriptions*.[76] Given such a general desire, it would be very easy to explain a correlation between people's normative judgment and their motivation, or indeed a reliable change in people's motivations immediately following a change in their normative judgments. Another possible explanatory strategy would be to focus attention on moral (or more broadly normative) *training*, where typically the child *simultaneously* learns that an action of his or hers was wrong *and* is given some incentive not to perform it, or is encouraged to associate in the future this action and its wrongness with something he or she rather strongly dislikes (like his or her punishment). Given such training, what would be surprising – what would *really* call for explanation – is not the correlation between people's normative judgments and their motivations, but rather a lack thereof.[77] Other possible explanations of the correlations between people's motivations and their normative judgments may be suggested in terms of a psychological mechanism that pushes our normative judgments in the direction of our motivations (and not the other way around), or in terms of other desires – not a desire to follow reasons de dicto – to which following reasons is typically instrumental (like perhaps the desire to take part in certain relationships that require this kind of dependability). Notice that this kind of explanation – and to a lesser extent also the previous one – can, if they can be made to work, explain also Smith's explanandum.[78] And of course, if normative beliefs can themselves motivate, or perhaps bring about desires that motivate, noticing this would be a promising first step in explaining the target correlation. All of these explanation-schemas (and presumably there are others) are perfectly compatible with Robust Realism.[79] All but the last one are neutral on questions in the theory of motivation. Of course, none of these stories – even when filled out with the necessary empirical

[76] For suggestions along these lines, see, for instance, Svavarsdóttir (1999). And for Kantian variants, see Rawls (2000, 214) and (1980, 525), here utilizing also higher-order desires. Darwall (1995, 6) finds a similar suggestion in Grotius.

[77] A point emphasized by Burgess (2007, 431) and Railton (1993, 296).

[78] So Smith is wrong to insist (e.g. 1997, 112–17) that the *only* possible explanation (other than his own) is in terms of a desire (understood de dicto) for the good.

[79] Some of these explanations can also explain why normative judgments would come to have motivational stuff as their pragmatic implicatures, even if not as a matter of their content. The suggestion that the plausibility of something in the vicinity of judgment-internalism comes from conflating pragmatics and semantics is made by Copp (2001, 12).

details – can vindicate Really Strong Judgment-Internalism. But we've already deserted that view. And when focusing on just the relevant empirical regularities, such psychological stories – all, to repeat, perfectly consistent with Robust Realism – can do the work.

Michael Smith famously objects to the first of these – the explanation in terms of (roughly) a de dicto desire for the good, or the right, or the reason-supported, or some such.[80] On this explanation, argues Smith, the virtuous person (someone who would presumably help his neighbor simply because the neighbor could use some help, or because he likes him, or some such) ends up looking more like a rightness-fetishist (someone who helps his neighbor because that would be a way of acting rightly). But we can now dismiss this objection, for the following reasons.[81] First, for reasons that are not altogether clear to me, Smith (1997, 113) rejects a possible reply in terms of motivational overdetermination, according to which the virtuous person has *both* a de re *and* a de dicto desire for the good. But once we allow for this possibility, there is really nothing offensive about describing the virtuous person as someone who is *also* concerned with the good as such.[82] And second, and relatedly, we can see that there's something wrong with Smith's objection by considering the parent example again. For in many cases, the parent who loves his daughter would have loved whatever child were to be born. Initially, the thought may go, the parent may be accused of parenthood-fetishism, as he cares for his child de dicto, under the description of "a child whose parent I am". But of course, often parenthood develops in other directions, including the perfectly particular direction of caring for *this particular girl*, plausibly as de re an attitude as is humanly possible. And my point now is not just that the two kinds of attitudes can happily co-exist (this would be the overdetermination point again), but also that there's quite a natural relation between them – namely, that given some features of human psychology, the de dicto attitude naturally develops into and reinforces the de re attitude. What starts as a de dicto interest in my child as such, naturally develops into a de re interest in *this child*. Wouldn't it be plausible, then, to see the virtuous person's relation to the good as analogous to the good parent's relation to his daughter in this respect? It seems utterly unsurprising – given what we know of human psychology – that a person who cares about the good de dicto will with time also develop attitudes towards the good, understood de re, and perhaps also vice versa.[83] (This is compatible, of course, with many different ways of explaining the emergence of the de dicto desire.)

---

[80] This point is made especially clearly in Smith (1997, 112–17), which follows up on Smith (1994).

[81] As already stated, an explanation in terms of the de dicto desire for the good (and so on) is only *one* possibility here, and there are others. So even if this one fails, still Smith doesn't get his (mitigated) internalist conclusion.

[82] This is a point Darwall (2002, 267) emphasizes, though he thinks that it fails to account for the full motivational force of normative judgment. And for the overdetermination point, see also Svavarsdóttir (1999, 215).

[83] See in this context Svavarsdóttir's (1999, 170) related suggestion, that (roughly speaking) a desire for the good understood de dicto may be sustained by different other desires in different agents.

What *would* be offensive, let me concede, is if robust realists had to deny that the virtuous person helping her neighbor can do this for the reason that her neighbor needs help. But explaining the correlation between a (virtuous) person's desires and her normative judgments in any of the ways above – including in terms of a de dicto desire for the good or the right – does not have this troubling result. For as I've argued in section 9.1 above, on the most natural understanding of action for a (specific) reason, Robust Realism can easily accommodate it, and nothing in the way in which Robust Realism can accommodate action for a reason is lost when one of the explanations sketched above for the correlation is endorsed.

Empirical correlations should indeed be explained. But they should be explained empirically. And nothing in Robust Realism or its underlying motivations makes the most natural candidates for such empirical explanations unavailable to the robust realist. Here too, I conclude, there is no serious trouble for Robust Realism.

9.4.3 Going global

Suppose we leave behind, then, claims about the relation between specific normative judgment and motivation (because the stronger among these claims cannot be adequately supported, at least not without what in our context would amount to begging important questions, and the weaker among these are easily explained compatibly with Robust Realism). There is still a challenge here worth considering. For it may be thought that even if there is no necessary connection between specific normative judgments and motivations, still there is a necessary connection on some more global level. Perhaps, for instance, though one can make normative judgments without being motivated accordingly, one cannot be in the business of making normative judgments (or perhaps normative judgments of a certain kind) without having one's motivations in line with one's normative judgments at least in some central cases.[84] Or perhaps something close to a global, perhaps social, version of internalism is in some other way necessary for the practices of making normative judgments to even get off the ground.[85] The underlying intuition here is perhaps best presented by David Lewis (1989, 70), who suggests that but for such a connection (on some global, not local, level), "there would be no conceptual reason why valuing is a *favorable* attitude. We might not have favored the things we value. We might have opposed them, or been entirely indifferent." Importantly, even a connection on the global level calls for explanation, and it may be thought that no plausible explanation of this connection is forthcoming consistently with Robust Realism.

---

[84] I think – but I'm not sure – that a suggestion along these lines is made by Jackson and Pettit (1995, 35–9). A somewhat similar point is made by Gibbard (2003, 11) when discussing "hyperexternalists". I am grateful to John Ku for making me see that this is something I need to address.

[85] I think – but I'm not sure – that a suggestion along these lines is made by Greenspan (1998) and by Tersman (2006, 120). See also Blackburn (1998, 61).

I want to concede that there is *a* sense in which a fairly strong relation to motivation (understood globally, in a way that is consistent with local failures of such connection) may be necessary for the possibility of making moral and other normative judgments. Perhaps, for instance, it is humanly impossible for such a practice to emerge without some such connection to motivation. Or perhaps it is humanly impossible to learn and master (some) normative concepts without some relation to motivation. Or perhaps without a relation of this sort normative knowledge would have been impossible, because the harmony Chapter 7 utilizes would not in such a world have been pre-established. But such necessities are consistent with Robust Realism: it may be the case, for instance, that but for some a posteriori acquaintances with multitudes, we would not have been able to do number theory – perhaps not even to learn and master the concept of a number – but this is no reason to reject even the strongest kind of mathematical Platonism.[86] An a posteriori acquaintance with multitudes may be an enabling condition for us doing number theory, without having any conceptual relation to the nature of numbers. Similarly, perhaps given the psychological (and perhaps other) limitations of human beings, it would have been impossible for norma-tive discourse and practice to emerge without some ties to motivation (and feelings too, perhaps). And if this is so, this calls for explanations. But the explanations (as well as the determination whether this *is* so) are presumably matters for the empirical sciences. And nothing here need be conceptually related to the nature of normative truths and facts. The relation to motivations and feelings may be merely a (perhaps psychologic-ally necessary, but conceptually and metaphysically contingent) enabling condition for normative discourse and practice.

Lewis, though, clearly wants more; Lewis wants a *conceptual* reason why valuing must be a positive attitude. Now, we should take care not to let Lewis's point gain plausibility because of its problematic use of the word "valuing". Valuing, after all, may be thought of as tantamount to believing-of-value. But it needn't be thought of in this way, and may in fact be thought of as already incorporating a motivational element.[87] Our question is whether there should be a conceptual reason why judging-of-value is a positive attitude (and similarly for other normative or evaluative concepts).

Once again, though, we need to be careful about the normative–motivational distinction. For what does "positive attitude" come to in this context? If it is something normative – so that a positive attitude towards something amounts, roughly, to a belief that it is good, or ought to be done, or some such – then *of course* (positive) normative beliefs are positive attitudes, and *of course* there's a conceptual reason for that – namely, their normative content is of this positive type. But if "positive attitude" is supposed to be understood motivationally (or in some other way essentially involving our

---

[86] I think – but I'm not sure – that this point suffices as a reply to the worry Greenspan (1998) mentions.
[87] For the distinction between valuing (a conative attitude) and judging valuable (arguably a cognitive attitude, as Lewis too will agree) see Svavarsdóttir (2009, 302, and the references at 318 n. 7).

responses), then we should simply reject the need for a conceptual reason to account for the relation between (for instance) judging of value and having a positive attitude. Of course, there may be *empirical* relations at work here, perhaps even nomically necessary ones. Perhaps, for instance, there can be no recognizably human community without such relations. And perhaps, given what we know about humans, there is an important sense in which our understanding of cases where positive motivational attitudes are not in line with normative judgments must be parasitic on our understanding of cases in which the relation between normative judgment and motivation is stronger. But these are not conceptually necessary relations between normative judgment and motivation – not even on the global level – and so they are explainable consistently with Robust Realism.

9.4.4 φ-ing because one believes one ought to

But there is another common intuition that threatens to push us in internalist directions, and it's one that often comes from the friends of realism, not its foes. This is the thought that it must be at least sometimes sufficient – in order to explain an agent's action – to cite her relevant normative belief or judgment, that at least sometimes no extra desire (or whatever) is needed for the relevant explanation of action. The thought seems to be that "it would be a hollow victory for the realist to get objectivity without motivational effect",[88] with the "motivational effect" here understood as sufficiency as an explanation of action. Can this intuition be made compatible with Robust Realism? Let me make the following points.

First, I'm not sure about this intuition. If we're trying to understand why someone strongly cares about a certain child's well-being, is it sufficient by way of explanation to cite the fact that that person is the child's parent? The answer is not clear, because the idea of sufficiency for explanation is not clear. We may fill in the details here in a way that will make "yes" the right answer to my question. On other ways of understanding this sufficiency, a "no" would presumably be more appropriate. If we answer "yes" this must be because we are willing to take for granted certain (conceptually contingent) fairly strong empirical regularities as the background for further explanations, against which all that needs to be cited to explain the relevant phenomenon is the fact that the relevant person is the relevant child's parent. But if this is so, then given the results of section 9.4.2, we should be able to say something precisely analogous about citing normative beliefs as sufficient explanation for action (against a certain empirically rich background). If, on the other hand, we answer "no" (so that "he's his father" is not a sufficient explanation of why he cares rather strongly for the child's well-being), then I do not see why we should think about the purported insufficiency of normative beliefs in explaining actions as at all a price. I am happy to tie the respectability of

---

[88] I heard Tom Nagel make this point in a seminar several years ago. For similar claims, see Rawls (2000, 255), Scanlon (1998, 33–4).

explanations of actions in terms of normative beliefs to that of "he's the child's father" as explaining why he cares for him.

Second, our context is where discussions in the theory of motivation are going to be most clearly relevant. In particular, if sometimes beliefs (for instance, normative ones) can themselves motivate without the aid of independent desires, then there is no general difficulty in normative beliefs' (even robustly realistically understood) being sufficient for the explanation of action. As promised, I am not going to engage these discussions here. But I want to note that if the anti-Humeans win this battle, then this would open the door for another way of reconciling Robust Realism with the thought that a normative belief can suffice as an explanation of action.

Third, let us again draw on the resources now – after the discussion in section 9.1 – available to us. Robust Realism, we already know, is consistent with action on a (specific) reason, and with the thought that so acting amounts to responding both to the relevant reason and to it being a reason. When A φ-s for R, A's φ-ing is caused in an appropriate way by A's belief that R is a reason for her to φ. In such cases, at least one natural way of describing the situation would be that A φ-s because she believes she has a reason to φ. And this now starts to sound awfully like explaining A's φ-ing (merely?) by reference to a normative belief.[89] I don't know whether this will completely satisfy those who feel the force of the intuition I started this sub-section with. But it cannot seriously be denied, I think, that it goes some way towards accommodating this intuition.

9.5 Existence-internalism

Existence-internalists believe that there is a necessary connection between the relevant normative judgments that apply to one and one's desires, or motivating states, or motivational set, or some such. As an example – a rather influential one, of course – we can take Bernard Williams's (1980) suggestion that one has a reason[90] to φ (perhaps if and anyway) only if there is a sound deliberative route from one's actual "motivational set" to one's φ-ing, where one's motivational set consists of some of one's psychological states (say, one's desires, with this word rather broadly understood), and where a sound deliberative route consists of the elimination of false factual beliefs, perhaps the introduction of some true (perfectly factual) beliefs, some exercises of the imagination, and that's pretty much it.[91] Typically, though, existence-internalists want much more than merely this necessary connection. Typically they also think of the normative

---

[89] This is especially clear with Broome's (1997, 139) way of putting the Nagel-intuition I started this section with: " . . . for reason to be practical, it must be *possible* for people to do what they believe they ought to do because they believe they ought to do it".

[90] Officially, this is what Williams says about *internal* reasons, but because he believes there are no external reasons, the formulation in the text is close enough.

[91] In the terms Parfit (1997, 101; 2011, vol. 1, ch. 3) introduces, a sound deliberative route may include improvements in procedural but not in substantive rationality.

truths that apply to one as somehow *grounded* in, or *explained* by, or *made true* by the relevant parts of one's psychology.[92] Here too, of course, there is room in logical space for a tracking internalism of sorts, but here too a robust realist will be well advised not to take that route. When arguing against existence-internalism below, I will be arguing against this necessary connection, regardless of what on top of it existence-internalists typically want.

Existence-internalism too comes in a variety of strengths. Thus, we can imagine a Really Strong Existence-Internalism, according to which (for instance) one has reason to φ only if one wants to φ. But no one, as far as I know, holds such a view. And so mitigated existence-internalist views can utilize any number of mitigating devices. Thus, they can employ some idealization, insisting that what is necessary for having a reason to φ is not that the agent wants or be motivated to φ, but rather that she *would* want or be motivated to φ if idealized in some suitable way. Of course, this existence-internalist then owes us an account of the relevant idealization, and there may be problems in filling in the details here. For reasons that are by now familiar to us, if the idealization or hypotheticalization is specified in normative terms ("insofar as she's rational", say), it will be hard to see the externalist thesis as anything but a substantive, intra-normative thesis which robust realists should in principle have no problem with.[93] And if the idealization is specified in non-normative terms (as perhaps in Williams[94]), then other problems arise. First, typically counterexamples are rather easy to come by (more on this shortly). And second, the idealization then seems suspiciously ad hoc, as an attempt to block counterexamples rather than as a part of a unified theory motivated by the relevant underlying rationales. I am not going to pursue this second difficulty here – I do it at some length elsewhere.[95] Let me just note here, then, that there is this general worry, but also that the extent to which it's a problem for the relevant existence-internalist view may differ according to its details.[96] Existence-internalists can mitigate their internalism in other, not-quite-idealizing ways as well. For instance, they can claim that the condition necessary (and perhaps also sufficient) for your having a reason to φ is not that you can be brought to φ somehow, but simply that φ-ing will promote the satisfaction of one of your desires (whether or not you understand, or even can understand, that this is so).[97] And there may be other ways of mitigating existence-internalism.

---

[92] Though see Dancy (2000, ch. 1) for the claim that existence-internalism must not be understood as necessarily committed to these further claims.

[93] For a related point made in the context of criticizing Korsgaard's internalism, see Shafer-Landau (2003, 172–4).

[94] See Williams (1989, 36) for an explicit acknowledgment of the need to avoid any normative terms in specifying the idealization.

[95] In "Why Idealize" (2005).

[96] For the claim that full-information idealizations can rather easily escape the Why-Idealize challenge, see Sobel (2009). For my attempt at a reply, see my "Idealizing Still Not Off the Hook" (manuscript).

[97] This suggestion is inspired by Schroeder's (2007) hypotheticalism.

Is existence-internalism – if true – a problem for Robust Realism? The answer depends on the details of the mitigating device employed by the existence-internalist. But I want to concede that if existence-internalism were true – and so long as the necessary mitigating device was not one that rendered such internalism trivial – this would indeed refute Robust Realism. For on Robust Realism normative truths are response-independent. But on existence-internalism normative truths are made true by the motivations or other psychological states of the agents to whom they apply. Or – if we go for the mere necessary relation understanding of existence-internalism – existence-internalism postulates a relation between normative truths and motivation of the kind that robust realists cannot possibly explain without resorting to a highly implausible tracking-internalism according to which our motivations miraculously line up with the normative judgments that apply to us (at least in the relevant idealized conditions). So it is clear how I must proceed – I must reject existence-internalism.[98]

The first step towards doing that is noting how bad existence-internalism is as a starting point. Some existence-internalists sometimes write as if existence-internalism is just *obvious*, a claim any reasonable thinker will immediately agree with, and so one that should be taken as a starting point in metanormative discussions.[99] But existence-internalism is a highly theory-laden, almost technical thesis. For this reason alone it is not a good candidate for the status of an intuitive starting point. That robust realists are committed to rejecting existence-internalism is no doubt an interesting fact about Robust Realism, and it may yet be a liability – but nothing here is obvious. Existence-internalism is badly in need of argumentative support (more on which shortly).

The problem is exacerbated by the fact that existence-internalism is prima facie vulnerable to rather obvious – and extremely strong – counterexamples.[100] Thus, and again assuming that the relevant mitigating device is not one that renders the relevant existence-internalist theory trivial, we can always describe a Sufficiently Bad Bad-Guy[101] in whose motivational set (or some such) there is just no ground for some normative judgments that – as pre-theoretically we would insist rather uncompromisingly – apply to him. If, for instance, Sufficiently Bad Bad-Guy doesn't care at all about Victim's well-being, and if there is nothing qualifying as sound deliberative route that can lead him to care about Victim's well-being or in some other way to avoid hurting her, then Sufficiently Bad Bad-Guy has – Williams is committed to saying – no reason not to hurt Victim. And assuming some rather close connections between moral

---

[98] The strategy of what follows resembles that of Shafer-Landau (2003, ch. 8) – he too emphasizes the intuitive plausibility of existence-externalism, and rejects the (four) arguments for internalism he can think of. But there are many differences in details here, mostly because of the way in which what I end up saying in rejecting arguments for internalism will depend on results achieved previously in this chapter and in previous chapters.

[99] Cullity and Gaut (1997, 3). And see Korsgaard (2008, 209 n. 2) for the claim that something very close to existence-internalism is "of course tautological".

[100] Here and in what follows I focus on prima facie counterexamples in just one direction – examples where it seems to us that there are reasons, but the existence-internalist is committed to denying that claim.

[101] See, for instance, Shafer-Landau (2003, 187–8).

judgments and reason-judgments (perhaps of the kind argued for in Chapter 4, section 4.3), it would also follow that it's not the case that Sufficiently Bad Bad-Guy ought not to hurt Victim, or that it's wrong for him to hurt her, and so on. Now, I want to keep as open a mind as I can, and so I am willing to accept the possibility that a thesis with such surprising results may yet be true (although you have to admit it loses significant plausibility points here, doesn't it?). But if nothing else, a theory that has such results cannot claim the status of an intuitively obvious starting point for philosophical discussion, or an adequacy constraint on theories of the normative.

Different existence-internalists respond to such counterexamples in different ways. Some respond with breathtaking bullet-biting, accepting the surprising results from the previous paragraph.[102] I find it hard to take such a response seriously, especially when made in the kind of intonation that suggests that there's something obvious about existence-internalism. For which are you pre-theoretically more confident in – something along the lines of existence-internalism, or that Sufficiently Bad Bad-Guy has a reason not to hurt Victim? If we are to take seriously this way of responding to the obvious counterexamples, then, some rather strong argument for existence-internalism must be presented.

Other – perhaps more intellectually honest – existence-internalists acknowledge that the bullet that would have to be bitten here is just too much to stomach, and so they try to show that their existence-internalism does not commit them to these problematic results. The main – Kantian – way of doing this is by insisting that some motivations or desires are constitutive of agency, so that there can be no agent who lacks it; and then reasons that are grounded in *these* desires can be both "internal" and universal or objective.[103] There is now in the literature[104] also another way for existence-internalism to resist such counterexamples: it may be argued that even though there are no desires that are constitutive of agency, still quite universal reasons can be grounded in contingent desires, though perhaps in different desires in different cases. If there are some actions, for instance, that promote satisfaction of your desires *whatever your desires may be*, there can be a reason for you and for everyone else to perform such actions that is still necessarily connected to and grounded in a desire (though perhaps different desires in different cases).

I don't know of a quick way of dismissing such ways of defending existence-internalism against counterexamples. The thing to do here, it seems, is to carefully engage the details of the relevant theories (in the case of the constitutivist, Kantian strategy, there are many different variants of this strategy – so even more work needs to

---

[102] I used Sufficiently Bad Bad-Guy rather than the obvious Hitler example because I accept the rule that the first one to mention the Nazis loses the argument. But it's OK – Harman used it first. For Harman's famous bullet-biting (regarding the Hitler example), see Harman (1977, 107).

[103] For the worry that existence-internalism may lead to something like the counterexamples in the text as an explicit motivation for going constitutivist (the motivation I called in "Agency, Shmagency" (2006) "quasi-externalism"), see Velleman (1996).

[104] Schroeder (2007).

be done). For reasons that I cannot elaborate on here (I have offered detailed argumentation against constitutivism and against Schroeder's version of Humeanism elsewhere,[105] I am not optimistic about the prospects of any of these projects. Here I just want to note two points, then. First, if any of these strategies succeeds, then existence-internalism (perhaps of some specific kind) can avoid the problematic results in the Sufficiently Bad Bad-Guy and related cases. And second, even if this is so, we have still not been given a reason to believe existence-internalism. All we have (so far) is a way of dealing with an initially strong objection to it. But this still doesn't suffice to vindicate existence-internalism, much less to vindicate its status as an adequacy constraint on metanormative theories, or an intuitive starting point for the debate.[106]

Either way, then – whether existence-internalists bite the bullet on the Sufficiently Bad Bad-Guy counterexample or attempt to resist it – existence-internalism is badly in need of argumentative support (and notice that in supporting this claim I have not relied in any way on Robust Realism). And some such arguments can indeed be found in the literature.[107] But we are now in a position to reject at least some of them rather quickly. (See? The hard work of previous chapters and sections pays off.)

Thus, Williams (1981, 109–10; 1989, 39) sometimes writes as if there is nothing that a claim about reasons could even mean or be about if it didn't mean something about internal reasons, that is, somewhat roughly, reasons that satisfy existence-internalism. But of course, there *is* something such a claim can mean or be about. It can be a normative claim. Paraphrasing Bishop Butler, it can mean and be precisely what it means, and not some other thing.[108] And Williams's refusal to consider this a serious option amounts to nothing more than the Sheer Queerness worry, which I've rejected in Chapter 6 (section 6.1).[109]

[105] In "Agency, Shmagency" (2006) and "On Mark Schroeder's Hypotheticalism" (forthcoming).

[106] But this doesn't mean that the people employing these strategies do not have more to say by way of vindication here. Thus, if I understand correctly Velleman's (2009, 135–46) response to my Shmagency challenge, it comes down to an insistence on the holistic value of his theory, on all of the phenomena it nicely explains. In our context, we can think of this as the claim that the reason to believe existence-internalism is that it is entailed by a theory which delivers much by way of explanatory payoff. For my attempt at a reply, see my "Shmagency Revisited" (2010b), especially sections 7–8. And Mark Schroeder explicitly rejects existence-internalism (or "the classical argument" supposedly supporting it) as acceptable starting points. He starts from different, much simpler and less theory-laden starting points, eventually *ending up* with a theory that is also existence-internalist. So the only way of rejecting his way of motivating existence-internalism, as far as I can see, is to engage his theory in detail and find it wanting. Again see my "On Mark Schroeder's Hypotheticalism" (forthcoming).

[107] Darwall (1995, 12) complains that there is little by way of argument either for or against existence-internalism. I think he's right that many here are willing to take internalism (or its denial) for granted, but I think it is no longer true to say that there are no relevant arguments (on either side) in the literature. For helpful surveys of arguments here see Rosati (1996), Shafer-Landau (2003, ch. 8), and Heathwood (forthcoming).

[108] Parfit (1997, 111 and on) insists on this point against Williams, as does Fitzpatrick (2004, 301–2).

[109] See Parfit (1997, 121) for a related point.

Similarly, Darwall (1983, 55)[110] emphasizes the metaphysically naturalist motivation for existence-internalism. Assuming a naturalist metaphysics, what else could normativity come to if it's not something about agents' motivations? But this way of arguing for existence-internalism is in our context problematic, not just because of its problematic argument-form,[111] but mainly because given the metaphysical picture defended in Chapters 5–6 (and motivated by the chapters preceding them), that Robust Realism is inconsistent with a thesis perhaps motivated by metaphysical naturalism is not a further dialectical price.

And sometimes (e.g. Darwall (1995, 11)) something like existence-internalism is supposed to be motivated by thoughts about practicality and bindingness on one's will. But given the discussion of section 9.2, we already know better than to let this kind of rhetoric blur the normative–motivating distinction.[112]

Perhaps the best-known argument for existence-internalism (about reasons) is another argument coming from Williams (1980). According to this argument, for it to be the case that an agent A has a reason R to ϕ it must be possible for A to ϕ for R; for that, it must be possible for R to explain why A ϕ-ed (if she ϕ-ed); but the only things that can explain actions are the motivating states of the agent (like perhaps her desires); so reasons must be grounded in the motivating states of the agent whose reasons they are. My way of rejecting this argument[113] should come as no surprise to you, given the discussion in section 9.1. I agree (for the sake of argument, at least) that for it to be the case that R is a reason for A to ϕ it must be possible for A to ϕ for R. But I disagree with the transition from this to the claim that it must be possible for R to explain why A ϕ-ed (if she did). For it to be the case that it is possible for A to ϕ for R, it's sufficient that A's *belief* that R is a reason for her to ϕ played an appropriate causal role in bringing her to ϕ-ing.[114]

These, I think, are the main lines of thought in the literature that are supposed to convince us to endorse existence-internalism. But they are quite unconvincing, certainly if they are supposed to be understood (as they have to be in our context) as the first step in what is ultimately to be an objection to Robust Realism. One can find in the literature some other considerations that are supposed to motivate existence-

[110] See also Darwall (1995, 14) and the historical references there; and Rosati (1996, 313–14).

[111] It has the same form as the proof-that-*p* attributed to Sydney Morgenbesser: "If not *p*, what? *q*, maybe?" See http://consc.net/misc/proofs.html

[112] Here also sometimes claims are being made about autonomy and its relation to existence-internalism (for instance, see Darwall (1995, 16–17), and Rosati (1996, 322)). Needless to say, far from being a plausible premise on which to ground existence-internalism, such claims about autonomy themselves are highly problematic and desperately in need of argumentative support.

[113] It is equally, I think, a way of rejecting Darwall's (1983, ch. 3) improved version thereof.

[114] Alternatively, if we're going to be a little looser in our use of the word "explanation", the classical argument can be seen to equivocate: there is *a* sense of "explanation" in which action for a reason requires that the reason play an explanatory role in bringing about the action, and there is (perhaps) *a* sense of "explanation" in which the only things that can explain an agent's actions are his psychological states, but there is no *one* sense of "explanation" that renders both these judgments true.

internalism – I very briefly discuss some in a lengthy footnote[115] – but they too, as far as I can see, cannot succeed. And so existence-internalism remains pretty much a dogma, one that robust realists should indeed reject, but the rejection of which does not amount to a price at all.

This has been a terribly long chapter. So it may not be redundant to offer a bird's eye view of what has been, I hope, achieved. The worry was that Robust Realism cannot respect some plausible relations between normativity and motivation. But I have argued that Robust Realism can accommodate action for a specific reason – and a good thing, too, because had it not been able to accommodate that, this *would* have been a devastating blow to Robust Realism. I then argued that thoughts about the practicality of (practical) normative judgments cannot justify any stronger relation between normativity and motivation than the one that Robust Realism accommodates by accommodating action for specific reasons. If the challenge is put in terms of a why-be-moral or perhaps why-do-what-I-have-reason-to-do question, then it is importantly ambiguous: it can represent a legitimate intra-normative challenge to morality, one about which Robust Realism remains largely silent (as it should); or it may represent a request for an incentive or some other way of motivating the moral or rational skeptic, in which case Robust Realism has no reply, just like any other metanormative view (this is where it's important to remember that philosophy cannot replace the hangman); or it may be understood as conceptually confused. So there is no real challenge to Robust Realism in the vicinity. Strong versions of judgment-internalism are indeed incompatible with Robust Realism, but they are implausible and ought to be rejected on independent grounds. Weaker versions of judgment-internalism may indeed have some plausibility to them, but they are not ones robust realists are committed to denying. And existence-internalism – which is indeed, in

---

[115] Thus, if we restrict our attention to just judgments about personal good (what is good for a person), Railton (1986b, 9) emphasizes the thought that one's good must be made for one, and Velleman (1998) introduces an ought-implies-can argument, according to which one ought to care about one's good, so it must be possible for one to care about one's good, so it must be possible (roughly speaking) for one to be motivated by one's good. I am not sure about any of these two ways of motivating existence-internalism, but for my purposes here suffice it to say that even if they succeed, they establish at most (as both these writers acknowledge) internalism only about a person's good, not about oughts, or reasons, or the right. So perhaps the best way to explain the phenomena here is not by endorsing some metanormative internalism, but rather some relevant intra-normative claim. (For a survey of arguments for existence-internalism about personal good that develop Railton's intuition here, see Rosati (1996).)

Sometimes existence-internalism is supported by an inference to the best explanation, either from the correlation between people's motivations and the reasons that apply to them (perhaps this is what Darwall (1983, 56–7) has in mind), or from judgment-internalism (Rosati (1996, 310–11)). But in both cases the relevant explanandum can be doubted (in the case of judgment-internalism, it *has* been doubted in section 9.4 above; see here also Parfit (1997, 114); but note that Rosati offers a more general version of the argument that doesn't depend on the truth of judgment-internalism), and attractive alternative explanations can be thought of.

There is also Williams's (1980, 105–6) "brow-beating" argument, attempting to support existence-internalism by noting the (supposed) inappropriateness of certain accusations or pronouncements. But as Shafer-Landau (2003, 176–8) notes, this argument seems to conflate questions of the truth of a judgment with questions of the desirability of pronouncing it.

non-trivial versions, incompatible with Robust Realism – is implausible right off the bat, and the attempts to support it in the literature do not succeed (though let me remind you that for this claim to be fully vindicated, we need also a refutation of some competing theories (like Velleman's and Schroeder's) that may be represented as yielding existence-internalism as a conclusion, not relying on it as a premise).

As far as I can see, then, Robust Realism doesn't lose significant plausibility points on account of thoughts about motivation. Indeed, here I am willing to stake out a stronger claim: nothing about the relation between normativity and motivation ends up costing Robust Realism any plausibility points at all.

10

Tallying Plausibility Points

This concludes, then, my defense of Robust Realism. As you may recall, it consists neither of a conclusive proof of Robust Realism, nor of a set of knock-down arguments against all competing views. Rather, it consists, first, of placing the concerns that motivate Robust Realism in clear view and attempting to generate reasonably precise positive arguments for Robust Realism that are sensitive to these concerns, and second, in responding to objections to Robust Realism, showing that none of them is as devastating as some of those rejecting Robust Realism (and related views) seem to think.

In the metaphorical terms I've been using throughout this book, my case for Robust Realism consists in showing where it gains plausibility points, and in showing that it doesn't lose too many plausibility points elsewhere. But the plausibility-points game is comparative: the view that we should endorse is the one that has – when all considerations are taken into account – the most plausibility points overall. And this means that even if you think that my reply to one of the objections leaves something to be desired, you should still check to see whether your favorite view does better – both vis-à-vis that specific objection, and in general. So the remaining task is that of tallying and comparing plausibility points: We should, as it were, reach Robust Realism's final score, and compare it to that of all competing views.

I hope you will forgive me if I don't actually go through the comparative part of this task. I do acknowledge, though, that this is what the fate of Robust Realism ultimately depends on – we should endorse it as our view of morality and normativity if and only if its plausibility score is on the whole higher than that of any competing view. (How surprising is it that we should endorse the philosophical view that is overall most plausible?) What I will do here, though, is quickly to go through the results of the previous chapters, thus helping you reach an overall plausibility estimate for Robust Realism. I do not have a method I can offer you of tallying plausibility points (or, for that matter, of comparing the overall plausibility scores of competing theories), other than trying to keep all relevant considerations clearly in mind, and asking oneself how plausible the whole story is (or which story is on the whole more plausible). You already know where I stand on this – after all, this book is a defense of Robust Realism. But let me briefly run through the considerations discussed in this book, and how I think they bear on the plausibility of Robust Realism – I hope this will make it easier for you to reach an on-the-whole-plausibility judgment, maybe even such a judgment that is somewhat similar to mine.

268 TALLYING PLAUSIBILITY POINTS

The main underlying motivation for Robust Realism was the need to take morality – and to an extent, normativity in general – seriously. I tried to present arguments that precisify this slogan in the earlier chapters of the book.[1]

Thus, I argued (in Chapter 2) that non-objectivist views of morality imply – together with IMPARTIALITY, a plausible moral principle – unacceptable moral judgments in cases of interpersonal disagreement and conflict. There is, I conceded there, a way for such views to avoid such unacceptable results: they can declare – by fiat, as it were – that the responses that constitute moral judgment are different in the relevant ways from other ones, the ones to which IMPARTIALITY applies. But the objectivist has more to say here, she has a more satisfying explanation of the distinction between cases in which something like IMPARTIALITY applies and cases in which this is not the case. So Robust Realism – together with other objectivist views of morality – earns here plausibility points compared to the competition.

In Chapter 3 I argued that normative truths are indispensable for deliberation, and that such indispensability suffices to justify the kind of ontological commitment that is part of Robust Realism. Establishing this result required a general epistemological detour about the justification of basic belief-forming methods, a phenomenological discussion of deliberation, and a discussion of the nature of indispensability and indispensability arguments. Given the results of all of these, if normative truths are indispensable for deliberation, this suffices, so I've argued, to justify belief in them. Now, perhaps other views can – to an extent – accommodate deliberation. But they do so far less naturally than Robust Realism does. Here too, then, Robust Realism earns plausibility points.

In Chapter 4 I argued that if you're already an objectivist about morality (perhaps under the pressure of Chapter 2), and a robust realist about normativity (perhaps under the pressure of Chapter 3), then even though you are not forced on pain of inconsistency to endorse Metaethical Robust Realism, still it's hard to see why you would rationally stop short of so doing. And in Chapter 5 I argued that there is no way of getting all we want from Robust Realism for a cheaper metaphysical price, by going reductionist, fictionalist, or quietist, or by endorsing an error theory. I hope that the combined strength of Chapters 2–5 suffices to establish a considerable advantage in plausibility points for Robust Realism.

From that point on the project turned defensive. In Chapter 6 I conceded that Robust Realism has anti-naturalist metaphysical implications, and proceeded to defend them, partly relying on the positive arguments of previous chapters. I argued that the Sheer Queerness worry can be rather quickly dismissed[2] (especially given the argument

---

[1] Pre-theoretically, I think that there is a sense in which taking morality seriously seems appropriate, but taking aesthetics seriously does not. And I think it's a virtue of my attempts at precisifying the taking-morality-seriously thought that they do not (I am here merely asserting) straightforwardly apply to aesthetics.

[2] I also suggested that one charitable reading of the queerness worry is not as an independent argument, but rather as a summary of other arguments – the claim, roughly, that the theoretical benefits of Robust Realism do not outweigh its costs. This is a legitimate worry, of course. And it is precisely the job of this chapter to address it, or indeed to show how this book addresses it.

of Chapter 3), and tried to respond to more focused metaphysical worries (having to do with the supervenience of the normative).

In Chapter 7 I dismissed as at the very least theoretically unhelpful several common ways of understanding "the" epistemological challenge to Robust Realism (and related views), and proceeded to present what I take to be the most important challenge here – namely, the need to explain, consistently with Robust Realism, at least some correlation between the normative truths and our normative judgment. I then suggested a moderately speculative explanation of the correlation, utilizing a small remaining miracle and a Godless pre-established-harmony mechanism. This, I argued, together with the arguably positive effect of subjecting our normative starting points to reflection and discussion, suffices in order to explain the limited correlation we do in fact observe (and cannot deny on pain of skepticism) between our normative judgments and the normative truths. In a final section I addressed – in an unsatisfyingly preliminary way – the worry that robust realists have no way of explaining, even in the broadest of outlines, the semantic access we presumably have to the normative properties they are robust realists about. But I hope I said enough to show that there is reason for cautious optimism here too.

Chapter 8 – the most disjunctive one in this book – surveys different ways in which moral and more broadly normative disagreement may be thought to pose a problem for Robust Realism, concluding that some of them are downright confused, that others serve to highlight problems or initial challenges discussed elsewhere in this book, and that in dealing with yet others Robust Realism does lose some – but not too many – plausibility points.

Chapter 9 was a long discussion of the relations between normativity and motivation, and the way in which thinking about such relations may be thought to highlight some problems for Robust Realism. In the positive part of this chapter, I presented (somewhat tentatively) an analysis of action for a (specific) reason, and showed that Robust Realism can easily accommodate such action. In the negative parts of the chapter I showed how – especially given this result – nothing at all plausible remains of the attempts to criticize Robust Realism along such motivation-related lines. Here, I insisted, Robust Realism does not lose any plausibility points.

If I am right, then, Robust Realism loses some plausibility points on account of not being metaphysically naturalist, but not too many (the loss here is similar to the loss in plausibility points of any theory that requires new ontological commitments – other things being equal, we should prefer a theory that doesn't require new ontological commitments, but other things are rarely equal). Depending on the size of the remaining miracle mentioned in Chapter 7, Robust Realism may lose some plausibility points there too, but again, not too many. There is a *very* mild loss of plausibility points that comes from thoughts about apparently rationally irresolvable disagreement (simply because Robust Realism incurs here an explanatory task that competing views do not have to address), and hardly any loss when it comes to thoughts about motivation.

Philosophers (myself included, I'm sure) often write with a confident tone that they themselves will acknowledge (perhaps in a quieter, more reflective, and perhaps more private moment) is not in place. Philosophy is hard, philosophical disagreement is everywhere, and for just about every claim I put forward in this book, there will be excellent philosophers who will reject it. So strong confidence in the truth of one's philosophical theories cannot be warranted. In fact, often a writer knows better than all others what the weaker points in his or her arguments are. We are all disposed (when defending a paper, say) to hide these weaknesses, and highlight the strengths of our views. But it is a disposition that I think we should resist. So, in order not to display more confidence than is genuine and warranted here, and in the spirit of a collaborative attempt to arrive at the relevant truths,[3] let me quickly state the points in the discussion of which I am least confident:

- I am somewhat worried about IMPARTIALITY (in Chapter 2): I am pretty confident there is something important and true in its vicinity, but I am not sure how precisely to capture it. (But I am reasonably confident that there is a distinction relevant to the truth in the vicinity of IMPARTIALITY between mere preferences and moral judgments, and it was this distinction that the argument of Chapter 2 relied on.)
- I am reasonably confident that the subjectivist reply to the argument from IMPARTIALITY – in terms of a normative distinction between preferences (and the like) to which IMPARTIALITY applies and those to which it doesn't apply – costs the subjectivist plausibility points. But I am not as confident that it costs the subjectivist *sufficiently many* plausibility points.
- I am not confident regarding the general epistemic story in section 3.4, on which (to an extent) the indispensability argument for Robust Realism relies. (But I am reasonably confident in the following conditional: If IBE can justify ontological commitment, so can arguments from deliberative indispensability.)
- I would like to have more to say by way of a general criticism of objectivist naturalist reductions. And while I am reasonably confident in the denial of such reductions (this is just a restatement of the just-too-different intuition from Chapter 5), I am not as confident that no such reduction can be close enough to what we want, in a way that could justify the kind of gentle revision that we would not be inclined to view as an error theory.[4]
- I am not sure how significant the explanatory burden is that robust realists incur because of the need (mentioned at the conclusion of section 8.7) to explain apparently rationally irresolvable disagreement.

---

[3] I am being sincere here. I hope the response this will give rise to is not the one Parfit (2011, vol. 1, xxxix) brings from James: "Sidgwick displayed that reflective candour that can at times be so irritating. A man has no right to be so fair to his opponents."
[4] This is the kind of revision David Lewis (1989, 93) presumably has in mind when he writes: "Shock horror: no such thing as simultaneity! Nobody ever whistled while he worked!"

- I am not as confident as I would like to be in the analysis of action for a specific reason in section 9.1.2 (I feel especially vulnerable to the unwilling-alcoholic example I discuss there). But I am reasonably confident that the conditions there specified are at least *sufficient* for action for a specific reason, and this suffices for the rest of the argument to go through, I think.
- Needless to say, I am not confident about the sketchy discussion of semantic access in section 7.6.

In most of these points I am not confessing some specific argumentative weaknesses I am aware of. I am just letting you know what points I am less confident in, thereby inviting you to focus your critical attention on these points.

Nevertheless, when I look at the project as a whole, I find myself reasonably confident in it and its conclusion. Perhaps somewhat paradoxically, I find myself more confident in the general picture than in some of its details. Trying to tally plausibility points, then, I find myself thinking that Robust Realism does pretty well, better, in fact, than competing views. Don't you?

References

Attfield, R. (1979) "How not to be a Moral Relativist," *The Monist* 62, 510–23.

Audi, R. (1995) "Intuitionism, Pluralism, and the Foundations of Ethics," in W. Sinnott-Armstrong and M. Timmons (eds.), *Moral Knowledge? New Readings in Moral Epistemology* (Oxford and New York: Oxford University Press), 101–36; reprinted in Audi (1997), 32–65.

—— (1997) *Moral Knowledge and Ethical Character* (Oxford: Oxford University Press).

Ayer, A. J. (1946) *Language, Truth and Logic*, 2nd ed. (London: Victor Gollancz).

Baker, A. (2004) "Simplicity," in *The Stanford Encyclopedia of Philosophy*, http://plato.stanford.edu/entries/simplicity/index.html#note-6

Bedke, M. S. (2009) "Intuitive Non-Naturalism Meets Cosmic Coincidence," *Pacific Philosophical Quarterly* 90, 188–209.

Bennigson, T. (1996) "Irresolvable Disagreement and the Case against Moral Realism," *Southern Journal of Philosophy* 34, 411–37.

Blackburn, S. (1973) "Moral Realism," in J. Casey (ed.), *Morality and Moral Reasoning* (London: Methuen); reprinted in Blackburn (1993), 111–29.

—— (1981) "Reply: Rule-Following and Moral Realism," in S. H. Holtzman and C. M. Leich (eds.), *Wittgenstein: To Follow a Rule* (London: Routledge & Kegan Paul), 163–87.

—— (1985) "Supervenience Revisited," in I. Hacking (ed.), *Exercises in Analysis* (Cambridge: Cambridge University Press); reprinted in Blackburn (1993), 130–48.

—— (1988) "How to be an Ethical Antirealist," *Midwest Studies in Philosophy* 12, 361–75; reprinted in Blackburn (1993), 166–81.

—— (1991a) "Just Causes," *Philosophical Studies* 61, 3–17.

—— (1991b) "Reply to Sturgeon," *Philosophical Studies* 61, 39–42.

—— (1993) *Essays in Quasi-Realism* (Oxford: Oxford University Press).

—— (1995) "Securing the Nots: Moral Epistemology for the Quasi-Realist," in W. Sinnott-Armstrong and M. Timmons (eds.), *Moral Knowledge? New Readings in Moral Epistemology* (Oxford and New York: Oxford University Press), 82–100.

—— (1998) "Moral Relativism and Moral Objectivity," *Philosophy and Phenomenological Research* 58, 195–8.

—— (1999) "Is Objective Moral Justification Possible on a Quasi-realist Foundation?," *Inquiry* 42, 213–27.

Block, N. (1998) "Conceptual Role Semantics," in E. Craig (ed.), *The Routledge Encyclopedia of Philosophy* (London: Routledge).

Bloomfield, P. (2001) *Moral Reality* (Oxford and New York: Oxford University Press).

—— (2003) "Is There Moral High Ground?," *Southern Journal of Philosophy* 41, 511–26.

—— (2009) "Archimedeanism and Why Metaethics Matters," *Oxford Studies in Metaethics* 4, 283–302.

Boghossian, P. (1989) "The Rule Following Considerations," *Mind* 98, 507–49.

—— (2000) "Knowledge of Logic," in P. Boghossian and C. Peacocke (eds.), *New Essays on the Apriori* (Oxford: Clarendon Press), 229–54.

Bond, E. J. (1983) *Reason and Value* (Cambridge: Cambridge University Press).

Bonjour, L. (1988) *In Defense of Pure Reason* (Cambridge: Cambridge University Press).

Boyd, R. N. (1988) "How to Be a Moral Realist," in G. Sayre-McCord (ed.), *Essays on Moral Realism* (Ithaca and London: Cornell University Press), 181–228.

Brandt, R. (1944) "The Significance of Differences of Ethical Opinion for Ethical Rationalism," *Philosophy and Phenomenological Research* 4, 469–95.

Brink, D. O. (1989) *Moral Realism and the Foundations of Ethics* (Cambridge and New York: Cambridge University Press).

—— (1997a) "Kantian Rationalism: Inescapability, Authority, and Supremacy," in G. Cullity and B. Gaut (eds.), *Ethics and Practical Reason* (Oxford: Clarendon Press), 255–91.

—— (1997b) "Moral Motivation," *Ethics* 108, 4–32.

—— (2001) "Realism, Naturalism, and Moral Semantics," *Social Philosophy and Policy* 18(2), 154–76.

Broome, J. (1997) "Reason and Motivation," *Proceedings of the Aristotelian Society* (Supp.) 71, 131–46.

—— (2007) "Wide or Narrow Scope?," *Mind* 116, 359–70.

Brown, C. (forthcoming) "A New and Improved Supervenience Argument for Ethical Descriptivism," *Oxford Studies in Metaethics* 6.

Burgess, J. (2007) "Against Ethics," *Ethical Theory and Moral Practice* 10, 427–39.

Burgess, J. and G. Rosen (1997) *A Subject With No Object* (Oxford: Clarendon Press).

Carnap, R. (1956) "Empiricism, Semantics, and Ontology," in his *Meaning and Necessity*, 2nd ed. (Chicago: University of Chicago Press), 205–21; reprinted in P. Benacerraf and H. Putnam (eds.), *Philosophy of Mathematics: Selected Readings* (2nd ed.) (Cambridge: Cambridge University Press, 1983), 241–57.

Carroll, L. (1895) "What the Tortoise Said to Achilles," *Mind* 4, no. 14 (April), 278–80.

Cassam, Q. (1986) "Necessity and Externality," *Mind* 95, 446–64.

Chang, R. (1997) "Introduction," in Chang (ed.), *Incommensurability, Incomparability, and Practical Reason* (Cambridge, Mass.: Harvard University Press), 1–34.

Cohen, S. (2002) "Basic Knowledge and the Problem of Easy Knowledge," *Philosophy and Phenomenological Research* 65, 309–28.

Colyvan, M. (2001) *The Indispensability of Mathematics* (Oxford: Oxford University Press).

Copp, D. (1990) "Explanation and Justification in Ethics," *Ethics* 100, 237–58.

—— (1997) "Belief, Reason and Motivation: Michael Smith's *The Moral Problem*," *Ethics* 108, 33–54.

—— (2001) "Realist Expressivism: A Neglected Option for Moral Realism," *Social Philosophy and Policy* 18(2), 1–43.

—— (2003) "Why Naturalism?," *Ethical Theory and Moral Practice* 6, 179–200.

—— (2006) "Introduction: Metaethics and Normative Ethics," in D. Copp (ed.), *The Oxford Handbook of Ethical Theory* (Oxford and New York: Oxford University Press), 3–35.

—— (2008a) "Do We Have Any Justified Moral Beliefs?," *Philosophy and Phenomenological Research* 77(3), 811–19.

—— (2008b) "Darwinian Skepticism about Moral Realism," *Philosophical Issues* 18(1), 186–206.

Crimmins, M. (1992) "Tacitness and Virtual Beliefs," *Mind and Language* 7, 240–63.

Cullity, G. and B. Gaut (1997) "Introduction," in Cullity and Gaut (eds.), *Ethics and Practical Reason* (Oxford: Clarendon Press), 1–28.

Cuneo, T. (2007a) *The Normative Web: An Argument for Moral Realism* (Oxford: Oxford University Press).

—— (2007b) "Recent Faces of Moral Nonnaturalism," *Philosophy Compass* 2(6), 850–79.

Cuneo, T. and S. Christy (2010) "The Myth of Moral Fictionalism," in M. Brady (ed.), *New Waves in Metaethics* (Basingstoke: Palgrave Macmillan), 85–102.

Dancy, J. (1986) "Two Conceptions of Moral Realism," *Proceedings of the Aristotelian Society* (Supp.) 60, 167–88.

—— (1995) "Why There Is Really No Such Thing as the Theory of Motivation," *Proceedings of the Aristotelian Society* 95, 1–18.

—— (1996a) "Real Values in a Humean Context," *Ratio* 9, 171–83.

—— (1996b) "In Defence of Thick Concepts," *Midwest Studies in Philosophy* 20: *Moral Concepts*, 263–79.

—— (2000) *Practical Reality* (Oxford: Oxford University Press).

—— (2005) "Nonnaturalism," in David Copp (ed.), *The Oxford Handbook of Ethical Theory* (Oxford: Oxford University Press), 121–44.

Darwall, S. L. (1983) *Impartial Reason* (Ithaca and London: Cornell University Press).

—— (1992) "Internalism and Agency," *Philosophical Perspectives* 6: *Ethics*, 155–74.

—— (1995) *The British Moralists and the Internal "Ought"* (Cambridge: Cambridge University Press).

—— (1998) *Philosophical Ethics* (Oxford: Westview Press).

—— (2002) "Ethical Intuitionism and the Motivation Problem," in P. Stratton-Lake (ed.), *Ethical Intuitionism: Re-evaluations* (Oxford: Oxford University Press), 248–70.

Darwall, S. L., A. Gibbard, and P. Railton (1992), "Toward Fin De Siècle Ethics: Some Trends," *Philosophical Review* 101(1), 115–89; reprinted in Darwall, Gibbard, and Railton (eds.), *Moral Discourse and Practice* (Oxford and New York: Oxford University Press, 1997).

Donagan, A. (1981) "W. A. Frankena and G. E. Moore's Metaethics," *Monist* 64, 293–304.

Dorr, C. (2002) "Non-Cognitivism and Wishful Thinking," *Nous* 36(1), 97–103.

Dreier, J. (1992) "The Supervenience Argument against Moral Realism," *Southern Journal of Philosophy* 30, 13–38.

—— (2002) "Meta-Ethics and Normative Commitment," *Philosophical Issues* 12: *Realism and Relativism*, 241–63.

Dworkin, R. (1996) "Objectivity and Truth: You'd Better Believe It," *Philosophy and Public Affairs* 25, 87–139.

—— (forthcoming) *Justice for Hedgehogs*.

Eklund, M. (2007) "Fictionalism," in *The Stanford Encyclopedia of Philosophy*, available at http://plato.stanford.edu/entries/fictionalism/

Elster, J. (1983) *Sour Grapes* (Cambridge: Cambridge University Press).

Enoch, D. (2003a) "An Argument for Robust Metanormative Realism" (Dissertation, NYU), available at http://law.huji.ac.il/upload/Thesis.doc

—— (2003b) "How Noncognitivists Can Avoid Wishful Thinking," *Southern Journal of Philosophy* 41(4), 527–45.

—— (2005) "Why Idealize?," *Ethics* 115, 759–87.

—— (2006) "Agency, Shmagency: Why Normativity Won't Come from What is Constitutive of Agency," *Philosophical Review* 115, 169–98.

Enoch, D. (2007a) "An Outline of an Argument for Robust Metanormative Realism," *Oxford Studies in Metaethics* 2, 21–50.

—— (2007b) "Rationality, Coherence, Convergence: A Critical Comment on Michael Smith's *Ethics and the A Priori*," *Philosophical Books* 48, 99–108.

—— (2007c) "Epistemicism and Nihilism about Vagueness: What's the Difference?," *Philosophical Studies* 133(2), 285–311.

—— (2009a) "How Is Moral Disagreement a Problem for Realism?," *Journal of Ethics* 13(1), 15.

—— (2009b) "Can there be a Global, Interesting, Coherent Constructivism about Practical Reason?," *Philosophical Explorations* 12(3), 319–39.

—— (2010a) "The Epistemological Challenge to Metanormative Realism: How Best to Understand It, and How to Cope with It," *Philosophical Studies* 148(3), 413–38.

—— (2010b) "Shmagency Revisited," forthcoming in M. Brady (ed.), *New Waves in Metaethics* (Basingstoke: Palgrave Macmillan), 208–33.

—— (2010c) "How Objectivity Matters," in R. Shafer-Landau (ed.), *Oxford Studies in Metaethics*, vol. 5 (Oxford: Oxford University Press), 111–52.

—— (2011) "Not Just a Truthometer: Taking Oneself Seriously, but not Too Seriously, in Cases of Peer Disagreement," *Mind* 119, 953–97.

—— (forthcoming) "On Mark Schroeder's Hypotheticalism: A critical Notice of *Slaves of the Passions*," *The Philosophical Review*.

—— (manuscript) "Idealization Still Not Off the Hook: A Reply to Sobel's Reply."

Enoch, D. and J. Schechter (2008) "How Are Basic Belief-Forming Methods Justified?," *Philosophy and Phenomenological Research* 76(3), 547–79.

Ewing, A. C. (1947) *The Definition of Good* (London: Routledge & Kegan Paul).

Fantl, J. (2006) "Is Metaethics Morally Neutral?," *Pacific Philosophical Quarterly* 87, 24–44.

Feigl, H. (1952) "Validation and Vindication: An Analysis of the Nature and Limits of Ethical Argument," in W. Sellars and J. Hospers (eds.), *Readings in Ethical Theory* (New York: Appleton-Centur-Crofts), 667–80.

Ferrero, L. (2009) "Constitutivism and the Inescapability of Agency," *Oxford Studies in Metaethics* 4, 303–33.

Field, H. (1980) *Science Without Numbers: A Defence of Nominalism* (Oxford: Blackwell).

—— (1989) *Realism, Mathematics, and Modality* (New York: Basil Blackwell).

—— (1991) "Metalogic and Modality," *Philosophical Studies* 62, 1–22.

—— (2000) "Apriority as an Evaluative Notion," in P. Boghossian and C. Peacocke (eds.), *New Essays on the Apriori* (Oxford: Clarendon Press), 117–49; reprinted with an appendix in H. Field (2001) *Truth and the Absence of Fact* (New York: Oxford University Press), 361–92.

Fine, K. (2001) "The Question of Realism," *Philosophers' Imprint* 1, 1–30.

—— (2002) "The Varieties of Necessity," in T. S. Gendler and J. Hawthorne (eds.), *Conceivability and Possibility* (Oxford: Oxford University Press), 253–82; reprinted in K. Fine (2005) *Modality and Tense* (Oxford: Oxford University Press), 235–60.

Finlay, S. (2010) "Normativity, Necessity, and Tense: A Recipe for Homebaked Normativity," in R. Shafer-Landau (ed.), *Oxford Studies in Metaethics*, vol. 5 (Oxford: Oxford University Press), 57–85

Fitzpatrick, W. J. (2004) "Reasons, Value, and Particular Agents: Normative Relevance without Motivational Internalism," *Mind* 113, 285–318.

—— (2005) "The Practical Turn in Ethical Theory: Korsgaard's Constructivism, Realism and the Nature of Normativity," *Ethics* 115, 651–91.

Fitzpatrick, W. J. (2008) "Robust Ethical Realism, Non-Naturalism and Normativity," *Oxford Studies in Metaethics* 3, 159–206.

—— (2010) "Ethical Non-Naturalism and Normative Properties," in M. Brady (ed.), *New Waves in Metaethics* (Basingstoke: Palgrave Macmillan), 7–35.

Foot, P. (1972) "Morality as a System of Hypothetical Imperatives," *Philosophical Review* 81, 305–16.

Frankena, W. K. (1958) "Obligation and Motivation in Recent Moral Philosophy," in A. I. Melden (ed.), *Essays in Moral Philosophy* (Seattle: University of Washington Press), 40–81.

Fumerton, R. (1992) "Inference to the Best Explanation," in J. Dancy and E. Sosa (eds.), *A Companion to Epistemology* (Oxford: Blackwell), 207–9.

Gampel, E. H. (1996) "A Defense of the Autonomy of Ethics: Why Value Is Not Like Water," *Canadian Journal of Philosophy* 26, 191–209.

Garner, R. (2007) "Abolishing Morality," *Ethical Theory and Moral Practice* 10, 499–513.

Gert, J. (2002) "Expressivism and Language Learning," *Ethics* 112, 292–314.

Gewirth, A. (1960) "Meta-Ethics and Normative Ethics," *Mind* 69, 187–205.

Gibbard, A. (1990) *Wise Choices, Apt Feelings* (Cambridge, Mass.: Harvard University Press).

—— (1992) "Reply to Blackburn, Carson, Hill and Railton," *Philosophy and Phenomenological Research* 52, 969–80.

—— (2003) *Thinking How to Live* (Cambridge, Mass.: Harvard University Press).

Goldman, A. H. (1990) "Skepticism about Goodness and Rightness," *Southern Journal of Philosophy* (Supp.) 29, 167–83.

Gowans, C. W. (2000) "Introduction," in C. W. Gowans (ed.), *Moral Disagreements: Classic and Contemporary Readings* (London and New York: Routledge, 2000), 1–43.

—— (2004) "*A Priori* Refutations of Disagreement Arguments against Moral Objectivity: Why Experience Matters," *Journal of Value Inquiry* 38, 141–57.

Greenspan, P. S. (1998) "Moral Responses and Moral Theory: Socially-Based Externalist Ethics," *Journal of Ethics* 2, 103–22.

Grice, P. (1975) "Method in Philosophical Psychology (From the Banal to the Bizarre)," *Proceedings and Addresses of the American Philosophical Association* 48, 23–53.

Hampton, J. (1998) *The Authority of Reason* (Cambridge: Cambridge University Press).

Hare, R. M. (1952) *The Language of Morals* (Oxford: Clarendon Press).

Harman, G. (1965) "The Inference to the Best Explanation," *Philosophical Review* 74, 88–95.

—— (1977) *The Nature of Morality* (Oxford: Oxford University Press).

—— (1984) "Is There a Single True Morality?," in D. Copp and D. Zimmerman (eds.), *Morality, Reason and Truth: New Essays on the Foundations of Ethics* (Totowa: Rowman & Allanheld), 27–48.

—— (1986a) "Moral Explanations of Natural Facts – Can Moral Claims Be Tested Against Moral Reality?," *Southern Journal of Philosophy* (Supp.) 24, 57–68.

—— (1986b) "Willing and Intending," in R. Grandy and R. Warner (eds.), *Philosophical Grounds of Rationality* (Oxford: Oxford University Press), 363–80.

—— (1998) "Responses to Critics," *Philosophy and Phenomenological Research*, 58, 207–13.

Harman, G. and J. J. Thomson (1996) *Moral Relativism and Moral Objectivity* (Oxford: Blackwell).

Heathwood, C. (2009) "Moral and Epistemic Open-Question Arguments," *Philosophical Books* 50, 83–98.

—— (forthcoming) "Desire-Based Theories of Reasons, Pleasure, and Welfare," *Oxford Studies in Metaethics*.

Heuer, U. (2004) "Reasons for Actions and Desires," *Philosophical Studies* 121, 43–63.

Hieronymi, P. (manuscript) "Reasons for Action."

Horgan, T. (1993) "From Supervenience to Superdupervenience: Meeting the Demands of a Material World," *Mind* 102, 555–86.

Horgan, T. and M. Timmons (1991) "New Wave Moral Realism Meets Moral Twin Earth," *Journal of Philosophical Research* 16, 447–65.

—— (1992) "Troubles on Moral Twin Earth: Moral Queerness Revived," *Synthese* 92, 221–60.

—— (2006) "Expressivism, Yes! Relativism, No!," *Oxford Studies in Metaethics* 1, 73–98.

Horwich, P. (1998) *Meaning* (Oxford: Oxford University Press, 1998).

Huemer, M. (2006) *Ethical Intuitionism* (Basingstoke: Palgrave Macmillan).

Hume, D. (1751/1957) *An Enquiry Concerning the Principles of Morals* (Liberal Arts Press).

Hurley, S. L. (1989) *Natural Reasons* (Oxford and New York: Oxford University Press).

Hursthouse, R. (2004) "On the Grounding of the Virtues in Human Nature," in J. Szaif and M. Lutz-Bachmann (eds.), *What is Good for a Human Being?* (Berlin: Walter de Gruyter), 263–75.

Jackson, F. (1998) *From Metaphysics to Ethics* (Oxford: Oxford University Press).

Jackson, F. and P. Pettit (1995) "Moral Functionalism and Moral Motivation," *Philosophical Quarterly* 45, 20–40.

Johnston, M. (1989) "Dispositional Theories of Value," *Proceedings of the Aristotelian Society* (Supp.) 63, 139–74.

Joyce, R. (2001) *The Myth of Morality* (Cambridge: Cambridge University Press).

—— (2006) *The Evolution of Morality* (Cambridge, Mass.: MIT Press).

Kalderon, M. E. (2005) *Moral Fictionalism* (Oxford: Oxford University Press).

Kant, I. (1783) *Prolegomena to Any Future Metaphysics*, trans. P. Carus, rev. J. W. Ellington (Indianapolis and Cambridge, Mass.: Hackett, 1977).

—— (1785) *Groundwork of the Metaphysics of Morals*, trans. M. Gregor (Cambridge: Cambridge University Press, 1997).

Kim, J. (1998) "Reasons and the First Person," in J. Bransen and S. E. Cuypers (eds.), *Human Action, Deliberation and Causation* (Dordrecht: Kluwer Academic), 67–87.

Kitcher, P. (1989) "Explanatory Unification and the Causal Structure of the World," in P. Kitcher and W. C. Salmon (eds.), *Scientific Explanation* (Minneapolis: University of Minnesota Press), 410–505.

Klagge, J. (1988) "Supervenience: Ontological and Ascriptive," *Australasian Journal of Philosophy* 66, 461–70.

Kolodny, N. (2005) "Why Be Rational?," *Mind* 114, 509–63.

Kolnai, A. (1962) "Deliberation is of Ends," *Proceedings of the Aristotelian Society* 62, 195–218.

Korsgaard, C. M. (1983) "Two Distinctions in Goodness," *Philosophical Review* 92, 169–95.

—— (1996) *The Sources of Normativity*, ed. Onora O'Neill (Cambridge: Cambridge University Press).

—— (1997) "The Normativity of Instrumental Reason," in G. Cullity and B. Gaut (eds.), *Ethics and Practical Reason* (Oxford: Clarendon Press), 215–54.

—— (2008) "Acting for a Reason," in *The Constitution of Agency: Essays on Practical Reason and Moral Psychology* (Oxford: Oxford University Press, 2008), 207–29.

—— (2009) *Self-Constitution: Agency, Identity, and Integrity* (Oxford: Oxford University Press).

Kramer, M. H. (2009) *Moral Realism as a Moral Doctrine* (Chichester and Malden, Mass.: Wiley-Blackwell).

Kripke, S. (1972) *Naming and Necessity* (Cambridge, Mass.: Harvard University Press).

Leibniz, G. W. (1686) *Discourse on Metaphysics*, trans. R. N. D. Martin and S. Brown (New York and Manchester: Manchester University Press, 1988).

Leiter, B. (2001a) "Moral Facts and Best Explanations," *Social Philosophy and Policy* 18(2), 79–101.

—— (2001b) "Objectivity, Morality, and Adjudication," in his *Objectivity in Law and Morals* (Cambridge: Cambridge University Press), 66–98.

Lenman, J. (2009) "Reasons for Action: Justification vs. Explanation," *The Stanford Encyclopedia of Philosophy*, available at http://plato.stanford.edu/entries/reasons-just-vs-expl/index.html#note-2

Lewis, D. (1982) "Logic for Equivocators," *Noûs* 16, 431–41; reprinted in his *Papers in Philosophical Logic* (Cambridge: Cambridge University Press, 1998), 97–110.

—— (1986) *On The Plurality of Worlds* (Oxford: Blackwell).

—— (1989) "Dispositional Theories of Value," *Proceedings of the Aristotelian Society* (Supp.) 63, 113–37; reprinted in his *Papers in Ethics and Social Philosophy* (Cambridge: Cambridge University Press, 2000), 68–94.

—— (1996) "Desire as Belief II," *Mind* 105, 303–13; reprinted in *Papers in Ethics and Social Philosophy* (Cambridge: Cambridge University Press, 2000), 55–67.

Lewis, D. and S. Lewis (1983) "Holes," in David Lewis, *Philosophical Papers*, vol. 1 (Oxford: Oxford University Press, 1983), 3–9.

Liggins, D. (2006) "Is there a Good Epistemological Argument Against Platonism?," *Analysis* 66 (2), 135–41.

Lillehammer, H. (2004) "Moral Error Theory," *Proceedings of the Aristotelian Society* 104, 95–111.

Lipton, P. (1991) *Inference to the Best Explanation* (London and New York: Routledge).

Loeb, D. (1998) "Moral Realism and the Argument from Disagreement," *Philosophical Studies* 90, 281–303.

Lycan, W. G. (1985) "Epistemic Value," *Synthese* 64, 137–64.

—— (1986) "Moral Facts and Moral Knowledge," *Southern Journal of Philosophy* (Supp.) 24, 79–94.

—— (2002) "Explanation and Epistemology," in Paul Moser (ed.), *The Oxford Handbook of Epistemology* (Oxford: Oxford University Press), 408–33.

McDowell, J. (1985) "Values and Secondary Qualities," in T. Honderich (ed.), *Morality and Objectivity* (Boston: Routledge & Kegan Paul), 110–29.

—— (1987) "Projection and Truth in Ethics," The Lindley Lecture, University of Kansas, in S. Darwall, A. Gibbard, and P. Railton (eds.), *Moral Discourse and Practice* (Oxford and New York: Oxford University Press), 215–25.

McGinn, C. (1997) *Ethics, Evil, and Fiction* (Oxford and New York: Clarendon Press).

Mackie, J. L. (1977) *Ethics: Inventing Right and Wrong* (Harmondsworth: Penguin Books).

McLaughlin, B. and K. Bennett (2005) "Supervenience," in *The Stanford Encyclopedia of Philosophy*, available at http://plato.stanford.edu/entries/supervenience/

McPherson, T. (2008) "Metaethics and the Autonomy of Morality," *Philosophers' Imprint* 8, 1–16.

—— (2009) "Moorean Arguments and Moral Revisionism," *Journal of Ethics and Social Philosophy* 3(2), 1–23.

—— (2011) "Against Quietist Normative Realism," *Philosophical Studies* 154, 223–40.

—— (manuscript) "Ethical Non-Naturalism and the Metaphysics of Supervenience."

Majors, B. (2005) "Moral Discourse and Descriptive Properties," *Philosophical Quarterly* 55, 475–94.

Manley, D. (2009) "Introduction: A Guided Tour of Metametaphysics," in D. Chalmers, D. Manley, and R. Wasserman (eds.), *Metametaphysics: New Essays on the Foundations of Ontology* (Oxford: Oxford University Press, 2009), 1–37.

Miller, A. (2003) *An Introduction to Contemporary Metaethics* (Cambridge: Polity Press).

Milo, R. (1995) "Contractarian Constructivism," *Journal of Philosophy* 92, 181–204.

Moody-Adams, M. M. (1997) *Fieldwork in Familiar Places: Morality, Culture and Philosophy* (Cambridge, Mass.: Harvard University Press).

Moore, G. E. (1903) *Principia Ethica* (Cambridge: Cambridge University Press; rev. ed., T. Baldwin ed. and intro., 1993).

—— (1939) "Proof of an External World," *Proceedings of the British Academy* 25, 273–300; reprinted in his *Philosophical Papers* (London: Allen & Unwin, 1959), 127–50.

Moore, M. S. (1992) "Moral Reality Revisited," *Michigan Law Review* 90, 2425–533.

Moran, R. (1994) "Interpretation Theory and the First Person," *Philosophical Quarterly* 44, 154–73.

Nagel, T. (1970) *The Possibility of Altruism* (Princeton: Princeton University Press).

—— (1979) *Mortal Questions* (Cambridge: Cambridge University Press).

—— (1986) *The View From Nowhere* (New York and Oxford: Oxford University Press).

—— (1987) "Moral Conflict and Political Legitimacy," *Philosophy and Public Affairs* 16, 215–40.

—— (1991) *Equality and Partiality* (New York and Oxford: Oxford University Press).

—— (1996) "Universality and the Reflective Self," in C. M. Korsgaard, *The Sources of Normativity*, ed. Onora O'Neill (Cambridge: Cambridge University Press), 200–9.

—— (1997) *The Last Word* (Oxford: Oxford University Press).

Nolan, D., G. Restall, and C. West (2005) "Moral Fictionalism versus the Rest," *Australasian Journal of Philosophy* 83(3), 307–30.

Oddie, G. (2005) *Value, Reality and Desire* (Oxford and New York: Oxford University Press).

Olson, J. (2010) "In Defense of Moral Error Theory," in M. Brady (ed.), *New Waves in Metaethics* (Basingstoke: Palgrave Macmillan), 62–84.

—— (forthcoming) "Getting Real about Moral Fictionalism," *Oxford Studies in Metaethics*.

Olson, J. and F. Svensson (2005) "Regimenting Reasons," *Theoria* 71, 203–14.

Parfit, D. (1997) "Reasons and Motivation," *Proceedings of the Aristotelian Society* (Supp.) 71, 99–130.

—— (2006) "Normativity," *Oxford Studies in Metaethics* 1, 325–80.

—— (2011) *On What Matters* (Oxford: Oxford University Press).

Peacocke, C. (2004) *The Realm of Reason* (Oxford: Oxford University Press).

Pettit, P. and M. Smith (1990) "Backgrounding Desire," *Philosophical Review* 99, 565–92.

—— (1998) "Freedom in Belief and Desire," in J. Bransen and S. E. Cuypers (eds.), *Human Action, Deliberation and Causation* (Dordrecht: Kluwer Academic), 89–112.

Plantinga, A. (2010) "Naturalism, Theism, Obligation and Supervenience," *Faith and Philosophy* 27, 247–72.

Platts, M. (1980) "Moral Reality and the End of Desire," in Platts (ed.), *Reference, Truth and Reality: Essays on the Philosophy of Language* (London: Routledge & Kegan Paul), 69–82.

Prichard, H. A. (1912) "Does Moral Philosophy Rest on a Mistake," *Mind* 21, 21–37.

Pritchard, D. (2007) "How to Be a Neo-Moorean," in S. Goldberg (ed.), *Internalism and Externalism in Semantics and Epistemology* (Oxford: Oxford University Press).

Pryor, J. (2000) "The Skeptic and the Dogmatist," *Nous* 34(4), 517–49.

—— (2001) "Highlights of Recent Epistemology," *British Journal for the Philosophy of Science* 52, 1–30.

Putnam, H. (1995) "Are Moral and Legal Values Made or Discovered?," *Legal Theory* 1, 5–19.

Quine, W. V. O. (1960) *Word and Object* (Cambridge, Mass.: MIT Press).

Quinn, W. (1986) "Truth and Explanation in Ethics," *Ethics* 96, 524–44.

—— (1993) "Putting Rationality in Its Place," in *Morality and Action* (Cambridge: Cambridge University Press), 228–55.

Rachels, J. (1999) *The Elements of Moral Philosophy*, 3rd ed. (New York: McGraw-Hill).

Railton, P. (1986a) "Moral Realism," *Philosophical Review* 95, 163–207.

—— (1986b) "Facts and Values," *Philosophical Topics* 14, 5–31.

—— (1993) "What the Non-Cognitivist Helps Us to See the Naturalist Must Help Us to Explain," in J. Haldane and C. Wright (eds.), *Reality, Representation, and Projection* (New York and Oxford: Oxford University Press), 279–300.

—— (1997) "On the Hypothetical and Non-Hypothetical in Reasoning about Belief and Action," in G. Cullity and B. Gaut (eds.), *Ethics and Practical Reason* (Oxford: Clarendon Press), 53–79.

—— (1998) "Moral Explanation and Moral Objectivity," *Philosophy and Phenomenological Research* 58, 175–82.

—— (2009) "Internalism for Externalists," *Philosophical Issues* 19: *Metaethics*, 187–202.

Rasmussen, S. A. (1985) "Quasi-Realism and Mind-Dependence," *Philosophical Quarterly* 35, 185–90.

Rawls, J. (1980) "Kantian Constructivism in Moral Theory," *Journal of Philosophy* 77, 515–72.

—— (2000) *Lectures on the History of Moral Philosophy*, ed. B. Herman (Cambridge, Mass.: Harvard University Press).

Raz, J. (1990) "Facing Diversity: The Case of Epistemic Abstinence," *Philosophy and Public Affairs* 19, 3–46.

—— (1998) "Disagreement in Politics," *American Journal of Jurisprudence* 43, 25–52.

—— (2000) "The Truth in Particularism," in B. Hooker and M. O. Little (eds.), *Moral Particularism* (Oxford: Clarendon Press), 48–78.

—— (2001) "Notes on Value and Objectivity," in B. Leiter (ed.), *Objectivity in Law and Morals* (Cambridge: Cambridge University Press), 194–233; reprinted in J. Raz (1999) *Engaging Reason* (Oxford: Oxford University Press), 118–60.

—— (2005) "The Myth of Instrumental Rationality," *Journal of Ethics and Social Philosophy* 1(1).

—— (2010) "On the Guise of the Good," in S. Tenenbaum (ed.), *Desire, Practical Reason, and the Good* (Oxford: Oxford University Press), 111–37.

Regan, D. H. (2003) "How to be a Moorean," *Ethics* 113, 651–77.

Reichenbach, H. (1938) *Experience and Prediction* (Chicago: University of Chicago Press).

Reynolds, S. L. (2009) "Making Up the Truth," *Pacific Philosophical Quarterly* 90, 315–35.

Ridge, M. (2007) "Anti-Reductionism and Supervenience," *Journal of Moral Philosophy* 4(3), 330–48.

Rosati, C. S. (1995) "Naturalism, Normativity, and the Open Question Argument," *Nous* 29, 46–70.

—— (1996) "Internalism and the Good for a Person," *Ethics* 106, 297–326.

Rosati, C. S. (2003) "Agency and the Open Question Argument," *Ethics* 113, 490–527.

Rosen, G. (1994) "Objectivity and Modern Idealism: What is the Question?," in `M. Michael and J. O'Leary-Hawthorne (eds.), *Philosophy in Mind* (Dordrecht: Kluwer Academic), 277–314.

—— (1998) "Blackburn's *Essays in Quasi-Realism*," *Nous* 32, 386–405.

—— (2001) "Nominalism, Naturalism, Epistemic Relativism," *Philosophical Perspectives* 15: *Metaphysics*, 69–91.

Sayre-McCord, G. (1988a) "Moral Theory and Explanatory Impotence," *Midwest Studies* 12, 433–57; reprinted in Sayre-McCord (ed.), *Essays on Moral Realism* (Ithaca and London: Cornell University Press, 1988), 256–81.

—— (1988b) "Introduction: The Many Moral Realisms," in *Essays on Moral Realism* (Ithaca and London: Cornell University Press), 1–23.

—— (1992) "Normative Explanations," *Philosophical Perspectives* 6: *Ethics*, 55–71.

—— (1995) "Coherentist Epistemology and Moral Theory," in W. Sinnott-Armstrong and M. Timmons (eds.), *Moral Knowledge? New Readings in Moral Epistemology* (Oxford and New York: Oxford University Press), 137–89.

—— (1997) "The Metaethical Problem," *Ethics* 108, 55–83.

Scanlon, T. M. (1995) "Moral Theory: Understanding and Disagreement," *Philosophy and Phenomenological Research* 55, 343–56.

—— (1998) *What We Owe to Each Other* (Cambridge, Mass.: Harvard University Press).

—— (2009) "Being Realistic about Reasons," The Locke Lectures 2009.

Schechter, J. B. (2006) *Two Challenges to the Objectivity of Logic* (Dissertation, NYU).

Schiffer, S. (2003) *The Things We Mean* (Oxford: Oxford University Press).

Schmitt, J. and M. Schroeder (forthcoming) "Supervenience Arguments under Relaxed Assumptions," *Philosophical Studies*.

Schneewind, J. B. (1998) *The Invention of Autonomy: A History of Modern Moral Philosophy* (Cambridge: Cambridge University Press).

Schroeder, M. (2005) "Realism and Reduction: The Quest for Robustness," *Philosophers' Imprint* 5(1), 1–18.

—— (2007) *Slaves of the Passions* (Oxford: Oxford University Press).

—— (2008a) "Having Reasons," *Philosophical Studies* 139(1), 57–71.

—— (2008b) "What Is the Frege–Geach Problem?," *Philosophy Compass* 3(4), 703–20.

Scott, R. B. Jr. (1980) "Five Types of Ethical Naturalism," *American Philosophical Quarterly* 17, 261–70.

Seabright, P. (1988) "Objectivity, Disagreement, and Projectibility," *Inquiry* 31, 25–51.

Setiya, K. (2003) "Explaining Action," *Philosophical Review* 112, 339–93.

—— (2007) *Reasons without Rationalism* (Princeton: Princeton University Press, 2007).

Shafer-Landau, R. (1994) "Ethical Disagreement, Ethical Objectivism and Moral In-determinacy," *Philosophy and Phenomenological Research* 54, 331–44.

—— (2003) *Moral Realism: A Defence* (Oxford and New York: Oxford University Press).

—— (2005) "Precis of *Moral Realism: A Defence*," *Philosophical Studies* 126, 263–7.

—— (2006) "Ethics as Philosophy: A Defense of Ethical Nonnaturalism," in T. Horgan and M. Timmons (eds.), *Metaethics after Moore* (Oxford and New York: Oxford University Press), 209–32.

Shafer-Landau, R. (2007) "Moral and Theological Realism: The Explanatory Argument," *Journal of Moral Philosophy* 4(3), 311–29.

—— (2010) "The Possibility of Metaethics," *Boston University Law Review* 90, 479–96.

Simon, C. J. (1990) "The Intuitionist Argument," *Southern Journal of Philosophy* 28, 91–114.

Singer, P. (1972) "Famine, Affluence and Morality," *Philosophy and Public Affairs* 1, 229–43.

Sinnott-Armstrong, W. (2006) *Moral Skepticisms* (Oxford and New York: Oxford University Press).

—— (2008) "Replies to Copp, Timmons, and Railton," *Philosophy and Phenomenological Research* 77(3), 820–36.

Sinnott-Armstrong, W. and M. Timmons (eds.) (1995) *Moral Knowledge? New Readings in Moral Epistemology* (Oxford and New York, Oxford University Press).

Skarsaune, K. O. (2011) "Darwin and Moral Realism: Survival of the Iffiest," *Philosophical Studies* 152, 229–43.

Slors, M. V. P. (1998) "Two Claims that Can Save a Nonreductive Account of Mental Causation," in J. Bransen and S. E. Cuypers (eds.), *Human Action, Deliberation and Causation* (Dordrecht: Kluwer Academic), 224–48.

Smith, D. (2006) "Ronald Dworkin and the External Sceptic," *Canadian Journal of Law and Jurisprudence* 19, 433–57.

Smith, M. (1994) *The Moral Problem* (Oxford: Blackwell).

—— (1997) "In Defense of *The Moral Problem*: A Reply to Brink, Copp, and Sayre-McCord," *Ethics* 108, 84–119.

—— (2007) "In Defence of *Ethics and the A priori*: A Reply to Enoch, Hieronymi, and Tannenbaum," *Philosophical Books* 48, 136–49.

Sobel, S. (2001) "Subjective Accounts of Reasons for Action," *Ethics* 111, 461–92.

—— (2009) "Subjectivism and Idealization," *Ethics* 119(2), 336–52.

Sorensen, R. (1988) "Dogmatism, Junk Knowledge, and Conditionals," *Philosophical Quarterly* 38 (October), 433–54.

Sosa, D. (2001) "Pathetic Ethics," in B. Leiter (ed.), *Objectivity in Law and Morals* (Cambridge: Cambridge University Press), 287–329.

Stratton-Lake, P. (2002) "Introduction," in Stratton-Lake (ed.), *Ethical Intuitionism: Re-evaluations* (Oxford: Oxford University Press), 1–28.

Street, S. (2003) "Evolution and the Nature of Reasons" (Ph.D. thesis, Harvard University).

—— (2006) "A Darwinian Dilemma for Realist Theories of Value," *Philosophical Studies* 127, 109–66.

—— (forthcoming) "Evolution and the Normativity of Epistemic Reasons," *Oxford Studies in Metaethics.*

Streumer, B. (2008) "Are There Irreducibly Normative Properties?," *Australasian Journal of Philosophy* 86, 537–61.

Stroud, B. (1968) "Transcendental Arguments," *Journal of Philosophy* 65, 241–56.

Sturgeon, N. S. (1984) "Moral Explanations," in D. Copp and D. Zimmerman (eds.), *Morality, Reason and Truth: New Essays on the Foundations of Ethics* (Totowa: Rowman & Allanheld), 49–78.

—— (1986a) "Harman on Moral Explanations of Natural Facts," *Southern Journal of Philosophy* (Supp.) 24, 69–78.

Sturgeon, N. S. (1986b) "What Difference Does It Make whether Moral Realism is True?," *Southern Journal of Philosophy* (Supp.) 24, 115–41.

—— (1991) "Content and Causes: A Reply to Blackburn," *Philosophical Studies* 61, 19–37.

—— (1992) "Nonmoral Explanations," *Philosophical Perspectives* 6: Ethics, 97–117.

—— (1998) "Thomson against Moral Explanations," *Philosophy and Phenomenological Research* 58, 199–206.

—— (2006) "Ethical naturalism," in D. Copp (ed.), *The Oxford Handbook of Ethical Theory* (Oxford and New York: Oxford University Press), 91–121.

—— (2007) "Doubts about the Supervenience of the Evaluative," *Oxford Studies in Metaethics* 3, 53–90.

Suikkanen, J. (2009) "The Subjectivist Consequences of Expressivism," *Pacific Philosophical Quarterly* 90, 364–87.

Sumner, L. W. (1967) "Normative Ethics and Metaethics," *Ethics* 77, 95–106.

Svavarsdóttir, S. (1999) "Moral Cognitivism and Motivation," *Philosophical Review* 108, 161–219.

—— (2001) "Objective Values: Does Metaethics Rest on a Mistake?," in B. Leiter (ed.), *Objectivity in Law and Morals* (Cambridge: Cambridge University Press), 144–93.

—— (2009) "The Practical Role Essential to Value Judgments," *Philosophical Issues* 19: Metaethics, 299–320.

Swinburne, R. (1976) "The Objectivity of Morality," *Philosophy* 51, 5–20.

Tännsjö, T. (1990) *Moral Realism* (Savage, N.J.: Rowman and Littlefield).

—— (2010) *From Reasons to Norms: On the Basic Question in Ethics* (Dordrecht: Springer).

Tersman, F. (2006) *Moral Disagreement* (Cambridge: Cambridge University Press).

Thagard, P. R. (1978) "The Best Explanation: Criteria for Theory Choice," *Journal of Philosophy* 75, 76–92.

Thomson, J. J. (1996) (contributor) in G. Harman and J. J. Thomson, *Moral Relativism and Moral Objectivity* (Oxford: Blackwell).

Timmons, M. (1990) "On the Epistemic Status of Considered Moral Judgments," *Southern Journal of Philosophy* (Supp.) 29, 97–131.

Tolhurst, W. (1987) "The Argument from Moral Disagreement," *Ethics* 97, 610–21.

Ullmann-Margalit, E. and S. Morgenbesser (1977) "Picking and Choosing," *Social Research* 44, 757–85.

Unger, P. (1996) *Living High and Letting Die* (New York and Oxford: Oxford University Press).

Van Cleve, J. (2003) "Is Knowledge Easy – or Impossible? Externalism as the Only Alternative to Skepticism," in S. Luper (ed.), *The Skeptics: Contemporary Essays* (Aldershot: Ashgate), 45–60.

Van Fraassen, B. C. (1980) *The Scientific Image* (Oxford: Clarendon Press).

—— (1989) *Laws and Symmetry* (Oxford and New York: Clarendon Press).

Van Inwagen, P. (1994) "Composition as Identity," *Philosophical Perspectives* 8, 207–20.

Van Roojen, M. (1996) "Moral Functionalism and Moral Reductionism," *Philosophical Quarterly* 46, 77–81.

Velleman, J. D. (1989) *Practical Reflection* (Princeton: Princeton University Press).

—— (1992) "The Guise of the Good," *Nous* 26, 3–26, reprinted in Velleman (2000), 99–122.

—— (1996) "The Possibility of Practical Reason," *Ethics* 106, 694–726, reprinted in Velleman (2000), 170–99.

Velleman, J. D. (1998) "Is Motivation Internal to Value?," in C. Fehige, G. Meggle, and U. Wessels (eds.), *Preferences* (Berlin: de Gruyter), reprinted in Velleman (2000), 85–98.

—— (2000) *The Possibility of Practical Reason* (Oxford and New York: Oxford University Press).

—— (2009) *How We Get Along* (Cambridge: Cambridge University Press).

Vogel, J. (2008) "Epistemic Bootstrapping," *Journal of Philosophy* 105, 518–39.

Waldron, J. (1992) "The Irrelevance of Moral Objectivity," in R. P. George (ed.), *Natural Law Theory: Contemporary Essays* (Oxford: Clarendon Press), 158–87 .

Wallace, R. J. (2001) "Normativity, Commitment, and Instrumental Reason," *Philosopher's Imprint* 1(3), 1–26.

Wedgwood, R. (2001) "Conceptual Role Semantics for Moral Terms," *Philosophical Review* 110, 1–30.

—— (2006) "How We Know What Ought to Be," *Proceedings of the Aristotelian Society* 106(1), 61–84.

—— (2007) *The Nature of Normativity* (Oxford and New York: Clarendon Press).

Weirich, P. (2008) "Causal Decision Theory," in *The Stanford Encyclopedia of Philosophy*, at http://plato.stanford.edu/entries/decision-causal/#NewPro

Wielenberg, E. (2010) "On the Evolutionary Debunking of Morality," *Ethics* 120, 441–64.

Wiggins, D. (1987) "A Sensible Subjectivism?," in his *Needs, Values, Truth: Essays in the Philosophy of Value* (New York: Oxford University Press), 185–214.

—— (1990) "Moral Cognitivism, Moral Relativism and Motivating Moral Beliefs," *Proceedings of the Aristotelian Society* 91, 61–86.

Williams, B. (1980) "Internal and External Reasons," reprinted in his *Moral Luck* (Cambridge: Cambridge University Press, 1981), 101–13.

—— (1981) *Moral Luck* (Cambridge: Cambridge University Press).

—— (1985) *Ethics and the Limits of Philosophy* (Cambridge, Mass.: Harvard University Press).

—— (1989) "Internal Reasons and the Obscurity of Blame," reprinted in his *Making Sense of Humanity* (Cambridge: Cambridge University Press, 1995), 35–45.

Wilson, J. (2010) "What Is Hume's Dictum, and Why Believe It?," *Philosophy and Phenomenological Research* 80, 595–637.

Wittgenstein, L. (1953) *Philosophical Investigations*, trans. G. E. Anscombe (Oxford: Blackwell).

Wong, D. B. (1984) *Moral Relativity* (Berkeley: University of California Press).

Woodbridge, J. (2005) "Truth as a Pretense," in M. E. Kalderon (ed.), *Fictionalism in Metaphysics* (Oxford: Oxford University Press), 134–77.

Wright, C. (1988) "Moral Values, Projection, and Secondary Qualities," *Proceedings of the Aristotelian Society* (Supp.) 62, 1–26.

—— (1992) *Truth and Objectivity* (Cambridge, Mass.: Harvard University Press).

—— (1993) "Realism: The Contemporary Debate – W(h)ither Now?," in J. Haldane and C. Wright (eds.), *Reality, Representation, and Projection* (New York and Oxford: Oxford University Press), 63–84.

—— (2004) "Warrant for Nothing (And Foundations for Free?)," *Proceedings of the Aristotelian Society* (Supp.) 78(1), 167–212.

Yablo, S. (1998) "Does Ontology Rest on a Mistake?," *Proceedings of the Aristotelian Society* (Supp.) 72, 229–62.

—— (2001) "Go Figure: A Path through Fictionalism," *Midwest Studies in Philosophy* 25, 72–102.

Yablo, S. (2005) "The Myth of the Seven," in M. E. Kalderon (ed.), *Fictionalism in Metaphysics* (Oxford: Oxford University Press), 88–115.

Yasenchuk, K. (1994) "Sturgeon and Brink on Moral Explanations," *Southern Journal of Philosophy* 32, 483–502.

Zangwill, N. (1992) "Quietism," *Midwest Studies in Philosophy* 17, 160–76.

Zimmerman, D. (1984) "Moral Realism and Explanatory Necessity," in D. Copp and D. Zimmerman (eds.), *Morality, Reason and Truth: New Essays on the Foundations of Ethics* (Totowa: Rowman & Allanheld), 79–103.

Index

Page references in bold indicate a substantive discussion of a thinker's views or arguments (rather than more incidental references).

Lightning Source UK Ltd.
Milton Keynes UK
UKOW06f0331170815

256996UK00001B/2/P